Peer-to-Peer Application Development

Peer-to-Peer Application Development

Cracking the Code

Dreamtech Software Team

Hungry Minds™

Best-Selling Books • Digital Downloads • e-Books • Answer Networks •
e-Newsletters • Branded Web Sites • e-Learning

New York, NY ◆ Cleveland, OH ◆ Indianapolis, IN

Peer-to-Peer Application Development: Cracking the Code

Published by
Hungry Minds, Inc.
909 Third Avenue
New York, NY 10022
www.hungryminds.com

Library of Congress Control Number: 2001095941

ISBN: 0-7645-4904-9

Printed in the United States of America

10 9 8 7 6 5 4 3 2 1

1B/QZ/RR/QR/IN

Distributed in the United States by Hungry Minds, Inc.

Distributed by CDG Books Canada Inc. for Canada; by Transworld Publishers Limited in the United Kingdom; by IDG Norge Books for Norway; by IDG Sweden Books for Sweden; by IDG Books Australia Publishing Corporation Pty. Ltd. for Australia and New Zealand; by TransQuest Publishers Pte Ltd. for Singapore, Malaysia, Thailand, Indonesia, and Hong Kong; by Gotop Information Inc. for Taiwan; by ICG Muse, Inc. for Japan; by Intersoft for South Africa; by Eyrolles for France; by International Thomson Publishing for Germany, Austria, and Switzerland; by Distribuidora Cuspide for Argentina; by LR International for Brazil; by Galileo Libros for Chile; by Ediciones ZETA S.C.R. Ltda. for Peru; by WS Computer Publishing Corporation, Inc., for the Philippines; by Contemporanea de Ediciones for Venezuela; by Express Computer Distributors for the Caribbean and West Indies; by Micronesia Media Distributor, Inc. for Micronesia; by Chips Computadoras S.A. de C.V. for Mexico; by Editorial Norma de Panama S.A. for Panama; by American Bookshops for Finland.

For general information on Hungry Minds' products and services please contact our Customer Care department within the U.S. at 800-762-2974, outside the U.S. at 317-572-3993 or fax 317-572-4002.

For sales inquiries and reseller information, including discounts, premium and bulk quantity sales, and foreign-language translations, please contact our Customer Care department at 800-434-3422, fax 317-572-4002 or write to Hungry Minds, Inc., Attn: Customer Care Department, 10475 Crosspoint Boulevard, Indianapolis, IN 46256.

For information on licensing foreign or domestic rights, please contact our Sub-Rights Customer Care department at 212-884-5000.

For information on using Hungry Minds' products and services in the classroom or for ordering examination copies, please contact our Educational Sales department at 800-434-2086 or fax 317-572-4005.

For press review copies, author interviews, or other publicity information, please contact our Public Relations department at 317-572-3168 or fax 317-572-4168.

For authorization to photocopy items for corporate, personal, or educational use, please contact Copyright Clearance Center, 222 Rosewood Drive, Danvers, MA 01923, or fax 978-750-4470.

Hungry Minds™ is a trademark of Hungry Minds, Inc.

Credits

Acquisitions Editor
Chris Webb

Project Editor
Chandani Thapa

Technical Editor
Dr. K.V.K.K. Prasad

Copy Editor
C. M. Jones

Media Development Specialist
Travis Silvers

Permissions Editor
Laura Moss

Media Development Manager
Laura Carpenter VanWinkle

Project Coordinator
Dale White

Cover Design
Anthony Bunyan

Proofreader
Anne Owen

Indexer
Johnna VanHoose Dinse

Cover
Vault door image used courtesy of
Brown Safe Manufacturing
www.BrownSafe.com

Dreamtech Software India, Inc., Team

dreamtech@mantraonline.com
www.dreamtechsoftware.com

Dreamtech Software India, Inc., is a leading provider of corporate software solutions. Based in New Delhi, India, the company is a successful pioneer of innovative solutions in e-learning technologies. Dreamtech's developers have over 50 years of combined software-engineering experience in areas such as Java, wireless applications, XML, voice-based solutions, .NET, COM/COM+ technologies, distributed computing, DirectX, Windows Media technologies, and security solutions.

About the Authors

Lead Author Team

Vikas Gupta, Co-founder and President. Vikas holds a B.E. in electronics, with a postgraduate diploma in sales and marketing and in publishing and printing studies. Actively engaged in developing and designing new technologies in wireless applications, e-learning, and other cutting-edge areas, he is also the Managing Director of IDG Books India (P) Ltd.

Avnish Dass, Co-founder and CEO. Avnish is a talented and seasoned programmer who has 15 years of experience in systems and application/database programming. Avnish has developed security systems, antivirus programs, wireless and communication technologies, and ERP systems.

Harpreet Singh Matharu, Sr. Software Developer. Harpreet holds a B.Tech. in computer science. Harpreet specializes in COM services and Windows Systems Programming, including Network Programming and Windows Security Systems.

Ankur Verma, Sr. Software Developer. Ankur has expertise in technologies such as Windows Media, Direct X (Direct Show), and Windows Shell Programming Services for Windows NT series. Ankur also provides the commercial COM/DCOM solutions to Dreamtech Software India, Inc.

Yashraj Chauhan, Sr. Software Developer. Yashraj has an advanced diploma in software development from IBM, with over three years of experience in Java, XML, and C++, and is pursuing his Masters in computer science.

Other Contributors

Pooja Aggarwal and Manish Aggarwal, Technical writers. They have contributed to developing the contents of this book.

Gaurav Malhotra, Pankaj Kumar, Manish N. Srivastav, A team of programmers of Dreamtech Software India, Inc. They contributed to the development of software in this book.

Acknowledgments

We acknowledge the contributions of the following people for their support in making this book possible:

John Kilcullen for sharing his dream and providing the vision for making this project a reality.

Mike Violano and **Joe Wikert** for believing in us.

M.V. Shastri, Asim Chowdhury, V.K. Rajan, Sanjeev Chatterjee, and **Priti** for their immense help in coordinating various activities throughout this project.

To our parents and family and beloved country, India,
for providing an excellent environment
for nurturing and creating world-class IT talent.

Preface

The Internet evolved out of the need to access information from one computer through another or over a network of computers. In the beginning, the Internet was a modest network of a few computers allowing access to data through any of its terminals. Gradually, the concept opened endless possibilities, and the Internet emerged as a super network — a network of networks — spanning the globe and involving millions of machines over which information could be shared, accessed, or communicated freely by the user.

Today, with the Internet's having graduated to the status of a religion that promises to fulfill the needs of everyone, regardless of caste, creed, or color, and having become potent enough to grant anything beseeched, you can find yourself quite lost in its world. Consequently, the need for personal attention and smaller subnetworks has risen once again. A handful of people got wise to this idea and developed software that allowed users to share data and to communicate with a set of selective people only: friends, relatives, or colleagues.

This has become among the most sought-after software on the IT market. A big user group is benefiting from such software, and many companies are venturing into the concept and capitalizing on it.

In this scenario, an application made on the concept of Peer-to-Peer (P2P), written in popular languages such as Java and C#, with its foundations for database interaction and communication laid in a platform as ubiquitous as XML and, above all, with open-source code and elaborate code explanations, is what developers of such software ultimately dream of. This may sound idealistic, but it is exactly such an application that this book is all about.

What This Book Covers

This book covers the technology of P2P programming. This is the first book to cover the entire code behind a Napster-style, file-sharing model. It contains unique coverage of Windows Media Technology development for making your P2P application multimedia aware. The book is loaded with code, keeping theory to a minimum. The applications, for which the source code is given in the CD accompanying this book, are 100 percent tested and working at Dreamtech Software Research Lab. The source code provided in the book is based on commercial applications, which have been developed by the software company. Each program of the application is explained in detail so that you gain insight into the implementation of the technology in a real-world situation. At the end of the book, some add-ons to this application are provided so that you can further explore new developments.

This book deals with the design, implementation, and coding of the latest form of the client/server model, the P2P model. The book serves to equip you with enough know-how on the subject so as to enable you to design a P2P model of your own.

The book begins with the history of the P2P model and goes on to explain the various types of P2P models, with detailed diagrams to elucidate the subject. After equipping you with basic concepts, it goes on to develop, step by step, a full-fledged application, which has the scope of being extended with add-ons.

This book is *not* meant for beginners. It teaches you the basics of specific technologies only. The *Cracking the Code* series is meant for software developers/programmers who wish to upgrade their skills and understand the secrets behind professional-quality applications. This book starts where other tutorial books end. It enhances your skills and takes them to the next level as you learn a particular technology. A thorough knowledge of the Java or C# programming languages is the prerequisite for benefiting the most from this book. Experience in network programming is an added advantage. For developing streaming applications, knowledge of Visual C++ is a must. At least a nodding acquaintance with the XML markup language is desirable, although the book includes a section on XML. Instructions for embedding existing chat-client and audio/video components have been included. You can craft this application in such a way that you are able to send your files to be printed to any part of the globe. Besides Globalized Printing, you can make the application run on wireless models, too. The opportunity is open for you to assess your networking skills and to improve them.

The pivotal feature of the book is that it offers a complete, ready-to-deploy application with source code. The purpose of this book is to acquaint programmers with the subject thoroughly so that they are in a position to write their own codes to build P2P applications. Detailed explanations of the steps involved in writing your own code to build a P2P application in Java as well as in C # have been furnished.

Although the topic is highly technical, every effort has been made to make the presentation lucid, interesting, and reader friendly.

How This Book Is Organized

Chapter 1 begins with a discussion of various P2P models, goes on to consider design parameters (including the target audience, the environment, and the possible range this application may be required to serve), and finally covers the implementation aspects of one of the aforementioned models. The last chapter is devoted to the add-ons incorporated in the application.

Chapter 2 explains designing the application you intend to develop. Having provided a basic overall view and the technical background of the application, the process of designing the application is taken up in this chapter. The chapter begins with a reiteration of design considerations and parameters. The sort of communication sought and the means to achieve it by way of this P2P application are detailed. The XML design specifications are given in detail, as the interoperability of the P2P application has been achieved by using them. The server side is discussed with a description of using the database, the table design, the XML implementation in SQL Server 2000, and so on. The client side is described with details of the two modules the client is made up of — the browser and the listener — along with the techniques for handling XML parsing, managing peers, connecting to the server and other peers, and finally searching.

It is imperative to mention here that the core of this application is discussed in Chapter 2, and it is exceptionally beneficial and mandatory for product designers and programmers aspiring to develop similar applications to peruse this chapter thoroughly.

Chapter 3 contains every detail of the server in reference to the P2P application. Various aspects of using SQL Server 2000, such as table creation with reference to this application and writing queries for retrieving data from tables, have been discussed in this chapter. This chapter also walks the reader through XML-related capabilities of SQL Server 2000.

Apart from giving you a comprehensive picture of the entire development cycle of the server for this application, this chapter presents a few facts about SQL Server 2000. It elaborates on the complete cycle of database structure tailoring, mounting it, and writing ASPs over it for connected users to be able to interact with it easily.

A sound command of RDBMS concepts helps you get the maximum benefit from this chapter.

Chapter 4 introduces you to the task of real cracking of code and illustrates all aspects of high-level programming. In the Java version of the P2P application, all codes carry a detailed explanation wherever needed so that you can fully appreciate the code.

The code explanation starts with a discussion of classes pertaining to operations on XML involved in the application.

After discussing the building blocks of our application, we discuss the application itself. This comprises the listener module and the browser module (client). These two interact with each other to give the final shape to this P2P application.

Apart from covering the entire application development in Java, this chapter describes the use of some of the XML parsers offered by IBM through Java. A firm command of Java and a nodding acquaintance with IBM Xerces XML parser is desirable, as this chapter deals primarily with implementation without giving any tutorial of either the language or the parser.

If you intend to make your application in C#, skip this chapter and proceed to the next chapter.

Chapter 5 covers the C# version of this P2P application. All codes and documentation processes carry a detailed commentary whenever needed so as to enable you to gain a sound understanding of the concept in question. The code in this chapter has been written using Microsoft Visual Studio .NET (Beta 2).

This application constitutes a listener module and a browser module (client), which interact with each other to effect the completion of this P2P application. While taking you through the development of the essential modules of this application, this chapter provides you with the opportunity to evaluate your skills in the C# language and to improve them. It lets you know how COM components are used in C#, how windows APIs (such as ShellExec()) can be used with interoperable namespaces, and how delegates can be used judiciously in programs.

A working knowledge of C# and MS XML parser is expected, as this chapter deals primarily with implementation without giving a tutorial of either the language or the parser. If you envisage your application in Java, skip this chapter.

Chapter 6 begins with an elaboration of streaming and goes on to discuss the tools, libraries, and resources required for extending this application to be able to stream audio/video data. The chapter concludes by explaining, in steps, the development of a streaming add-on for this P2P application.

The understanding of Windows Media technologies you gain through this chapter can be directed toward developing or extending applications. This knowledge can be used as a bridge to gain access to even better applications of Windows Media technologies and DirectX.

Because the SDKs involved for developing this add-on are available for VC++ only as of now, you need to know VC++ to understand or develop this add-on. This chapter makes use of Windows Media Encoder SDK. Familiarity with Windows Media technologies is expected of you.

Chapter 7 offers you an opportunity to be innovative in extending this so-far-elementary P2P application. It provides a deeper insight into the flexibility and the prudence of the design of this application that makes it possible for you to incorporate add-ons to the application even at an advanced stage in its development cycle. The implementations of the following add-ons have been described and serve as practical guidelines if you want to explore the possibilities offered by this application:

- Chat client
- Globalized Printing
- P2P wireless search (Java version only)

The fully functional chat client incorporated in this application provides you with an understanding of fundamental techniques such as socket programming and introduces you to .NET's powerful resource designer. Globalized Printing convinces you how easily a new idea can be incorporated into an application if some care is taken to keep the foundation of the application ubiquitous. This notion is further substantiated by the incorporation of the P2P wireless search, which is written in Java and therefore calls for a working knowledge of CLDC (Connected Limited Device Configuration) for a complete appreciation of this extension.

The other two add-ons discussed are developed in C#, and you are expected to possess a working knowledge of this language.

Who Should Read This Book

This book is intended for those aspiring to learn specific technologies. It is meant for developers who wish to join the evolutionary pathway of innovative software that gives new dimensions to existing technology.

The book primarily targets programmers and project designers who wish to learn the concept of P2P thoroughly so as to be able to develop their own applications.

This book offers code-intensive coverage of Windows Media technologies. It presents a revolutionary combination of two nascent technologies: P2P and Windows Media. The two have been interlaced so that you can extend your applications in a number of ways by using the code for streaming audio/video over the network furnished herein.

This book provides programmers of Java and C# the opportunity to assess their skills and to improve them.

This book also throws light on aspects of CLDC required by a CLDC programmer to appreciate a case study, which demonstrates the technique of enabling a device to communicate with a desktop computer by means of simple-socket programming using XML as the language for communication. The pertinent tool kits and the CLDC VM have been detailed.

The overall objective of this book is to acquaint you with developing cutting-edge P2P applications and creating and extending other software that keeps you in the vanguard of the technical race.

Contents

Chapter 1

An Introduction to the
Peer-To-Peer Programming Model

This book discusses the design, implementation, and coding of the peer-to-peer programming model (P2P). It equips you with enough know-how on the subject to enable you to design your own unique P2P model by offering you a complete, ready-to-deploy application with source code. This application, the Dreamtech P2P application, incorporates some interesting features. For instance, it enables you to send your files to be printed to any part of the globe. In addition to globalizing printing, you can make the application run on wireless models.

A thorough knowledge of the XML, Java, and C# programming languages is the prerequisite for getting the maximum benefit from this book. At least rudimentary knowledge of the XML mark-up language is desirable. The opportunity is open for you to assess your networking skills and to improve them.

Although the subject is highly technical, we have made every effort to make our presentation lucid, friendly, and interesting. Since the purpose of this book is to help you to write your own code to build P2P applications, it introduces you to the vital concepts of P2P and briefly goes over networking and networking protocols besides explaining, in detail, the various components of P2P and their designs. Further, it offers an exhaustive description of the steps involved in building a P2P application in Java as well as in C#.

This book deals with the concept of P2P programming that holds immense utility, scope for innovation, and enough potential to change the entire complexion of networking procedures as they stand today.

A Brief History of P2P

P2P is not an altogether novel concept. It has existed since the Internet was taking form in the 1970s. Recent changes in technology and the improved computing capability of desktops have brought about P2P's revival on a larger scale.

Until the recent past, similar systems were used primarily for sharing files within a closed circle of known users over LANs, BBSs, and FTPs. As such, the reach of the P2P model-based applications is confined to sharing files within a known group of computer users. If one wants to transfer files with unknown users, one has to use IRC (Internet Relay Chat) or other BBSs (Bulletin Board Services). In the '80s, the restriction of mainframes to nongraphical user interfaces and the increase of online users created a rush to wire PCs to one another and, more important, to a new class of server computers.

Individual computers were assigned permanent IP addresses until 1994. Newer browser software, such as Mosaic and Netscape, were introduced to access the Web from PCs. These PCs, unlike older mainframe computers, were not always on and entered and exited the Web unpredictably. The sudden gush of Web users caused a scarcity of IP addresses. ISPs (Internet Service Providers) began assigning new IP addresses to users for each session. The temporary IP addresses, in turn, prevented users from hosting any data or Web-enabled application for other peers.

As a result of the increased demand for Web-based services, users felt the need to control, exchange, and share resources directly. In the meantime, in the late 1990s, PCs became increasingly powerful in terms of speed and processing power. Hence, software developers realized that they could put server software on individual PCs and initiate a direct two-way flow of information between peers. This led to the revival of P2P.

Interestingly, the IP routing infrastructure is still P2P. Internet routers act as peers in finding the best route from one point on the net to another. Yet overlaid on this structure are several layers of hierarchy. Users get their Internet connectivity from ISPs who, in turn, connect to each other in hierarchies hidden from the end user. These ISPs depend on the same P2P architecture. Similarly, a network of peered-mail servers routes e-mail. Between 1999 and 2000, when Napster was revolutionizing the way users shared music on the Internet, people began to realize the true potential of P2P. Napster is the first large-scale commercial success of P2P in resource sharing.

From the Client/Server Model to P2P

As against the client/server architecture, the greatest strengths of P2P-based models are their decreased dependency on the server and their decentralization of control from servers, which used to be workstations, to peers. Some P2P models do not require servers. End users can directly establish connections with other users without involving servers. Users have more command in P2P-based models than in the typical client /server architecture, in which conventional rules must be followed. Unlike in the C/S system, there is no single point of failure in P2P; in some models, in which P2P puts the server in place, the role of the server is restricted to a bare minimum. To share files, users do not have to seek the help of the server, as they can do this directly among themselves.

In view of these advantages, many corporate houses and computing firms consider the P2P model to be as important as the C/S model. Both models have advantages as well as disadvantages. For example, in the C/S model, the server becomes a bottleneck when too many users log in to download information. In contrast to the P2P model, too many requests sent across the network among users keeps network administrators busy and puts a load on the network itself. Besides, in terms of financial management and administration, the P2P model definitely has an edge over the C/S model. However, practical realization of the pure P2P model still remains to be achieved. Companies such as Intel and IBM are spending millions of dollars and expending significant labor on P2P applications.

In the 1990s, client/server computing architecture was at the peak of its popularity. It attained popularity because it broke down the regime of monopoly of a few data providers across the world; also, it encouraged resource sharing and provided various firewalls to its users. However, in 1999 Napster challenged the C/S architecture. Napster, a P2P-based application, stretched the meaning of sharing beyond the imagination of the C/S creators. With its file-sharing system of MP3 files, Napster gave a new boost and dimension to the network and optimized its role toward greater scalability.

With regard to P2P's popularity and utility, many business organizations are seeking to incorporate it in their purview. Another advantage of P2P is that companies can build collective computing powers and thereby forget servers and expensive storage devices. P2P has shaken the boundaries of networking in terms of sharing resources and costs incurred on servers. Compared with the C/S model, P2P is the better alternative, being more flexible and versatile.

Various P2P Models

P2P models can be divided into the following categories:

♦ Pure peer-to-peer

♦ Peer-to-peer with a simple discovery server

- ◆ Peer-to-peer with discovery and lookup servers
- ◆ Peer-to-peer with discovery, lookup, and content servers

Pure P2P Model

The pure P2P model entirely depends on computers (*clients* in the C/S model). This may seem contradictory because each networking model involves both the computer and the server, like the typical client/server architecture. But the pure P2P model works *without relying on any central server*. Once the P2P application is downloaded in the memory of the machine, peers find other connected peers on the network dynamically. The entire communication occurs among connected peers without any assistance from a server (see Figure 1-1). By communication, we mean transferring data in the form of uploading and downloading files, carrying out on-line activities, sending requests, receiving responses, and so on.

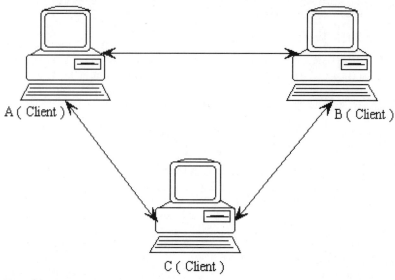

Figure 1-1: The pure peer-to-peer model

This feature of the pure P2P-based model breaks the conventional method of communication in client/server-based models in which the entire communication process between the client and server takes place based on rules the server sets. The pure P2P-based model allows users to set their own rules and to set up their own networking environments. The P2P model completely eliminates the headache of becoming part of any server or ISP to utilize the Internet.

Pure P2P models provide almost plug-and-play features for working with the Internet, in the sense that you just connect to the Internet and you can use the P2P feature. Another advantage of the pure P2P model is that it not only works efficiently for the Internet but also is quite beneficial for LAN or an intranet.

The only problem with the pure P2P model is finding peers on the network. Because no central administration registers the entry of peers that log in to the network, the users themselves have to locate other peers.

P2P with Simple Discovery Server

The very name of this model suggests its constitution. Such P2P models do not actually involve a server. To affect some administration, server boundaries have been laid down in this model. But the role of the server in this model is restricted to providing the names of already connected peers to the incoming peer, which notifies the server about its presence by logging in. It must be noted that the server only assists peers by providing a list of connected peers and that establishing connection and communication still remains the job of the peers (see Figure 1-2). Such P2P models surpass the pure P2P model by providing peers the list of already connected peers, which increases the chances of finding a larger number of peers on the network. To download a resource, a peer has to approach each connected peer individually and post its request, which makes the process time consuming.

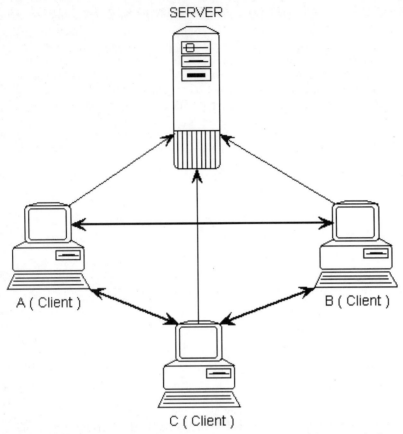

Figure 1-2: Only the discovery of clients occurs via the server; the rest of the communication occurs among peers.

In contrast, in the client/server-based models, any peer looking for resources needs not go around other connected peers, as the server itself maintains all the required content.

P2P with a Discovery and Lookup Server

In this model, the server is used to provide the list of connected peers along with the resources available with each of them (refer to Figure 1-2). Hence, this model integrates the features of the pure P2P and the P2P with simple discovery server models for enhanced functionality of the server.

This model reduces the burden on peers, as there is no longer a need to visit each peer personally for the required information. The server in such a model initiates communication between two peers; once again, the two connected peers establish communication, keep it alive, and perform various activities, like logging into the database the information about the connecting peers, entering an index of resources shared by them, and so on.

P2P with a Discovery, Lookup, and Content Server

In this model, the server dominates as in a typical client/server architecture. All the facets of catering to the requests of peers are removed from the purview of peers and reside with server (see Figure 1-3).

Also, peers are not permitted to connect with each other directly, as all resources are stored in the database of the centrally located server. If a peer requires information, instead of communicating with another peer, it approaches the server. The server processes requests and displays sources of information.

The major disadvantage of this model is that the server slows down if too many requests come up simultaneously. Another disadvantage of such models is high cost because the server has to manage and store data, and cater to all requests, by itself.

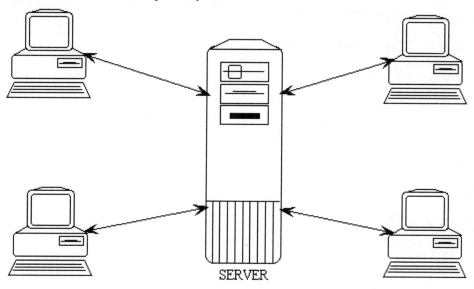

Figure 1-3: P2P with a discovery, lookup, and content server

Because such models are entirely dependent on the central server, chances of failure through a single point increase, affecting the entire system. This is not the case with the previously discussed P2P models.

Existing P2P Applications

Now that we have described the various P2P models, let's proceed to examine two well known P2P applications: Napster and Gnutella.

Napster

Napster, which is based on the third variety of the P2P models we discussed, is the first commercial success of P2P on a big scale. Shawn Fanning, Napster's developer, was 19 when he invented it in 1999. Napster's style model focuses on sharing a particular file extension. Executable files or simple document files can be shared. This is the concept we have used in our application so that files can easily be downloaded or uploaded among computers.

Because Napster allows only files with MP3 extensions, whenever you decide to look for a song, you open the Napster utility. Napster logs on to the central server via the user's Internet connection. This central server keeps an index of all the registered users that are online. It also maintains directories of the MP3 music files stored on the machines of users. These directories are updated every time you log onto or off of the Napster server.

When you send a request or search for a particular song, the central Napster server looks for the song in the indexes of the users currently online. The Napster server then displays the list of the currently connected users whose collections contain the song you request.

You can then click any name from the list and open a direct link with that user. The central server connects you to the user and gets out of the way. The file is downloaded from one user to the other. The actual file is never stored on the Napster server.

Napster does not sell, store, or transfer music files. It is only a platform to enable you to find a file that is requested by the peer. The Napster server enables you to search music available on other PCs and allows direct traffic among users. The Napster central server records its registered users and the music files available on their hard disks. This record is updated each time you log in. When you download and install the Napster program on your PC, it asks you which folders you want to share with other users.

Gnutella

In 1999, Napster forced serious thinkers to reconsider what network is and how Napster had redefined it by stretching the rules of the information technology industry. In spite of criticism from various copyright lawyers and music industries, Napster's popularity never diminished but kept increasing. Inspired by the way Napster changed the rules, another P2P-based mode, Gnutella, entered the market. It went one step beyond Napster. Napster was the catch phrase of the late '90s, but this century belongs to Gnutella.

Gnutella works more or less like a pure P2P model. Gnutella is downloaded and installed on the computer. Once the computer on which you have installed Gnutella, is connected with the network, a message is sent to a computer, which passes it to the other computers, which are also connected to the Gnutella network via the Internet, to let them know about your presence. Message forwarding works this way: You get connected on the network and inform a computer, which, in turn, informs 10 others. These 10 computers inform 9 more computers, and so on.

Gnutella is a client-based software that has a file-sharing service and a mini search engine. Once Gnutella is installed on your local machine, you can serve the requests of other users, acting somewhat like a server and, on the other hand, can find the desired content by sending requests on the Gnutella network for locating the user who has the requested content. You can directly download the content from its machine. Searching on Gnutella is almost like working with any other search engine. In the same way, Gnutella works on the network processes and shows the client what has been requested. Searching on Gnutella is more convenient and promising, as the search occurs directly on Gnutella users' computers without involving any centralized server search. One limitation is that if the load on the server increases or the server slows down due to some technical problem, all services slow down or come to a halt. Though the searching service in Gnutella is free, this also has some limitations. From the data seeker's point of view, there is no certainty of the direction in which the request is proceeding, as many data providers are on the network, making it impossible for the client to discover who fulfills the request. This information may be needed for future references. From the data provider's point of view, there is no guarantee that you hear all the queries.

But in terms of its file-sharing system, Gnutella certainly maintains an edge over other P2P models. Napster encourages its users to share music files via the centralized server solely. Gnutella facilitates not only your ability to share music files but also to share all kinds of files, from MP3 to executable files, without a server.

Some key terms often used in Gnutella networking are the following:

♦ **Servent:** Because in Gnutella architecture users can be either clients or service providers, depending on the situation, they are collectively referred to as *servents*.

♦ **Horizon:** A horizon refers to a group of servents. A horizon does not represent the entire Gnutella network but is itself divided into various horizons.

- **Firewall:** A firewall is a shield that protects users inside the Gnutella network. Users outside the firewall cannot send requests to servents inside the firewall, and servents cannot send requests/responses to users or servents outside the firewall.

- **Broadcasting:** Broadcasting is just like the messaging service servents carry out within themselves across Gnutella network. Broadcasting can be done in two ways: send messages over the entire network, or send messages to a particular location.

- **Dropped Packets:** Dropped packets are small packages of data that have been lost or dropped across the Gnutella network. This happens because the client connected to the other end does not keep pace with the data flow. Dropped packets can be minimized by revisiting servents and asking them for dropped packets.

- **Push Request:** Whenever a client behind the firewall is unable to download a file from a servent, the firewall sends a request to the server for uploading the file. This is called a push request.

- **Port:** An application on a computer is assigned a specific port number. For example, the default port number for Gnutella servents is 6346. This means a servent running Gnutella software is available on port 6346.

Although Gnutella is gaining popularity, it is also encountering several bugs in its functioning across the network. Gnutella is still in its infancy and has not matured enough to match its popularity. Some of the major drawbacks of Gnutella are the following:

- The Gnutella protocol, being very simple, knows only how data is transferred from one location to another. It does not guarantee that each site interprets data. The number of lost packets in Gnutella is quite high. In addition, no provision stops requests that keep crowding a servent. In such situations, the servent can easily become a bottleneck.

- The fixed time to remain an eligible user of the Gnutella network imposes a limit on its users.

The biggest drawback of Gnutella is that it is very hard for the user to verify the source of information, that is, the peer on which the client's information is processed, as security is not addressed adequately. In other words, it is very difficult to find the server where the client's request is being processed.

Yet, in spite of all its limitations and the criticism it faces from the IT gurus, Gnutella and Napster are in the race neck and neck. It is very hard to judge which one is better, because in one way or another, each is maintaining an edge over the other. A brief comparison is presented for you to decide whether Gnutella or Napster deserves the higher pedestal (see Table 1-1).

Table 1-1: Pros and Cons of Napster and Gnutella

Napster	*Gnutella*
Positive	
Gives material to its customer in the form of MP3 music files all across the continents. This is the key reason for its popularity.	Truly decentralized network due to the absence of the server. Chances of failure at single point to affect services is completely ruled out.
Provides a protective layer to its user due to the involvement of a server. Fully authenticated data travels on Napster network.	Shares not only MP3 files but also other files such as .exe, jpg, and so on.
User friendly and easy to download on your computer.	Has a provision for redirecting the request, plus supports HTTP protocol.
Negative	
Server presence slows down or brings services to a halt in case of a technical problem. Server can	No provision for stopping the flood of requests.

easily become the bottleneck once requests flood it, as there is no provision for redirecting the requests.	
Works for only MP3 files. It does not share any other files on its network.	Absence of the server makes user feel unsafe, as it is tough to find out on Gnutella network where data is sent from.
Facing the opposition of copyright lawyers and the music industry.	Encounters many bugs in its application, such as lost packets.

Working of Various P2P Models

Whether it is a P2P-based application or a typical client/server-based application, the way an application works matters a lot. A typical P2P-based application can be based on any of the models discussed previously, but some prerequisites exist for an application to be an ideal P2P application. Some of the key features every model P2P application should have are the following:

- ◆ **Tracing out other peers:** Finding other peers connected to the server
- ◆ **Querying peers for required content:** Getting lists of shared resources from other peers
- ◆ **Sharing content/resources with other peers:** Learning how contents are shared among the peer network

In the upcoming discussion, a comprehensive explanation makes you more familiar with how various P2P models work (that is, how P2P-based applications incorporate these essential features).

Tracing Out Other Peers

Tracing out other peers is an essential feature of every P2P-based application. This feature is discussed with reference to different P2P models in the following sections.

- ◆ **Discovering other peers in pure P2P-based model:** Because this model is without a server, peers find others dynamically and communicate between themselves directly. This communication, therefore, is not restrained by the terms and regulations that the conventional methods impose. However, though local configuration schemes and network messaging services are available, a user logging on to a pure P2P model may not always obtain a substantial number of peers to cater to the request posted. Besides, the direct communication between peers affects security.
- ◆ **Discovering peers in P2P with simple discovery server-based model:** This model incorporates a centrally located server. This server, in its database, stores the information related to all registered users. Any query for searching a particular peer is processed by the server, which returns a list of other peers from its database. The main advantages with this method are enchanced security and the availability of a large number of peers to the requesting peer. However, if the server slows down or crashes, locating peers becomes difficult, and other peers are also affected.
- ◆ **Discovering peers in P2P with a discovery and lookup server-based model:** In this model, the server provides a list of services as well as a list of peers. All users are required to notify their presence to the server while they log in. The server not only discovers other peers but also returns vital information regarding all logged in peers. Therefore, this model reduces time consumption considerably as compared to the other models.
- ◆ **Discovering peers in P2P with a discovery, lookup, and content server-based model:** This model traces out peers in response to a request much like the others. The centrally located server in this case maintains all the vital information and also furnishes the content to requesting peers. Each peer is registered with the server, and the server handles all requests on its own and serves responses. The dependency on the server is therefore very high.

Querying Peers for Required Content

The user initiates the request for content. Any application can make a request for content to a peer once a peer has been traced and located. Only a peer can provide the content required. A peer might not entertain the query the user presents or might not have the information the user seeks. In such cases, the better option is to utilize the server to send the request over the network, as in the pure P2P model, than to approach a single peer.

Yet the strong point of the P2P model is that against conventional models, which invariably require a centrally located server for communication among peers, it allows direct communication among peers. If the approached peer has the requested content and it is willing to furnish it, the positive points of this architecture become evident. The relegation of the server to the background pre-empts the situation in which overload on the server renders it a bottleneck. Because the load on the server is reduced, the overheads to be incurred on account of the server are reduced. Also, if the server breaks down, services are not halted. Apart from tracing out potent peers and initiated connections, the role of the server is not significant. Once connection among peers has been established, communication takes place among peers, and the server is not in the picture.

Tracing out other peers and initiating connections are the server's tasks. Peers query directly with each other once the preceding two tasks are complete. The process by which peers query one another for content also varies slightly depending on the P2P model being employed:

- **Querying peers for content in the pure P2P model:** A peer passes its request for content to another peer, the latter being referred to as the host peer. If the host peer contains the required information and it is within the scope of its criteria for shared resources, the latter satisfies the former's query. Thus, a peer can procure an executable file from another peer, which is found dynamically. This model provides an interchangeability of the role of peers. Thus, when a peer requests information, it acts as client; and when a peer is providing information, it assumes the role of a server. In effect, this model permits the exchange of the client/server functions.

- **Querying peers for content in the P2P model with a simple discovery server:** This model uses the functionality of a server (that is, of providing the list of logged-in peers to a requesting peer); however, another peer provides this service. The most patent advantage of this model over the pure P2P model is that because the presence of a centrally located peer acts as a server, a requesting peer always gets a large number of peers of interest so it can communicate with them. The main disadvantage is that because the requesting peer has to contact each peer in the list by itself and individually for processing the information, processing time is abundant. Overheads are the regular maintenance required for the infrastructure, such as data-storage capability and related peripherals.

- **Querying peer for content in P2P with a discovery and lookup server:** This model provides additional advantages over the previous models, attributed to the more pronounced role of the server. The role of the server is not limited here to just maintaining a list of registered users but extends to processing queries for the content the requesting peer seeks. The requesting peer in this case passes its query to the server, not to individual peer. The server processes the query to locate the peer that has matching contents, and this information is returned to the requesting peer. The searching path of a peer seeking content is thereby shortened. But with this model, the server is taxed, and its increased demands are liable to affect its speed and general performance. This shortcoming is more than offset by the drastic reduction in network traffic.

- **Querying for content in P2P with a discovery, lookup, and content server:** In this model, the role of the server is the most significant. The requesting peers approach the server, and the server not only processes the request but also procures the result and returns it to the requesting peer. The server not only maintains a list of registered users but also undertakes the entire connection management to provide the content by itself. Because the server has to manage the whole session for providing the content, it is prone to become a gridlock. Also, costs on account of the server are high. However, this method protects information from invasion. This advantage is substantial. The server ensures reliable, uniform process handling coupled with caution that makes for high security.

Sharing Contents with Other Peers

Sharing refers to how contents are asked for, how resources are shown and shared, and how connected peers share resources over the network on locating each other. As mentioned previously, the role of the server is not mandatory with some P2P models. Files can be passed between peers without resorting to the server, except for some cases in which the server initiates connection. Thus, information and resources are shared among peers over the network. The peer provides the resource that parses the query of a requesting peer to return the result. This must not be confused with the result(s) the server provides. The server provides information about connected peers only. Note that in the P2P model, with a discovery, lookup, and content, the server controls all the operations and that this model is an exception.

♦ **Sharing resourcea with peers in the pure P2P model:** When a peer sends a request for content to another peer, if the desired content is available with the latter, it is downloaded across the network. In the case of the pure P2P model, peer is the service provider which has shared resources. The requesting peer just sends its request to the peer it approaches. It is the peer that has the requested information that opens the connection.

♦ **Sharing resources in the P2P model with a simple discovery server:** Here, a peer that requires content sends its query to the server. The server, in response, returns the list of all connected peers. The requesting peer approaches peers individually from this list for required content. Once the requesting peer locates the content required, the server connects them. The requesting peer downloads the required content from the network. Though the process is lengthy, the requesting peer obviously has a substantial number of peers it may approach. Uploading content cannot occur in this model. We discuss this limitation in the following section.

♦ **Sharing resources in the P2P model with a discovery and lookup server:** As with the previous model, in this model the requesting peer approaches the server but differently. The server doesn't just furnish the list of peers; it carries out the search on the basis of the search criteria and traces out peers of relevance. The requesting peer downloads the required content from the network stream. Uploading is also possible with this method. A peer can upload contents to the server as well as to other peers. The availability of both uploading and downloading makes this model highly flexible as compared with the other P2P models.

♦ **Sharing resources in P2P with a discovery, lookup, and content model:** This P2P model is almost like the C/S computing architecture. In this model, all information is housed in the centrally located server. Here, the peer that requires content passes its request to this centrally located server. The server processes the request, procures the result, and returns it to the requesting peer. The server itself carries out both uploading and downloading. For retrieving content over the network easily, this is the best-suited option. This model offers high security to users. Uniformity in accessing the contents and information reliability are other advantages, whereas high costs due to the server might be daunting.

Searching for Shared Resources

Searching is a term every computer user is familiar with, but it has many subtle connotations that are often overlooked. Generally, it means searching for a file or a folder by using a user-entered phrase. Search engines such as Google or even the local machine itself may be used for this purpose. Searching is used mainly to save time and to reduce effort. Thus, a search technique may win a required file from a large database of files in no time. But searching techniques are best appreciated if you consider how to sort out a situation over a network when you know what you want but do not know where to find it in the vast diversity of randomly distributed files. Here, you may type the phrase that you want to search, and the server will do the searching and return the results. All Web sites and service providers incorporate searching facilities as imperative features because they accumulate an otherwise unfathomable ocean of information.

Searching may be divided into two distinct categories:

- Server-side searching
- Client-side searching

Server-Side Searching

Networks such as LAN, MAN, WAN, and so on, employ server-side searching. In general, a server, wherever present in computing architecture, acts as the reservoir of all information. Often, data integrity, consistency, and security a computing architecture can boast of can be ascribed to a server acting as a centralized data-management unit. Multiple-user requests are processed on the common platform the server offers. Server-side searching always results in the most updated information. Search criteria have to be passed to the server, and the server must refer to its database or file system to cater to the request. The search result is returned to the user as the response. The greatest advantage of server-side searching is that the user need not worry about the location of a file. Connection may be made only to peers that possess required content. This is particularly relevant in a situation in which many users are connected and are liable to modify a file. Although safe and descriptive, the requesting clients may send an avalanche of requests and may slow down server's services.

Client-Side Searching

Client-side searching comes into play when peers are connected with each other and are communicating without the involvement of any other machine or server. But even with client-side searching, things can look a bit cluttered if too much of the information is shared by any of the peers involved in communication. Thus, the search facility finds its relevance at this level, too. Usually, client-side searching is performed on the basis of prior information about the contents residing on one peer. Other peers connected to such peers may search at this level to make their work easier. Once they are connected to the peer that has the required information, they don't need to look for that information on that computer; search facility, at this level, expedites the process of finding information.

Such surfing occurs on a local machine (that is, a search is confined to a particular computer only). It is not concerned with network searching performed on a server. Here you search for a particular file or folder within your machine. Client-side searching reflects the changes and modifications you have made before saving the document. In addition, client-side searching is limited to the user's machine but is faster than server-side searching because it occurs on a single machine, and a single user performs it.

Searching Techniques in P2P Models

In the P2P model, the search for content keeps changing according to the applicability of the model. Some models of the P2P architecture follow client-side searching, others follow server-side searching, and others follow both types of searching. Searching facilities always have to strike a balance between the merits of speed and reliability on the one hand and the flaws of nonpertinent information and unreliability on the other. Advantages are speed, direct communication, and reliability; disadvantages are unreliable and nonapplicable information. The following are the types of searching techniques various models follow:

- **Searching for content in the pure P2P model:** Because this model is without a server, it employs the client-side searching model. If a requesting peer has prior information regarding the location of another peer, which has the required content, the process provides unsurpassed speed. There is no queuing of requests on a server to rank priority, as with the conventional client/server models, for procuring the content is a matter of direct communication among peers. However, the absence of a server imposes a dearth of peers that may be approached for content.

- **Searching contents in the P2P with a simple discovery server model:** This model does have a server, yet it employs the client-side searching technique. The server presents the requesting peer a list of connected users. The requesting peer finds which peer has the required information, approaches it, and procures content. Obviously, the process is lengthy as far as the requesting peer is considered. The advantage of this method is that it provides a large number of peers that may be approached for the required content.

♦ **Searching contents in P2P with a discovery and lookup server model:** This model follows both client-side searching and server-side searcling. Among all P2P models, this model is the most efficient and flexible. Whenever a peer wishes to find or search some particular content, it can search directly on the already connected peers on the server, or it can simply query the server to reply with the results of the required information. In this model, apart from connected peers over the network, the server remains available to serve the requesting peer. Such a searching facility is possible on the server because whenever a registered peer logs on to it, apart from authentication, it sends the list of shared resources on the server along with its login name. Hence, it becomes easier for the requesting peer to search the content instead of approaching each peer individually. In case the requesting peer does not want to take the assistance of the server, it can directly approach the peer and can pass search criteria to it. The advantage of this search technique is a flexible approach that facilitates the requesting peer with both searching options. The time consumed to search information decreases rapidly in this model. But in spite of the heavy cost the server incurs, this model of P2P computing architecture is still the favorite among developers and users.

♦ **Searching contents in P2P with a discovery, lookup, and content server model:** This model restricts all client-side searching techniques, as the centrally located server takes command of the entire network. Here, the requesting peer is not required to contact other peers for information, as the server caters to all search processes. This model is completely based on the server-side searching technique. Whenever a peer requires information, it simply contacts the server, as the server keeps the entire information in database, ranging from information about the registered peers to all possible contents. Because the entire network in such models remains in the hands of the server, it is very easy for the server to become a bottleneck. If too many peers approach the server for content, its processing speed decreases and so do other related services. The positive side is that peers perform in a uniform way and receive results in the same way. Besides, there is no risk that any malicious peer is sitting at the other end, thereby shielding users.

A Brief Description of Our P2P Application

The application developed in this book involves various high-level programming techniques: C# and Java programming; socket programming; Web requests and responses; threading; and XML documents. You must have a working knowledge of the preceding concepts to understand the application developed in this book. Because XML communication is the backbone of our application, allowing an interoperable design, you must know XML thoroughly. The application also involves wide usage of threading and sockets.

We have discussed developing this application in Java as well as in C#. The software requirements for the Java version are JDK1.3, Apache Xerces XML Parser, CLDC 1.0.2, and KXML Parser. For the C# version, the software requirements are Microsoft Visual Studio .NET (Beta2) and MS XML Parser3.0. The hardware requirements for both the versions are Pentium1 or above, 128MB RAM or more, 1.4G or more of free hard disk space, and an Internet connection. The Operating System is Windows 2000 (Professional Edition) for both versions.

Our P2P application is based on the third model (P2P with discovery and lookup server model) of the P2P hierarchy. In our application, file sharing takes place between two connected peers regardless of their file extensions. The application consists of three components:

♦ **Listener:** Handles requests of incoming peer connections

♦ **Server:** Maintains the database required for the application

♦ **Browser:** Shows results to the peer through a user-friendly interface and acts as an interactive layer for the client

Though applications in the P2P model can be built without involving the server, in the long run it may cause problems for end users and at the network-traffic-management level. Moreover, with the presence of a server, users automatically feel secure, as it protects them and applications from any invasion such as unauthorized access and downloading files. This application is the first step toward resource sharing in a true sense; from server technology to client technology, every bit of information is provided for the user in an interactive and user-friendly manner. Application components handle and perform the following tasks described in the following section.

Role of Each Component

Each of the preceding components performs a specific role to enable the application to run smoothly. The boundaries and roles of each component are described sequentially.

The listener

The first jobs the listener performs are logging on to the server, notifying the server about its own presence, and listing its shared resources. After logging on, the listener can handle the requests of clients the server passes to it. The listener downloads files whenever a client approaches it. Along with the downloading process, a listener can easily handle multiple clients with their requests. In essence, while handling multiple clients, the listener acts like a server. While accepting requests and responding to clients, the listener, like a server, enables you to use the search option in an expanded way. As mentioned previously, the server performs only root-level searches (searching for the shared resources at the basic level). To search beyond the root level, the listener helps you.

If the listener declares any folder directly as a shared resource, you can easily open the folder for details and view all files listed under it. Such a search is much faster than a root search performed at the server level. At the listener level, the search occurs on a single machine with prior information about the location of content. One important feature of the listener is that it can run in *unattended mode*; that is, in the absence of the user.

The server

The server holds the list of all registered listeners along with the detailed description of their resources, which listeners offer to share with other peers. Notice that a file on the client or the listener machine never passes through the server. After providing the list of listeners, the server initiates a connection between the listener and the client. The rest remains in the hands of the listener and the client. If the client wants to download a file from the listener machine, it does so directly without involving the server. A client can query the server to show the list of listeners, which can fulfill its request.

In the P2P environment, such searching is called a *global request*. Another term associated with searching while using the server is *root search*, which occurs while the listener declares its shared resources. In simple terms, after establishing a connection between the listener and the client, the server points out the folder or directory that contains the required content for the client. It does not facilitate an in-depth search facility of every folder or directory. To do this, you have to understand the listener's role detailed in the previous section.

The browser

The browser acts as the interface between the user and the computer. Through the browser, the client sends its requests and receives the listener's response. Unlike the listener, the browser always runs in *attended mode*. The browser shows the list of listeners logged in and sends all requests to the listener, which the listener itself processes. Once the listener processes the request, the browser shows the results at the user end. Note that it is not the browser that does the processing; the listener does this. The user sees only the result of the query. *Processing content is kept encapsulated from users.*

You can search for shared contents based on various criteria with the help of the browser. For instance, a client can request that the listener show only document files or request that only executable files be displayed. Along with a search based on some criteria, you can prompt the browser to make a global search on the server to fetch the list of active listeners, apart from querying listeners for contents only.

Some of the highlights of this application are as follows:

- ♦ Downloading and uploading files is possible.
- ♦ Intense search-option facilities are available to easily locate files ranging from document files to executable files and Dynamic Link Libraries.
- ♦ The interface is user friendly with online help to guide you.
- ♦ High-speed connectivity with the server is available.
- ♦ Easy chatting over the network is possible.

This is our first step toward redefining the network, and we expect a positive response from our users.

The Relationship of Three Components

Apart from performing their individual tasks, the server, listener, and browser bear some relationship to each other. Based on this application's P2P computing architecture, we categorize the relationship of the three components in the following way:

- ♦ Listener to server relationship
- ♦ Listener to broswer relationship
- ♦ Browser to server relationship

Listener to server relationship

In this relationship, the server maintains the database of all listeners along with their names, IP addresses, and, most important, their shared resources. After being logged on to the server and declaring its shared resources, the listener sends only the names of files and folders along with their destined locations, not the contents of files and folders. By disposing of all files and folders and their contents, the server becomes a bottleneck; plus, the entire load of file sharing and downloading is the server's burden, degrading its performance. Another important point is that the server gives you the list of listeners currently online only, not the list of logged-out listeners.

Listener to browser relationship

The relationship between the browser and listener, to a great extent, is a request/response relationship in which the browser sends all requests to the listener and receives a response in the form of a processed query or message. In this relationship, the listener processes all requests at the listener level, and the browser receives the result at the client end. The client can send requests in various forms:

- ♦ The client can show all the shared files and folders.
- ♦ The client can search or ask the listener to show contents in files and folders, which can't be done at the server level.
- ♦ The client can download the contents by passing a downloading request to the listener.
- ♦ The client can upload its files into the listener's account.
- ♦ When it comes to downloading and uploading files from listener by client, the listener has an upper edge since while sharing contents with the client, the listener has the right to impose its content or information as readable only or readable as well as writable. These rights can be put along with the folder as its property. With these rights, the listener can restrict malicious clients from uploading unnecessary files into its account as well as restrict clients from downloading important information.

Browser to server relationship

In this relationship, the browser brings the list of the listeners at the user end from the server, and it checks with the list with which the listener is sharing resources. Along with retrieving the list of listeners from the server, the browser can pass the root-level search requests. In other words, the browser can search all listeners for the content you require and can inform the client about all eligible listeners as the client demands or requests.

How to Achieve the Preceding Design

To achieve the preceding design, you need three components: the server, listener, and browser. But before proceeding, be aware that, unlike in the pure P2P model, this model incorporates the role of a server. Though the role of the server in this model is not as active as in the C/S architecture, to some extent peers do need to rely on the server for first-hand connection. Sharing of files occurs between the listener (peer) and the client (peer) without involving the server. Contents cannot pass through the server while they are going through the exchange between one peer and another. This model extends the role of the server to include content lookup services.

In this case, the peer-to-peer application not only registers with a server but also uploads the lists of its contents at regular intervals. When an application (client) is looking for some particular content, it queries the central server rather than sending the query to each client. The central server responds with a list of clients (listeners) that contain the requested content, and the peer application (listener) can contact these clients directly to retrieve the content. This model proves to be more efficient than the pure P2P model because it reduces the number of requests going over the network. But, of course, the reduction in load over the network is offset by the higher cost of the server.

Figure 1-4 shows a server (listener) and four separate peers that run the browser software. In fact, the listener can be a browser for other listeners also in cases where one listener is drawing services from the other listener (services can include any of those that a browser can ask for). In this case, after getting the list of the currently active listeners from the server, the browser establishes a direct connection with the listener. More than one browser can be connected to one listener, as shown in Figure 1-4. The browser computer (the client) sends a request to the listener computer in the XML format, and the listener computer responds with the result to the request. If any error occurs in the middle, the listener sends an error-XML response to the browser, and the browser informs the user. This communication is open both ways, from the listener to browser and vice-versa. Exchanging information takes place by using the standard XML document format. Every connection is socket oriented. The listener listens on a particular socket for the browser to connect.

The Purpose of Using the Three Components

In our application, we are using three modules acting like three pillars, which hold the application. These modules are the server, the browser, and the listener, each having a specific role. While preparing the application, we made thorough considerations to enable the application to move among distributed users and various operation systems. Languages such as XML, C#, and Java have been incorporated for easy debugging and increased modularity. Code written for this application is not confined to it, but users can implement code into their own applications. For instance, an audio/video module written as an extension to this application can be used in its existing form — no change made — in any new application to support audio/video streaming. Almost all functions used in this application are implemented and written in such a way that with minor changes in naming conventions, anyone can use them in an application. Whenever the *Java* appears, interoperability follows. Java makes this application more flexible, as it is not restricted to any operating system.

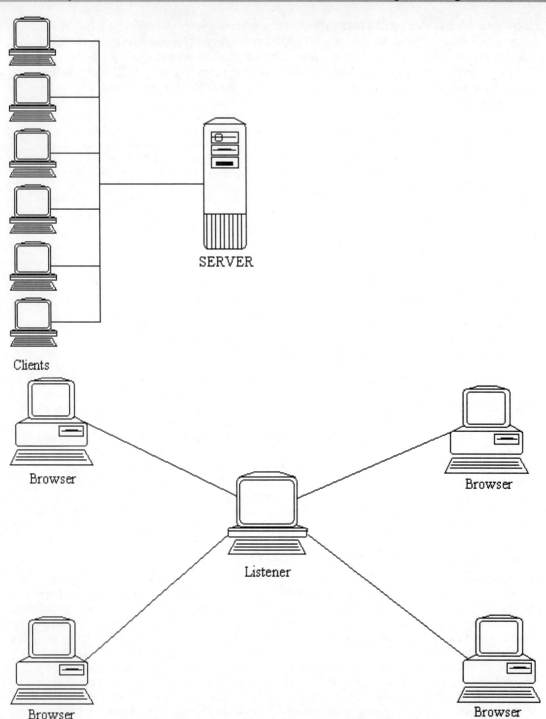

Figure 1-4: Once the list of active listeners is obtained, browsers establish direct connections with them.

Various features are in this application to make it more scalable for the near future. Our application has been designed to survive the changes foreseen in the near future. A server component in our application reduces the traffic over the network and provides protection and performance speed to its users. On behalf of the end user, the server handles the searching process quickly and efficiently, thereby reducing the need for front-end processing. Because our application is distributive, the server can handle multiple clients at any particular moment, thereby increasing the reach of the application.

Summary

In this chapter, we have gone through the history of the evolution of the P2P model. We have discussed the types of P2P models to enable you to understand every aspect of P2P technology. Moreover, we have had a short discussion of the existing P2P models so that you may understand the application better. In addition, we have mentioned the basic technologies you must acquire before exploring application development by using the P2P model. In the following chapters, you find the details of the design of our P2P application, complete coding, and an exercise to help you explore your own skills.

Chapter 2

Designing the P2P Application

This chapter explains the process of designing the P2P application described in the previous chapter. Having provided a basic overview and the technical background of the application and considerations for designing the application in the previous chapter, here the actual process of designing the application is taken up. The chapter begins with a reiteration of design considerations and design parameters. The communication requirements and the means to achieve them by way of this P2P application are detailed. XML design specifications are provided in detail, as the interoperability of the P2P application has been achieved through XML. The server side has been discussed with descriptions of the database, table design, XML implementation in SQL Server 2000, and so on. The client side has been described with details of the browser and the listener, such as handling XML parsing, managing peers, connecting to the server and other peers, and searching.

Design Considerations for the P2P Application

While designing this application, the following key points have been borne in mind.

Applications of this kind are likely to be used on global scale. Thus, it is quite probable that the application will encounter networking problems. Its global nature also leads to a situation in which a good number of users are communicating with one another simultaneously. Therefore, network traffic may exceed the limits estimated to deploy the application to handle data without facing memory problems.

Eventually, users of the application interact with it. Thus, the design should be equipped to be of use in a variety of environments, whether it is used by users at the individual level or by corporate organizations at the enterprise level. Users might propose to avail the design for maintaining their own universities, schools, or community-level networks. Thus, the design has to be flexible enough to easily scale down to work under smaller networks such as LANs.

Without altering its foundation, the application should have the flexibility to be molded as required by the ever-changing technology. This application may serve the basic purpose of resource sharing, but the possibility of the user extending its scope and usability by incorporating additional functionality cannot be overlooked. Because this application is chiefly devoted to educating readers about the idea and the practical implementation of P2P, the design must be such that it easily offers itself to any programmer seeking to add modules written in any language in the existing model of this application. This can be made possible by using ubiquitous techniques legible to all programming languages and platforms. The application should be able to support sharing of all file extensions, not just a few specific ones, and the design must tide over the obstacles imposed by the previously mentioned design considerations.

Constraints

In view of the preceding considerations, it is quite obvious that very little latitude was available as far as the designing process is concerned. The application had to regard and honor all the aspects of design considerations and make its way through the restrictions imposed by them.

Proxy IP Resolution

Because the proxy server serves many nodes through a single Internet connection, individual IP addresses no longer have meaning while working on the Internet. The proxy server recognizes all IP addresses behind it by using its own IP address. On behalf of the user, the proxy server sends and receives data. In essence, the proxy server acts as a layer between the end user and the Internet. In the absence of a proxy server, all machines are free to establish connections directly on the Internet. So this is a scenario in which dynamic IP addresses assigned to the machine are being used for communication through sockets. How do you make this application work behind a proxy? This has been reserved as an interesting topic for you to explore.

Problems in Transfer of Data

Because users of this application are likely to be scattered around the globe, communication might be the main issue as the probability of a large number of users flocking to the server all the time is high. Download and upload processes are the most sensitive operations, being highly susceptible to communication problems. This problem is tackled to an extent in this application by keeping the connection open long enough only to serve the request. Keeping only the active connections (connections on which some operation is being carried out) open reduces the number of connections at a given time to be monitored, thus reducing load on the server.

Security

While discussing the possible users of this application under design considerations, we have considered whether this application will be used in corporate environments or by individuals. The main difference between the two is that under security-intensive corporate environments, in which corporate firewalls generally allow communication on a particular port only, this application may fail at times to communicate. If this application were aiming for a corporate audience, we would have to talk to the administrator of the concerned corporate network; then the application would have to communicate through corporate firewalls. But because this application is designed for users who are not likely to go through a firewall to find other peers, just about any port that is not already reserved for another protocol can work.

This kind of communication demands that you use registered ports ranging from 1024 to 49151 or dynamic or private ports ranging from 49152 to 65535.

For a list of the well-known and registered ports, an IANA port-assignments list is available at `http://www.iana.org/assignments/port-numbers`. For this application, port number 7070 has been declared.

Structure of the P2P Application

As mentioned in Chapter 1, our P2P application is based on three components: listener, browser, and server. In Figure 2-1 we depict two peers, the listener and the browser running our application from remote locations intending to share resources with each other. While sharing resources with each other, both peers perform two basic operations:

- ♦ **Making requests:** A process for establishing communication for further interactions
- ♦ **Responding:** A process for returning an appropriate response either through the messaging scheme or by simply returning the result corresponding to the request

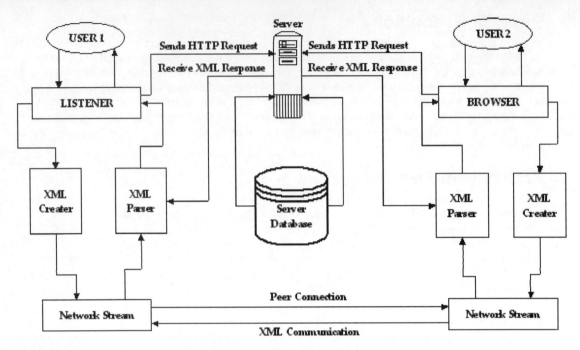

Figure 2-1: Listener and browser running the application from remote locations

In our application, the peer depicted as listener has been assigned the job of catering to the requests made by other peers, whereas the browser is the peer from which all requests are made.

The server maintains the database that holds records of information of all logged-in peers, such as their IP addresses and login names, along with summaries of their shared resources (resources peers have declared as *shared* for other peers). It is important to mention that all components involved in our application use XML. Our application heavily depends on XML, as whatever communication takes place between the components in the background is through XML documents. We have chosen XML as the communication medium for our application because XML is legible to all contemporary programming languages.

Two prewritten components are used for handling XML in our application:

♦ **The XML parser:** Used for parsing the responses and requests generated

♦ **The XML creator:** Used for creating appropriate requests and responses

At the start of the application, the listener logs on to the server by sending an HTTP request containing information such as the login name, the IP address, and a description of shared resources. The listener is required to make entries to the server, which authenticates the information it receives from the listener. Authentication by the server is successful if the information passed is correct; on the other hand, authentication fails if the server finds something wrong, such as duplicity, with the information sent. In both cases, the server returns the appropriate response in XML format, which is then forwarded to the XML parser for parsing. Finally, the appropriate message is displayed to the listener.

Now we assume that the peer acting as the listener has successfully logged on to the server. The listener is ready to cater to the requirements of other peers. Meanwhile, the browser looking for content approaches the server by sending an HTTP request.

Once again, the server responds to the peer in XML format but with a slight difference. In the former case, the XML response is returned subject to authentication. In case of a browser request, the server returns the XML response as the list of all connected peers. The server equips the browser with the list of the various listeners along with their shared resources and respective IP addresses.

Now, based on its requirement, the browser can choose the listener. From here on, the role of the server is absent, as it has completed the task of initiating communication between peers. It must be emphasized that the server initiates communication, whereas the browser establishes the connection between itself and the peer for further communication. The listener never initiates the connection with the browser; instead, it searches for the requests on the connection opened by browsers.

Thus, the browser performs two steps: It approaches the server and then establishes communication with the listener. Subsequently, the communication exists directly between the two peers (the listener and the browser). The browser opens the network streams for the listener for reading and writing data in XML format. Generally, uploading and downloading files/folders takes place between peers.

To retrieve content from the listener, the browser downloads specific information from the remotely located listener. For this, the browser creates the request XML by using the XML creator component and writes it on the network stream of the listener. The listener then parses the incoming request and finally judges which file needs to be uploaded for browser calls waiting on the XML parser. It can either be a response written for the request made by using XML creator or the file requested for download, which is then uploaded by writing it on the network stream of the browser. Finally, the browser reads the file uploaded at its end by the listener, checks whether the file is a response for the request the browser has made or a file the browser has requested for downloading, and the appropriate message is displayed.

Just as the browser downloads files from the listener, it can upload files to the listener. To achieve this, the browser selects a memory area that is shared by the other peer through its listener, selects a file that it intends to upload, and generates a request XML to the listener. Upon receiving such a request, the listener checks the shared memory area for the credentials for the file to be written. Upon finding sufficient credentials, it begins to read the file being written by the browser running on the other peer and writes the data coming its way. If adequate credentials are not found, a denial response is made and returned to the browser.

These two processes are described in more detail later in this chapter in the section titled "Downloading and Uploading Files."

Achieving Proper Communication among Modules

This application is designed to make room for third-party add-ons to be incorporated effectively. Achieving communication with add-ons written by third parties has been the major obstacle to accomplishing this design, as new extensions written for this application should be able to converse with it in its existing form. Also, the incorporation of new modules must not tax the performance and must be compatible with the application's existing design.

To construct such a flexible structure, there are only a few technical options to choose from. Foremost among such techniques is COM, which has been popular with programmers lately for such designs. COM is a popular model because of its capabilities place special emphasis on communication among different and distant modules. COM's competence in effective communication and callbacks, even across networks (through DCOM), makes it a good choice for the foundation of software.

But the biggest shortcoming of COM is that in its present form COM/DCOM is not well supported by languages other than those Microsoft has hybridized to support it, one such language being Java. Neither on technical grounds nor on commercial ones can it be assumed that Java programmers would never turn toward writing add-ons for this application. So COM has had to be ruled.

The option left is to custom craft an agile structure that perfectly suits the work at hand. This is not as difficult as it sounds. After a little thought and exploration, we have encountered SOAP (Simple Object Access Protocol), in which every software essentially stands on a basic exchange of data blocks called *events.* If this basic data exchange can be standardized, any kind of module is able to communicate with any other. This can be done by using XML as the mediator for communication. When we write *communication,* we actually mean firing events, handling them, and responding back. This idea has been chosen to be the foundation of our software. In the following sections, we explain how communication among different modules has been achieved.

Listener to Server Communication Using ASP

When the listener is initiated, a login window is displayed. In this login window, you are prompted to enter the name with which you want to be identified. Internally, the IP address of the listener, not the login name, is used for communication. After entering the login name, click the login button. The listener then calls an ASP page named Login.ASP. To register you on the server, the listener has to pass the shared resources list, your login name, and your IP address (see Figure 2-2). The login page and parameters are as follows:

```
http://abc/login.asp?USERID=username&IP=ip addresses SHARE=file1*file2*...*filen
```

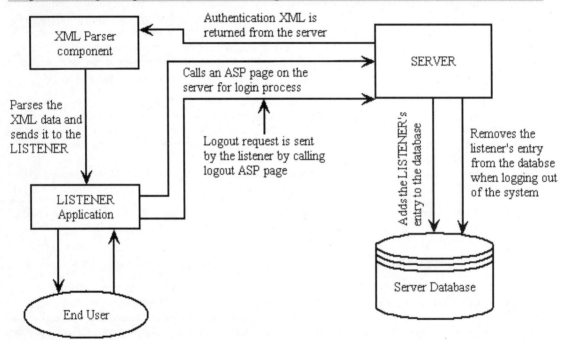

Figure 2-2: The user interacting with the Server through Listener.

Make all the necessary entries after validating each and every argument and then throw an XML as the response to the listener who has made the request. After this, the server is bypassed, and the listener never communicates with the server until it logs out. When the listener logs out, a request to unregister the listener from the server by removing all the relevant entries is sent via ASP. The parameter for log out is:

```
http://abc/logout.asp? IP=ip address of the user
```

Browser to Server Using ASP

After the listener has successfully connected with the server, the browser (client) communicates with the server (Figure 2-3). The browser obtains the list of all the currently running listeners and displays the list in its window. Then the browser sends a request to the server by loading an ASP page from the server. The address of the server's ASP page is as follows:

```
http://abc/userlist.asp
```

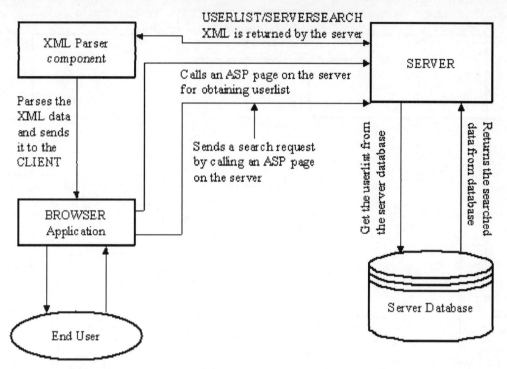

Figure 2-3: Server's ASPs entertaining the user running Browser

The server, in turn, retrieves the list of all the currently running listeners available in its database and passes the response to the browser in the form of an XML. The browser shows the list from this XML to the user after parsing it.

The server again enters the picture when the browser needs to search some file globally. In such a case, the browser sends a request to the server for the particular search by passing parameters to an ASP page. The address is as follows:

```
http://abc/search.asp?US="computername criteria"&FS="file search criteria"
```

The parameters passed to the ASP are the search criteria for the user names and the shared files. The server conducts the search by applying the search criteria passed by the browser in the database and returns the result in the form of an XML. When the user selects a name from the user list and connects to it, the browser establishes a connection with the selected listener. A direct communication is established between the listener and the browser by using the IP address from the user list. The server is bypassed for all further communication between the browser and the listener.

Listener to Browser Using XML

This communication in this application works on sockets, which uses the network stream of the system for communicating with each other. The listener and the browser software write to their respective streams and read from there. In this case, a request/response mechanism is involved. The browser sends requests in the form of XMLs to the listener by writing the request to the listener's network stream, and the listener reads from its network stream and processes the request (shown in Figure 2-4).

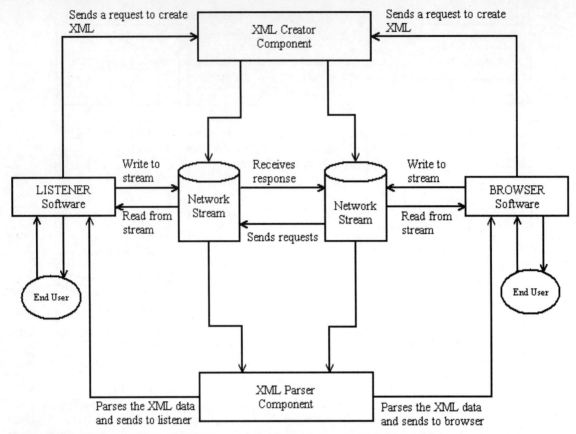

Figure 2-4: Listener and Browser exchange XML response/requests to communicate with each other.

The response is written by the listener on the browser's network stream over a socket connection, and the browser starts reading from its network stream to get the data the listener sends. The data can come in XML format or in standard-byte format. When XML data is received on any end, the XML parser parses that XML and sends it to its respective owner. The XML is created through the XML creator component of the system. If the browser wants to download or upload any file to the listener, it sends an XML request through the XML creator and transfers the file directly over the socket connection. The listener interprets this data and processes it accordingly.

XML Request and Response DesignSpecifications

As the first step, the software logs on to the server and is processed for authentication by the server. Authentication information is sent back to the requestor in XML format. From here after, modules communicate with each other in the form of making requests and getting the responses to them. XML mediations for communication designed for this purpose can be divided broadly into two categories: Request XMLs and Response XMLs.

Request XMLs are further elaborated to make different kind of requests; *Response XMLs* respond to different kinds of requests. Malfunctioning of the application at either end is signaled at the other end as an Error Response XML. Using this design and XML for communication make this application readable for modules and add-ons written in any programming language, as all the contemporary programming languages support XML.

Each request carries information in the form of attributes. This information is needed at the end where these requests are processed for responding accordingly.

Here is a search request XML, with search criteria specified as attributes of a scope child node:

```
<?xml version="1.0" encoding="utf-8" ?>
<p2p_lng>
 <request type="SEARCH">
  <scope type="C:\TempDownload\*.exe" mask="1" />
 </request>
</p2p_lng>
```

Response XMLs are created according to the requests made; information here also is passed as child nodes and their attributes. Here is an example of a SHOWFILES response:

```
<?xml version="1.0" encoding="utf-8" ?>
<p2p_lng>
 <response type="SHOWFILES">
  <fileinfo filename="C:\TempDownload\define1a.exe" mask="1"
  filesize="3072" />
  <fileinfo filename="C:\TempDownload\Define3.exe" mask="1"
 filesize="3584" />
  <fileinfo filename="C:\TempDownload\Ganesh.exe" mask="1"
 filesize="553788" />
 </response>
</p2p_lng>
```

The design of XMLs is flexible enough to incorporate any other kind of functionality to this application; you just have to add new request/response types and add-ons to process them.

Server Design

The server for this software is used for keeping track of online and offline users and to maintain the index of the resources they share. This temporary indexing mechanism has been used to expedite the overall working of this software and to provide useful facilities to the users. Instead of making use of Web services that would have been a good option to implement server side functionality, ASPs are written considering the fact that ASPs are a more common form of server side programming.

Because virtually nothing happens on the server side during a given session of this software, ASPs are better, as they are legible to all the contemporary programming techniques. This can be said about Web services, too, as SOAP services can always be applied to Web services to make them accessible to any platform; ASPs have a shorter learning cycle than Web services, so we have adhered to ASPs for this software. By temporarily indexing the shared resources of the connected users, this server has been enabled to provide a powerful global search facility to users.

SQL Server 2000

A few features of SQL Server 2000 are worth discussing here for you to appreciate why it has been preferred over other databases.

SQL Server 2000 offers the following features:

- ♦ **Internet Integration:** The SQL Server 2000 database engine provides integrated XML support.
- ♦ **Scalability and Availability:** The same database engine can be used across platforms, ranging from laptop computers running Microsoft Windows 98 to large, multiprocessor servers running Microsoft Windows 2000 Data Center Edition.
- ♦ **Enterprise-Level Database Features:** The SQL Server 2000 relational database engine supports the features demanded by enterprise data-processing environments. The database engine protects

data integrity while minimizing the overhead of managing thousands of users concurrently modifying the database.

♦ **Ease of Installation, Deployment, and Use:** SQL Server 2000 offers a set of administrative and development tools that improve installing, deploying, managing, and using SQL Server across several sites.

♦ **Data Warehousing:** SQL Server 2000 offers tools for extracting and analyzing summary data for online analytical processing. SQL Server 2000 also features tools for visually designing databases and analyzing data using English language-based questions.

Complete Database Design

In this section, the design of the database for our application is presented. The database consists of two tables: the Peer Table and the Share Table.

The structure of the Peer Table is shown in Figure 2-5 and Table 2-1.

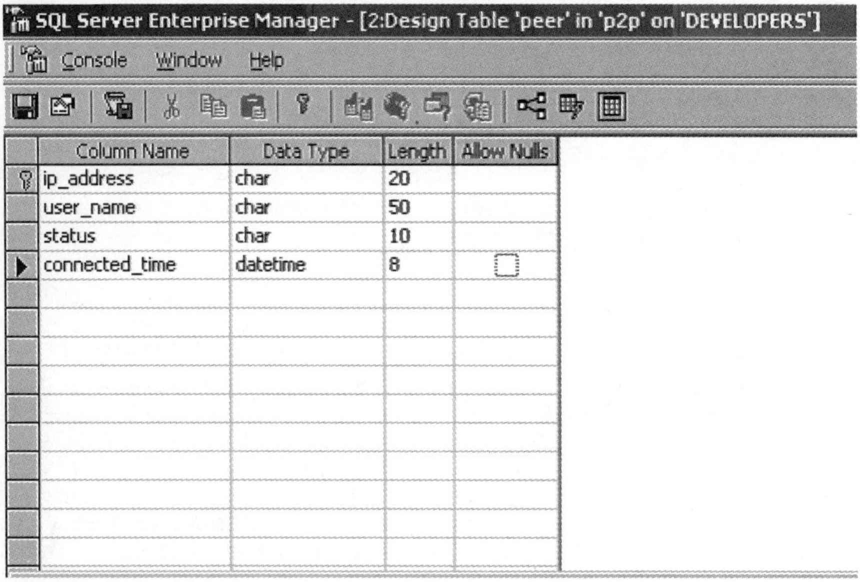

Figure 2-5: Peer Table

Table 2-1: Peer Table

Field Name	Description
ip_address	Stores the remote IP address of the user
user_name	Stores the name of the user
Status	Stores the status of the connection (0 or 1)
connected_time	Stores the time of connection

This Peer Table in our P2P application is used to store information related to the user who is logging through the application. The Peer Table stores the remote IP address, the user name, the status of the connection, whether it is active or not. For successful connection, it stores 1. The connected_time field is used to store the time of connection when the user has logged in.

When a user logs out of our P2P application, entries of that user are deleted from this Peer Table.

The Share Table structure is depicted in Figure 2-6 and Table 2-2.

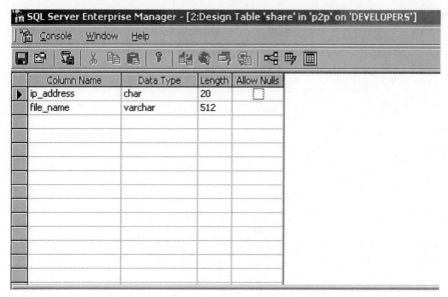

Figure 2-6: Share Table

Table 2-2: Share Table

Field Name	Description
ip_address	Stores the remote IP address for the user
file_name	Stores the file names shared by the user

This Share Table in our P2P application is used to store information of the files shared by users. Field ip_address is used to store the remote IP address of the user who has just logged in through our P2P application. This IP address is the same as the one we have entered in the Peer Table. The list of files shared by the user is stored using the field file_name. Any user availing the service of our application can search these files, which are shared by the other users who are availing the services of our application.

XML Implementation in SQL Server 2000

SQL Server 2000 introduces features that support XML functionality. The combination of these features makes SQL Server 2000 an XML-enabled database server. These new features are the following:

- ◆ The ability to access SQL Server using HTTP
- ◆ Support for XDR (XML-Data Reduced) schemas and the ability to specify XPath queries against these schemas
- ◆ The ability to retrieve and write XML data:
  - Retrieve XML data using the SELECT statement and the FOR XML clause.
  - Write XML data using OPENXML rowset provider and UpdateGrams.
  - Retrieve XML data using the XPath query language.
- ◆ Enhancements to the Microsoft SQL Server 2000 OLE DB provider (SQLOLEDB) that allow XML documents to be set as command text and to return the result sets as a stream

You can execute SQL queries to return results in XML format rather than standard rowsets. These queries can be executed directly or from within stored procedures. To retrieve results directly, you use the FOR XML clause of the SELECT statement, and within the FOR XML clause you specify an XML mode: RAW, AUTO, or EXPLICIT. For instance, FOR XML clause is used in the code given below to obtain the list of connected users at a particular time. This code can be used to replace userlist.asp on the server which is performing the same task.

The code for userlist.xml is the following:

```
 1 <?xml version ='1.0' encoding='UTF-8'?>
 2 <p2p_lng xmlns:sql="urn:schemas-microsoft-com:xml-sql">
 3   <response type="USERLIST">
 4     <sql:query>
 5        SELECT 1 as Tag,
 6          null as Parent,
 7          user_name as [userinfo!1!username],
 8          ip_address as [userinfo!1!ip]
 9  FROM peer
10 FOR XML EXPLICIT
11 </sql:query>
12 </response>
13 </p2p_lng>
```

The XML generated by this method is directly thrown by SQL server 2000 (that is, ASP is not used to generate this XML).

This userlist.xml file runs on a virtual path named template (for better understanding on the concept of virtual path, the reader can refer to the explanation for Listing 3-4 in Chapter 3) for XML support of SQL server 2000. When this file runs on this virtual path, it communicates with the Peer Table of the P2P database and shows the user information present in the Peer Table, such as username, IP address, and so on.

Client DesignClient side is made up of two modules: the listener and the browser. The design and the role of each has already been discussed in the sections. "Design Considerations for the P2P Application" and "Structure of the P2P Application," respectively, toward the beginning of this chapter. We will now go through the process of implementation of the design laid in previous sections.

Both the listener and the browser have two versions: one written in Java and the other in C#.

Java was chosen as a language to implement these modules due to the fact that it is comparatively easy to comprehend (easier than C or C++), thus providing the programmers some respite by keeping the intricacies of networking and other concepts hidden from them. Also, being a pure OOPS based language, Java helps a lot in modularizing the tasks. Besides, Java is not only gaining popularity among programmers but is also emerging as the language of choice among hardware vendors. Almost all the new devices (handheld devices, mobile phones, tabloid computers) that hit the market come up with some degree of support for Java.

C# seems to be Microsoft's answer to Java. With the same programming style and similar set of libraries as Java combined with native Microsoft techniques like COM and APIs, C# is has a lot of potential and offers immense scope for exploration. In view of these, we decided to develop the two modules of Client in these two languages.

The foremost functionality of the two modules is to be able to communicate with each other, which they do by exchanging XML request/response documents between each other. Exchanging XML documents involves two processes: creating XML and parsing XML.

Creating XML

This module is the generic XML creator for our application, and it handles all requests. The listener and the browser share this module for creating XML requests and responses. XML creator creates XML as indicated by the parameters sent by the browser or listener; then the XML creator writes the XML to the temporary file, which is processed accordingly by either module.

Parsing XML

This module helps the browser or listener in parsing the XML for values. This module can be called by the browser as well as by the listener. All XMLs received are passed to the XML parser for parsing, after which values are returned to the caller module. The values in these structures are used by the caller module for displaying data to the user.

Using IBM XERCES XML Parser (Java)

Modules written in Java make use of Xerces Java Parser 1.2.2, which supports XML 1.0 recommendations and contains advanced parser functionality, such as XML Schema, DOM Level 2 version 1.0, and SAX Version 2, in addition to supporting the industry-standard DOM Level 1 and APIs.

Using MS XML 3.0 component (C#)

Modules written in C# make use of the MS XML 3.0 component, which supports the World Wide Web Consortium (W3C) XML Recommendation specification. Namespace support is integrated into all aspects of the MS XML parser, including the Document Object Model (DOM) and Extensible Stylesheet Language (XSL) support.

Listener Design

Figure 2-7 shows how the listener prepares to listen.

First, the listener application logs on to the server. While logging on to the server, the listener opens share.ini (the file that keeps a record of all the files and folders shared by the listener), reads all shared files/folders, and makes a list of them. This list is then sent to the server, along with username and IP address as parameters, while calling login.asp (the ASP that handles the login process), residing on the server.

If the application is unable to make the call to login.asp, the application terminates (as it indicates some problem while establishing connection with the server and as there is no point in going further).

On the other hand, if login.asp is called successfully, it receives the response from the server and parses it to check whether the login has been authenticated. Authentication is done by imposing checks on the information passed by the listener, for duplication, like there may be a case where user is trying to log in with the name that already exists in the list of the names of connected users, in which case the application is rolled back, and the user is prompted to log on again. However, in the case of correct authentication, the listener is logged-on to the server successfully.

If desired, the listener can go for sharing resources before logging on to the server. The option for sharing resources has been given on the login screen itself, so that readers have the choice of logging in or to share the resources first.

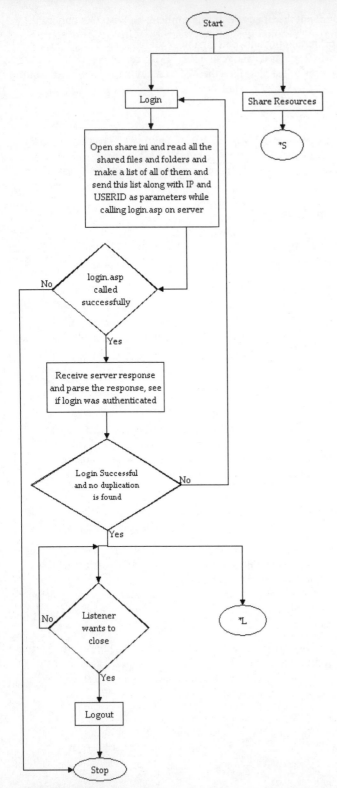

Figure 2-7: Listener start-up flow

This option is available to the listener throughout the life cycle of this application. With this option, the listener can select any folder or file residing on the computer and can share it if it has not been shared. Attempts to share anything twice will be discarded. Figure 2-8 shows how the sharing process is carried out.

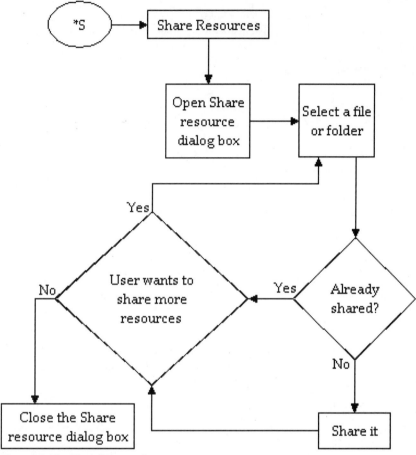

Figure 2-8: The Share Resource flow

Once the listener has successfully logged on to the server, its information is entered in the list of active listeners, and this entry remains there till the listener logs out calling logout.asp.

The listener that logs in has to prepare itself to answer peers who try to connect to it and post requests. Listener has to begin listening on a common port, which all other peers use for communication under a mutual agreement. Listener does this by using the various wrapper classes that Java and C# provide.

ServerSocket class (Java)

This class implements server sockets. A server socket waits for requests to come in over the network. It performs an operation based upon that request and possibly returns a result to the requester.

The actual work of the server socket is performed by an instance of the `SocketImpl` class. An application can change the socket factory that creates the socket implementation to configure itself to create sockets appropriate to the local firewall.

For the purpose of our application, we make an object of `ServerSocket` class, passing the port number to listen on and call its `accept()` function to initiate the process of monitoring for incoming connection requests as the listening process starts as soon as you instantiate this class, and we are through.

TCPListener class (C#)

The `TCPListener` class provides TCP services at a higher level of abstraction than the `Socket` class. `TCPListener` is used to create a host process that listens for connections from TCP clients. Application-level protocols such as FTP and HTTP are built on the `TCPListener` class.

TCPListener class is very easy to use and provides programmers respite from almost all the intricacies of socket programming, helping them concentrate on logic.

This class has a lot in common with Java's `ServerSocket` class. Both share almost the same set of functionality. We call its `Start()` functions to initiate the process of listening, and then we call the same `Accept()` functions to monitor for incoming connection requests. As soon as a connection is accepted, the `Accept()` function returns a `Socket` class object for that connection. Communication thereafter is done on the `Socket` class object returned.

Handling multiple connections

As in every ideally designed application, the listener component is capable of handling multiple connections, thereby widening the scope of its application and increasing the capability of the software as a whole.

For every connection received, a thread is created to cater to the requests. Under this thread, the connection is monitored for requests, and requests received are sent for parsing to determine the type of request. Once this is done, the appropriate response is made and written on the network stream for the browser to read it from there.

Because this software aims to cater to a good number of peers simultaneously, managing peers is an important feature of this application and is a vital factor that determines the efficiency of the software as a whole. Considering this, intense care has been taken to address each parallel communication effectively.

Some techniques for managing peers are discussed in the following sections.

Threading is a special technique for accomplishing multitasking. The main advantage of threading is that two or more tasks that originate from the same process can run simultaneously.

In simple words, a single program can handle multiple activities simultaneously. Multiple activities in our application pertain to the listener handling multiple connections. In other applications such as MS-Word, multiple activities could be printing one document while checking it for spelling mistakes.

As soon as a connection is detected, it is forwarded to a function called in a new thread, which takes on and serves all communication on that thread.

Requests obtained from browsers are sent for parsing and for determining the type of request. Once the request type is determined, the appropriate response is written and forwarded to the browser.

The listener runs its application to accept connections to fulfill requests coming its way. Notice that regardless of the request made by the browser, the listener always processes requests to generate appropriate responses and answers the browser's requests on its network stream. The listener waits for the connection to be made. Once the connection has been made and accepted by the listener to handle the requests from the browser, the listener reads the requests on that connection and parses the request to determine the type of request made by the browser. Requests made to listener can be any of the following types:

- ◆ Show files request for shared resources
- ◆ Search request along with search criteria
- ◆ Request for uploading files/folder
- ◆ Request for downloading files/folder

After reading and determining the request type, the listener reacts and responds accordingly.

If the request type generated by the browser is of Show File type, the listener simply responds correspondingly and returns the list of all shared resources, after which it closes the connection and starts waiting or serving the next request coming its way.

Instead of asking for the entire list of shared resources, the browser can also ask for a specific file/folder. This is usually done by sending the Search request to the listener. The browser sends the search request with criteria; in response, the listener returns the corresponding results, matching the search criteria passed to it by the browser.

Apart from a search request, an upload request can be placed to the listener if the browser is interested in giving rather than taking and is not interested in searching for any content. In such a situation, the listener first verifies whether the folder chosen by the browser for uploading has read/write permission or not. If the file/folder does not have enough credentials, the connection between the listener and the browser comes to a halt. On the other hand, if the selected file/folder has valid permission, the listener reads the file from its network stream, which is uploaded by the browser. Finally, the listener writes the file at the specified location.

Just as the browser can send requests for uploading, it can send the listener requests for downloading. In such a situation, the listener writes the requested file on the network stream for the browser to read and stores the downloaded file in the specific location. As usual, upon completing the downloading process, the connection between the listener and the browser is closed.

When a file/folder is uploaded, the browser writes and the listener reads from the stream. While downloading, the listener writes and the browser reads from the stream.

In an exceptional case in which the request type is not among those previously discussed, an error message is displayed to the user, indicating that the request type could not be resolved and that the connection has been terminated (Figure 2-9).

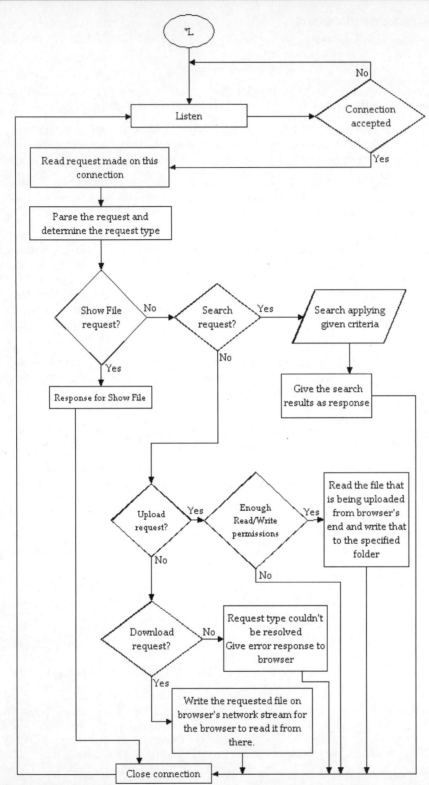

Figure 2-9: The Request Response flow

Searching for files and folders

Searching for the required information is one of the most prominent services this software offers its users. This application can be used on LANs such as an organization network, a university network, or a community network as successfully as it can be used on Wide Area Networks.

In these networking environments, with all the probabilities of a plethora of resources being shared by connected peers, it becomes pretty hard to search for the information you need without searching facilities. Hence, search processes receive a lot of emphasis in this software.

Once a peer is connected to another, searching for the required information from shared resources is very powerful and highly customizable in this application (see Figure 2-10). Upon connecting to a peer, users have all the search criteria at their disposal that can be used with the DIR command of MS DOS, making it a handy utility.

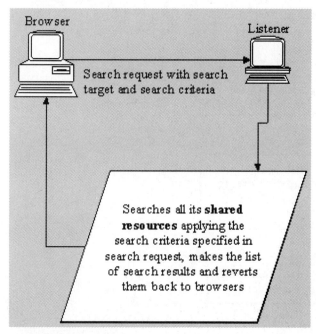

Figure 2-10: The search process

Browser Design

Figure 2-11 depicts how the client starts up gets to know the list of connected listeners and how the connection with any one of the connected listeners is established.

The browser part of this software provides the actual interface for all the activities and operations performed during the life cycle of any given session. This is a control panel for the user to leverage all the facilities that this software offers. It facilitates the user's effort to request the server for the list of listeners. Once the list is obtained, the user can select any one of them and establish connection with it.

Before you connect to any listener, you might want to see which listeners have the required information. For instance, if you are in search of the latest song of a particular group, it is possible that the listener you have approached has the songs of that group, but not the ones you want, or is not in a position to share it although it is there; worse, the listener might not have any songs of that group. To avoid such situations, you can fire a global search for the song. The list of all the listeners who have that song is at your disposal the very next moment. How this can be done is explained in the following paragraphs.

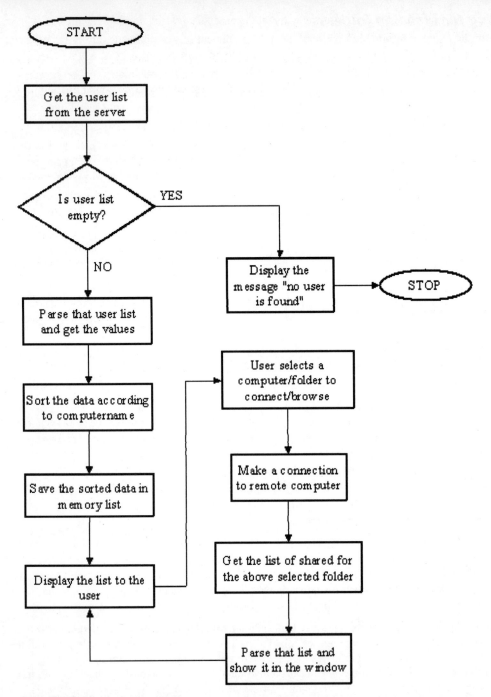

Figure 2-11: Flow of the browser module

Connecting to the server and retrieving lists of connected users

As the browser initiates, the list of all the users connected at that instant is picked up from the server calling userlist.asp. If the call is successful, it provides an XML response that constitutes the list of all the users connected at that moment. If no user is connected or, in other words, if the list of users is empty, an error message is displayed to the user, informing that at the particular instant, no user (listener) is available to listen to the request of the user.

If the user list is not empty, the list that will be in XML form will first be parsed to extracted values from it. The data or values extracted from the XML form of the list are sorted out alphabetically in accordance with the computer names of the users appearing in the list and are stored into the computer memory of the browser.

From the list, the user may select a computer to connect to or a file or folder to browse through. If a connection to a selected remote computer is made successfully, the browser picks up the list of the resources that are shared between the two ends. This list is parsed, and the values are extracted, sorted, and displayed to the user at the client end.

Calling ASP pages on the server has been made easy by a few classes C# and Java offer; such classes veil all the intricacies of making calls on the server. Some of these classes are explained in the next section.

For making calls on the server, .Net has provided a System.Net assembly that carries various useful classes and interfaces. One such class is `WebRequestFactory`. It is a static class that returns an instance of an object derived from `WebRequest`. The object returned is based on the URI scheme passed to its `Create` method.

The object returned this way can be type cast to the `HttpWebRequest` class, which contains support for the properties and methods defined in `WebRequest` along with additional properties and methods that enable the user to interact directly with the HTTP protocol.

By using its `GetResponse()` function, you can get a response for an Internet resource. `GetResponse()` function returns a `WebResponse` object that can be type cast to the `HttpWebRequest` class, which again is a descendent of the `WebResponse` class for better efficiency on HTTP protocol.

By calling the `GetResponseStream()` function, you can get the stream used for reading the body of the response from the server, which, in this case, is of XML format written in a temporary file for handing it over to the parsing mechanism for retrieving the list of connected users.

The java.net package in Java is the counterpart of the System.Net assembly of .Net. It also has classes with capabilities similar to those defined in System.Net, which are as suitable for our purpose as the C# classes are.

The URL class defined in this package can be used to establish connection with the concerned Internet resource. Its `openConnection()` function returns an object of type `URLConnection` whose `connect()` function can be used to make a call on the server and get the response. The response can then be read through its input stream obtained by calling the `URLConnection`'s `getInputStream()`, which makes placing calls on the server really hassle free.

Once the connection to the server has been established and userlist.asp has been called successfully, the XML returned as the response is parsed, and the list of connected users is displayed to the user, who may choose one to connect to.

Connecting to other peers

Once the list of listeners is obtained, the user is likely to connect to one of them. The list provides the user with the names and IP addresses of listeners. When the user double clicks or hits the Connect button after selecting a listener from the list, a socket connection is established with the concerned listener using its IP address.

Once the connection is successfully established, the first request sent to the connected listener is to show all the shared resources. When this list is displayed on the user's end, the user confirms that connection has been successfully made.

For communicating with different peers online, the wrapper classes provided by C# and Java are used.

This class is given as an implementation for clients' sockets. It has functions such as `getOutputStream()`, to get the output stream to write data for the connected person to read from there, and functions such as `getInputStream()`, to get the input network stream to read the data written by the person the user connects to from there.

This class is similar to Socket but provides TCP services at a higher level of abstraction. After initializing its object, you just have to call its `Connect()` function, give the IP address of the computer to connect to and the port number to communicate and the job is done. After getting connected, you can retrieve the network stream, calling its `GetStream()` function for writing to or reading from the stream accessible by the connected machine.

.Net's System.Net provides a static class called DNS that provides access to information from the Internet Domain Name System (DNS).

The information returned includes multiple IP addresses and aliases if the host specified has more than one entry in the DNS database.

The host information from the DNS queried by calling `GetHostByName()` is returned in an instance of the `IPHostEntry` class. This class enables you to provide a list of addresses with host names and aliases.

Java's way of resolving DNS is very similar to that of C#. Java's java.net.InetAddress package implements a very simple class called `InetAddress` for this purpose. This class represents an IP address. Applications should use the method `getLocalHostto` to create a new `InetAddress` instance and to get the local host.

```
InetAddress localHostAddress = InetAddress.getLocalHost();
```

Downloading and uploading files

The download procedure is initiated by the browser with the listener for downloading any file or folder (see Figure 2-12). This is the pivotal aspect of the P2P application: that files and folders get exchanged without going over to the server. Once the connection has been established, the server is bypassed and there is direct communication between the browser and the listener. The following diagram shows schematically how a user (client) downloads the file selected from the other user (listener) via the browser.

The end user (client) selects a file from the list provided by the server. The application first checks whether the selected file is available for downloading. If the file is available, details of the destination to which it is to be downloaded are determined. The file name, size, and permission are extracted from the relevant array that stores these details regarding the file.

Till this point, the user collects only the necessary information regarding the file that is to be downloaded. With these, the user determines whether or not downloading is valid; if it is, an XML request is sent to the user at the other end for downloading.

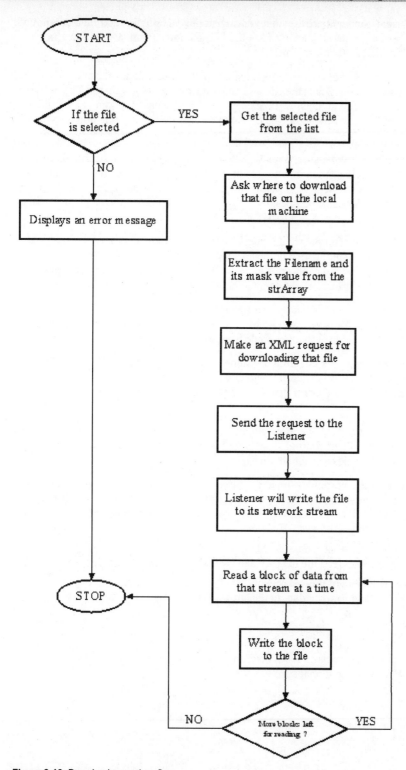

Figure 2-12: Download procedure flow

Once the request is sent, the user (listener) opens the networking stream to establish communication with the user at the client's end. The user (listener) starts writing the file into the stream. Meanwhile, the browser starts reading from the same network stream.

Thus, two-way communication occurs over this network stream. The listener uploads the file and writes it into the stream, whereas the browser downloads the file and reads it from the same stream. The browser reads blocks of data and writes to the file at the specified location. This process of reading and writing continues until the entire file has been downloaded. Once no more data is to be read, the downloading process stops.

The upload procedure is also initiated by the user, with the help of the browser, for uploading the file to the other user (listener) (see Figure 2-13). As in downloading, there is no need of the server for uploading files. When the user initiates to upload a file, it is determined whether or not the selected folder or file has rights for uploading. If the file or folder selected does not possess rights for uploading, an error message is generated, and the uploading process comes to a halt.

If, on the other hand, the file/folder satisfies the rights criteria, the file/folder is processed for uploading. Then the filename is converted into a string, which represents the remote filename. The browser then generates the XML request of uploading type and sends it to the listener. Upon receiving the request, the listener opens the stream, thereby preparing for communication with the user.

The browser, after the stream has been opened, starts writing data on the stream, and the listener starts reading data from the same stream. Again, two-way communication exists between the listener and the user. But this time the browser writes and the listener reads from the same stream.

Once data starts to flow through the network stream, the listener starts reading the block of data and writing the blocks on its local machine until the entire uploading process has been executed. After the process is complete, uploading stops. Whether for uploading or for downloading, the network stream is always opened by the listener.

Downloading and uploading are the two key operations likely to be carried out more often than any other processes this application is capable of performing. How these two services are incorporated in this application is veiled in a few wrapper classes, which are explained in this section.

- ◆ **NetworkStream (C#):** This class provides the underlying stream of data for network access. Each time the listener receives a connection, it obtains an object of this class by calling the method `GetStream()`. Through this class, you can very conveniently write to or read from the network stream by using its `Read()` and `WriteI()` functions.

- ◆ **InputStream (Java):** An object of this class is obtained by calling the socket's `getInputStream()` method to read the data written by the connected user on this stream.

- ◆ **OutputStream (Java):** An object of this class is obtained by calling the socket's `getOutputStream()` method to write data to the stream for the connected user to read it from there.

Searching

When it comes to searching, this software has a lot to offer to its users. Users have two options for searching information: a local search or a global search.

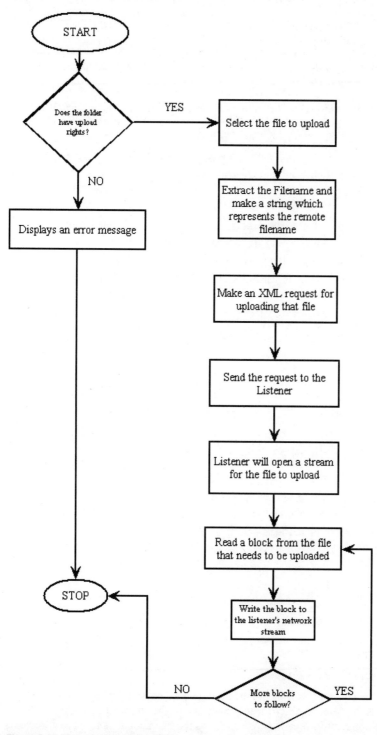

Figure 2-13: The upload procedure flow

After getting connected to a listener, you may want to search for files on your computer or to refine the list to show only a particular type of resources. This can be done by deploying a local search. Although the area to be searched for the resource in this case is restricted to the machine you are connected to, this search is powerful and works very effectively inside these demarcations. You are provided with all the search options you can use with the DIR command in DOS.

When you wish to use this option, a request XML is created with information about the target to search and the search criteria. The rest of the process takes place on the listener's side. What happens can be seen in the section titled "Listener Design" in this chapter.

This service is the most conspicuous utility in this application. Before you connect to a listener listed in the list of connected listeners, you can search for the information of your interest and its presence on these listeners. This option helps you in deciding which listener to connect to.

When you initiate this kind of search, an ASP called Search.asp is called, passing the search criteria as the parameter to this ASP. This ASP provides results in an XML format that contains information about listeners, where the concerned information is spotted, and the number of instances of information on each listener. The global search operation is depicted in the Figure 2-14.

Having discussed in detail all programming techniques, tools, intercomponent communication, and architecture, the user interface that finally presents the application to you is discussed here.

Now we are in position to appreciate what is required of the user interface for this application. Every constituent of the user interface displayed to you at various stages of the life cycle of this application has been meticulously worked out to help you derive the maximum benefit from this application. Every attempt has been made to render this interface as powerful and intuitive as possible.

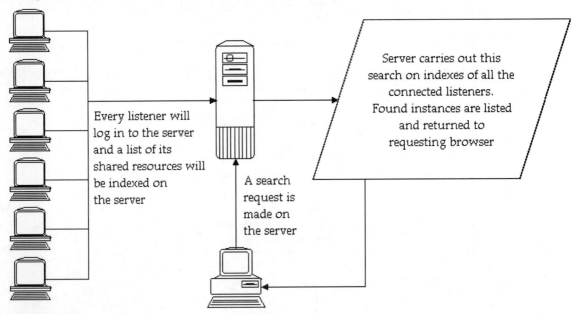

Figure 2-14: Global search flow

Client: A Comprehensive View

The following sequence depicts the entire flow of the application with all possible information. In our P2P application, the listener holds the responsibility for the execution of the application. Unless the listener logs on to the server, the application cannot move ahead, as the listener caters to all requirements coming its way and initiates the requesting peer in data transfer, downloading, uploading, and searching.

An overview of the application is given here. However, technical aspects are not discussed here, as they are detailed in upcoming chapters. Before proceeding, a few points must be clarified to achieve a better understanding of the application.

Throughout the lifecycle of this application, the listener can declare desired resources (files/folders) as *shared* without logging on to the server. The sharing process can be carried out after logging on to the server as well.

Any file or folder can be declared as *shared* only for once. Once declared as *shared*, these files/folders are available to all incoming clients.

At the start up of the application, a window is displayed (see Figure 2-15) prompting the client to enter the *Login ID* in the textbox.

Figure 2-15: The peer to peer login window

You will find a few more buttons on the displayed window apart from Login Button (that is, Share Files /Folder, Quit, and a Checkbox named Remember My Login ID. After typing the Login ID and clicking the Login button, an icon appears in the system tray, indicating that the user has successfully logged in (see Figure 2-16). However, this tray icon will not be available in the Java version of this application.

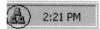

Figure 2-16: This icon in the system tray indicates that you have succesfully logged in.

You may declare some file or folder as *shared* before logging on to the server. For this, execute the following steps:

1. Click the Share Files/Folders button at the start up window. A Share dialog box is displayed on the screen (see Figure 2-17).

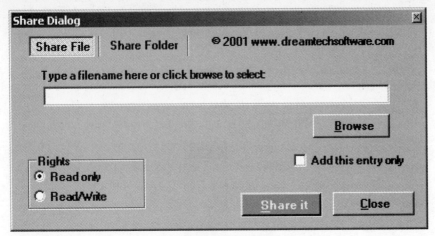

Figure 2-17: Share Dialog allows the user to share files of folders.

There is a Checkbox on the Share File/Folder dialog box named *Add this entry only,* which helps you determine whether you would like to continue with sharing resources or terminate the process (when you are through with sharing a particular file/folder). By checking it, you close the dialog box and share only the currently selected file or folder; otherwise, you can continue the sharing process.

2. From the Share dialog box, choose the Share File box and click the Browse button. The Select a file to share dialog box is displayed (see Figure 2-18), from which you can choose the file for sharing.

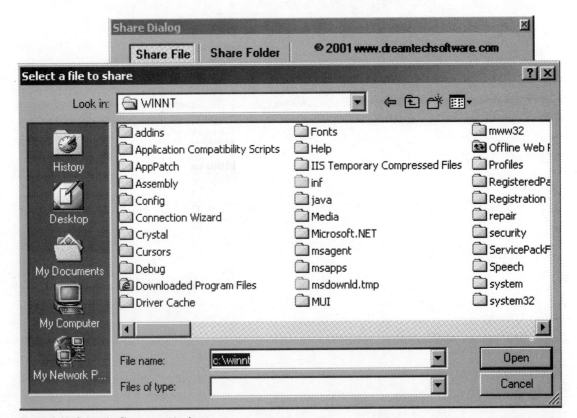

Figure 2-18: Select the file you want to share.

3. From the File dialog box, choose the file you'd like to share, and click the Open button. Again, the Share dialog (refer to Figure 2-17) box is displayed, and this time you are required to assign some rights or properties to the selected file. You can do so by checking the appropriate Radio button from the Rights option field.

4. Finally, click the Share it button.

A confirmation message is shown, indicating whether the file has been successfully shared or not (see Figure 2-19).

Figure 2-19: User is notified if the resource selected to share gets shared successfully.

To set any folder as *shared*, you need not take any step apart from those mentioned for setting any file as *shared*. For the convenience of all users who use this application, the steps to declare a folder as *shared* are as follows:

1. On the Share File Folder dialog box choose, the Share Folder tab, and click the Browse button (see Figure 2-20).

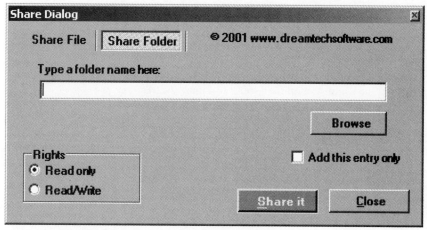

Figure 2-20: Share dialog to let the user share his files or folders

2. A window is displayed (see Figure 2-21) from which you are required to select a folder. Apart from selecting the already available folders, you can create a new folder instantly by clicking the New folder button placed on the current window. After selecting the appropriate folder, click the Open button.

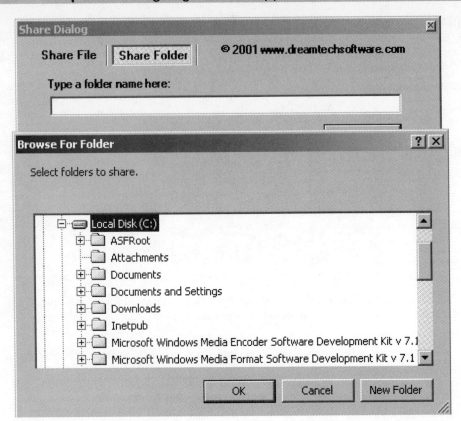

Figure 2-21: Select the folder you want to share.

3. Once again, the Share dialog window is displayed, out of which the selected folder has to be assigned some rights from the Rights option field (refer to Figure 2-20).

4. Finally, click the Share it button placed on the Share dialog window.

A confirmation message is displayed, indicating whether the folder has been successfully shared or not, just as in the case of the sharing file. If the folder has been shared already, an error message is shown (see Figure 2-22).

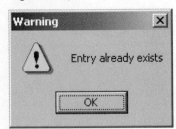

Figure 2-22: Attempt to share any resouce twice will be discarded, and the user will be notified regarding the reason.

Once you are through with sharing and login, you are listed on the server as a connecting peer with some shared resources to distribute among users who require them. As a result of successful login on the server, a window comes up showing the list of all other peers who are already connected with the server along with their IP addresses (see Figure 2-23).

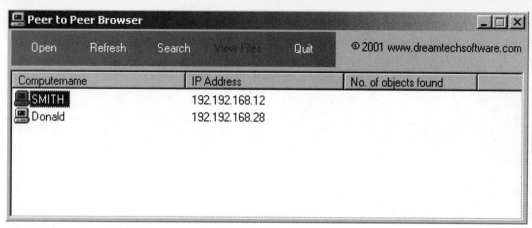

Figure 2-23: Conncted peers get listed in this window.

Now an end user can establish connection with the listed peers. Any requesting peer can search for the contents of his or her interest before establishing a connection with one of the listed peers. The following steps establish such a connection:

1. Click the Search button (see Figure 2-23). A Search dialog box is displayed, containing *Search on* and *Search for* fields representing "search to be made on which peer" and "what content should be searched," respectively (see Figure 2-24). A search can be made either by passing full phrases or by using wildcard patterns.

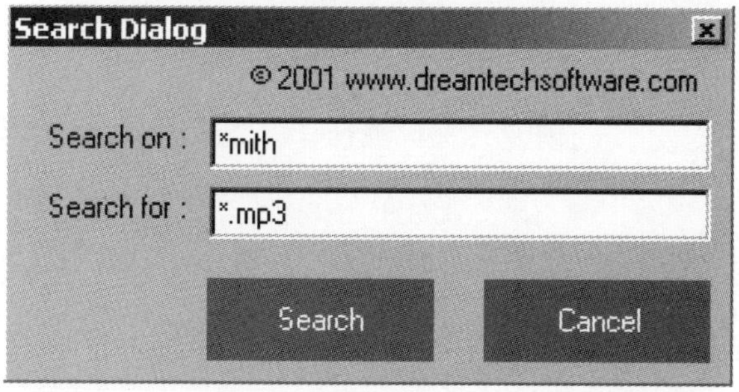

Figure 2-24: One can specify the search criteria in this widow.

2. After passing the desired searching criteria, click the Search button.

3. Search results are displayed, along with the number of instances found on corresponding peers (see Figure 2-25).

In case the requesting peer does not want to go through the search option but would like to initiate a direct communication with the listed peers, the following steps suffice:

1. Select the peer name from the computer name list displayed in the window and click the Open button to start communication (see Figure 2-23).

2. Or simply double click the peer name from computer name list in the window and move forward.

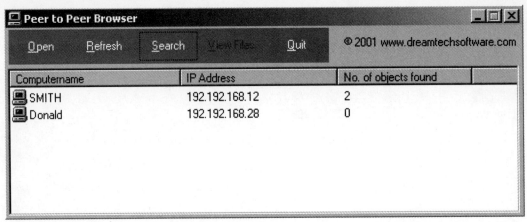

Figure 2-25: The number of times the information (satisfying the search criteria you specified) was found and peers (other than you) this information was found on are listed in this window.

After selecting and opening the peer, the shared contents on the window shows all the *shared resources* of the corresponding peer (see Figure 2-26).

File / Folder	Size	Type
D:\Drive F\Temporary floppy\Temp		Folder
C:\TempDownload		Folder
BrowseThroughVB.htm	676	htm File
define1a.exe	3072	exe File
ATLDuck.txt	3939	txt File
Sample.jpg	9894	jpg File
ADMixer_Mute.zip	74766	zip File
RANDOM.bmp	80862	bmp File
Ganesh.exe	553788	exe File

Shared contents on: SMITH (192.192.168.12)
Upload   Download   Search   Chat   Close   © 2001 www.dreamtechsoftware.com
Root

Figure 2-26: Resources shared by the peer you are connected with are shown in this window.

From this window, you perform the following:

1. Select any file you want to download.
2. Click the Download button.

Upon clicking the Download button, the Select Location dialog box window appears for you to mention the location at and the name with which the user wants the downloaded file to get saved on the hard disk. From the Select Location dialog box window, click the Save Button to download the shared content at the desired location (see Figure 2-27).

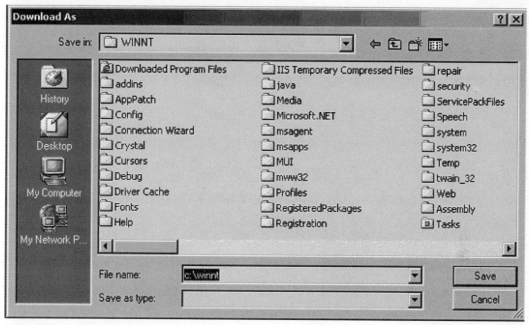

Figure 2-27: File dialog box to specify the location at and the name with which the user wants the downloaded file to get saved on the hard disk.

Just as content can be downloaded from a peer, it can easily be uploaded to the peer you are connected with. To do this, follow these steps:

Decide what you want to upload on the connected peer's machine:

1. Click the Upload button from the Shared contents window.

2. The Select File dialog box is displayed.

3. Select a file from the box, and click the Open button on the current window.

This uploads the selected file to the selected folder in the shared resource list or to the remote folder that is currently open. It is also worthwhile to mention that files can be uploaded to specific remote folders only if they are user-shared with write permission assigned (see Figure 2-28).

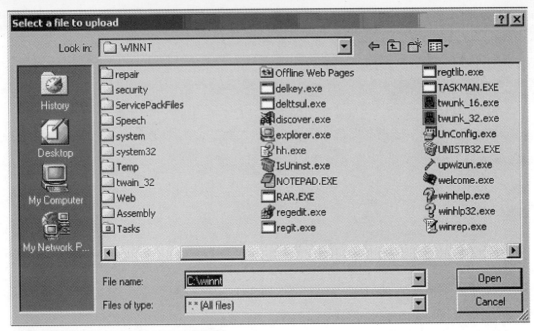

Figure 2-28: File dialog to select the file to upload

Once you are connected to a peer, you may find yourself in a situation in which you are looking at a list of shared resources that is too long for you to find the desired information. You can narrow down this list to those entries that concern you (see Figure 2-29). To do this, you can do the following:

Figure 2-29: Search dialog allows the user to search for particular information out of the resources shared by the peer the user is connected with.

1. Click the Search button. It shows you a small Search dialog box similar to the one we encounter while doing a global search, with the first Edit box disabled. The second textbox allows you to type a search criteria, for example, *.exe.

2. Click the Search button of current window (Search dialog box).

3. Results satisfying the criteria are displayed.

To quit the application, simply right-click the Application icon placed on the system and select quit from the pop-up menu (see Figure 2-30).

Figure 2-30: Listener can quit from the system tray menu option.

A confirmation dialog box is displayed to indicate that the application has successfully logged out (see Figure 2-31). This means the application is no longer connected and is no longer on the server list.

Figure 2-31: User is notified that the listener has successfully logged out.

Summary

In this chapter, we have presented the complete design of our P2P application. The architecture of the software is such that the design is modular with features of expandability and scalability. The communication mechanism involved among the three components (server, listener, and browser) was discussed in detail. The various classes and methods used for the implementation in both Java and C# were also discussed. The user interface for the application is also described so that you get a feel for running the application.

Now that you are familiar with the design of our application, the following chapters are dedicated to its implementation aspects.

Chapter 3

Understanding the P2P Server

SQL Server 2000 (Structured Query Language Server 2000) is a novel concept in database management and data-accessing methods. Although the previous version of SQL Server (SQL 7.0) continues to challenge other RDBMS, SQL Server 2000 can claim an edge over it. SQL Server 2000 has reduced the need for lengthy programming to access data, and it addresses data in sets rather than by constructing typical tools. The language SQL Server 2000 provides to access data from the server is known as SQL, a short form of Structured Query Language. There are numerous benefits to using SQL Server 2000, some of which are the following:

♦ It translates a logical name into a linked set of physical locations, thereby reducing the need to refer to the physical location of data.

♦ It manages all locks and, as a result, eliminates the need for explicit locking statements.

♦ It identifies the most efficient method of finding the required data without specifying the index of search strategy.

As mentioned previously, SQL Server 2000 is more versatile than SQL 7.0. Apart from reducing the length of the programming required for accessing data, SQL Server 2000 has come up with a technique for accessing data over HTTP by passing URLs to it. The main reason for using SQL Server 2000 in our application is its compatibility with XML language, the feature which enhances the usability of SQL Server 2000 in Web-development environments. Various new features are incorporated in SQL Server 2000 to extend its role in Web development while supporting XML. Some of these features are the following:

♦ The `ForXML` clause has been equipped to the `select` statement for retrieval of data in XML format.

♦ With `OpenXML` rowset provider, SQL Server 2000 can write XML data. This enables responding in XML format.

♦ SQL Server 2000 can be accessed through URL.

♦ To set an XML document as command text, SQL Server 2000 OLEDB has been enhanced.

Creating Tables in SQL Server 2000

A table in an SQL Server is the object that contains data residing on a database. A database can have more than one table. Similarly, a table can have one or more than one attribute, commonly known as fields and columns. The structure designs of database tables used in P2P applications are shown in Figures 3-1 and 3-2.

Column Name	Data Type	Length	Allow Nulls
ip_address	char	20	
user_name	char	50	
status	char	10	
connected_time	datetime	8	

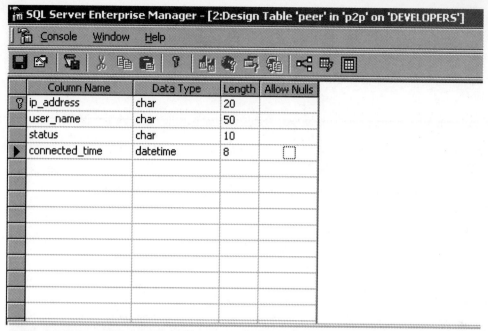

Figure 3-1: Structure design of a peer table

Column Name	Data Type	Length	Allow Nulls
ip_address	char	20	
file_name	varchar	512	

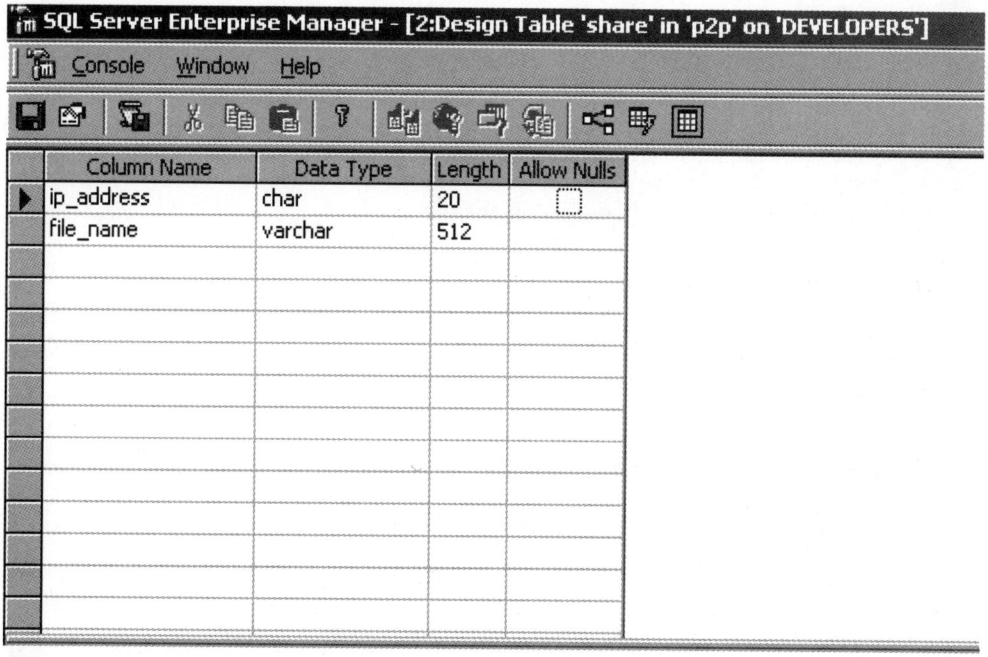

Figure 3-2: Structure design of a share table

To create tables in SQL Server 2000, simply type the name of your choice preceded with the key words "Create Table." The complete description follows:

To create tables, follow this path: "Start ⇨ Programs ⇨ MicrosoftSQLServer ⇨ Query Analyzer".

You find the screen divided into two parts. In the upper part, start creating the table by following this example where we are creating the peer table used in our P2P database:

```
create table        peer
(
ip_address char (20) primary key
user_name char (50)
status char (10)
connected_time datetime (8)
)
```

In the previous example, `create table` is the key word and `peer` is the name of the table. Notice that every table requires information such as the following: names of the columns, their data types, and column properties. These properties can convey whether or not a column allows null values and so on. While mentioning data types for a column, its length should be mentioned against them.

A *key* identifies and defines a specific set of one or more columns in a table that serves a specific purpose. In SQL Server 2000, two types of keys exist:

- ♦ Primary key
- ♦ Foreign key

Primary Key

A *primary key* refers to one or more columns in a table that uniquely identify its rows. There can't be more than one primary key in any table. If you take a look at the structure of the peer table explained in the preceding section, you will notice that the `ip_address` field has a key sign preceding it, which indicates that this field is the primary key for the table it belongs to. The field can be declared as primary at the time of creation of the table by adding the key word `primary  key` after it.

Foreign Key

When the primary key of one table appears as an attribute in another table, it is called a foreign key in the second table. A *foreign key* is used to relate two tables. For every value of the foreign key, there is a matching value of the primary key. Unlike the primary key, a table can contain any number of foreign keys, depending on database design and data-access requirements.

Select Statement in SQL Server 2000

SQL Server 2000 provides the `select` statement to access and retrieve data from the server. A `select` statement prompts the server to prepare a result and to return it to the client application. The key words `select`, `from`, and `where` make up the basic `select` statement.

Selecting a column

The select statement can be used to retrieve specific columns from the table by specifying the column names from the table. The column names specified in the select statement are separated by a comma (,). There is no need to insert a comma after the last column name. The syntax is the following:

```
Select column1, column2From <tablename>
```

Selecting all columns

The `select` statement, along with the asterisk symbol (*), produces the result in the form of detailed data. The asterisk symbol, when used with the `select` statement, ensures that the column listing of data is in same sequence as the one used at the time of table creation. For instance, for retrieving the records from the peer table, the statement would be

```
Select * from peer
```

Description of the ASP Files with Flowcharts

This section explains the asp files at the server end that enable the user to interact with the underlying database apart from bearing the logic for user authentication, resource sharing, and data integrity.

login.asp

This file is used to make entries in the peer table of the user who has just logged in to our P2P application. This file generates an XML document that communicates whether or not the logging of that user has been successful.

This program enables users to enter our server's peer table by using our P2P application. The result of the login, whether it has been successful or not, is displayed to the user by using XML.

Flowchart description of login.asp

This flow chart (see Figure 3-3) explains how the SQL server enters the user in the peer table of the database, which is requesting for login from the P2P application. The result of login, whether it is successful or not, is in XML format.

The program fills the variables sUserID, sIPaddress, and sharestring with the values USERID, IP, and SHARE, respectively, extracted from the querystring of login.asp. It then obtains the remote IP address of the client machine from where this login.asp page has been called. Next, it checks the values of sUserID, sIPaddress, and remote-IP. If any of these values are empty, the program generates an XML response for unsuccessful login, and the program is terminated. If the values of these variables are valid, the program creates new instances of ADODB connection to establish the connection with the P2P database residing in SQL Server 2000. After that, the program executes an SQL query that selects all the records from the peer table in which the ip_address is equal to the value of remote_IP variable. If any record exists in the recordset opened with the preceding SQL query, the program deletes all records from the peer table in which the IP_address is equal to remote_IP. Then a new record is added to the peer table in which the IP_address and user_name are added, respectively, to the values of remote-IP and sUserID. The connected_time field is set to the current time. Now the program deletes all the entries of remote_IP in the share table and makes new entries for this remote_IP with the list of shared filenames in the share table. Lastly, the program generates an XML document for successful login and terminates the process.

Correct Usage

The correct syntax for login.asp is:

```
http://192.168.1.12/login.asp?USERID="Username"&IP="ip
address"&Share="File1*file2*..........*.
```

If the USERID parameter is missed in the preceding address, the following error XML is generated:

```xml
<?xml version='1.0' encoding='utf-8'?>
<p2p_lng>
<response type='AUTH'>
 <connection code ="1" status="User Id can't be blank." ip="0" />
</response>
</p2p_lng>
```

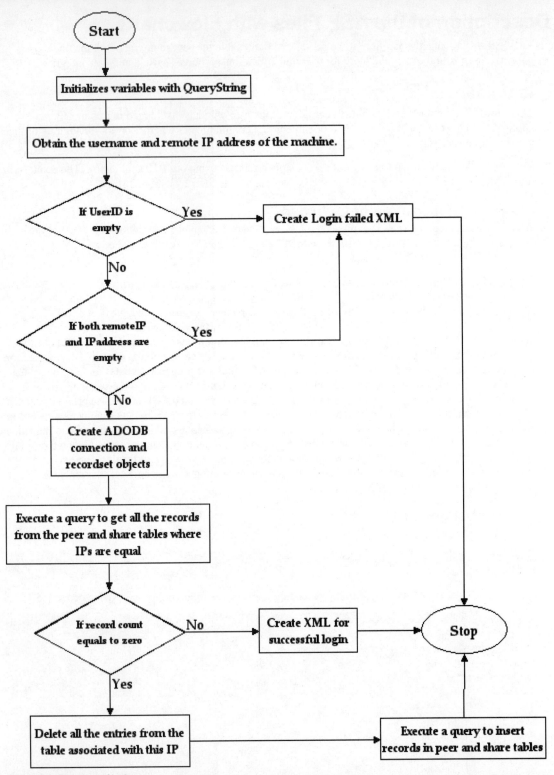

Figure 3-3: Flowchart of login.asp

Listing 3-1 contains the code for login.asp.

Listing 3-1: login.asp

```
 1 <%@ Language=VBScript %>
 2 <!--#include file="adovbs.inc"-->
 3
 4 <%
 5 '//Variable declaration----------//
 6  dim sUserId,sIPaddress,sError,str,sharestring,count,iloop,remoteIP
 7  dim conn,rsUser,rsIP,rsPeer
 8  dim sqlUser,sqlIP,sqlPeer
 9  dim bError,bUserExist,bIPexist
10  dim tConnectedTime
11 '//--------------------------//
12
13
14 '//Getting values from Query String variables-------------//
15  sUserId = Ucase(trim(Request.QueryString("USERID")))
16  sIPaddress = trim(Request.QueryString("IP"))
17  sharestring = trim(Request.QueryString("share"))
18 '//----------------------------------------------//
19
20
21 '//Getting the remoteIP address of the machine--------//
22  remoteIP = trim(Request.ServerVariables("REMOTE_ADDR"))
23 '//----------------------------------------------//
24
25
26
27 '//Check for userid, if empty initialize variables for error message-----//
28  if sUserId="" then
29    bError=true
30    sError="User Id can't be blank."
31  end if
32 '//------------------------------------------------------------------//
33
34
35 '//Check for IPaddress and remoteIP, if both are empty then initialize
variables for error message-----//
36  if (sIPaddress="" and remoteIP ="")then
37    bError=true
38    sError=sError & "IP can't be blank."
39  end if
40 '//------------------------------------------------------------------//
41
42
43
44
45 '//Writing XML if either userid or IPaddress does not exist---//
46  if bError then%>
47
48  <?xml version='1.0' encoding='utf-8'?>
49  <p2p_language>
```

```
50   <response type='AUTH'>
51     <connection code ="1" status="<%=sError%>" ip="0" />
52   </response>
53   </p2p_language>
54
55   <%
56   Response.End
57   end if
58
59   '//----------------------------------------------------------//
60
61
62
63   '//Creating object for connection string------------//
64   set conn = Server.CreateObject("ADODB.Connection")
65   conn.ConnectionString = "Provider=SQLOLEDB.1;Persist Security
     Info=False;User ID=sa;Initial             Catalog=p2p;Data
     Source=developers"
66   conn.Open
67
68   '//----------------------------------------------------------//
69
70
71
72   '//Creating objects for recordset--------------------//
73   Set  rsIP= Server.CreateObject("ADODB.Recordset")
74   Set rsPeer = Server.CreateObject("ADODB.Recordset")
75   Set  rsShare= Server.CreateObject("ADODB.Recordset")
76   Set  rsDeleteShare= Server.CreateObject("ADODB.Recordset")
77   rsPeer.CursorType=adOpenDynamic
78   rsIP.CursorType=adOpenStatic
79   '//----------------------------------------------------------//
80
81
82
83   '//Writing SQL queries and open recordset-------------//
84   sqlIP = "SELECT * from peer where ip_address='"  & remoteIP & "'"
85   rsIP.Open sqlIP,conn
86   rsPeer.open "peer",conn,adOpenDynamic,adLockOptimistic
87   '//----------------------------------------------------------//
88
89
90   bIPexist=false
91
92
93
94   '//Check for no. of records in both the recordsets-----//
95   if rsIP.RecordCount<>0 then bIPexist=true
96   '//----------------------------------------------------------//
97
98
99
100
101  '//Delete the record if IP address already exists----//
102  if(bIPexist) then
103    conn.Execute "Delete from peer where ip_address='" & remoteIP & "'"
```

```
104   end if
105  '//----------------------------------------------------//
106
107
108
109  '//Close and destroy objects of recordsets------------//
110   rsIP.Close
111   set rsIP=Nothing
112  '//----------------------------------------------------//
113
114
115
116  '//Add a new record in peer table-----------------//
117   rspeer.AddNew
118   rsPeer("ip_address")=remoteIP
119   rsPeer("user_name")=sUserId
120   rsPeer("status")=1
121   rsPeer("connected_time")=now()
122   rsPeer.Update
123  '//------------------------------------------//
124
125
126
127  '//Writing XML if neither userid nor IPaddress already exists--//
128  %>
129     <?xml version='1.0' encoding='utf-8'?>
130     <p2p_language>
131     <response tag='AUTH'>
132     <connection code ="0" status="Successful" ip="<%=remoteIP%>" />
133     </response>
134     </p2p_language>
135
136  <%
137
138  '//----------------------------------------------------------//
139
140
141
142
143  '//Delete records from share table where that IPaddress already exists--//
144  Set rsShare = conn.Execute("delete share where ip_address='" & remoteIP &
     "'")
145  '//----------------------------------------------------------//
146
147
148
149  '//Findout the filenames from the QuerySting variable------//
150  sharestring = CStr((trim(sharestring)))
151  count = 0
152  str = split(sharestring, "*")
153
154  '//----------------------------------------------------------//
155
156
157
158
```

```
159 '//Insert ipaddress and filenames in share table----------//
160 For iloop = LBound(str) To UBound(str)
161   Set rsShare = conn.Execute("INSERT share (ip_address,file_name) VALUES ("
      & "'" & remoteIP  & "' , '" &              str(iloop) &  "')")
162
163 Next
164 '//-----------------------------------------------------//
165
166
167
168 '//Close the connection----------//
169 conn.Close
170 set conn=Nothing
171 '//--------------------------//
172
173 %>
```

Code description

♦ Lines 6-10: Variables are declared here to store the values of the username, IP address, and so on.

♦ Lines 15-17: Variables are initialized here with the values of the QueryString variables USER ID, IP, and share.

♦ Lines 22: Value of REMOTE_ADDR ServerVariable is set into remoteIP. REMOTE_ADDR returns the remote IP address of the machine requesting for the ASP page.

♦ Lines 28-31: If sUserId is empty, sError variable is initialized with an error message. It generates an error message by setting the boolean variable bError as true and setting the variable sError as User Id can't be blank.

♦ Lines 36-39: If both sIPaddress and remoteIP are empty, sError variable is initialized with an error message. This checks if both the variables sIPaddress and remoteIP (value acquired in line 22 as remote IP address of the machine) are not blank. In case both the variables are blank, it presents an error message by setting the boolean variable bError as true and setting the value of variable sError as IP address can't be null.

♦ Lines 46-57: If bError is equal to TRUE, XML is generated with the message for unsuccessful login, and the process ends. This code checks if the value of boolean variable bError is set to true; then an error message is generated using XML. After this, the program stops. (This is required, as both userId and IP address are null in lines 36-39).

♦ Lines 64-66: An ADODB connection object with the name conn is created here, which is used to establish the connection with the P2P database that is on SQLServer2000.

A connection object represents an open connection to a data source. Here, the ADODB connection object is used to establish a connection with SQL Server 2000. A connection object is needed to access data using the data environment and represents a connection to a database residing on the server that is used as a data source. An alternative way of establishing the connection is through DSN. For this, remove the connection string statement and while calling the open function on the connection object, pass the DSN name as the only parameter.

```
conn.Open ("P2Pdsn")
```

Replace the P2Pdsn with the name of the DSN created by you.

The same would work wherever you are establishing a connection with the server.

♦ Lines 73-78: The new instances of the ADODB recordset are created here and set their CursorType as adopenstatic.

(A cursor type is a way to cache data on the client machine and to provide local scrolling, filtering, and sorting capabilities. adopenstatic is a static copy of a set of records that can be used to find data or generate reports; changes made by other users are not visible.)

♦ Lines 84-110: The following section checks for instances of multiple records in which the IP address is equal to the remote IP value (84-86). Eventually, our program deletes all records from the peer table having an ip_address equal to the remote IP.

  • 84-86: An SQL query is defined in the variable sqlIP, which has selected all the records from the peer table in which the ip_address field value is equal to the remote_IP value. Then the selected record is opened in the rsPeer recordset.

  • 95: If more than one record is in the rsPeer recordset, the bIPexist variable is set to true.

♦ Lines 102-104: If bIPexist is true, an SQL is executed that deletes all the records from the peer table in which the ip_address field value is equal to the remoteIP.

♦ If the value of bIPexist is true (from line 95, in which multiple records exist in rsPeer), an SQL query is executed that deletes all the records from the peer table in which ip_address is equal to remoteIP value.

♦ Lines 110-111: An instance of the recordset rsIP is closed and destroyed here.

♦ Lines 117-122: A new record is added in the peer table by using rsPeer recordset object in which ip_address and user_name are added with the values of the remoteIP and sUserId, respectively. connected_time field is equal to the current time.

♦ Lines 129-134: An XML response is generated here, having the message for successful login. These lines generate a message by using XML to inform the user that the login is successful.

♦ Lines 144: An SQL query is executed here that deletes all the entries from the share table where ip_address is equal to the remoteIP value.

♦ Lines 150-152: A data type of the sharestring variable is converted into a string type by using the CStr function. After that, the value of the sharestring variable is split on the * in that string by using the split function. The resulting values are stored in the str variable.

♦ Lines 160-163: The number of filenames stored in the str variable is entered into the share table, with the ip_address stored in the remote_IP variable, by executing an SQL query.

♦ Lines 169-170: The instance of the connection with the name conn is closed and destroyed here.

These lines help close the connection object and set the value of conn to null.

logout.asp

This file is used to delete the entry of a user from the peer table at the time of logout.

Flowchart description of logout.asp

The flowchart shown in Figure 3-4 explains how to delete the entry from the peer table of the user, requesting for logout from the P2P application.

First, the program gets the value of the IP address from the QueryString variable and assigns it to the sIPaddress variable. Next, the program checks the value of sIPaddress. If it is empty, the program terminates the process; otherwise, it creates the ADODB connection and recordset objects to establish the connection with the P2P database residing on SQL Server 2000, and also the connection with the tables of that P2P database. After that, the program executes an SQL query to delete the entry of the user from the peer table, which is requesting for logout from the P2P application. After deleting the records from the peer table, the program terminates the process.

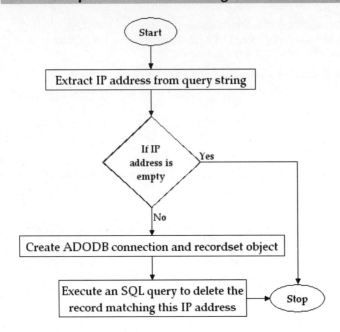

Figure 3-4: Flowchart of logout.asp

The correct syntax of the logout.asp page is

```
http://p2pserver/logout.asp&IP='IP address of the machine'.
```

Listing 3-2 describes the code of logout.asp.

Listing 3-2: logout.asp

//© 2001 Dreamtech Software India Inc.
// All rights reserved

```
1 <%@ Language=VBScript %>
  2 <!--#include file="adovbs.inc"-->
  3
  4 <%
  5 '//Variable declaration----------//
  6  Dim sIPaddress
  7  Dim conn
  8 '//---------------------------//
  9
 10
 11 '//Getting the IPaddress from queryString variable-----//
 12 sIPaddress = trim(Request.QueryString("IP"))
 13 '//--------------------------------------------------//
 14
 15
 16 '//If sIPaddress variable is empty then end the process--//
 17  if sIPaddress="" then
 18    Response.End
 19  end if
 20 '//--------------------------------------------------//
```

```
21
22
23 '//Create the connection object and open it --------------------//
24  set conn = Server.CreateObject("ADODB.Connection")
25  conn.ConnectionString = "Provider=SQLOLEDB.1;Persist Security
    Info=False;User   ID=sa;Initial                  Catalog=p2p;Data
    Source=developers"
26  conn.Open
27 '//------------------------------------------------------------//
28
29 '//Delete the records from peer table for that ip address--//
30  conn.execute "delete from peer where ip_address='" & sIPaddress & "'"
31 '//------------------------------------------------------------//
32
33
34 '//Close and destroy the connection object--------------------//
35  conn.Close
36  set conn=Nothing
37 '//------------------------------------------------------------//
38 %>
```

Code description

♦ Lines 6-7: Variables sIPaddress and conn are declared here. sIPaddress is for storing the value ip_address. conn is used to establish connection with the database kept on the server.

♦ Line 12: Variable sIPaddress is initialized with the value of QueryString variable IP. These lines initialize the value of variable sIPaddress with the value of QueryString variable IP retrieved from the client.

♦ Lines 17-18: The value of sIPaddress variable is checked. If it is empty, the process is terminated. These lines check whether there is a value for IPaddress; if the value of sIPaddress is null, the process of logout is terminated.

♦ Lines 24-26: An ADODB connection object with the name conn is created here, which is used to establish the connection with the P2P database on SQL Server 2000.

♦ Line 30: The connection object executes an SQL query, in which all the records in the peer table are deleted that have an IP address equal to the value of the sIPaddress variable.

♦ Lines 35-36: The established connection object conn is closed and destroyed here. These lines close the connection object conn and the value of the conn variable is set to null.

userlist.asp

This program is used to generate an XML document that shows the userlist in XML format that has the information username and the IP address from the peer table.

This code displays a list of users currently logged on to the P2P application by using XML. This userlist is displayed in XML format, showing user information including the username and the IP address from the peer table.

Flowchart description of userlist.asp

The flow chart shown in Figure 3-5 explains that the currently logged user information on the P2P application is displayed in XML format. User information includes the username and the IP address of the logged users from the peer table.

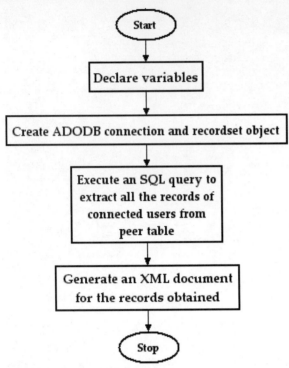

Figure 3-5: Flowchart of userlist.asp

First, the program declares all the variables used in the file. Then the ADODB connection and recordset objects are created to establish the connection with SQL Server 2000 and with the peer table present in the P2P database. After that, the program executes an SQL query to select all records from the peer table of the database having IP address, user_name, and connected_time fields. All the records selected by the query are opened by a recordset object and then displayed in XML format.

The correct syntax of the userlist.asp is

```
http://p2pserver/userlist.asp
```

It does not have any parameters to be passed to it.

Listing 3-3 displays the code of userlist.asp.

Listing 3-3: userlist.asp

//© 2001 Dreamtech Software India Inc.
// All rights reserved.

```
 1 <%@ Language=VBScript %>
 2 <%Option Explicit%>
 3 <!--#include file="adovbs.inc"-->
 4 <%
 5 '//Variables declaration---------------------//
 6   dim conn,sqlPeer,rsPeer
 7   dim sUserId,sIP,sString
 8 '//-------------------------------------------//
 9
10
11 '//Establish the connection creating connection object--------//
12   set conn = Server.CreateObject("ADODB.Connection")
```

```
13   conn.ConnectionString = "Provider=SQLOLEDB.1;Persist Security
     Info=False;User ID=sa;Initial                    Catalog=p2p;Data
     Source=developers"
14   conn.Open
15 '//---------------------------------------------------------//
16
17
18 '//create a recordset object and open it with peer table--------//
19   Set rsPeer = Server.CreateObject("ADODB.Recordset")
20   rsPeer.CursorType = adOpenStatic
21   sqlPeer="select * from peer"
22   rsPeer.Open sqlPeer,conn
23 '//---------------------------------------------------------//
24
25
26
27
28 '//Creating XML for no. of users present in the peer table------//
29
30 %><?xml version='1.0' encoding='utf-8'?>
31 <p2p_lng>
32   <response type="USERLIST">
33 <%
34   while not(rsPeer.EOF)
35   sUserId=trim(rsPeer.Fields("user_name"))
36   sIP=trim(rsPeer.Fields("ip_address"))
37 %>      <userinfo username='<%=sUserId%>' ip='<%=sIP%>' />
38 <%
39     rsPeer.MoveNext
40   wend
41 %></response>
42 </p2p_lng>
43
44 <%
45
46 '//---------------------------------------------------------//
47
48
49
50 '//Close and destroy the connection and recordset objects---------------//
51   rsPeer.Close
52   set rsPeer=Nothing
53   conn.Close
54   set conn=Nothing
55   Response.End
56 '//---------------------------------------------------------------//
57
58 %>
```

Code description

♦ Lines 6-7: Variable names are declared here.

♦ Lines 12-14: An ADODB connection object with the name conn is created here, which is used to establish the connection with the P2P database on SQL Server 2000. A connection object represents an open connection to a data source. Here, the ADODB `connection` object is used to establish a connection with SQL Server 2000. A `connection` object is needed to access data using the data environment and represents a connection to a database residing on server used as a data source.

♦ Lines 19-22: A new instance of the ADODB recordset is created with the name `rsPeer` and `CursorType adopenstatic`. An SQL query is defined in the variable `sqlPeer`, which selects all the records from the peer table. Then the selected record is opened in the `rsPeer` recordset.

♦ Lines 30-42: An XML document is generated here on the basis of records selected in the `rsPeer` recordset. The XML document has the username and IP address of the users present in the peer table.

This code displays a list of currently logged on peers to the user using XML. This user list is displayed in XML format that has the information username and IPaddress from the peer table using the object `rsPeer` of recordset.

♦ Lines 51-55: The instances of the recordset and connection created in the beginning of the file are closed and destroyed here.

These lines help in closing the connection `conn` and recordset `rsPeer` created earlier. Both of these are initialized to a null value.

userlist.xml

The other way of getting the list of currently logged in users in XML format is to configure SQL Server 2000 for XML query support. This is done by creating a virtual directory and mapping it to the server path where the XML query files (`userlist.xml` in this case) are kept. Now the virtual name template for this virtual directory is again mapped to the directory to which the virtual directory was mapped. For more generic discussions, refer to the SQL documentation.

```
http://<SERVERNAME>/<virtual directory name>/template/userlist.xml
```

Having done this when userlist.xml runs on this virtual path, it communicates with the peer table of the P2P database and shows the user information present in the peer table, such as the `username`, `ip_address`, and so on. Listing 3-4 shows the code of userlist.xml.

Listing 3-4: userlist.xml

//© 2001 Dreamtech Software India Inc.
// All rights reserved.

```
 1 <?xml version ='1.0' encoding='UTF-8'?>
 2 <p2p_lng xmlns:sql="urn:schemas-microsoft-com:xml-sql">
 3   <response type="USERLIST">
 4     <sql:query>
 5        SELECT 1 as Tag,
 6         null as Parent,
 7         user_name as [userinfo!1!username],
 8         ip_address as [userinfo!1!ip]
 9  FROM peer
10 FOR XML EXPLICIT
11 </sql:query>
12 </response>
13 </p2p_lng>
```

Code description

♦ Line 1: This line describes the processing of the instruction that shows that the code written in this file is an XML format.

♦ Line 2: There is a tag defined with the name <p2p_lng>.

♦ Line 3: A tag named <response> is defined here with an attribute named type having the value USERLIST.

♦ Line 4: The <sql:query> tag is defined here. This is an XML built-in tag used to define the SQL query in an XML file.

♦ Lines 5-10: An SQL query is defined here in explicit mode of the response. This query selects user_name and IP address from the peer table of the P2P database and shows the resulting data in XML format set by the developer.

♦ Line 11: The </sql:query> tag is defined here that indicates the end of the <sql:query> tag.

♦ Line 12: The </response> tag is defined here that indicates the end of the <response> tag.

♦ Line 13: The </p2p_lng> tag is defined here that indicates the end of the <p2p_lng> tag.

search.asp

This file is used to generate an XML response on the basis of search criteria. This XML shows the listing of the usernames and the shared file or folder names in XML format.

Flowchart description of search.asp

The flow chart shown in Figure 3-6 explains how the list of user names and file names shared by the users, using some match criteria, is obtained in XML format from the peer and the share tables.

First, the program gets the value of user_name and filenames from the Querystring variables and then assigns them to the UserID and filename variables, respectively. After that, the program calls the function replacestar, which is defined to replace *into %in the string of the filename variable, which holds the value of the search string sent by the user who has been allowed to use * as the wildcard. This is because * is a common wildcard in various forms of search utilities, including the windows file search and in many of the better known search engines. This search string thus has to be parsed to replace * (which is not legible to SQL queries) with % (which is legible). The program then creates the ADODB connection and recordset objects to establish connection with the P2P database residing in SQL Server 2000 to be able to access the peer and the share table. Next, the program executes an SQL query that selects every user_name from the peer table having the userID similar to the one specified in the search string. Then the program executes another SQL query that selects all the filenames shared by the users selected in the previous query. The output of this program is in XML format having the list of user names and the shared filenames. After throwing this XML document, the program terminates the process. Listing 3-5 contains the code for search.asp.

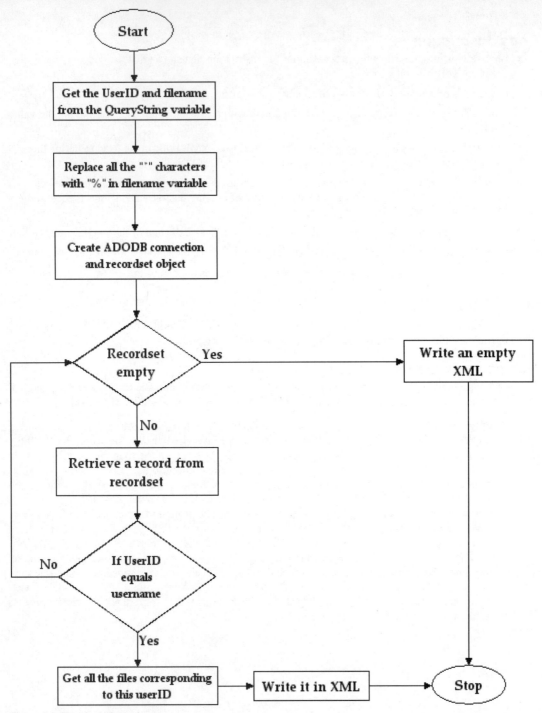

Figure 3-6: Flowchart of search.asp

Listing 3-5: search.asp

```
 1<%@ Language=VBScript %>
 2 <!--#include file="adovbs.inc"-->
 3 <%
 4
 5 '//Getting the values of variables from QueryString-----------//

 6  UserId = trim(Request.QueryString("US"))
 7  filename = UCase(trim(Request.QueryString("FS")))
 8 '//----------------------------------------------------------//
 9
10
11
12 '//Calling the function replacestar-----------//
13  filename = replacestar(filename)
14  UserId = replacestar(UserId)
15 '//-----------------------------------------//
16
17 '//Definition of the function replacestar that replace "*" with "%" --------
//
18  Function replacestar(tmpstring)
19   tmpstring = REPLACE(tmpstring,"*","%")
20   replacestar = tmpstring
21  End Function
22
23 '//------------------------------------------------------------------------
//
24
25
26 '//Create and open the connection object-----------------//
27  set conn = Server.CreateObject("ADODB.Connection")
28  conn.ConnectionString = "Provider=SQLOLEDB.1;Persist Security
Info=False;User ID=sa;Initial Catalog=p2p;Data Source=developers"
29  conn.Open
30 '//-------------------------------------------------------//
31
32
33 '//Create and open the recordset object with peer table-----------------//

34  Set  rsUser= Server.CreateObject("ADODB.Recordset")
35  Set  rsFile= Server.CreateObject("ADODB.Recordset")
36  sqlIP = "SELECT ip_address,user_name from peer where user_name like '" &
UserId & "'"
37  rsUser.Open sqlIP,conn
38 '//----------------------------------------------------------------//
39
40
41
42
43 '//Create an XML for the search result---------------------------//
44 %>
45
46  <?xml version='1.0' encoding='utf-8'?>
```

```
47   <p2p_language>
48   <response type='SERVERSEARCH'>
49
50   <%while not(rsUser.EOF)
51        sqlFile = "SELECT * from share where ip_address='" &
rsUser.Fields("ip_address") & "' and file_name like '" & filename & "'"
52        rsFile.Open sqlFile,conn
53        ip = rsUser.Fields("ip_address")
54        uname = rsUser.Fields("user_name")
55        while not(rsFile.EOF)
56             fname = rsFile.Fields("file_name")%>
57             <result ip="<%=ip%>" username="<%=uname%>"
filename="<%=fname%>" />
58
59        <%rsFile.MoveNext
60        wend
61        rsFile.Close
62
63   rsUser.MoveNext
64   wend
65
66
67
68
69   %>
70   </response>
71   </p2p_language>
72
73   <%
74   '//-----------------------------------------------------------------------//
75
76
77   '//Close and destroy the connection object----------------------//
78   conn.Close
79   set conn=Nothing
80   '//--------------------------------------------------------//
81   %>
```

Code description

♦ Lines 6-7: The values of the `userId` and `filename` variables are set with the values of the `QuerySting` variables `US` and `FS`, respectively.

♦ Lines 13-14: The user-defined function `replacestar` is called here to replace * text with % text in the string of the `filename` and `userID` variables. Resulting strings are stored in their respective variable userIDs and filenames.

♦ Lines 18-21: The function `replacestar` is defined here. This function stores the passed parameter's value in the `tmpstring` variable. Then the built-in function `REPLACE` is used to replace * with % in the `tmpstring`. The resulting string is returned.

These lines define the function `replacestar`, called in lines 13-14. This function is used to replace * with %.

♦ Lines 27-29: An ADODB connection object with the name conn is created here, which is used to establish the connection with the P2P database on SQL Server 2000.

A connection object represents an open connection to a data source. Here, the ADODB connection object is used to establish a connection with SQL Server 2000. A connection object is needed to access data using the data environment and represents a connection to a database residing on the server used as a data source.

♦ Lines 34-37: The new instances of the ADODB recordset are created with names `rsUser` and `rsFile`. An SQL query is defined in the variable `sqlIP`, which selects all the records from the peer table in which `username` is similar to the value of the `userId` variable. Then the selected record is opened in the `rsUser` recordset.

♦ Lines 46-71: An XML response is generated on the basis of the records selected in the `User` recordset. An SQL query is defined in the variable `sqlFile`, which selects all the records from the share table in which `file_name` is similar to the value of the `filename` variable. Then the selected records are opened in the `rsFile` recordset. The search result having user names and shared filenames is displayed in XML format.

♦ Lines 78-79: The instance of the connection created in the beginning of the file is closed and destroyed here.

♦ These lines help in closing the connection `conn` created earlier and set it to a `null` value.

This asp has two parametes that are to be passed to it. These parameters are US and FS. The US and FS parameters are for `User Search` and `File Search`, respectively. In the US parameter, the scope for the computer name is passed (for example US=f* means all the computer names starting with *f*), similarly the parameter FS is used. The correct syntax for the search.asp page is

```
http://p2pserver/search.asp&US=f*?FS=*
```

This will search for all the files shared by the computers with names starting with the letter *f*.

Summary

In this chapter, we have studied the details of server-side coding required for the full and proper functioning of the server. The server used here has Microsoft SQL Server 2000 installed on it. You can use any database you want and can change the ASPs accordingly for the purpose of making this system run. This is because no special feature of SQL Server 2000 is being used as such, except for the example userlist.xml that emphasizes the usage of XML awareness of SQL Server 2000. In addition, we have discussed programming of ASPs in detail as we have walked the user through the process of how different ASP programs responsible for different tasks are coded. The flowcharts in this chapter help you understand coding details and the logical flow of the programs.

Chapter 4

The P2P Application in Java

We have selected Java to build our P2P application in this chapter. The same application can be built by using C#. Building the application in C# can meet the purpose quite well and has the advantage that the final application will be in the form of an EXE file. However, there are a few disadvantages with C#. A C# application is not available to the user as a compiled file, because not all people have the C# compiler. Moreover, such a compiler can run only with Visual Studio 6. This means that the user is required to install Visual Studio 6 so as to provide the Common Language Runtime (CLR) required to run the C# code. Of course, this situation changes as C# gains more acceptance. Because C# has the patronage of Microsoft behind it, we can reasonably expect that running C# applications without having to first compile them will become quite common in the near future. But for the time being, Java is the best option.

It is not impossible to build P2P applications using other programming languages, but Java gives us all the advantages associated with it, the major one being portability across all platforms. One argument that may slightly go against Java is performance, but the difference in performance between C# and Java is not significant. Java provides us with a fairly well-established platform with an exhaustive range of APIs. One more feature in favor of Java is that its combination with XML is considered ideal by many people because Java is a portable language and XML is portable data which can be easily ported to any platform. This makes Java and XML a perfect match.

We have used the same design for our application for both Java and C#. The architectures, as well as the programming logic, are similar. Only the implementation is different. XML is used as the data carrier in both the cases. The same project has been implemented using the Java 2Micro Edition platform. To have a look at the application, you can refer to *Wireless Programming with J2ME: Cracking the Code*. We discuss implementation of this application by using C# in the next chapter.

This chapter introduces you to the task of cracking code and illustrates all aspects of high-level programming. All programs carry a detailed explanation wherever needed so that you are able to understand and appreciate the code better.

The code explanation starts with a discussion of the XML classes involved in the application. The two major XML classes are SParser and xmlwriter. The Sparser class is a wrapper to the XML parser class. The name of the XML file to be parsed is to the Sparser.java class, and the XML parser is called from it. The XML parser parses the file and stores the parsed data in an object of the class Vector, which is returned to the calling program.

The xmlwriter class, on the other hand, is used to handle responses and requests to and from the browser, as well as to and from the listener, in XML format. The functions of this class take some parameters, and, depending upon the parameters, a request or response is generated.

After discussing the building blocks of our application, we go on to the application itself. This consists of a listener software and a browser software (client). These two interact with each other to give the final shape to this P2P application. The listener, as the name suggests, listens to the request sent by the browser (client) and then sends the response back to the client in XML format. The client, on the other hand, is responsible for showing the response to users.

Listener Source Code: XMLParserServer.java

The input to this Class is the name of the XML file passed as a string, and the output of the class is a `Vector` object containing all the information from a parsed XML file. This class acts as a wrapper class to the XML parser (it calls the XML parser and stores the results generated by the parser in a `Vector`). Listing 4-1 contains the source code for XMLParserServer.java.

Listing 4-1: XMLParserServer.java

//© 2001 Dreamtech Software India Inc.
// All rights reserved

```
1.   //  parses XML File
2.
3.   import java.awt.*;
4.   import java.io.*;
5.   import java.util.*;
6.   import org.xml.sax.*;
7.   import org.apache.xerces.parsers.SAXParser;
8.   /* This is the wrapper class of the XML parser class as it calls the Xml
parser and in turn when
9.      the xml parser, parses the xml file it generates the call backs on the
class MyContentHandler...
10.     the various parsed documents can be used by using the varoius functions
in this class.
11.     This class returns a vector to the class which calls this class
XMLParserServer.java the vector
12.     consists of the data provided by the XML document.
13.
14.  */
15.  public class XMLParserServer
16.  {
17.   String attributevalue;
18.   Vector value1;
19.   // Function used for calling the parser it has a parameter called "uri"
which has the
20.   // information of the file to be parsed...
21.   public void perform(String uri)
22.   {
23.    System.out.println("Parsing XML File : " + uri + "\n\n" );
24.    try
25.    {
26.        // Generate an object of the XMLParser class..
27.        XMLReader parser = new SAXParser();
28.        // Generate an Object of the MyContentHandler Class it is in this
class that
29.        // the xml parser generates the call backs...

30.        MyContentHandler contHandler = new MyContentHandler();
31.        parser.setContentHandler(contHandler);
32.        // call the parse function of the XMLParser class with the file
information
33.        //as the parameter...
34.        parser.parse(uri);
35.        value1 = contHandler.returnvector();
36.    }
37.    catch(IOException e)
```

```java
38.     {
39.          System.out.println("Error reading uri : " +e.getMessage());
40.     }
41.    catch(SAXException e)
42.     {
43.          System.out.println("Error in parsing : " +e.getMessage());
44.     }
45.    }
46.    // This function returns the vector generated after xmlparsing is
complete..
47.    public Vector yakreturn()
48.    {
49.     return value1;
50.    }
51.  }
52.
53.
54.  class MyContentHandler implements ContentHandler
55.  {
56.   private Locator locator;
57.   Vector value = new Vector();
58.   public Vector returnvector()
59.   {
60.     return value;
61.   }
62.   // Only this function is used by us for our purpose....
63.   public void startElement(String namespaceURI, String localName, String
rawName, Attributes atts) throws SAXException
64.   {
65.     System.out.println("Name of the tag " + localName);
66.     System.out.println(" NO of Attributes " + atts.getLength());
67.
68.     for(int i= 0; i<atts.getLength();i++)
69.     {
70.
71.          System.out.println("Value of i :" + i);
72.          if(atts.getValue(i) == null)
73.          {
74.                 System.out.println("Entered if Statement");
75.
76.          }
77.          else
78.          {
79.                 System.out.println(" Attribute : "  + atts.getLocalName(i) +
atts.getValue(i));
80.                 value.add(atts.getValue(i));
81.
82.          }
83.     }
84.
85.     if(!namespaceURI.equals(""))
86.     {
87.     }
88.     else
89.     {
90.     }
```

```
91.    }
92.
93.
94.    public void  characters( char[] ch, int start , int end )
95.    {
96.     //empty
97.    }
98.    public void  startDocument() {}
99.    public void  endDocument() {}
100.     public void endElement(String nameSpaceURI, String localName, String
rawName) {}
101.     public void startPrefixMapping(String prefix, String uri) {}
102.     public void endPrefixMapping(String prefix) {}
103.     public void ignorableWhitespace(char[] ch, int start, int end) {}
104.     public void processingInstruction(String target, String data) {}
105.     public void setDocumentLocator(Locator locator) {}
106.     public void skippedEntity(String name) {}
107.     static String ty;
108.    }
```

Code description

♦ Lines 3-5: This portion includes the basic packages used by the various classes to build this application. The packages include `java.io` (file streams), `java.util` (various utilities), and so on.

♦ Lines 6-7: This part lists the basic packages used by the various classes of the XML parser. These packages are `org.xml.sax.*` and `org.apache.xerces.parsers.SAXParser`.

♦ Lines 15-18: This code declares a public class (`XMLParserServer`) that represents the base class for this file and declares the user-defined variables, which are used for various purposes during the course of the program. These include Vector-type variables into which the result of the parsed XML file is stored.

♦ Lines 21- 45: The code here defines a function of the name perform. This function is used for calling the parser. It take a parameter called `uri`, which has the information of the file to be parsed.

  • 27: This generates an object of the `XMLParser` class.

  • 30-31: This generates an object of the `MyContentHandler` class. In this class, the XML parser generates the callbacks. The method `setContentHandler` is called, with object of `MyContentHandler class` as parameter. This assigns the handler to the parser.

  • 34: This calls the `parse` function of the `XMLParser` class with the file information as the parameter.

  • 35: The content handler's attributes are stored in the variable called `value1`.

  • 37-44: Exception Handling code.The code makes sure the appropriate message is shown, depending on whether the error is in parsing or reading.

♦ Lines 47-50: The code here defines a function of the name `yakreturn()`. This function returns a vector object `value1` containing data after XML parsing.

♦ Lines 54-108: The code here pertains to the declaration of a `MyContentHandler` class. In this class, the callback from the XML parsing is handled and stored in appropriate data structures. For our requirements, we use a `startElement` function (69-77) and store the values in the `Vector` object, which is returned to the calling class in the end.

  • 57: A new `Vector` object is instantiated.

  • 58-61: This defines the method `returnvector`, which returns the Vector values.

- 63: A method `startElement` is defined. It takes the parameters `namespaceURI`, `localname`, `rawName` and `atts` (attributes).

- 68 - 83: Values of attributes are obtained by calling the `getValue` method and are added to the `Vector` object after casting them as object. A `for loop` runs till the count becomes equal to the length of `atts` parameter.

- 94-108: This is the implementation of the methods of the `ContentHandler` interface.

Login.java

Login is the first class to be invoked when the application starts. This is a GUI class. The user is shown a window containing a text field for entering the user name, three buttons, and a checkbox.

- **Shared Files button:** This button is used to share files. When the user presses this button, the `Shareddilog` class is called. This contains a new window through which the user can select the file or folder to be shared.

- **Login button:** This is used to invoke the listener. Pressing this button calls Login.asp on the server, which makes an entry of the user name entered and the IP address of the system. This also invokes listener in a new thread by calling the `IDGMultiServer` class.

- **Cancel button:** This is used to close the application. Pressing this button calls Logout.asp on the server, which removes the user entry from the server.

- **The checkbox "Remember my Login ID":** This checkbox is used to store user information. Checking the box creates a UserInfo.ini file, which contains the user name. If unchecked, the file is deleted (see Figure 4-1).

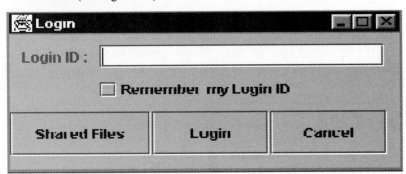

Figure 4-1: The Login dialog box

Listing 4-2 describes the code of login.java.

Listing 4-2: Login.java

```
1.  /*
2.   * This is login class. This class is used to login.The user has to enter
his login name
3.   * and through this Frame user can open the Share frame . The ip address of
the System and
4.   * login is sent to the Server (Login.asp).When the user wants to logout
again the
5.   * information is sent to the Server (Logout.asp)
6.   */
7.
```

```
8.   import java.util.*;
9.   import java.net.*;
10.  import java.io.*;
11.  import javax.swing.*;
12.  import javax.swing.event.*;
13.  import java.awt.*;
14.  import java.awt.event.*;
15.
16.  public class  Login extends JFrame implements ActionListener
17.  {
18.
19.  // This is Constructor part of this login class
20.   public Login()
21.  {
22.
23.    // set the title of this frame
24.         setTitle("Login");
25.
26.    // set layout to null
27.    getContentPane().setLayout(null);
28.
29.    // Set size to 310 and 150
30.         setSize(310,150);
31.
32.    // get the insets
33.    Insets insets = getInsets();
34.
35.    // write the window closing event.
36.    addWindowListener(new WindowAdapter()
37.    { public void WindowClosing(WindowEvent e)
38.         {
39.                 System.exit(0);
40.         }
41.    });
42.
43.     //This is the label displayed just befor the TextFeild
44.    l_login = new JLabel("Login ID :");
45.     //This method sets the coordinates where this label will be drawn
46.    l_login.setBounds( 10 + insets.left ,insets.top + 10, 60, 20);
47.    //Label is added to the Frame
48.    getContentPane().add(l_login);
49.
50.
51.    //This text field is for the user to enter his login name
52.    login_field = new JTextField(50);
53.    //This method sets the cordinates where this text field will be drawn
54.    login_field.setBounds( 70 + insets.left ,insets.top + 10, 220, 20);
55.        //TextFeild is added to the Frame
56.    getContentPane().add(login_field);
57.
58.   /*CheckBox is used to store login information
59.    * If Checked UserInfo.ini file is created which will store the user name
60.    */
61.    c_remember = new JCheckBox("Remember my Login ID");
62.    //This method sets the cordinates where this textfeild will be drawn
63.    c_remember.setBounds( 70 + insets.left ,insets.top + 40, 220, 20);
```

```
64.      //Registering this component for user events
65.      c_remember.addActionListener(this);
66.      //Text Field is added to the Frame
67.      getContentPane().add(c_remember);
68.
69.
70.      /* This button is for sharing a file. Pressing this button will open a
filechooser dialog
71.      * where the user can choose the files to be shared
72.      */
73.       bshared_files = new JButton("Shared Files");
74.     //This method sets the cordinates where this text field will be drawn
75.      bshared_files.setBounds( 0 + insets.left ,insets.top + 70, 110, 40);
76.       //Registering this component for user events  */
77.      bshared_files.addActionListener(this);
78.      //TextField is added to the Frame
79.      getContentPane().add(bshared_files);
80.
81.
82.      //This button is for Login. Pressing this button will register the user
with the server
83.      blogin = new JButton("Login");
84.       //This method sets the cordinates where this textfield will be drawn
85.      blogin.setBounds( 111 + insets.left ,insets.top + 70, 90, 40);
86.      //Registering this component for user events
87.      blogin.addActionListener(this);
88.      //TextFeild is added to the Frame
89.      getContentPane().add(blogin);
90.
91.      /*This button is for Logout. Pressing this button will make the user
logout and his entry will
92.      *  be removed from the server
93.      */
94.      bcancel = new JButton("Cancel");
95.      // This method sets the cordinates where this textfield will be drawn
96.      bcancel.setBounds( 202 + insets.left, insets.top + 70 , 90, 40);
97.     // Registering this component for user events
98.      bcancel.addActionListener(this);
99.      // TextField is added to the Frame
100.         getContentPane().add(bcancel);
101.
102.     try
103.     {
104.         // Store the ip address of local host
105.         InetAddress localHostAddress = InetAddress.getLocalHost();
106.
107.         // local ip address converted into string
108.         String local_address = localHostAddress.toString();
109.
110.         // its local ip address seperated by "/"
111.         st = new StringTokenizer(local_address, "/");
112.
113.         // While loop run till tokens are present
114.         while(st.hasMoreTokens())
115.         {
116.             // login computer name stored in this variable
```

```
117.                  machine_owner_name = st.nextToken();
118.
119.                  // login computer ip address stored in this variable
120.                  ip_address = st.nextToken();
121.          }
122.
123.        }
124.
125.    catch (Exception e)
126.    {    System.out.println("Error: " + e);
127.    }
128.
129.    try
130.    {
131.
132.        String r_line = "";
133.
134.        // Opened a Stream to read from UserInfo.ini file
135.        user_stream = new DataInputStream(new BufferedInputStream(new
FileInputStream("UserInfo.ini")));
136.
137.   / Buffered reader object instantiated to read from the stream
138.        name_in_buffer_stream = new BufferedReader(new
InputStreamReader(user_stream));
139.
140.        // This loop runs until the end of the stream
141.        while((r_line = name_in_buffer_stream.readLine()) != null)
142.        {
143.            // string divide on the basis of " = "
144.            r_st = new StringTokenizer(r_line, " = ");
145.
146.            // while loop run till any token present
147.            while(r_st.hasMoreTokens())
148.            {
149.                // store the text "username"
150.                user = r_st.nextToken();
151.
152.                // store the name of the user
153.            name = r_st.nextToken();
154.
155.                // display the name of login user in textfiled
156.                login_field.setText(name);
157.
158.                // checkbox  c_remember set true
159.                c_remember.setSelected(true);
160.            }
161.
162.        }
163.
164.        // close the user_stream
165.        user_stream.close();
166.
167.        // close the name_in_buffer_stream
168.        name_in_buffer_stream.close();
169.    }
170.    catch (IOException e)
```

```
171.    {
172.    }
173.  }
174.  /* This method is used to handle the user generated events  */
175.  public void actionPerformed(ActionEvent e)
176.  {
177.    //The getSource method returns the object of the component which has
generated an event
178.    Object pan =e.getSource();
179.
180.    //The code in the if condition is executed if the user clicks the login
button
181.    if(pan.equals(blogin))
182.    {
183.    try
184.    {
185.
186.    int count = 0;
187.    full_string = "";
188.    String search_name = "";
189.
190. // First time search the "Share.ini" file open the stream for it
191. BufferedReader first_search = new
192. BufferedReader(new FileReader("Share.ini"));
193.
194.         // while loop run till first_search stream not become null
195.    while ((search_name = first_search.readLine())  != null)
196.    {
197.
198.        count++;
199.        String filename = "";
200.        String filesize = "";
201.        String mask = "";
202.
203.    // String divided in the basis of "="
204.    st_xml = new StringTokenizer(search_name, "=");
205.
206.    // while loop run till tokens present in StringTokenizer
207.    while(st_xml.hasMoreTokens())
208.     {
209. // in this variable store the file name and directory
210.    filename = st_xml.nextToken();
211.
212.    /* if filename string not end by "\" then enter in this condition
213.     * otherwise go to else part */
214.     if( !filename.endsWith("\\") )
215.        {
216.    // store the rights of file
217.        mask = st_xml.nextToken();
218.
219.    // Store the file size in this variable
220.        filesize = st_xml.nextToken();
221.
222.    // take only file name
223.    String  word = filename.substring((filename.lastIndexOf("\\")  + 1 ));
```

```
224.
225.      // store the file name with "*"
226.      full_string = full_string + word + "*";
227.
228.
229.    }
230.    else
231.    {
232.          // store the rights of file
233.            mask = st_xml.nextToken();
234.
235.      // store the directory with full path name "*"
236.      full_string = full_string + filename + "*";
237.
238.    }
239.     }
240.
241.  }
242.    }
243.    catch(IOException ex)
244.    {
245.    }
246.
247.    try
248.    {
249.          // store the user name which is enterd by user in textfield
250.          name = login_field.getText();
251.
252.
253.  // full_string value is null means first time "Share.ini" file does not
exist
254.    if (full_string.equals(""))
255.    {
256.
257.    full_string = "";
258.    }
259.    else
260.        {
261.    // make one string for share.ini file list
262.    full_string = full_string.substring(0, (full_string.length()- 1));
263.                 }
264.    /* Login.asp file on the server is called and three parameterd are passed
ip_address,share file
265.        * and directory list
266.        */
267.    urlName = "http://www.s-cop.com/login.asp?USERID=" + name + "&IP=" +
ip_address + "&share=" + full_string;
268.        // maket the object for URL and send the asp path
269.          URL url = new URL(urlName);
270.
271.          // open the connection of url
272.          URLConnection connection = url.openConnection();
273.
274.          // connect with url
275.          connection.connect();
276.
```

```
277.            //Open a stream to read from the URL
278.            BufferedReader response_stream = new BufferedReader(new
InputStreamReader(connection.getInputStream()));
279.
280.            // Character array created
281.            char[] b = new char[32];
282.            int i =0;
283.
284.   // Make the string buffer object which stores the response sent by server
285.       StringBuffer sb = new StringBuffer();
286.       while ((i = response_stream.read(b,0,32))>0)
287.          {
288.                // charecter by charecter append in the string buffer
289.              sb = sb.append(b,0,i);
290.          }
291.
292.          // make the object of newstsrtclass
293.          newstartclass = new StartNewClass();
294.
295.          //call the constector of that class
296.          newstartclass.startnew();
297.
298.      }
299.   catch(Exception exception)
300.      {
301.            System.out.println("Error :" + exception);
302.      }
303.
304.
305.      }
306.
307.   // if user clicks on "shared files" button  then enter in this condition
308.   else if(pan.equals(bshared_files))
309.      {
310.          // make the object of Shareddilog class
311.            sh_files = new Shareddilog();
312.
313.          // calling the function of this Shareddilog class
314.            sh_files.shared_files();
315.      }
316.
317.   // if user click on "cancel" button this code is executed
318.   else if(pan.equals(bcancel))
319.      {
320.          try
321.          {
322.
323.   // Call the logout.asp file giving parameter the ip address of the system
324.          urlName = "http://www.s-cop.com/logout.asp?IP=" + ip_address;
325.
326.
327.          // url object instantiated
328.            URL url = new URL(urlName);
329.
330.          // URL called by opnening a Stream
331.                url.openStream();
```

```
332.          }
333.        catch(Exception exception)
334.        {
335.            System.out.println("Error :" + exception);
336.        }
337.        System.exit(0);
338.   }
339.
340.   // if user checks "Remember my Login ID" checkbox the code in this
condition is executed
341.   else if(pan.equals(c_remember))
342.   {
343.
344.              if(c_remember.isSelected())
345.              {
346.
347.                  String u_name = "";
348.
349.   /* login text field is not null then enter in this condition otherwise
enter in
350.     * else condition */
351.   if((u_name = login_field.getText()) != null)
352.   {
353.       try
354.       {
355.
356.   // open the stream of "UserInfo.ini" for writing the file
357.          out = new DataOutputStream(
358.           new FileOutputStream("UserInfo.ini"));
359.
360.   // write in this file Byte by Byte
361.          out.writeBytes("username = " + u_name);
362.
363.   //close the out Stream
364.          out.close();
365.   }
366.   catch (IOException tr)
367.   {}
368.   }
369.   }
370.   else
371.   {
372.
373.   // Make the file object store the "UserInfo.ini" data into this variable
374.   File user_list = new File("UserInfo.ini");
375.
376.   // Find the path of the file
377.          String actual_path = user_list.getAbsolutePath();
378.
379.
380.            //Make the object for deleting  the file
381.          File delete_file = new File(actual_path);
382.          String d_file = "";
383.   if((d_file = login_field.getText()) != null)
384.   {
385.       // delete the file
```

```
386.            boolean io = delete_file.delete();
387.
388.    // The textfeild is cleared (blank)
389.        login_field.setText("");
390.    }
391.  }
392. }
393.}
394.
395.    // The main function of the application
396.    public static void main(String[] args)
397.    {
398.
399.
400.                    JFrame login = new Login();
401.                    login.show();
402.    }
403.
404.        // Declraing login button
405.        JButton blogin;
406.
407.        // Declaring cancel button
408.        JButton bcancel;
409.
410.        // Declaring ShareFile button
411.        JButton bshared_files;
412.
413.        // Declaring TextFeild for entering username
414.        JTextField login_field;
415.
416.        // Label declared
417.        JLabel l_login;
418.
419.        // declaring Checkbox
420.        JCheckBox c_remember;
421.
422.        // This string will contain the url address
423.         String urlName;
424.
425.        // Declaring StringTokenizer
426.        StringTokenizer st_xml;
427.
428.        // Declaring StringTokenizer
429.        private StringTokenizer st;
430.
431.        // Declaring StringTokenizer
432.         private StringTokenizer r_st;
433.
434.    // This string contains the ip address of the User's System
435.        static private String ip_address;
436.
437.        static private String machine_owner_name;
438.
439.        // Store the "UserName"
440.        static private String user;
441.
```

```
442.        // Store the login name
443.          static private String name;
444.        //Declaring DatadInputStream
445.        private DataOutputStream out;
446.          //Declaring DatadInputStream
447.        private DataInputStream user_stream;
448.          //Declaring Buffered Reader
449.        private BufferedReader name_in_buffer_stream;
450.
451.        // Declaring StartNewClass which call the listener
452.          StartNewClass newstartclass;
453.
454.        // Declaring Shareddilog which call the filechooser frame for sharing
file & directory
455.          Shareddilog sh_files;
456.
457.        String full_string;
458.    }
459.
460.
461.    /* this class starts another Thread.In the application login screen runs
on one thread and listener
462.    * runs on another Thread
463.    */
464.    class StartNewClass extends Thread {
465.    public void startnew()
466.    {
467.        // call the run function
468.          start();
469.    }
470.
471.    public void run()
472.    {
473.        try
474.        {
475.
476.              // make the object for MultiServer class
477.              server = new MultiServer();
478.              // call the function of this class
479.              server.multiaccess();
480.        }
481.        catch(IOException ex)
482.        {}
483.    }
484.    // defined the object of this class
485.          public MultiServer server;
486.    }
```

Code description

♦ Lines 8-14: Import statments. This imports basic classes needed for the application.

♦ Line 20: The constructor is called.

♦ Lines 24-33: This sets the size of the Frame (Container) and the text, which is displayed as the title of the Frame.

♦ Lines 36-41: This part handles window-closing events.

♦ Lines 44-100: This declares GUI objects, defines the coordinates where the component is drawn on the screen, registers the component to handle user events, and draws all GUI objects on Frame.

- 44-48: A label is instantiated, its bounds (coordinates) are set, and it is added to the content pane.

- 52-56: A text field for login is instantiated, its bounds are set, and it is added to the content pane.

- 61-67: A checkbox is instantiated, its bounds (coordinates) are set, and it is added to the content pane. An ActionListener is added to it.

- 73-100: Three buttons (Shared Files, Login, and Cancel) are added in the same way as previously. An ActionListener is added to this button, too.

♦ Lines 102-123: A try... catch block is used to store the IP address of the local host and to convert it into a string. StringTokenizer and a while loop are used to store the login computer name and the login computer's IP address in variables. The Code also handles any exception.

♦ Lines 129-172: This code reads the UserInfo.ini file and gets the user name from that file and stores it in a string, which is displayed in the textfield. This is done inside a try...catch block. A stream is opened to read from the UserInfo.ini file, and a BufferedReader reads from this stream. A StringTokenizer and a while loop are used to divide the string and store the user name. The name of the login user is displayed in the textfield, and the state of the checkbox c_remember is set to true.

♦ Lines 175: This method is used to handle action events usually generated when the user clicks some button. Any event generated invokes this method.

♦ Lines 181-305: This `if` condition is true when the user presses the Login button. In this if condition, the Share.ini is read, and the entries are appended in a String object. This String object is sent as the third parameter to Login.asp. The other two parameters are IP address and user name. If the Shared.ini does not exist, the the String is blank. This also invokes the listener by intantiating a MultiServer class.

- 183-245: This is a try...catch block, inside which the Share.ini file is searched and a stream is opened for it. Then a StringTokenizer inside a while loop is used to divide the string. The rights of the file, the file size, the file name, and so on are stored.

- 247-302: This try... catch block stores the user name entered in the textfield. It then checks whether the full_string has a null value. If it has, the Share.ini file doesn't exist. The Login.asp file on the server is called and three parameters are passed to it — the IP address, the share file, and the directory list. A connection is opened with the URL, and a stream is opened to read from the URL. A `newstartclass` object is created.

♦ Lines 308-315: This if condition is true when the user presses the Shared File button. In this if condition, the `Shareddilog` class `shared_files` method is called, which will generate the `Shareddilog` frame.

♦ Lines 318-338: This if condition is true when the user presses the Cancel button. In this if condition, Logout.asp is called and the IP address is passed as a parameter, which removes the entry from the server.

♦ Lines 341-392: This if condition is true when the user clicks the checkbox. If the checkbox is checked, the user name is entered in the UserInfo.ini file; if it is unchecked, the UserInfo.ini file is deleted.

♦ Lines 396-458: This is the main method. In this method, the login class is instantiated and objects are declared.

♦ Lines 464-486: This is an inner class and invokes the listener in a new thread. This class calls the object of the class `MultiServer`.

Shareddilog.java

This class is used for sharing files and folders and is GUI class (see Listing 4-3). The window contains five buttons, a textfield, two radio buttons, and one checkbox.

- **ShareFile Button:** The user presses this button if he or she wants to share files only. After pressing this button, if the user presses the Browse button, the file is displayed (see Figure 4-2).

- **ShareFolder Button:** The user presses this button if he or she wants to share folders only. After pressing this button, if the user presses the Browse button, folders are displayed.

- **Browse Button:** The user presses this button to select the files and folders to be shared. Pressing this button displays a file chooser dialog box from which the user can select the file or folder.

- **Shareit Button:** Pressing this button makes the file and folder entries in Share.ini file. If the Share.ini file does not exist, this creates it.

- **Close Button:** This button closes the window.

- **TextField:** The textfield displays the full path of the files or folder selected.

- **Radio Buttons:** There are two radio buttons. One is read only. If this radio button is checked, it means that the shared file is given a ReadOnly permission. The second radio button is Read/Write; if this button is checked, it means that the shared file is given Read/Write permission.

- **CheckBox:** If the checkbox "Add this entry only" is checked, after pressing Share button, the window closes. The user doesn't have to press the Close button.

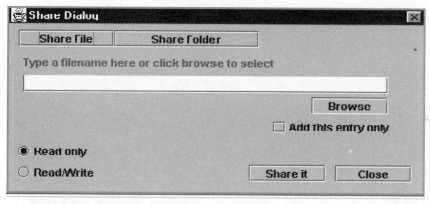

Figure 4-2: Share file/folders

Listing 4-3: Shareddilog.java

//© 2001 Dreamtech Software India Inc.
// All rights reserved

```
1.   import java.util.*;
2.   import java.awt.*;
3.   import java.awt.event.*;
4.   import java.io.*;
5.   import javax.swing.*;
6.   import javax.swing.event.*;
7.   import javax.swing.border.*;
8.
9.   /*
10.   * This class mainly used for sharing files and directories for user to
use.Through this class
```

```
11.   * the listener can add the files and directory. The major disadvantage is
that the listener
12.   * cannot remove the already shared file/folder.
13.   */
14.
15.  class  Shareddilog extends JDialog  implements ActionListener
16.  {
17.
18.  public void shared_files()
19.          {
20.     // Create an object of the class JDialog
21.          sharedilog = new JDialog();
22.     // Set the Layout as null then draw the gui components according to our
need
23.          sharedilog.getContentPane().setLayout(null);
24.     sharedilog.setTitle("Share Dialog");
25.
26.     // Adding the window  Listener to the gui window
27.     // ie. Code for the "cross"...
28.     addWindowListener( new WindowAdapter()
29.          { public void windowClosing(WindowEvent e)
30.                  {
31.                       dispose();
32.                  }
33.          });
34.     share_file = new JButton("Share File"); // Initializing the GUI
Component.
35.     share_file.setBounds(10,7,100,20);       // Positioning the GUI Component.
36.     share_file.addActionListener(this);// Add action listener
37.     sharedilog.getContentPane().add(share_file);    //     Adding the GUI
Buttons.....
38.
39.     share_folder = new JButton("Share Folder");// Initializing the GUI
Component.
40.     share_folder.setBounds(110,7,150,20);// Positioning the GUI Component.
41.     share_folder.addActionListener(this);// Add action listener
42.     sharedilog.getContentPane().add(share_folder);//      Adding the GUI
Buttons.....
43.
44.     l_type = new JLabel();// Initializing the GUI Component.
45.     l_type.setText("Type a filename here or click browse to select");
46.     l_type.setBounds(15,35, 380, 20);// Positioning the GUI Component.
47.     sharedilog.getContentPane().add(l_type);//      Adding the GUI Component
48.
49.
50.     t_type = new JTextField(150);     // Initializing the GUI Component
51.     t_type.setBounds(15,60, 380, 20);// Positioning the GUI Component.
52.     sharedilog.getContentPane().add(t_type);//      Adding the GUI Component
53.
54.     browse = new JButton("Browse");// Initializing the GUI Component
55.     browse.setBounds(315,85, 80, 20);// Positioning the GUI Component.
56.     browse.addActionListener(this);// Add action listener
57.     sharedilog.getContentPane().add(browse);//      Adding the GUI Component
58.
59.
```

```
60.      c_entry = new JCheckBox("Add this entry only");// Initializing the GUI
Component
61.     c_entry.setBounds(275,110, 150, 20);// Positioning the GUI Component.
62.     sharedilog.getContentPane().add(c_entry);//     Adding the GUI Component
63.
64.     // When this button is pressed then the information regarding the
file/folder shared will be added on to shard.ini file.
65.     shared_it = new JButton("Share it");// Initializing the GUI Component
66.     shared_it.setBounds(250,165, 80, 20);// Positioning the GUI Component.
67.     shared_it.addActionListener(this);// Add action listener
68.     sharedilog.getContentPane().add(shared_it);//   Adding the GUI Component
69.
70.     // This button for close the Dialog
71.     close = new JButton("Close");// Initializing the GUI Component
72.     close.setBounds(340,165, 80, 20);// Positioning the GUI Component.
73.     close.addActionListener(this);// Add action listener
74.     sharedilog.getContentPane().add(close);//         Adding the GUI Component
75.
76.     // This RadioButton to give read only permission to the file
77.     read_only = new JRadioButton("Read only", true);// Initializing the GUI
Component
78.     read_only.setBounds(10,140,80,20);// Positioning the GUI Component.
79.     sharedilog.getContentPane().add(read_only);//   Adding the GUI Component
80.
81.     // This RadioButton to give the read & write  permission to the file
82.     read_write =new JRadioButton("Read/Write", false);
83.     read_write.setBounds(10,165,80,20);// Positioning the GUI Component.
84.     sharedilog.getContentPane().add(read_write);// Adding the GUI Component
85.     group = new ButtonGroup();
86.
87.     group.add(read_only); // Add the radiobutton to the radiobuttongroup
88.     group.add(read_write);// Thereby enabling only one button at a time.
89.
90.     // Make vector to read Share.ini file and insert into it.
91.     v_file_list = new Vector();
92.
93.
94.   try
95.    {
96.        // String r_line iniatialize as null;
97.        String r_line = "";
98.
99.    // Open a DataInputStream to the file "Share.ini" for Reading the data
from the file.
100.    data_in = new DataInputStream(new BufferedInputStream(new
FileInputStream("Share.ini")));
101.    // Open a bufferedreader to the file "Share.ini" for Reading the data from
the file.
102.    data_buffer_in = new BufferedReader(new InputStreamReader(data_in));
103.
104.        // Reading the file buffer
105.        while((r_line = data_buffer_in.readLine()) != null)
106.            {
107.                // add the data into a vector
108.                    v_file_list.add(r_line);
109.                }
```

```
110.
111.                    // close DataInputStream
112.                    data_in.close();
113.                    // close the input Buffer
114.                    data_buffer_in.close();
115.         }
116.         catch (IOException e)
117.         {}
118.
119.
120.
121.
122.        sharedilog.setSize(440, 225);
123.        sharedilog.show();
124.
125.    }
126.
127.    // The part Below pertains to the Action Performed when a Button is
pressed...
128.
129.    public void actionPerformed(ActionEvent e)
130.        {
131.                Object source = e.getSource();
132.
133.        // When User clicks on "Share file" Button
134.        if(source == share_file)
135.            {
136.    l_type.setText("Type a filename here or click browse to select");
137.    b_cho_f = true;
138.
139.            }
140.        // When user clicks on "Share folder" Button
141.        else if(source == share_folder)
142.            {
143.        l_type.setText("Type a folder name here:");
144.        b_cho_d = true;
145.            }
146.        else if(source == browse)
147.            {
148.    // Initialize object for JFileChooser
149.    fileselection = new JFileChooser();
150.    fileselection.setCurrentDirectory(new File("."));
151.
152.        //              File pp1 = fileselection.getCurrentDirectory();
153.
154.        if ( b_cho_f == true )
155.            {
156.                    fileselection.setFileSelectionMode(0);
157.                    b_cho_f = false;
158.            }
159.        // When c_cho_d the set mode is "1" .It means show the directroy
160.        else if(b_cho_d == true )
161.            {
162.                    fileselection.setFileSelectionMode(1);
163.                    b_cho_d = false;
164.            }
```

```
165.
166.         // Readonly right means the mask is set to 0;
167.         if (read_only.isSelected())
168.             {
169.                     r_reights = "0";
170.             }
171.     // readwrite right means the mask is set to 1;
172.         else if (read_write.isSelected())
173.             {
174.                     r_reights = "1";
175.             }
176.             // show the JFileChooser
177.             int  pp = fileselection.showOpenDialog(this);
178.         if (pp == 0)
179.             {
180.                     // selected the current file or directroy
181.                     file_list = fileselection.getSelectedFile();
182.                     // Find the length of the file
183.                     lengthoffile = file_list.length();
184.
185.                     t_type.setText("");
186.                     // Display the  text on to the JTextField..
187.                     t_type.setText(file_list.toString());
188.
189.
190.         try
191.             {
192.
193.                     s_line = "";
194.
195. // Open a DataInputStream to the file "Share.ini" for Reading the data from
the file.
196.   data_in = new DataInputStream(new BufferedInputStream(new
FileInputStream("Share.ini")));
197.   // Open a Inputbuffer to the file "Share.ini" for Reading the data from
the file.
198.
199.   data_buffer_in = new BufferedReader(new InputStreamReader(data_in));
200.                     //
201.         value_all_ready_present = false;
202.
203.   while((s_line = data_buffer_in.readLine()) != null)
204.   {
205.                 //
206.   first_time_entry = true;
207. //Divide String on the basis of "="
208.   st = new StringTokenizer(s_line, "=");
209. // while loop run tile token present
210.   while(st.hasMoreTokens())
211.   {
212.
213. if (st.nextToken().equalsIgnoreCase(file_list.toString())  == true )
214.                                             {
215.
216.   value_all_ready_present = true;
217.   Box b = Box.createVerticalBox();
```

```
218.    b.add(Box.createGlue());
219.    b.add(new JLabel("This file is all ready exits"));
220.    getContentPane().add(b, "Center");
221.    setSize(180, 100);
222.    setVisible(true);
223.    JPanel p2 = new JPanel();
224.    // Press the "OK" button then close the messagebox
225.    JButton ok = new JButton("OK");
226.    p2.add(ok);
227.    getContentPane().add(p2, "South");
228.    ok.addActionListener(new ActionListener()
229.    { public void actionPerformed(ActionEvent evt)
230.    {    setVisible(false);
231.        }
232.    });
233.    System.out.println("This file is already exists");
234.    }
235.    else
236.    {
237.    }
238.    }
239.
240.    }
241.    // close DataInputStream
242.        data_in.close();
243.    // close the input Buffer
244.    data_buffer_in.close();
245.    }
246.    catch (IOException ex)
247.    {}
248.
249.
250.    // if files and directories are not present in share.ini
251.    if(value_all_ready_present == false || first_time_entry == false)
252.    {
253.    // Check whether file_list is directroy or file
254.    if (!file_list.isDirectory())
255.        {
256.    // Add Files list in vector
257.    v_file_list.add(file_list.toString() + "=" + r_reights + "=" +
lengthoffile);
258.        }
259.    else
260.    {
261.        // Add directories list in vector
262.     v_file_list.add(file_list.toString() + "\\=" + r_reights );
263.    }
264.    }
265.    }
266. }
267.
268. else if(source == shared_it) // When share button  is pressed.
269.    {
270.    try
271.      {
```

```
272.     // Open a DataOutputStream to the file "Share.ini" for Reading the data
from the file.
273.     data_out = new DataOutputStream(
274.     (new FileOutputStream("Share.ini")));
275.
276.     for (int t = 0; t < v_file_list.size() ; t++)
277.         {
278.  // Write the all data present in the vector byte-by-byte in the Share.ini
file
279.  data_out.writeBytes(v_file_list.get(t) + "\n");
280.  }
281.  // Close the object of DataOutputStream
282.     data_out.close();
283.     }
284.     catch (IOException ex)
285.     {}
286.
287.     if (c_entry.isSelected()) // When add this file only checkbox is checked
288.         {
289.                  // Close the share dialog box
290.                  sharedilog.dispose();
291.
292.         }
293.
294.         }
295.
296.         else if(source == close)      // Close button is pressed.
297.         {
298.
299.                  sharedilog.dispose();
300.  }
301.
302.     }
303.
304.
305.         JFileChooser fileselection;
306.         JButton share_file;
307.         JButton share_folder;
308.         JLabel l_type;
309.         JTextField t_type;
310.         JButton browse;
311.         JCheckBox c_entry;
312.         JButton shared_it;
313.         JButton close;
314.         JRadioButton read_only ;
315.         JRadioButton read_write ;
316.         ButtonGroup group;
317.         static boolean  b_cho_f = false;
318.         static boolean b_cho_d = false;
319.         static boolean first_time_entry = false;
320.         static boolean value_all_ready_present = false;
321.         DataOutputStream data_out;
322.         DataInputStream data_in;
323.         BufferedReader data_buffer_in;
324.         StringTokenizer st;
325.         // list of files
```

```
326.        static File file_list;
327.        // Store the length of files
328.        long lengthoffile;
329.        // Store the list all files which are all ready shared
330.        Vector v_file_list;
331. // Give the rights to the file and Directroy, "0" for read only and "1"
for read and write
332.        String r_reights;
333.        // Main Dialog box
334.        JDialog  sharedilog;
335.        String s_line;
336.    }
```

Code description

+ Lines 1-7: Import statements to import basic classes for the application.

+ Line 18: shared_files method declared.

+ Lines 21-24: The Jdialog class is instantiated and the title of the dialog is set, which is displayed as the title of the window.

+ Lines 28-33: This handles the window-closing event.

+ Lines 34-91: This code declares and initializes the components. The components insets are set. This sets the coordinates where the Component is drawn and also registers these components to handle user events and the Component is then added to the container.

+ Lines 94-125: This appends the data in the Share.ini file.

+ Line 129: This method handles the events generated on the GUI components.

+ Lines 134-139: This if condition is executed if the user presses the ShareFile button.

+ Lines 141-145: This if condition is executed if the user presses the ShareFolder button.

+ Lines 146-266: This if condition is executed if the user presses the Browse button. This opens a file-chooser dialog box from which the user can select the files to be shared. Every entry is stored in the Vector with full path, permissions, and size.

  • 154-164: File selection mode is set depending on which of the b_cho_f and b_cho_d variables is true.

  • 168-175: File permissons are checked and the mask is set to 0 or 1 accordingly. Setting the mask to 1 means read and write permission.

  • 180-187: The currently selected file or directory is found out, and its size is obtained with getLength method. The text is displayed on the text field.

  • 196-247: A stream is opened to read from the file Share.ini. It is divided up on the basis of "=" by using a StringTokenizer. The OK button is created, and an ActionListener is attached to it. The stream is closed when the while loop responsible for reading runs out.

  • 251-266: This checks whether files and directories are not present in Share.ini file. If they are not, they are added to Vector.

+ Lines 268-294: This if conditon is true if the user presses the Share It button. In this case, the values from the Vector are read and written in Share.ini.

+ Lines 296-302: This if condition is true if the user presses the Close button. It also disposes of the dialog box.

+ Lines 305-335: Objects and variables declaration.

MultiServer .java

This class handles the client requests such as show file, download file, Search files and directories, and upload (see Listing 4-4). To read the request and to respond to clients, this class has to parse and write an XML file. For parsing, it calls the Sparser class and for writing it calls the XMLWriter class. For searching requests, this class calls the check_directory class.

Listing 4-4: MultiServer.java

//© 2001 Dreamtech Software India Inc.
// All rights reserved

```
1.   import java.io.*;
2.   import java.net.*;
3.   import java.util.*;
4.
5.   /*  This Class is the listener class of the application. This class handles
the request from clients
6.     * the class extends Thread class because any new request runs in a new
thread .
7.   */
8.   class  OneServer extends Thread {
9.
10.     // Make object for client socket
11.     private Socket socket;
12.
13.     // Make object for tokenizer
14.         private StringTokenizer st_xml;
15.
16.     // Make object for parser
17.     static  SParser sp;
18.     private BufferedOutputStream data_write;
19.
20.     // Return files and directroy names.Return the file size and rights of
the files
21.     String[][] returnvalueoffiles;
22.
23.     // Vector Declared
24.     static Vector v_file_name;
25.     //This class is used to write xmldata
26.     private XmlWriter xmlwriter;
27.
28.     private check_directory check;
29.
30.     //Declaring BufferedInputStream
31.     private BufferedInputStream in;
32.
33.     // Declaring BufferedOutputStream
34.     private BufferedOutputStream out;
35.
36.     // This String will contain the FileName
37.     String left_half;
38.
39.     // Store right part of the file it means after "."
40.     String right_half;
41.
42.     // Store detail path name of file & directories in file object
```

```
43.     File path_file;
44.
45.     // Store files and directories names in string array
46.     String[] files;
47.
48.     /* when search any word if any character present in  left of file
extension then  in that
49.     * condition this flag becomes true */
50.     boolean left_half_flag = false;
51.
52.     /* when search any word if any character present in right of file
extension then  in that
53.     * condition this flag becomes true */
54.     boolean right_half_flag = false;
55.
56.     // file and directory stored in this variable
57.     String filename;
58.
59.     // file size stored in this variable
60.     String filesize;
61.
62.     // file rights stored in this variable
63.     String filemask;
64.
65.     String stemp="";
66.
67.     /* from this fuction listener takes request from client and according to
the
68.     *  request listener gives the response */
69.     public OneServer(Socket soc) throws IOException
70.         {
71.
72.     // store the socket value which is connected by user
73.                 socket = soc;
74.
75.     // take the request from the user in the form of BufferInputStream
76.     in = new BufferedInputStream (socket.getInputStream());
77.
78. // give the response to the user from listener in form of BufferOutputStream
79.     out = new BufferedOutputStream(socket.getOutputStream());
80.
81.     // start the new thread for new user
82.     start();
83.         }
84.
85.
86.     // when any new user connects then this function call by start()
87.     public void run()
88.         {
89.     try
90.         {
91.         int i = 0;
92.         String value;
93.         byte [] a = new byte[1024];
94.
```

```
95.            // open main.xml file as BufferedOutputStream for writing data into
it
96.        data_write = new BufferedOutputStream(
97.              (new FileOutputStream("main.xml")));
98.
99.        // read data from user DataInputstream
100.              in.read(a,0,1024);
101.
102.            // Store reading value in temp String
103.            String temp = new String(a);
104.
105.            // Break the temp till last ">" + 1 value
106.            temp = temp.substring(0,(temp.lastIndexOf(">")+1));
107.
108.            // convert temp string value in Byte
109.            byte d[] = temp.getBytes();
110.
111.            // write converted value in "main.xml" file
112.            data_write.write(d, 0, d.length);
113.
114.            // Close the date_write stream
115.            data_write.close();
116.
117.            // Make the object of XmlWriter class
118.            xmlwriter = new XmlWriter();
119.
120.            // Make the object of SParser class
121.            sp = new SParser();
122.
123.            // call the function of class SParser and pass the argument
as  string
124.            sp.perform("main.xml");
125.
126.            // This function returns the file names as vector
127.            v_file_name = sp.yakreturn();
128.
129.        // This for loop runs the size of the vector
130.        for(int t = 0; t < v_file_name.size(); t++)
131.              {
132.
133.
134. // vector value stored is showfiles type then enter in this condition
135.    if((v_file_name.get(t).toString()).equalsIgnoreCase("SHOWFILES"))
136.    {
137.                String s = "";
138.
139.    // open stream      of "Share.ini" file for reading
140.                BufferedReader data_read = new
141.                BufferedReader(new FileReader("Share.ini"));
142.
143.    // This while loop runs till stream "data_read" not become null
144.        while ((s = data_read.readLine()) != null)
145.              {
146.                String filename = "";
147.                String filesize = "";
148.                String mask = "";
```

```
149.
150.  // divide string "s" on the basis of "=" and store in st_xml
151.  st_xml = new StringTokenizer(s, "=");
152.
153.  // This while loop runs till that tokenizer present in st_xml
154.   while(st_xml.hasMoreTokens())
155.              {
156.
157.   // Here store first token in variable filename
158.   filename = st_xml.nextToken();
159.
160.  /* This filename string ends with "\" then enter in this part otherwise enter
161.   * in else part. if filename string ends with "\" it means that is directroy there
162.   * oterwise that is file */
163.         if( !filename.endsWith("\\") )
164.   {
165.
166.   // Here store second token in variable mask. it is rights of file
167.        mask = st_xml.nextToken();
168.
169.  // Here store third token in variable filesize. it is writes of file
170.    filesize = st_xml.nextToken();
171.
172.  /* Call the returnHeader function from XmlWriter class this fuction returns
173.   * the header of xml file as string and stores this value in stemp variable. */
174.  stemp = xmlwriter.returnHeader(v_file_name.get(t).toString());
175.
176.  /* Call the responseFString function from XmlWriter class this fuction
177.   * writes the xml file for files. */
178. xmlwriter.responseFString(v_file_name.get(t).toString(), filename, filesize, mask);
179.  }
180.  else
181.  {
182.
183.  // Here store second token in variable mask. it is rights of file
184.      mask = st_xml.nextToken();
185.
186.  /* Call the returnHeader function from XmlWriter class this fuction return
187.   * the header of xml file as string and store this value in stemp variable. */
188.    stemp = xmlwriter.returnHeader(v_file_name.get(t).toString());
189.
190.  /* Call the responseFString function from XmlWriter class this fuction
191.   * writes the xml file for Directroy. */
192.
xmlwriter.responseFString(v_file_name.get(t).toString(), filename, "", mask);
193.                              }
194.              }
195.
196.
197.  }
```

```
198.
199.   /* Call the returnResponse function this function returns whole xml except
header of xml as
200.   * string.Store this value in wholexmlwithoutheader veriable */
201.   String wholexmlwithoutheader = xmlwriter.returnResponse();
202.
203.   /* Add two string veriable and store in any third string variable. This
variable stores whole
204.   * xml file */
205.   wholexmlwithoutheader = stemp+wholexmlwithoutheader;
206.
207.   // Find the length of xml file and send 0 to length of file xml file
bytes to user
208.
out.write(wholexmlwithoutheader.getBytes(),0,wholexmlwithoutheader.length());
209.
210.    // Close the data_read stream which read from file.
211.   data_read.close();
212.
213.   // Close the out stream which connected to user.
214.    out.close();
215.    }
216.
217.   // In this condition we do all download work related to user request
218.   else if((v_file_name.get(t).toString()).equalsIgnoreCase("DOWNLOAD"))
219.       {
220.
221.   // Store the file name in variable f_name. This file downloaded by user
222.   String f_name = v_file_name.get(1).toString();
223.
224.   // initilize the variable of len
225.   int len = 0;
226.
227.   // Open the file stream of stored file name which is present in f_name.
228.   FileInputStream fstream = new FileInputStream(f_name);
229.
230.   // Make variable c_write as Byte array which is sent to user
231.    byte[] c_write = new byte[32];
232.
233.    // While loop run upto 32 Byte of all stored array value
234.    while ((len = fstream.read(c_write,0,32))>0)
235.    {
236.
237.    // Send the out stream to user every 32 Byte
238.    out.write(c_write, 0, len);
239.    }
240.
241.   // Close the out Stream
242.   out.close();
243.
244.    }
245.
246.   // In this condition we do all search work related to user request
247.    else if((v_file_name.get(t).toString()).equalsIgnoreCase("SEARCH"))
248.       {
249.
```

```
250.   /* Make the object of check_directory which search file and diretory
251.    * which is requested by the user */
252.    check = new check_directory();
253.
254.   // Store file & directory name with path in whole_String variable
255.    String whole_String = v_file_name.get(1).toString();
256.
257.    // Store file & directory path in full_path
258.  String  full_path = whole_String.substring(0,
(whole_String.lastIndexOf("\\") + 1));
259.
260.   // Store file & directory name without path in word variable
261.  String  word = whole_String.substring((whole_String.lastIndexOf("\\")  + 1
));
262.
263.   // Make file object of file which path present in full_path
264.   path_file = new File(full_path);
265.
266.
267.   // Find the position of "." in file
268.   int dot_index = word.indexOf('.');
269.
270.  /* When "." not present in file then return -1 then enter in this condition
otherwise enter
271.   * in else part */
272.  if (dot_index == -1)
273.  {
274.
275.   // whole word value store in left_half variable
276.   left_half = word;
277.
278.   // write_half variable value become blank(" ")
279.   right_half = " ";
280.
281.   // Find the position of "*" in left_half variable and store that variable
in asterix_index
282.   int asterix_index = left_half.indexOf("*");
283.
284.   // if left_half variable not content any "*" then its return -1 then not
enter in this condition
285.   if (asterix_index != -1)
286.   {
287.   /* Store value in left_half first position to "*" position when check the
left_half_flag
288.    * flag to true */
289.    left_half = left_half.substring(0,asterix_index);
290.    left_half_flag = true;
291.   }
292.  }
293.  else
294.  {
295.   // Store file name beginning to "." position left part
296.   left_half = word.substring(0,word.indexOf('.'));
297.
298.   // Store file name last to "." position of right part of that file
299.  right_half = word.substring(word.indexOf('.') + 1);
```

```
300.
301.   // left_half is equal to "*" or left_half is equal to "" then enter in
this condition
302.   if ((left_half.equals("*"))||(left_half.equals("")))
303.   {
304.     // left_half string value insilize by null(" ")
305.     left_half = " ";
306.   }
307.   else
308.   {
309.   // Find the position of "*" in left_half variable and store that variable
in asterix_index
310.     int asterix_index = left_half.indexOf("*");
311.
312.   // if left_half variable not content any "*" then its return -1 then not
enter in this condition
313.     if (asterix_index != -1)
314.     {
315.
316.     /* Store value in left_half first position to "*" position when check the
left_half_flag
317.      * flag to true */
318.     left_half = left_half.substring(0,asterix_index);
319.     left_half_flag = true;
320.     }
321.   }
322.   // right_half is equal to "*" or right_half is equal to "" then enter in
this condition
323.     if ((right_half.equals("*"))||(right_half.equals("")))
324.     {
325.       // right_half string value insilize by null(" ")
326.       right_half = " ";
327.     }
328.   else
329.   {
330.   // Find the position of "*" in right_half variable and store that variable
in asterix_index
331.     int asterix_index = right_half.indexOf("*");
332.
333.       // if right_half variable does not contain any "*" then do  not enter
in this condition
334.     if (asterix_index != -1)
335.     {
336.     /* Store value in right_half first position to "*" position when check the
right_half_flag
337.      * flag to true */
338.     right_half = right_half.substring(0,asterix_index);
339.     right_half_flag = true;
340.     }
341.
342.   }
343.   }
344.
345.   // Store files name which are present in this path_file in files array
346.     files = path_file.list();
347.
```

```
348.
349.   // make object of String array which contains files & directories name
filesize and mask
350.   returnvalueoffiles = new String[files.length + 1][3];
351.
352.   // Store all values in returnvalueoffiles array which return by wild_card
function
353.   returnvalueoffiles =
 check.wild_card(1left_half,right_half,left_half_flag,right_half_flag,
path_file);
354.
355.
356.   for(int y = 0; y < files.length + 1; y++)
357.   {
358.   /* data in this array returnvalueoffiles[y][0] not present in this then
break the
359.    *  loop otherwise go to else part  */
360.   if(returnvalueoffiles[y][0] == null)
361.   {
362.    break;
363.   }
364.   else
365.   {
366.
367.     // Store full path with file & directories name in filename
368.     filename = path_file + "\\" + returnvalueoffiles[y][0];
369.
370.
371.     // Store size of file
372.     filesize = returnvalueoffiles[y][1];
373.
374.
375.     // Store the rights of the files
376.     filemask = returnvalueoffiles[y][2];
377.
378.
379.     /* Call the returnHeader function from XmlWriter class this fuction
returns
380.      * the header of xml file as string and stores this value in stemp
variable. */
381.     stemp = xmlwriter.returnHeader("SHOWFILES");
382.
383.     /* Call the responseFString function from XmlWriter class this fuction
384.      * writes the xml file for Directroy. */
385.     xmlwriter.responseFString("SHOWFILES", filename, filesize, filemask);
386.   }
387.   }
388.
389.   String wholexmlwithoutheader = "";
390.
391.   /* data in this array returnvalueoffiles[0][0] not present in this then
enter
392.    * in this condition it means there is no file and diretory  otherwise
393.    * go to else part of this condition*/
394.     if(returnvalueoffiles[0][0] == null)
395.     {
```

```
396.    // Make one xml file without any files & directries list
397.    stemp = xmlwriter.returnHeader("SHOWFILES");
398.    wholexmlwithoutheader = "</response></p2p_lng>";
399.     }
400.    else
401.    {
402.    /* Call the returnResponse function this function returns whole xml
except header
403.     * of xml as string.Store this value in wholexmlwithoutheader variable */
404.    wholexmlwithoutheader = xmlwriter.returnResponse();
405.    }
406.
407.    /* Add two string variables and store in any third string variable. This
variable stores whole
408.     * xml file */
409.    wholexmlwithoutheader = stemp+wholexmlwithoutheader;
410.
411.    // Find the length of xml file and send 0 to length of file xml file
bytes to user
412.
out.write(wholexmlwithoutheader.getBytes(),0,wholexmlwithoutheader.length());
413.
414.    // Close the data_read stream which read from file.
415.    out.close();
416.
417.    }
418.
419.
420.    // vector value store is upload type then enter in this condition
421.    else if((v_file_name.get(t).toString()).equalsIgnoreCase("UPLOAD"))
422.    {
423.    // Store file & directory name with path in whole_String variable
424.     String upload_name = v_file_name.get(1).toString();
425.
426.
427.    // initilize the variable  len
428.    int len = 0;
429.
430.    // Make variable c_write as Byte array which is sent to user
431.    byte[] c_write = new byte[32];
432.
433.    // open stream    of upload_name file for writing
434.    data_write = new BufferedOutputStream(
435.    (new FileOutputStream(upload_name)));
436.
437.    // While loop run upto 32 Byte of all stored array value
438.    while ((len = in.read(c_write,0,32))>0)
439.    {
440.       // Send the out stream to user every 32 Byte
441.       data_write.write(c_write, 0, len);
442.    }
443.
444.                    // Close the date_write stream
445.                    data_write.close();
446.
447.             }
```

```
448.
449.         }
450.     }
451.     catch (IOException e)
452.     {
453.         System.out.println("Exception ocurred" + e);
454.     }
455.
456.     }
457.
458. }
459.
460.
461. public class MultiServer
462.     {
463.
464.         // Here initialize the PORT
465.         static final int PORT = 7070;
466.
467.     MultiServer()
468.         {
469.         }
470.
471.     void multiaccess() throws IOException
472.         {
473.
474.     /* Create an object of server socket on this port any client can connect
and they can send
475.     * its request */
476.                 ServerSocket s = new ServerSocket(PORT);
477.                 System.out.println("Server Started");
478.         try
479.         {
480.                 while (true)
481.                 {
482.
483.                     // Create  a new socket for every client
484.                     Socket soc = s.accept();
485.
486.                     try
487.                     {
488.
489.     // Call the OneServer class and pass the connected client socket
490.         new OneServer(soc);
491.                 }
492.                     catch (Exception e)
493.                     {
494.
495.                     // Close the created socket
496.                     soc.close();
497.                 }
498.                 }
499.         }
500.         catch (Exception e)
501.         {}
502.
```

```
503.    }
504.    }
505.
```

Code description

♦ Lines 1-3: Import statements for importing basic class files.

♦ Lines 11-65: Declares variables and objects.

♦ Lines 69: Constructor is defined for OneServer, an inner class of MultiServer.

♦ Lines 72-82: Objects are defined to store the socket value, receive requests, and respond to them. The start method is called.

♦ Line 87: The run method is defined.

♦ Lines 89-134: The main.xml is parsed. A byte stream is read from the client, and the data read is written in main.xml; then this XML file is parsed, which provides the request type.

♦ Lines 135-215: This if condition is executed if the request type is SHOWFILES. In this case, the Share.ini file is read, and the entries (File Name, File Size, Permissions) are sent to the client as XML data, which is writen by the XmlWriter class. The same strategy of using a while loop and StringTokenizer is applied to break up the string and to read it.

♦ Lines 218-244: This if condition is executed if the request type is DOWNLOAD. In this case, a stream is opened from the file to be downloaded, and the object of the stream is sent to the client.

♦ Lines 247-417: This if condition is executed if the request type is SEARCH. In this case, the search string is compared with the files or directory name in Share.ini file, and the entries found are sent as XML data to the client.

♦ Lines 421-428: This if condition is executed if the request type is UPLOAD. In this case, a stream is opened by the client for the file to be uploaded. Through this stream, data is read, and the file is created with the same file name; data is written to the file.

♦ Lines 461-504: The MultiServer class is defined. A port is provided at which the listener runs. Method multiaccess is defined, in which the inner class OneServer is called.

check_directory.java

This class is used for searching. The search string is passed to this class, and this class searches for the file and directory with the search string and returns a 2D array containing the file name, file size, and permission on files and the directory (see Listing 4-5).

Listing 4-5: check_directory.java

//© 2001 Dreamtech Software India Inc.
// All rights reserved

```
1.   import java.io.*;
2.
3.   /*
4.    * This class is only for searching purpose . namely
5.    * ., *., .*, *.*, ja*.*, java.*, java., *.ja*, *.java, ja*.ja* etc. In this
case it can
6.    * search file as well directory .
7.    */
8.
9.
10.  public class check_directory
11.  {
12.
```

```
13.     // To store the list of files
14.     String[] files;
15.
16.     // to store the fillter files only
17.     String[] fillterfiles;
18.
19.
20.     String[][] all_details;
21.
22.     // Number of files.
23.     int count = 0;
24.
25.     //int  sizeoffile = 0;
26.
27.
28.     public String[][] wild_card(String left_half,String right_half, boolean
left_half_flag, boolean right_half_flag, File path_file)
29.     {
30.                         // store all the files  in files variable
31.                         files = path_file.list();
32.
33.                         fillterfiles = new String[files.length + 1];
34.
35.     // If search criteria is *.*
36.     if ((left_half.equals(" "))&&(right_half.equals(" ")))
37.     {
38.
39.             // Total number of files..
40.         for (int i = 0;i<files.length ;i++ )
41.         {
42.
43.                 // Search result..
44.                 fillterfiles[count] = files[i];
45.
46.                 count++;
47.
48.         }
49.     }
50.
51.     // right side of file is "" and "*"
52.     else if (right_half.equals(" "))
53.     {
54.         String temp = "";
55.                                 // Total number of files..
56.         for (int i = 0;i<files.length ;i++ )
57.         {
58.                 // Find the position of "." in file
59.                 int index_dot = files[i].indexOf(".");
60.
61.                 if (index_dot != -1) // "." is not found..
62.                 {
63.                     // Store the substring till the index of dot is reached.
64.                         temp = files[i].substring(0,index_dot);
65.                 }
66.                 else
67.                     // Store the first[i] in temp veriable
```

```
68.                      temp = files[i];
69.
70.               // temp variable is equal to left_half and "*" not present in
left side of file
71.    if ((temp.length() ==
(left_half.length()))&&(temp.equalsIgnoreCase(left_half))&&(!left_half_flag))
72.                {
73.
74.                      // files satisfying the search criteria.
75.                      fillterfiles[count] = files[i];
76.
77.                      // increment the count value by 1
78.                      count++;
79.                }
80.                      // * is present in left half
81.               if ((left_half_flag)&& (temp.length() >= left_half.length()))
82.                {
83.
84.
85.    if (left_half.equalsIgnoreCase(temp.substring(0,left_half.length())))
86.                   {
87.
88.                      //     files satisfying the search criteria
89.                      fillterfiles[count] = files[i];
90.
91.                      // increment the count value by 1
92.                      count++;
93.                   }
94.                }
95.
96.         }
97.    }
98.
99.    // left side of file is "" and "*"
100.        else if (left_half.equals(" "))
101.        {
102.
103.               String temp = "";
104.
105.               // total number of files
106.               for (int i = 0;i<files.length ;i++ )
107.               {
108.                      // Find the position of "." in file
109.                      int index_dot = files[i].indexOf(".");
110.
111.                      if (index_dot != -1) // if dot is found..
112.                      {
113.    // Store value in temp "." position + 1 to last charecter
114.                         temp = files[i].substring(index_dot+1);
115.                      }
116.                      else
117.                        temp = " ";
118.
119.// temp variable is equal to right_half and "*" not present in left side of
file
```

```
120.  if ((temp.length() ==
(right_half.length()))&&(temp.equalsIgnoreCase(right_half))&&(!right_half_flag))
121.                       {
122.        // files satisfying the search criteria
123.        fillterfiles[count] = files[i];
124.
125.        // increment the count value by 1
126.        count++;
127.    }
128.
129.    /* "*" present in right side and temp (length) is greater than right_half
length */
130.    if ((right_half_flag)&& (temp.length() >= right_half.length()) )
131.    {
132.
133.    if (right_half.equalsIgnoreCase(temp.substring(0,right_half.length())))
134.    {
135.
136.    // files satisfying the search criteria
137.    fillterfiles[count] = files[i];
138.
139.  // increment the count value by 1
140.    count++;
141.    }
142.  }
143. } // End for loop....
144.
145.}        // Else if...
146.  else
147.  {
148.        /* some character and "*" present in left side and some character and
"*" present in right side */
149.    if ((right_half_flag)&&(left_half_flag))
150.  {
151.        // total number of files..
152.        for (int i = 0;i<files.length ;i++ )
153.        {
154. /*  if file files[i] length is grater and equal to left_half length
155.   * then enter in this condition */
156.    if (files[i].length() >= left_half.length())
157.        {
158.        if
(left_half.equalsIgnoreCase(files[i].substring(0,left_half.length())))
            {
159.
160.     // Find the position of "." in file
161.        int index = files[i].indexOf(".");
162.
163.        if (index != -1)
164.        {
165.     // Store value in temp "." position + 1 to last charecter
166.        String temp = files[i].substring(index+1);
167.
168.    /*  if file temp length is grater and equal to right_half length
169.     */
170.        if (temp.length()>=right_half.length())
```

```
171.                     {
172.
173.
174.    if (temp.substring(0,right_half.length()).equalsIgnoreCase(right_half))
175.      {
176.
177.
178.    // files satisfying the search criteria
179.      fillterfiles[count] = files[i];
180.
181.     // increment the count value by 1
182.      count++;
183.      }
184.
185.    }
186.    }
187.  }
188. }
189.}
190.}
191.
192.  /* only characters are  present in left side and some character and "*"
present in right side */
193.    else if ((right_half_flag)&&(!left_half_flag))
194.    {
195.
196.    // make complete filename out of the criteria.
197.    String filename = left_half+"."+right_half;
198.
199.    // total number of files..
200.    for (int i = 0;i<files.length ;i++ )
201.    {
202.                // if search criteria is less than the file length
203.       if (files[i].length() >= filename.length())
204.       {
205.       if
(filename.equalsIgnoreCase(files[i].substring(0,filename.length())))
206.        {
207.
208.
209.      // files satisfying the search criteria
210.      fillterfiles[count] = files[i];
211.
212.      // increment the count value by 1
213.      count++;
214.    }
215.   }
216.   }
217. }
218.
219.  /* only characters are present in right side and some character and "*"
present in left side */
220.  else if ((!right_half_flag)&&(left_half_flag))
221.    {
222.    // total number of files.
223.    for (int i = 0;i<files.length ;i++ )
```

```
224.            {
225.     /*  if length of files[i] is greater and equal to left_half length
226.      */
227.     if (files[i].length() >= left_half.length())
228.            {
229.      /* If left_half is equal to substring of files[i] first position to
length of left_half */
230.     if (left_half.equalsIgnoreCase(files[i].substring(0,left_half.length())))
231.     {
232.       // Find the position of "." in file
233.       int index = files[i].indexOf(".");
234.
235.
236.     if (index != -1)
237.         {
238.     // Store value in temp "." position + 1 to last charecter
239.      String temp = files[i].substring(index+1);
240.
241.     // right_half is equal to temp then enter in this condition
242.     if (temp.equalsIgnoreCase(right_half))
243.     {
244.
245.     //     files satisfying the search criteria
246.     fillterfiles[count] = files[i];
247.
248.                     // increment the count value by 1
249.             count++;
250.
251.         }
252.       }
253.                                     }
254.                             }
255.                         }
256.                     }
257.                 else
258.                     {
259.                         // Make complete filename to add strings
260.                         String filename = left_half+"."+right_half;
261.
262.                         // all files
263.     for (int i = 0;i<files.length ;i++ )
264.     {
265.     // filename is equal to files[i] then enter in this condition
266.     if (filename.equalsIgnoreCase(files[i]))
267.         {
268.
269.
270.     //    files satisfying the search criteria
271.         fillterfiles[count] = files[i];
272.
273.       // increment the count value by 1
274.         count++;
275.
276.         }
277.     }
278.     }
```

```
279.
280.   }
281.
282.
283.        long selectedfilesize = 0;
284.
285.
286.        String filesizereturn = "";
287.
288.
289.        String maskoffile= "" ;
290.
291.        all_details = new String[fillterfiles.length][3];
292.
293.        // run till the length of fillterfiles array..
294.        for(int i = 0; fillterfiles[i] != null; i++)
295.        {
296.                //Make the file object by appending path of files
297.                File finallist = new File(path_file + "\\" +
fillterfiles[i]);
298.
299.
300.                // if current file object is directory then
301.                if (finallist.isDirectory())
302.                {
303.                        // no filesize
304.                        filesizereturn = "";
305.
306.                        //mask = 0
307.                        maskoffile = "0";
308.
309.                        // in case of directroy add "\" in last
310.                        fillterfiles[i] = fillterfiles[i] + "\\" ;
311.
312.
313.                }
314.
315.                // if a file then
316.                else
317.                {
318.                        if (finallist.canRead())
319.                        {
320.                                // read mask
321.                                maskoffile = "0";
322.                        }
323.
324.                        else if(finallist.canWrite())
325.                        {
326.                                // write mask
327.                                maskoffile = "1";
328.                        }
329.
330.                // find the file size
331.                selectedfilesize = finallist.length();
332.
333.
```

```
334.              filesizereturn=      Long.toString(selectedfilesize);
335.              }
336.
337.   /// Store the information in array..
338.
339.              all_details[i][0]= fillterfiles[i];
340.              all_details[i][1]= filesizereturn;
341.              all_details[i][2]= maskoffile ;
342.          }
343.      // Return the array to the calling programme..
344.      return all_details;
345.   }
346.
347.  }
```

Code description

◆ Line 1: A single import statement that imports the java.io class.

◆ Lines 14-23: Arrays and variables are declared.

◆ Lines 28-345: This is the method wild_card definition. This method searches for files and directories based on the search string and stores the entries in a 2D array and returns that array. The array contains the full path of the file or directory, the file size, and permissions.

  • 36-49: This is an if block to show search results if the serach criterion is *.*.

  • 52-70: This shows results if the search criterion is that the right side of the file specified is "" and the left part is "*". The left side of a file is the file name and the right side is the extension of the file. Say, for example, if the file name is Help.doc the left side is "Help" and the right side is ".doc".

  • 71-79: The code for the case when "*" is not present in the left half.

  • 81-94: The code for the case when "*" is present in the left half.

  • 98-145: The code for the case when the left side of the file is "" and the right side is "*".

  • 149-190: The code for the case when some characters and "*" are present on both the right and the left side.

  • 192-217: The code for the case when only characters are present on the left side and characters as well as "*" are present on the right side.

  • 220-256: The code for the case when only characters are present on the right side and characters as well as "*" are present on the left side.

  • 257-280: Complete filenames are formed, and files satisfying the preceding seach criteria are stored in an array.

  • 294-347: The second dimension of the array is used to store information about the files found during a search.

Browser/Client Source Code: SParser.java

The input to the SParser class is the name of the XML file passed as a string, and the output of the class is a Vector object containing all the information from a parsed XML file. This class acts as a wrapper class to the XML parser (it calls the XML parser and stores the results generated by the parser in a Vector). Listing 4-6 contains the source code for SParser.java.

Listing 4-6: SParser.java

```
1.   import java.awt.*;
2.   import java.io.*;
3.   import java.util.*;
4.   import org.xml.sax.*;
5.   import org.apache.xerces.parsers.SAXParser;
6.
7.   /* This is the wrapper class of the XML parser class as it calls the Xml
parser and in turn
8.      when the xml parser, parses the xml file it generates the call backs on
the class
9.      MyContentHandler... the various parsed documents can be used by using the
various functions in this class.
10.
11.     This class returns a vector to the class which calls this class
SParser.java the vector
12.      consists of the data provided by the XML document.
13.
14.  */
15.
16.  public class SParser
17.  {
18. Vector values = new Vector();
// Initialzing a object(values) of the class vector...
19.  // It is this object which is returned to the class
20.  // called...
21. public Vector perform(String uri)
// Function used for calling the parser
22.      {   // it has a parameter called "uri" which has the
23.         // information of the file to be parsed...
24.
25.     try
26.     {
27. XMLReader parser = new SAXParser();
     // Generate an object of the
28. // XMLParser class...
29.
30.// Generate an Object of the MyContentHandler Class it is in this class that
31.// the xml parser generates the call backs...

32.
33.  MyContentHandler contHandler = new MyContentHandler();
34.
35.    parser.setContentHandler(contHandler);
36. parser.parse(uri);     // call the parse function of the XMLParser class with
the
37.                                          // file information as the
parameter...
38.
39.        values = contHandler.values_attributes();
40.
41.      }
42.     catch(IOException e)
```

```
43.    {
44.         System.out.println("Error reading uri : " +e.getMessage());
45.    }
46.    catch(SAXException e)
47.    {
48.         System.out.println("Error in parsing : " +e.getMessage());
49.    }
50.
51.        return values; // Return the vector generated after xmlparsing is
complete..
52.
53.    }
54.
55.
56.  }
57.
58.  class MyContentHandler implements ContentHandler
59.  {
60.   private Locator locator;
61.
62.      Vector values = new Vector();
63.    int j = 0;
64.
65.    public Vector values_attributes()
66.    {
67.      return (values);
68.    }
69.    public void startElement(String namespaceURI, String localName, String
rawName, Attributes atts) throws SAXException  // Only this function is used by
us for our
70.    // purpose....
71.    {
72.    for(int i= 0; i<atts.getLength(); i++)
73.    {
74.     values.add(j,(Object)atts.getValue(i)) ;
75.     j++;
76.    }
77.    }
78.    public void  characters( char[] ch, int start , int end )
79.    {}
80.    public void  startDocument() {}
81.    public void  endDocument() {}
82.    public void endElement(String nameSpaceURI, String localName, String
rawName) {}
83.    public void startPrefixMapping(String prefix, String uri) {}
84.    public void endPrefixMapping(String prefix) {}
85.    public void ignorableWhitespace(char[] ch, int start, int end) {}
86.    public void processingInstruction(String target, String data) {}
87.    public void setDocumentLocator(Locator locator) {}
88.    public void skippedEntity(String name) {}
89.
90.  }
```

Code description

♦ Lines 1-3: This portion includes the basic packages used by the various classes to build this application. The packages include `java.io` (file streams), `java.util` (various utilities), and so on.

♦ Lines 4-5: This part lists the basic packages used by the various classes of the XML parser. These packages are `org.xml.sax.*` and `org.apache.xerces.parsers.SAXParser`.

♦ Lines 16-18: This code declares a public class (`SParser`) that represents the base class for this file and declares the user-defined variables, which are used for various purposes during the course of the program. These include Vector-type variables into which the result of the parsed XML file is stored.

♦ Lines 21-53: The code here defines a function of the name perform. This function is used for calling the parser. It take a parameter called `uri`, which has the information of the file to be parsed.

  • 27: This generates an object of the `XMLParser` class.

  • 33-35: This generates an object of the `MyContentHandler` class. In this class, the XML parser generates the callbacks. The method `setContentHandler` is called, with object of `MyContentHandler class` as parameter. This assigns the handler to the parser.

  • 36: This calls the `parse` function of the `XMLParser` class with the file information as the parameter.

  • 39: The content handler's attributes are stored in the variable called `value`.

  • 42-49: Exception Handling code.The code makes sure the appropriate message is shown, depending on whether the error is in parsing or reading.

  • 51: Once XML parsing is complete, the `Vector` object generated is returned.

♦ Lines 58-90: The code here pertains to the declaration of a `MyContentHandler` class. In this class, the callback from the XML parsing is handled and stored in appropriate data structures. For our requirements, we use a `startElement` function (69-77) and store the values in the `Vector` object, which is returned to the calling class in the end.

  • 62: A new `Vector` object is instantiated.

  • 65-68: This defines the method `values_attributes`, which returns the Vector values.

  • 69: A method `startElement` is defined. It takes the parameters `namespaceURI`, `localname`, `rawName` and `atts` (attributes).

  • 72-76: Values of attributes are obtained by calling the `getValue` method and are added to the `Vector` object after casting them as object. A `for` loop runs till the count becomes equal to the length of `atts` parameter.

  • 78-88: This is the implementation of the methods of the `ContentHandler` interface.

XMLWriter.java

The `XMLWriter` class is common to both the client and the listener, as it is used to send requests and responses to the listener and the client, respectively (see Listing 4-7). It has four important functions to perform. Two are used to send requests, and two are used to send responses.

Two functions are used for sending requests:

♦ `requestFString()`

♦ `returnRequest()`

Two functions are used for sending responses:

- responseFString()
- returnResponse()

Listing 4-7: XMLWriter.java

//© 2001 Dreamtech Software India Inc.
// All rights reserved

```
1.   //class for xml writer(returns a String for generating an XML File)
2.
3.   import java.awt.*;
4.   import java.io.*;
5.   import java.util.*;
6.   import java.lang.*;
7.
8.
9.   public class XmlWriter
10.  {
11.    int flag = 1 ;
12.    StringBuffer sbuf  = new StringBuffer();
13.
14.   String name1 =  "", fame =  "", type = "", size = "", mask = "" ;
15.
16.   void requestFString(String filetype, String filename)
17.   {
18.    sbuf = sbuf.delete(0, sbuf.capacity());
19.    //String ch = filetype;
20.    sbuf.append("<?xml version=\"1.0\" encoding=\"utf-8\"?>");
21.    sbuf.append("<p2p_lng>");
22.    sbuf.append("<request type=\"" +filetype+ "\">");
23.
24.    if (filetype.equals("SEARCH") || filetype.equals("DOWNLOAD") ||
filetype.equals("UPLOAD") )
25.    {
26.        sbuf.append("<scope type=\"" +filename+"\" mask=''>");
27.        sbuf.append("</scope>");
28.    }
29.  }
30.
31.   void  responseFString(String filetype, String filename, String filesize,
String mask)
32.   {
33.       //System.out.println(" Last : " + filetype ) ;
34.    //String ch = filetype;
35.    //if (flag == 1)
36.    //{
37.    //   flag = 0;
38.    //}
39.
40.    if (filetype.equals("SHOWFILES") || filetype.equals("SEARCH") )
41.       {
42.        if (filesize.trim().length() == 0)
43.        {
44.            sbuf = sbuf.append("<fileinfo filename=\"" +filename+"\"
mask=\"" +mask+"\"/>");
```

```
45.          }
46.      else
47.      {
48.          sbuf = sbuf.append("<fileinfo filename=\"" +filename+"\" mask=\""
+mask+"\" filesize=\"" +filesize+ "\"/>");
49.          //System.out.println(" Last : " + sbuf.toString()) ;
50.      }
51.  }
52.  if (filetype.equals("ERROR") )
53.  {
54.      //sbuf.append("<errorinfo errcode=\"" +extended error code+"\"
severity=\"" +message+"\" description=\"" +description of possible error+
"\">");
55.  }
56.
57.  }
58.
59.  public String returnHeader(String filetype) throws IOException
60.  {
61.      StringBuffer sb = new StringBuffer();
62.      sb.append("<?xml version=\"1.0\" encoding=\"utf-8\"?>");
63.      sb.append("<p2p_lng>");
64.      sb.append("<response type=\"" +filetype+ "\">");
65.
66.      String temp_s = sb.toString();
67.          sb = sb.delete(0,sb.capacity());
68.      return(temp_s);
69.  }
70.
71.  public  String returnResponse() throws IOException
72.  {
73.    String tt;
74.    sbuf.append("</response>");
75.    sbuf.append("</p2p_lng>");
76.    tt = sbuf.toString();
77.    //System.out.println(sbuf.toString()) ;   // last response Statement to
print
78.    sbuf = sbuf.delete(0, sbuf.capacity());
79.    return tt;
80.
81.  }
82.
83.  public  String returnRequest() throws IOException
84.  {
85.    String tt;
86.    sbuf.append("</request>");
87.    sbuf.append("</p2p_lng>");
88.    tt = sbuf.toString();
89.    //System.out.println(sbuf.toString()) ;   // last request Statement to
print
90.    sbuf = sbuf.delete(0, sbuf.capacity());
91.    return tt;
92.
93.  }
94. }
```

Code description

♦ Lines 3-6: This includes the basic packages used by various classes included to build this application. The packages include `java.io` (file streams), `java.util` (various utilities), `java.lang` (string), and so on.

♦ Lines 11-14: This declares the user-defined variables, which are used for various purposes during the course of the program. These include String types (`name`, `fame`, `type`, `size`, `mask`, `int flag`, `stringbuffer sbuf`, and so on).

♦ Lines 16-29: This includes the code for generating the XML request sent by the client to the listener (`requestFString`); the client passes parameters according to the request to be generated: Search, Download, Upload, Showfiles, and so on.

  • 18: Delete the String buffer initially.

  • 20-21: Append to the String buffer the initial tags common to all the requests, such as XML tags, `p2p_lng` tags, and so on.

  • 22: Append the request type according to the parameter passed.

  • 24-28: Whether or not the filetype equals SEARCH, DOWNLOAD or UPLOAD, the scope type is appended accordingly.

♦ Lines 31-57: This includes the code for generating the XML response sent by the listener to the client (`responseFString`). The listener passes the parameters according to the response to be generated. For example: Search, Download, Upload, Showfiles, and so on.

  • 40-45: If the response to be generated is of the type showfiles or Search and the file size is zero, (that is, it is a folder), append `fileinfo tag` in the string buffer, with a filename mask written to it. This information is passed as parameter to the `responseFString` function.

  • 46-50: Otherwise, append the string buffer with a `fileinfo` tag with a filename, mask, and file size written to it.

  • 52-57: This shows an error message if the filetype is ERROR.

♦ Lines 59-69: This includes the code for generating the XML response sent by the listener to the client (`returnHeader`). This code returns the header information of the XML file to be generated.

♦ Lines 71-81: This includes the code for generating the XML response sent by the listener to the client (`returnResponse`). This code returns the end tag information of the XML file to be generated.

♦ Therefore, a complete XML response is generated by combining three functions: `returnHeader` (59-69), `responseFString` (31-57), and `returnResponse` (59-69).

♦ Lines 83-93: This includes the code for generating the XML request sent by the client to the listener (`returnRequest`). This code returns the end tag information of the XML file to be generated.

Therefore, a complete XML request is generated by combining two functions: `requestFString` (16-29) and `returnRequest` (83-93).

client.java

This is the main class of the client. It requests the server for the list (userlist) of all the listeners connected at a particular time (see Listing 4-8). After receiving the response from the server, the `client.java` class displays the list of listeners connected to the user (see Figure 4-3) and provides the user with certain options:

♦ To connect to a particular listener

♦ To refresh the list so as to see whether any other entry is added to the list or not

♦ To search for files on all the listeners' (server-level search) machines or to search by specifying search criteria

♦ To view the files (which are searched during the search option)

♦ To exit the client application

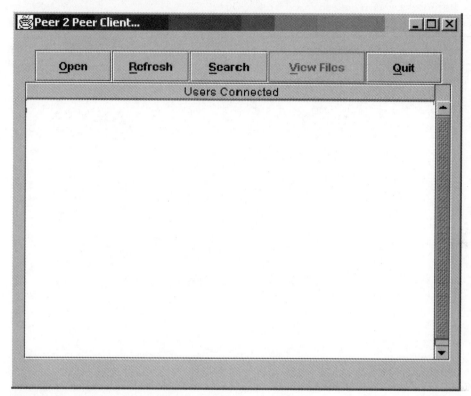

Figure 4-3: Starting screen of the peer-to-peer client

Listing 4-8: client.java

//© 2001 Dreamtech Software India Inc.
// All rights reserved

```
1.   import javax.swing.*;
2.   import javax.swing.event.*;
3.   import java.awt.event.*;
4.   import java.awt.*;
5.   import java.net.*;
6.   import java.io.*;
7.   import javax.swing.table.*;
8.   import java.util.*;
9.
10.  /* This is the main Class: it caters to the GUI and the starting the Peer 2
Peer Client */
11.
12.  public class client extends JFrame implements ActionListener
13.  {
14.   private JButton client_open;                    //
15.   private JButton client_refresh;                 //
```

```
16.    private JButton client_search;                    //
17.    private JButton client_quit;                       //   GUI Components for
various purposes..
18.    private JButton client_view_files;      //
19.    private JTable client_listing;                     //
20.    private JScrollPane client_scroller;      //
21.    int count = 0;
22.    Container contentpane;                                    //   For  placing
the GUI Componemnts
23.
24.    TableModel default_table;                          //
25.    String names[] = {"Users Connected"};      //      For JTable GUI Component
26.    Object data[][] ={{null},{null},{null},{null},{null},{null},

{null},{null},{null},{null},{null},{null},{null},{null},{null},{null},{nu
ll}};
27.
28.    private URLConnection urlconnection;      //
29.    private InputStream url_inputstream;      // For Connecting and gaining the
information..
30.    private Socket client_socket;
31.
32.    boolean go_on = true;
33.    boolean check = true;
34.
35.    Vector values = new Vector();
36.
37.
38.    String information[][];
39.    int g;
40.    add_on connection;
41.
42.    /* The constructor for the Main Class Takes Four Arguments.....*/
43.
44.    //    param ... For the state in which this class is called (Search / Other
).
45.    //    us ... Will come into use when param is in Search Mode..
46.    //    fs ... Will come into use when param is in Search Mode..
47.    //    present_users ... Will come into use when param is in Search Mode..
48.
49.    client(String param, String us, String fs, String present_users[][])
50.    {
51.
52.
53.          setTitle ("Peer 2 Peer Client...");
54.
55.      contentpane = getContentPane();
56.      contentpane.setLayout(null);                      // Setting the Layout to Absolute
Layout..
57.
58.
59.      client_open = new JButton("Open");      // Initializing the GUI
Component.
60.      client_open.setMnemonic('O');                      // Setting the Mnemonic..
61.      client_open.setBounds(20,20,80,35);      // Positioning the GUI Component.
62.
```

```
63.     client_refresh = new JButton("Refresh"); // Initializing the GUI
Component.
64.     client_refresh.setMnemonic('R');            // Setting the Mnemonic..

65.     client_refresh.setBounds(100,20,80,35); // Positioning the GUI Component.
66.
67.     client_search = new JButton("Search");   // Initializing the GUI
Component.
68.     client_search.setMnemonic('S');                    // Setting the Mnemonic..
69.     client_search.setBounds(180,20,80,35);   // Positioning the GUI Component.
70.
71.     client_view_files = new JButton("View Files"); // Initializing the GUI
Component.
72.     client_view_files.setMnemonic('V');                      // Setting the
Mnemonic..
73.     client_view_files.setBounds(260,20,100,35);        // Positioning the GUI
Component.
74.     client_view_files.setEnabled(false);
75.
76.     client_quit = new JButton("Quit");        // Initializing the GUI
Component.
77.     client_quit.setMnemonic('Q');                  // Setting the Mnemonic..
78.     client_quit.setBounds(360,20,80,35);// Positioning the GUI Component.


79.
80.     //   Initializing the Table
81.
82.     default_table = new AbstractTableModel()
83.     {
84.         // These methods always need to be implemented.
85.         public int getColumnCount() { return names.length; }
86.      public int getRowCount() { return data.length;}
87.         public Object getValueAt(int row, int col) {return data[row][col];}
88.
89.      // The default implementations of these methods in
90.         // AbstractTableModel would work, but we can refine them.
91.         public String getColumnName(int column) {return names[column];}
92.         public Class getColumnClass(int col) {return
getValueAt(0,col).getClass();}
93.         public boolean isCellEditable(int row, int col) {return (col==4);}
94.         public void setValueAt(Object aValue, int row, int column) {
95.             data[row][column] = aValue;
96.             fireTableCellUpdated(row, column);
97.         }
98.       };
99.
100.       // Positioning and Initializing the GUI Component (Table)...
101.
102.       client_listing = new JTable(default_table);
103.       client_listing.setSelectionMode(ListSelectionModel.SINGLE_SELECTION);
104.       client_listing.getTableHeader().setReorderingAllowed(false);
105.        client_listing.setBounds(10,55,440,300);
106.       client_listing.setGridColor(new Color(255,255,255));
107.       client_listing.setBackground(new Color(255,255,255));
108.
```

```
109.      // Adding Scroll Facility to the JTable by adding JScrollpane
Component
110.
111.
112.        client_scroller = new JScrollPane();
113.        client_scroller.setBounds(10,55,440,300);
114.        client_scroller.setViewportView(client_listing);// Adding the
Table...
115.
116.        contentpane.add(client_scroller);   // Placeing the scroller on to
the gui window..
117.
118.      // The Rest of the GUI conponents will be placed on the window as and
when needed.
119.
120.        information = present_users;  // A String array(2 D) is initialized
with the
121.                                               // present_users
for reference..
122.
123.      // The Class add_on is a muli utility class which has fuctions
defined in it which
124.      // are used by many other classes in this peer 2 peer client
project...
125.
126.       connection = new add_on();//Object Connection of class add_on is
created..
127.
128.      // A function start_connection of the class add_on is called... which
performs
129.      // 2 tasks on the basis of parameters passed on to it...
130.
131.      //      param ... For the state in which this class is called (Search
/ Other ).
132.      //      us ... Will come into use when param is in Search Mode..
133.      //      fs ... Will come into use when param is in Search Mode..
134.      //      present_users ... Will come into use when param is in Search
Mode..
135.
136.   information = connection.start_connection(param,us,fs,present_users);
137.
138.// The function returns a String 2 D Array which has the users list along
with the
139.  // shared files (if the param was Search) and the ip address of the user..
140.
141.  // Another function of this class is called which is responsible for
placing the ]
142.  // information provided by the above function on to the Table...
143.
144.        place_info_table(information);
145.
146. // Now according to the parameters passed in the class the various GUI
components
147.  // are enabled or disabled....
148.
149.        if (param.equalsIgnoreCase("search"))
```

```
150.              {
151.                  client_view_files.setEnabled(true);      // View Files Button is
Enabled...
152.              }
153.
154.          // Adding the window  Listener to the gui window
155.          // ie. Code for the "cross"...
156.          addWindowListener (new java.awt.event.WindowAdapter () {
157.              public void windowClosing (java.awt.event.WindowEvent evt) {
158.              System.exit(0);
159.              }
160.              }
161.              );
162.
163.          contentpane.add(client_open);              //
164.          contentpane.add(client_refresh);     //
165.          contentpane.add(client_search);            //       Adding the GUI
Buttons.....
166.          contentpane.add(client_view_files); //
167.          contentpane.add(client_quit);              //
168.
169.      }           // End of the constructor.......(client)...
170.
171.// The part Below pertains to the Action Performed when a Button is
pressed...
172.
173.      public void actionPerformed(ActionEvent ae)
174.      {
175.      if (ae.getSource() == client_open)       // When open Button is pressed...
176.      {
177.          int row = 0;                                   // Temporary
variable to get the index...
178.          check = true;
179.          row = client_listing.getSelectedRow();   // To get the index of the
row which
180.
  // is selected by the user...
181.          try
182.          {
183.              if(information[row][1] != null) // If the user index is not
null...
184.                  {
185.                  try
186.                  {
187.                      InetAddress inet =
InetAddress.getByName(information[row][1]);
188.                      client_socket = new Socket(inet,7070);      // Create a
client_socket on the
189.
  // Listener's machine at port 7070.
190.
191.  // Get The output as well as the input Streams on that socket...
192.BufferedOutputStream out = new
BufferedOutputStream(client_socket.getOutputStream());
193.
```

```
194.BufferedInputStream br_socket = new
BufferedInputStream(client_socket.getInputStream());
195.
196.    // Now a request is sent to the Listener to show all the shareable files
197.    // of the particular user which was selected by the user..
198.
199.    // To send a request a class of the name xmlwriter is used which has two
200.    // functions of interest they are... requestFString(String, String) and
201.    // returnRequest(), this xmlwriter is a versatile class as it is used to
202.    // generate xml requests for various purposes... SEARCH,UPLOAD, DOWNLOAD
203.    // and SHOWFILES... therefore accordingly the requestFString takes two
204.    // parameters in case of SHOWFILES the second parameters is not used.
205.
206.  XmlWriter writer = new XmlWriter();        // Initializing a object of
xmlwriter..
207.  writer.requestFString("SHOWFILES"," "); //calling the function...
208. String file_data = writer.returnRequest(); // getting the request in a
209.// temp variable file_data.
210.
211.  byte file_bytes[] = file_data.getBytes();// getting byte array of string
212.
213.  int file_size = file_bytes.length; // Getting the length of byte array
214.
215. byte b[] = new byte[1024];   // Initializing a new byte array of 1024.
216.
217.  // another method of the class add_on is used now (apporpriatelength) this
218. // is  used so as to make the request sent by the client to the listener
219. // 1024 in length..(for c#) listener's...
220.
221. // The methos takes a byte array and its length as parameters and return
222.  // a byte array of length 1024 bytes....
223.
224.   add_on upload = new add_on();
225.  b = upload.appropriatelength(file_bytes, file_size);
226.
227. out.write(b,0,1024); // The byte array is written on the output stream
228.
229.
230.// An output stream is also initialized this is used to store all the
response
231.  // from the listener..
232.
233.  BufferedOutputStream out_file = new BufferedOutputStream(new
FileOutputStream("response.xml"));
234.
235.  int y = 0;                              // Temporary variables....
236.   byte f[] = new byte[32];  // Temporary variables...
237.
238. while ((y = br_socket.read(f,0,32))>0)      // the socket input stream is
read
239.  {
240.  out_file.write(f,0,y);                  // written on to the file output
stream...
241.   }
242.
243.   out.close();                               //
```

```
244. //br_file.close();//    The filestream and socket streams are
245.    br_socket.close();                        //      closed...
246.    out_file.close();                         //
247.
248. }                                            // End try..
249.    catch(Exception e)
250.    {
251.    client_socket = null;
252.  check = false;                              // Check is made false...
253.    }
254.
255.    try

256.    {
257.     client_socket.close();                   // Close the Client_socket...
258.     }
259.     catch (Exception e)
260.     {
261.    row = 0;
262.    }
263.
264.    if (check)         // If the exception occurs then do not come here....
else
265.    {
266.  Vector parameters = new Vector();   // Temp Vector Declaration..
267.
268.  // A class SParser is also used here this class has a function/method of
269.  // the name perform which calls the xml parser to parse the xml file
270.  // generated by the response from the client soket...
271.
272.  // the function perform returns a Vector which has the files/directories,
273.  // along with their flag information and size in case of files....
274.
275.                      SParser sp = new SParser();
276.                      parameters = sp.perform("response.xml");
277.
278.  // The vector value returned by the xml parser is then passed as one of
279.  // the parameters to a class named file_gui this class is responsible for
280.  // displaying GUI consisting of a table and some buttons along with the
281.  // root information and flag..
282.
283.  // Initially since the class is called for the first time the parameter
284.  // for the root is given the name "ROOT" and the Flag is set to "0"..
285.
286.file_gui showfiles = new
file_gui(parameters,information[row][1],"Root","0");
287.        showfiles.show();
288.                  check = false;
289.            }              // End if ...
290.          }              // End If......
291.      }              // End Try.......
292.      catch(Exception e)
293.      {
294.        row = 0;
295.      }
296.    }                // End if of ae.getSource()...
```

```
297.
298.    else if (ae.getSource() == client_refresh)
299.    {
300.      this.setVisible(false);          //hide the present window.....
301.      String present_users[][] = {{" "," "},{" ", " "}};  // make the user
list empty
302.
303.      // Call the main class a  new ....
304.      client client = new client("start", " ", " ",present_users);
305.        client.setSize(465,410);
306.      client.show();
307.
308.    }                    // End if of ae.getSource()...
309.
310.    else if (ae.getSource() == client_quit)
311.    {
312.    System.exit(0);            // Close the connection and exit to system...
313.    }                  // End if of ae.getSource()...
314.
315.    else if (ae.getSource() == client_search)
316.    {
317. // If search button is pressed a new class called search_window is called
which
318. // is reponsible for client searching it caters to the gui of the
search_window
319.   // as well....
320.        search_window search_users = new search_window(this, information);
321.            search_users.show();
322.
323.    }            // End if of ae.getSource()...
324.
325.    else if (ae.getSource() == client_view_files)
326.    {
327.  // This button activates only after the client_search button is used for
328.  // searching the listener or a particular file name on all the possible
329.  // users...
330.
331. // When this button is activated the user will see all the names of the
users
332. // connected at that instant along with the number of files (satisfying a
333.// particular search criteria) enclosed in bracket to see those files the
user
334.// presses the viewfiles button after selecting a particular user and the
335. // list of the files is displayed to the user.The user is however not able
to
336. // download the files from that location...
337.  int row = 0;
338.
339.  row = client_listing.getSelectedRow();
340. // for this another function of the add_on class is used returnfilenames
which
341. // returns the filenames vector along with the name of the user..
342.            add_on search_result = new add_on();
343.            Vector filenames = search_result.returnfilenames();
344.            Vector results = new Vector();
345.            results.add(0,(Object)"files");
```

```
346.
347. // Out of this vector another vector is generated which consists of  files
348. // or folders pertaining to a paricular user who was highlighted when the
349.  // viewfiles is pressed... the delimiters used are "?".
350.
351.
352.              for (int i = 1;i<filenames.size() ;i++ )
353.              {
354.                  String temp = (String)filenames.get(i);
355.                  String name = " ";
356.                  name = temp.substring(0,temp.indexOf("?"));
357.                  name = name.substring(0,information[row][1].length());
358.                  if (name.equals(information[row][1]))
359.                  {
360.                      temp = temp.substring(temp.indexOf("?")+1);
361.                      StringTokenizer st = new StringTokenizer(temp,
"?");
362.                      while (st.hasMoreTokens())
363.                      {
364.                          results.add((Object)st.nextToken());
365.                      }
366.                      temp = "";
367.                  }
368.
369.              }
370.// when the vector is generated (results) it is passed on to the the
file_gui
371. // class which is responsible for displaying the files..., the root
parameter
372. // is given the value as search result and the flag information as "0"...
373. file_gui showfiles = new file_gui(results,information[row][1],"Search
Results","0");
374.              showfiles.show();
375.
376.    }             // End if of ae.getSource()...
377.
378.    }             // End Action Listener......
379.
380.    // The function below places the information on to the gui and enables
appropriate
381.    // buttons in between...
382.
383.    public void place_info_table(String information[][])
384.    {
385.        if (!(information.length > 1))              // If no information[][]
array is generated..
386.        {
387.            JOptionPane.showMessageDialog(this,"Sorry There is no server at
present to satisfy ur request. ","Peer 2 Peer
Client",JOptionPane.ERROR_MESSAGE);
388.            client_open.setEnabled(false);
389.            client_refresh.setEnabled(false);// all buttons except quit
are disabled.
390.            client_search.setEnabled(false);
391.            client_view_files.setEnabled(false);
392.            client_quit.setEnabled(true);
```

```
393.
394.          }
395.      else
396.      {
397.              client_open.setEnabled(true);
398.              client_refresh.setEnabled(true);
399.              client_search.setEnabled(true);
400.  client_view_files.setEnabled(false);        // else all the buttons except
view
401.  client_quit.setEnabled(true);                    // files are enabled...
402.
403.          }
404.      int j = 0;
405.
406.      for (int i = 0;i<information.length ;i++ )        // Loops through
information and
407.          {
    // put the value on to the table..
408.              client_listing.setValueAt(information[i][0],j,0);
409.              j++;
410.              client_quit.setEnabled(true);
411.              client_refresh.setEnabled(true);
412.          }
413.
414.      client_open.addActionListener(this);
415.      client_refresh.addActionListener(this);                    // Add
action listener to all the
416.      client_search.addActionListener(this);                    //
Buttons...
417.      client_view_files.addActionListener(this);
418.      client_quit.addActionListener(this);
419.
420.  }      // End... place_info_table()...
421.
422.
423.
424.   public static void main(String[] args)  // this is the main class
425.   {
426.          String present_users[][] = {{" " ," "},{" ", " "}};
427.          // Since client is called for the first time therefore the present
users
428.          // array is left empty...
429.          client client = new client("start", " ", " ",present_users);
430.            client.setSize(465,410);
431.          client.show();
432.   }
433.
434.  }      // End class client....
435.
```

Code description

♦ Lines 1-8: This code is for including the basic packages used by various classes to build this application. The packages include java.net (sockets), java.io (file streams), javax.swing (frames), javax.swing.event (event handling), and so on.

♦ Lines 12-27: This declares a public class (`Client`) that represents the base class for this file. All the variables defined here represent their respective controls pasted on the frame. These variables include `client_open`, `client_refresh`, `client_search`, `client_viewfiles`, and `client_quit` that are of the type `JButton`, `client_listing` that is of the type `Jtable`, and so on.

♦ Lines 28-48: This declares the user-defined variables used for various purposes during the course of the program; these are variables for `URLConnection`, `InputStream`, and variables of the type `boolean` for various checks during the program.

♦ Lines 49-125: The code between these lines pertains to initializing the GUI components (that is, the buttons, the table, and the scrollbar positioning). These GUI components on the frame are supplied with their mnemonics for faster access through the keyboard, and so on.

♦ Lines 126-136: Object connection of class `add_on` is created, and a method of the class `start_connection` is called, which returns a list of all the listeners connected at a particular time.

♦ Lines 144: The information, returned by the method, is then passed on to the function `place_information`, which is responsible for displaying the information in the Table for the user to understand easily.

♦ Lines 163-169: The code here pertains to adding the various GUI components to the frame.

♦ Lines 173-378: This includes the code for actions performed on various buttons.

♦ Lines 175-296: This includes the code executed when the client selects a particular listener from the list and presses the Open button (`client_open`).

  • 179: The row selected by the client is identified and based on the row from which the IP address of the listener is obtained .

  • 187-188: Create a `client_socket` on the listener's machine on the port 7070.

  • 192-195: Get the output as well as the input streams on that socket.

  • 206-208: Now a request is sent to the listener to show all the shareable files.

  • 224-225: A method of the class `add_on` is used now (`apporpriatelength`). This is used to make the request sent by the client to the listener 1024 bytes in length (for C# listeners).

  • 227: The byte array is written to the output stream.

  • 233: An output stream is also initialized. This is used to store all the responses from the listener.

  • 238-241: The socket-input stream is read and written to the file-output stream.

  • 243-263: This closes the file streams as well as the sockets and handles the exceptions through the try... catch blocks.

  • 266-276: A Temporary Vector (parameters) is declared. The `SParser` class is also used here. This class has a function/method of the name perform, which calls the XML parser to parse the XML file generated by the response from the client socket. The function returns a Vector, which is stored in the Temp Vector.

  • 286-287: The Vector value returned by the XML parser is then passed as one of the parameters to a class named `file_gui`. This class is responsible for displaying GUI consisting of a table and some buttons, along with the root information and flag.

♦ 298-308: This includes the code executed when the client presses the Refresh button, in which case the current frame is made to disappear and a new request is sent to the server for the list of all the available listeners.

♦ 310-313: This includes the code executed when the client presses the Quit button to quit the application.

- ◆ 315-323: This includes the code executed when the client presses the Search button on the main screen. Here a GUI appears above the main screen, which is responsible for performing server-level searches on file names and on users connected at a particular time.
- ◆ 325-376: This includes the code executed when the client presses the Viewfiles button. This button is initially disabled and only comes into use view when the user has used the Search button to perform a server-level search. This code is responsible for displaying the files of a particular user, which satisfy the search criteria.
  - • 339: The row selected by the client is identified and based on the selected row; the IP address of the listener is obtained.
  - • 342-343: Another function returnfilenames of the add_on class is used, which returns the filenames Vector along with the name of the user.
  - • 344-369: Out of this Vector, another Vector is generated that consists of files or folders pertaining to a particular user who has been highlighted when the Viewfiles button is pressed. The delimiter used is "?".
  - • 373-374: When the Vector is generated (results), it is passed to the file_gui class, which is responsible for displaying files; the root parameter is given the value as a search result and the flag information as "0."
- ◆ 383-420: This includes the code of a function, which places the information (number of users connected at a particular time) on the GUI and enables appropriate buttons in between.
  - • 406-412: This loops through information and puts the value on the table.
  - • 414-418: This adds an action listener to all the buttons.
- ◆ 424-432: The main function is declared, which is called at the start.
  - • 426: Because the client is called for the first time, the present users array is left empty.
  - • 429-431: The constructor is called, the size of the frame is set, and the frame is displayed.

search_window.java

This class is used when the user presses the Search button on the main screen, the class helps in server-level search after specifying certain search criteria (see Listing 4-9). The search criteria can be a particular file on all the listeners connected or can be a particular file with a subset of all listeners connected. The search window is shown in Figure 4-4.

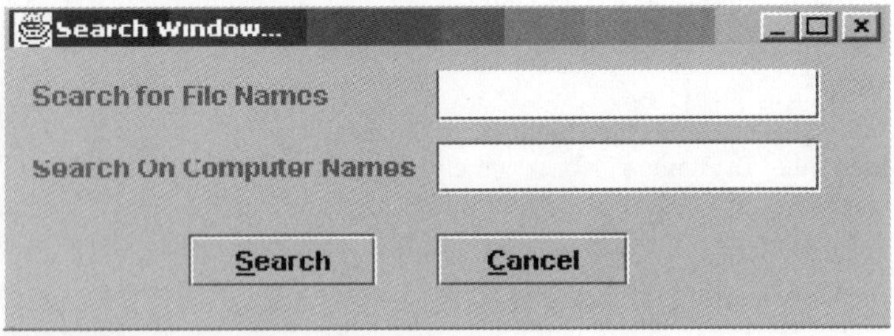

Figure 4-4: Server level search screen

Listing 4-9: search_window.java

```
1.  import javax.swing.*;
2.  import javax.swing.event.*;
```

```
3.    import java.awt.event.*;
4.    import java.awt.*;
5.    import java.util.*;
6.    import java.net.*;
7.    import java.io.*;
8.
9.    /* This Class is used to implement Client search on the p2p client... This
class has
10.      two main features....
11.       1. To search for a file on all the connected listeners...
12.       2. To search for a file on a particular subset of the connected
listeners...
13.   */
14.
15.   public class search_window extends JFrame implements ActionListener
16.   {
17.     JLabel label_file_name;                                    //
18.     JLabel label_computer_name;                        //
19.     JTextField search_file_name;                       //   GUI Components for
various purposes..
20.     JTextField search_computer_name;       //
21.     JButton search_ok,search_cancel;       //
22.
23.     Container contentpane;
24.
25.     String information[][];
26.     JFrame parent_window;                              // To Keep
information about the parent frame..
27.
28.     // The constructor of the class search window takes two arguments..
29.     // 1..  The parent frame...
30.     //2..  The names of  all the present liseners and their IP addresses stored
in
31.     //      2-D array info..
32.
33.     // The arguments are then initialized to the objects parent_window and
String 2-D array
34.     // information....
35.
36.     search_window(JFrame ancestor, String info[][])
37.     {
38.
39.       super("Search Window...");
40.       setSize(375,160);                              // Set The Size of the Frame...
41.       parent_window = ancestor;
42.
43.       contentpane = getContentPane();
44.       contentpane.setLayout(null);                   // Setting the Layout to Absolute
Layout..
45.
46.       label_file_name = new JLabel("Search for File Names "); // Initializing
the GUI.
47.       label_file_name.setBounds(10,10,130,25); // Positioning the GUI
Component.
48.
```

```
49.     search_file_name = new JTextField(30);       // Initializing the GUI
Component.
50.     search_file_name.setBounds(180,10,160,25);   // Positioning the GUI
Component.
51.
52.     label_computer_name = new JLabel("Search On Computer Names "); //
Initializing the
53.
          // GUI Component.
54.     label_computer_name.setBounds(10,45,170,25);    // Positioning the GUI
Component.
55.
56.     search_computer_name = new JTextField(30);       // Initializing the GUI
Component.
57.     search_computer_name.setBounds(180,45,160,25);// Positioning the GUI
Component.
58.
59.     search_ok = new JButton("Search");               // Initializing the GUI
Component.
60.     search_ok.setMnemonic('S');                           // Setting the
Mnemonic..
61.     search_ok.setBounds(75,90,80,25);                 // Positioning the GUI
Component.
62.
63.
64.     search_cancel = new JButton("Cancel");   // Initializing the GUI
Component.
65.     search_cancel.setMnemonic('C');                   // Setting the Mnemonic..

66.     search_cancel.setBounds(180,90,80,25);   // Positioning the GUI Component.
67.
68.
69.     search_ok.addActionListener(this);               // Add action listener to
all the
70.     search_cancel.addActionListener(this);   // buttons...
71.
72.
73.     // Adding the window  Listener to the gui window
74.     // ie. Code for the "cross"...
75.
76.     addWindowListener (new java.awt.event.WindowAdapter () {
77.         public void windowClosing (java.awt.event.WindowEvent evt) {
78.                 setVisible(false);
79.             }
80.         }
81.         );
82.
83.     contentpane.add(label_file_name);                 //
84.     contentpane.add(search_file_name);                //
85.     contentpane.add(label_computer_name);     //       Adding the GUI
Buttons.....
86.     contentpane.add(search_computer_name);   //
87.     contentpane.add(search_ok);                           //
88.     contentpane.add(search_cancel);                   //
89.
```

```
90.     information = info;        // Initializing the variable information with
the parameter
91.                               // info...
92.
93.   }
94.
95.   public void actionPerformed(ActionEvent ae)
96.   {
97.    if (ae.getSource() == search_ok)        // When Ok Button Is pressed....
98.    {
99.
100.        String us = " ";    // Two variables namely us(user search) and fs
(file search)
101.        String fs = " ";    // are used to store the value that the user
enters in the
102.                               // appropriate textfields...
103.
104.        boolean search = true;    // Temporary variable used in
computation..
105.
106.            us = search_computer_name.getText();  // Storing the value
107.            fs = search_file_name.getText();    // Storing the value
108.
109.
110.            if ((us.equals(""))&&(fs.equals("")))    // Apply check
condition
111.            {
112.            JOptionPane.showMessageDialog(this,"Please Enter some search
Criteria ","Peer 2 Peer Client",JOptionPane.ERROR_MESSAGE);
113.            search = false;
114.
115.            }
116.    else if (us.equals(""))                    // if any of the field is
left empty..
117.            {
118.                us = "*";
119.            }
120.    else if (fs.equals(""))                    // if any of the field is
left empty..
121.            {
122.            fs = "*";
123.            }
124.            if (search)        // Start the search procedure... as both
the variables
125.            {                               // have been assigned the
value...
126.    this.setVisible(false);    // hide the search window...
127.    parent_window.setVisible(false);   // Hide the parent window as well...
128.                    // Call the main class client with the parameters...
129.                    // 1.. Search..
130.                    // 2.. user search criteria..
131.                    // 3.. file search criteria..
132.                    // 4.. Information about the present users...
133.
134.    client search_result = new client("Search",us,fs,information);
135.    search_result.setSize(465,410);   // Set the size of the GUI called..
```

```
136.    search_result.show();                    // Display the GUI...
137.              }
138.
139.       }
140. else if (ae.getSource() == search_cancel)  // When Cancel Button Is
pressed....
141.        {
142.  this.setVisible(false);   // Hide this GUI screen
143.        }
144.    }
145.
146.  }
```

Code description

♦ Lines 1-7: This includes the basic packages used by the various classes used to build this application. The packages are java.net (sockets), java.io (file streams), javax.swing (frames), javax.swing.event (event handling), and so on.

♦ Lines 15-21: This declares a public class (search_window) that represents the base class for this file. All the variables defined here represent their respective controls pasted on the frame. These variables are label_file_name; label_computer_name of the type Jlabel; search_ok; search_cancel of the type JButton; search_file_name; search_computer_name of the type JtextField, and so on.

♦ Lines 36-70: The code between these lines pertains to initializing the GUI components (that is, the buttons, the table, the scrollbar positioning these GUI components on the frame, and their mnemonics for faster access through the keyboard, and so on.

♦ Lines 76-81: Adding window Listener.

♦ Lines 83-88: The code here pertains to adding the various GUI components to the frame.

♦ Lines 95-144: This includes the code for actions performed on various buttons.

♦ Lines 97-139: This includes the code executed when the client, after entering certain search criteria in the two JtextFields, presses the Search button to commence the searching operation.

  • 110-115: If both the JtextFields are left empty and the Search button is pressed, the Alert Box requisite pops up.

  • 116-123: If any of the JtextFields are left empty, a "*" is assigned to the variable of that field type.

  • 124-137: Start the search procedure by hiding the search GUI and the frame that has invoked the GUI. Then call the main class client with the parameters: 1. Search. 2. User search criteria. 3. File search criteria. 4. Information about present users.

♦ Lines 140-143: If the Cancel button is pressed, the search window hides.

file_gui.java

This class is used when the client/user decides to visit a particular listener to download/upload/search files (see Figure 4-5). This class, apart from showing the shared files of a particular listener, provides buttons to let the client perform various operations (see Listing 4-10). The operations might be the following:

♦ Open option (used when the user wants to browse the folders)

♦ Download option (used when the user wants to download a particular file)

♦ Upload option (used when the user, after having the proper permissions, wants to upload a file to the listener's machine)

♦ Search option (used when the user wants to search for a particular file on the listener's machine by specifying certain search criteria).

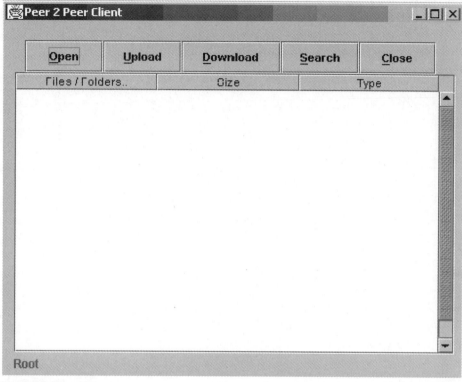

Figure 4-5: file_gui.java

Listing 4-10: file_gui.java

```
1.   import javax.swing.*;
2.   import javax.swing.event.*;
3.   import java.awt.event.*;
4.   import java.awt.*;
5.   import java.net.*;
6.   import java.io.*;
7.   import javax.swing.table.*;
8.   import java.util.*;
9.
10.  /* When the Client selects a particular Listener's name from the list of
the users
11.     connected and presses the button Open then this class is called. This
class helps
12.     the client directly connect to the Listener's machine and browse
through, download,
13.     upload, search for the files/folders shared by that particular
Listener....
14.
15.     This class provides the client facilities for download, upload, search
for files,move
```

```
16.      through shared folders facility...
17.  */
18.
19.
20.  public class file_gui extends JFrame implements ActionListener
21.  {
22.    private JButton file_open;                      //
23.    private JButton file_search;                    //
24.    private JButton file_close;                     //
25.    private JButton file_upload;                    //       GUI Components for
various purposes..
26.    private JButton file_download;                  //
27.    private JTable file_listing;                    //
28.    private JScrollPane file_scroller;      //
29.    private JLabel status;                                  //
30.
31.    Container contentpane;                              //  For  placing
the GUI Compomnents
32.    private Socket file_socket;                         //  To Declare the client
socket...
33.    Vector values = new Vector();                       //  To declare a vector
"values" for holding
34.                                                        // the results
of the xml response from
35.                                                        //  the
listener...
36.
37.    TableModel default_table;                       //       For JTable GUI
Component
38.    String names[] = {"Files / Folders..", "Size", "Type"};// Name of the
Columns in JTable
39.    Object data[][] ={{" "," "," " },{" ", " "," "}};// Initializing the
JTable Columns..
40.    String ip_address;                                      //
Variable to store the ip_address.
41.    String information[][];
42.    String file_name= new String();
43.    String status_text;                                 // Variable
to store the root information
44.    String flag_info;                                   // Variable
to store the flag information
45.    boolean done =  false;
46.
47.    /* Constructor is called with 4 parameters they are as follows...
48.1.This is the result of XML parsing done (and stored in a vector) at the
class
49.        files which calls this class.
50.  2.  The IP address of the Listener to which the client wants to connect...
51.  3.  The root information (ie . the directory in which the user is currently
52.        browsing..). initially this information is kept as "ROOT".
53.  4.  The flag Information about the directory in which the user is currently
54.        browsing,this is used for upload purposes.. initially this is kept as
0 as 0
55.        stands for no uploads and client cannot upload on listener's root
directory..
56.      */
```

```
57.
58.
59.    public file_gui(Vector parameter, String ip ,String stat_text, String
flag_info)
60.    {
61.    values = parameter;        //
62.    ip_address = ip;                    //                Initializing the variables
with parameters...
63.    status_text = stat_text;   //
64.    this.flag_info = flag_info; //
65.
66.        setTitle ("Peer 2 Peer Client");
67.    setSize(475,405);                              // Set The size of the frame...
68.
69.    contentpane = getContentPane();   //  Initialize the window for placing
the
70.                                                // components..
71.    contentpane.setLayout(null);       // Setting the Layout to Absolute
Layout..
72.
73.    file_open = new JButton("Open"); // Initializing the GUI Component.
74.    file_open.setMnemonic('O');                        // Setting the Mnemonic..
75.    file_open.setBounds(20,20,80,35);         // Positioning the GUI Component.
76.
77.    file_upload = new JButton("Upload");     // Initializing the GUI
Component.
78.    file_upload.setMnemonic('U');                      // Setting the Mnemonic..
79.    file_upload.setBounds(100,20,80,35);      // Positioning the GUI Component.
80.
81.    file_download = new JButton("Download");// Initializing the GUI
Component.
82.    file_download.setMnemonic('D');                        // Setting the
Mnemonic..
83.    file_download.setBounds(180,20,100,35);           // Positioning the GUI
Component.
84.
85.    file_search = new JButton("Search");     // Initializing the GUI
Component.
86.    file_search.setMnemonic('S');                          // Setting the Mnemonic..
87.    file_search.setBounds(280,20,80,35);     // Positioning the GUI Component.
88.
89.    file_close = new JButton("Close");// Initializing the GUI Component.
90.    file_close.setMnemonic('C');         // Setting the Mnemonic..
91.    file_close.setBounds(360,20,80,35);// Positioning the GUI Component.
92.
93.    status = new JLabel(status_text);// Initializing the GUI Component.
94.    status.setBounds(10,355,300,25); // Positioning the GUI Component.
95.
96.    //   Initializing the Table
97.
98.    default_table = new AbstractTableModel()
99.    {
100.         // These methods always need to be implemented.
101.         public int getColumnCount() { return names.length; }
102.       public int getRowCount() { return data.length;}
```

```
103.              public Object getValueAt(int row, int col) {return
data[row][col];}
104.
105.       // The default implementations of these methods in
106.             // AbstractTableModel would work, but we can refine them.
107.             public String getColumnName(int column) {return names[column];}
108.             public Class getColumnClass(int col) {return
getValueAt(0,col).getClass();}
109.             public boolean isCellEditable(int row, int col) {return (col==4);}
110.             public void setValueAt(Object aValue, int row, int column) {
111.                   data[row][column] = aValue;
112.                      fireTableCellUpdated(row, column);
113.                }
114.             };
115.
116.       /* This condition is applied so as to disable all the buttons except
the close
117.             button when view files button is pressed as while viewing the
files the client
118.             cannot make downloads/uploads etc...
119.           */
120.
121.       if (stat_text.equalsIgnoreCase("SEARCH RESULTS"))
122.       {
123.             file_open.setEnabled(false);
124.             file_download.setEnabled(false);
125.             file_upload.setEnabled(false);
126.             file_search.setEnabled(false);
127.       }
128.
129.       contentpane.add(file_open);                        //
130.       contentpane.add(file_close); //
131.       contentpane.add(file_download);       //
132.       contentpane.add(file_upload);//   Adding the GUI Components...
133.       contentpane.add(file_search);                      //
134.       contentpane.add(status);                           //
135.
136.       /* An important function "formating" is called with the parameter a
vector value
137.             this helps in extracting the information stored in the vector and
placing them
138.             in a string 2-Dimensional array in proper format for later
reference also
139.             placing the information on to the JTable...
140.           */
141.
142.       formating(values);
143.
144.       // Positioning and Initializing the GUI Component (Table)...
145.
146.       file_listing = new JTable(default_table);
147.       file_listing.setSelectionMode(ListSelectionModel.SINGLE_SELECTION);
148.       //file_listing.getTableHeader().setReorderingAllowed(false);
149.         //file_listing.setBounds(10,55,650,300);
150.       file_listing.setGridColor(new Color(255,255,255));
```

```
151.        //file_listing.setPreferredScrollableViewportSize(new Dimension(500,
70));
152.
153.        // Adding Scroll Facility to the JTable by adding JScrollpane
Component
154.
155.        file_scroller = new JScrollPane();//file_listing);
156.        file_scroller.setBounds(10,55,450,300);
157.        file_scroller.setViewportView(file_listing);
158.        file_scroller.setHorizontalScrollBarPolicy(
JScrollPane.HORIZONTAL_SCROLLBAR_AS_NEEDED);
159.        file_listing.setAutoResizeMode(JTable.AUTO_RESIZE_ALL_COLUMNS);
160.
161.        contentpane.add(file_scroller);              // Add the Scroll Bar...
162.
163.        // Adding the window  Listener to the gui window
164.        // ie. Code for the "cross"...
165.
166.        addWindowListener (new java.awt.event.WindowAdapter () {
167.          public void windowClosing (java.awt.event.WindowEvent evt) {
168.            setVisible(false);
169.          }
170.          }
171.          );
172.
173.        file_open.addActionListener(this);           //
174.        file_upload.addActionListener(this);         //
175.        file_download.addActionListener(this);//Add the  ActionListener...
176.        file_search.addActionListener(this);         //
177.        file_close.addActionListener(this);          //
178.
179.    }                  // End of Constructor file_gui...
180.
181.
182.    // The part Below pertains to the Action Performed when a Button is
pressed...
183.
184.    public void actionPerformed(ActionEvent ae)
185.      {
186.      if (ae.getSource() == file_open )// When open Button is pressed...
187.        {
188./* This button will function only in case when the user selects a folder and
189.    opens it for knowing the details of the folder.. If the client tries to
open
190.    a file a MessageBox is shown....
191.    */
192.
193.        try
194.          {
195.      int row = 0;
196.      row = file_listing.getSelectedRow();          // Get the Selection...
197.
198.    if (information[row][2].equalsIgnoreCase("Folder")) // Check whether
Folder
199.      {
200./* If a folder is selected and then pressed the open button then an object
```

```
201.   of the class add_on is created (request) This is responsible for sending
202.   the request to the Listener by using a function of the class of the name
203.   "search_request". The parameters passed on to the function are the folder
204.   name, followed by the search criteria here in this case it is *.*, foll-
205.   -owed by the ip_address of the listener, followed by the flag
206.    information of the folder searched for...
207.*/
208.     add_on open_request = new add_on();
209.
open_request.search_request(information[row][0],"*.*",ip_address,information[row
][3]);
210.           }
211.    else            // If a file is selected...
212.    {
213.                    // Alert / Message Box is displayed...
214.                    JOptionPane.showMessageDialog(this,"Cannot Open a File
Over Network. Try Downloading it.  ","Peer 2
Peer...",JOptionPane.INFORMATION_MESSAGE);
215.               }
216.        }
217.      catch(Exception es)
218.        {}
219.    }                // End File Open ....
220.   else if (ae.getSource() == file_close)  // If close button is pressed

221.    {
222.       this.setVisible(false);          // Hide this frame...
223.    }
224.   else if (ae.getSource() == file_download)     // If Download button is
pressed...
225. {
226. /* When download button is pressed a class called SwingWorker provided by
Sun is
227.    called this class helps in running a task in seperate thread thus helps
in gui.
228.       */
229.      final SwingWorker worker = new SwingWorker()
230.        {
231.            public Object construct()
232.            {
233.                // The function of the class is given a task to
perform (downloading).
234.                // By calling a class donload_file..
235.                // This downloading is done in a seperate thread...
236.              return new download_file();
237.            }
238.       };
239.      worker.start();      // Calling the start of the swingworker
240.
241.    }
242.   else if (ae.getSource() == file_upload)
243.    {
244.       done = false;
245.       /* When Upload button is pressed a class called SwingWorker provided
by Sun is
```

```
246.             called this class helps in running a task in seperate thread thus
helps in gui.
247.         */
248.         final SwingWorker upload = new SwingWorker()
249.         {
250.             public Object construct()
251.             {
252.                 // The function of the class is given a task to
perform (Uploading).
253.                 // By calling a class upload_file..
254.                 // This uploading is done in a seperate thread...
255.                 return new upload_file();
256.             }
257.         };
258.         upload.start();            // Calling the start of the swingworker
259.         if (done)
260.         {
261.             this.setVisible(false);        // Hide the window after
the upload...
262.         }
263.     } // End Upload.....
264.     else if (ae.getSource() == file_search) // When Search Button is
pressed...
265.     {
266.         /* When search button is pressed by the client then root information
is checked
267.             if root information is is "ROOT" then a message box is shown
indicating that
268.             no search can be done...
269.             else a class search screen is called... which caters to the search
...
270.         */
271.
272.         if (status_text.equalsIgnoreCase("Root"))  // If status_text is
"ROOT"
273.         {
274.             JOptionPane.showMessageDialog(this,"Cannot Search on Root.
Try searching in sub directories . ","Peer 2
Peer...",JOptionPane.INFORMATION_MESSAGE);
275.         }
276.         else   // If search Text is not root...
277.         {
278.             /* Create an Object of the class search_screen ..
279.                 the parameters passed on to the constructor are...
280.                 1. Status_text...
281.                 2. the ip address of the listener...
282.                 3. The flag_info of the folder on which search is
being performed...
283.             */
284.             search_screen search_now = new
search_screen(status_text,ip_address,flag_info);
285.             search_now.show();  // Show the frame...
286.         }
287.     }
288.
289.
```

```
290.   }                // End of Action Listener....
291.
292.
293.
294.   /* An important function "formating" is called with the parameter a
vector value
295.          this helps in extracting the information stored in the vector and
placing them
296.          in a string 2-Dimensional array in proper format for later
reference also
297.          placing the information on to the JTable...
298.       */
299.
300.   void formating(Vector values)
301.   {
302.       // To check whether the vector has more than one value or not.
303.
304.     if (values.size() > 1)
305.   {
306.       int array_size = values.size();
307.
308.       information = new String[array_size][4]; // Array in to which the
information
309.
  //   extracted is added...
310.       // Information to be placed on the Table is put into the array (2-D)
data...
311.
312.       if (array_size > 19)
313.       {
314.       data = new Object[array_size][3];
315.       }
316.       else
317.       {
318.       data = new Object[19][3];                    // Minimum size of
array...
319.       }
320.       boolean file_or_Folderectory;
321.
322.       int i = 1;
323.       int g = 0;
324.     while(i<array_size)
325.     {
326.     try
327.       {
328.         String temp = (String)values.get(i);
329.
330.         file_name = temp.substring(temp.lastIndexOf("\\")+1);
331.       if (file_name.equals(""))
332.       {
333.           information[g][0] = (String)values.get(i);

334.         data[g][0] = values.get(i);
335.           information[g][2] = "Folder";
336.         data[g][2] = "Folder";
337.           i++;
```

```
338.                     information[g][3]   = (String)values.get(i);

339.                     i++;
340.                     data[g][1] = (Object)" - ";
341.

342.                 }
343.             else
344.             {
345.                     information[g][0] = (String)values.get(i);
346.                     int index =file_name.lastIndexOf(".");
347.                     String gh = "";
348.                     if (index == -1)
349.                     {
350.                     information[g][2] = "";
351.                     data[g][2] = information[g][2]+" File";
352.                     gh = file_name;
353.                     }
354.                     else
355.                     {
356.                     information[g][2] =
file_name.substring(file_name.lastIndexOf(".")+1);
357.                     data[g][2] = information[g][2]+" File";
358.                     gh = file_name.substring(0,index);
359.                     }
360.                     data[g][0] = gh;
361.                     information[g][2] =
file_name.substring(file_name.lastIndexOf(".")+1);
362.                     data[g][2] = information[g][2]+" File";
363.                     i++;
364.                     information[g][3]   = (String)values.get(i);

365.                     i++;
366.                     information[g][1] = (String)values.get(i);
367.                     data[g][1] = values.get(i);
368.                     i++;
369.

370.             }
371.

372.         }
373.     catch (Exception e)
374.         {
375.          System.out.println( e );
376.         }
377.         g++;
378.         file_name = "";
379.     }           // End While.....
380.

381.     }           //  end if..
382.     else
383.      {
384.         information = new String[1][3];
385.         information[0][0] = "No Files are shareable";
386.         information[0][1] = " ";
387.         information[0][2] = " ";
388.

389.         data[0][0] = (Object)"No Files are shareable";
```

```
390.          data[0][1] =(Object)" - ";
391.          data[0][2] =(Object)" - ";
392.
393.     }
394.  }
395.
396.  /*  This class is used to download the file from the listener on to the
Client's
397.   machine....
398.   */
399.
400.    public class download_file extends JFrame
401.    {
402.      download_file()          // Constructor...
403.        {
404.        try
405.         {
406.             int row = 0;
407.             row = file_listing.getSelectedRow();        // Get the
selection of the user...
408.
409.             InetAddress inet = InetAddress.getByName(ip_address);
410.             file_socket = new Socket(inet,7070);        // Establish a
socket connection with
411.
  // the Listener on the port 7070
412.
  // address -- inet..
413.             // Get The output as well as the input Streams on that
socket...
414.
415.             BufferedOutputStream out = new
BufferedOutputStream(file_socket.getOutputStream());
416.
417.             BufferedInputStream br_socket = new
BufferedInputStream(file_socket.getInputStream());
418.
419.             // if the selection is a folder... then pop up  a message for
denial of
420.             // download..
421.             if (information[row][2].equalsIgnoreCase("Folder"))
422.             {
423.             JOptionPane.showMessageDialog(this,"Cannot  Download a Folder.
Try Opening it.  ","Peer 2 Peer...",JOptionPane.INFORMATION_MESSAGE);
424.             }
425.             else    // If the request is that of a file..
426.             {
427.             XmlWriter writer = new XmlWriter();  // Call a class
XMLWRITER to generate
428.   //  request by using a function
429.             writer.requestFString("DOWNLOAD",information[row][0]); //
requestFString...
430.             String file_data = writer.returnRequest();
431.             byte file_bytes[] = file_data.getBytes(); // get the Number
of bytes from the
```

```
432.
   // request...
433.            String temporary
=information[row][0].substring(information[row][0].lastIndexOf("\\")+1);
434.
435.            JFileChooser jfc = new JFileChooser();            // Call an
object of JFileChooser
436.
   // File Dialog to place the file.
437.
438.            File file = new File (temporary);
439.            jfc.setSelectedFile(file);
440.            jfc.ensureFileIsVisible(file);
441.            int button_pressed = jfc.showSaveDialog(this);
442.            String str1 = "";
443.            File file_final = jfc.getSelectedFile();
444.        if (button_pressed == JFileChooser.APPROVE_OPTION)
445.            {
446.                str1 = file_final.getPath();// Get the path where the
file is being saved..
447.            }
448.
449.            BufferedOutputStream out_file = new BufferedOutputStream(new
FileOutputStream(str1)); // Create an outputstream to that path...
450.
451.            int file_size = file_bytes.length;
452.
   // Adjust the request length to 1024
453.
   // (for c#) listener's...
454.            byte b[] = new byte[1024];
455.            // another method of the class add_on is used now
(apporpriatelength) this
456.            // is  used so as to make the request sent by the client to
the listener
457.            // 1024 in length..(for C#) listeners...
458.
459.            // The methos takes a byte array and its length as parameters
and return
460.            // a byte array of length 1024 bytes....
461.
462.            add_on download = new add_on();
463.            b = download.appropriatelength(file_bytes, file_size);
464.
465.            out.write(b,0,1024);   // The byte array is written on the
output stream
466.
467.            int y = 0;
468.            byte f[] = new byte[32];
469.            int file1_size = Integer.parseInt(information[row][1]);
470.            // Generate a progress monitor to monitor the request...
471.            ProgressMonitor pm = new ProgressMonitor(this,"Downloading
File..","Downloading Please Wait...",0,file1_size);
472.            int current = 0;
473.            pm.setMillisToPopup(5);
474.
```

```
475.                  while ((y = br_socket.read(f,0,32))>0)  // Read the socket and
write on to the
476.          // file...
477.                    {
478.                    out_file.write(f,0,y);
479.                    current = current + y;
480.                    pm.setProgress(current);                // Monitoring the progress

481.                                                                    //
monitor.,..
482.                    }
483.
484.                    out.close();                      //
485.                    br_socket.close();                // The filestream and
socket streams are
486.                    out_file.close();                 // Closed
487.
488.            }
489.        }
490.     catch(Exception es)
491.     {
492.     }
493.     try
494.     {
495.     file_socket.close();                    // Close the Client_socket...
496.     }
497.     catch (Exception e)
498.     {
499.        System.out.println( "Some Error while Closing : "+e );
500.     }
501.      }          // End Constructor..
502.   }                  // End Class Download_file...
503.
504.
505.  /*  This class is used to upload the file from the Client on to the
Listener's
506.   machine....
507.   */
508.
509.    public class upload_file extends JFrame
510.      {
511.    upload_file()              // Constructor...
512.      {
513.       String str1 ="";
514.       Vector parameters = new Vector();
515.       try
516.        {
517.                InetAddress inet = InetAddress.getByName(ip_address);
518.                file_socket = new Socket(inet,7070);// Establish a socket
connection with
519.   // the Listener on the port 7070
520.   // address -- inet..
```

```
521.                    // Get The output as well as the input Streams on that
socket...
522.
523.                    BufferedOutputStream out = new
BufferedOutputStream(file_socket.getOutputStream());
524.
525.                    BufferedInputStream br_socket = new
BufferedInputStream(file_socket.getInputStream());
526.
527.                    // if the upload is in a root... then pop up  a message for
denial of
528.                    // download..
529.
530.                    // if the flag is a 0... then pop up  a message for denial of
531.                    // download..
532.
533.                    if (status_text.equalsIgnoreCase("ROOT"))
534.                    {
535.                      JOptionPane.showMessageDialog(this,"Cannot  Upload In Root.
Try sub Folders .  ","Peer 2 Peer...",JOptionPane.INFORMATION_MESSAGE);
536.                    }
537.                    else if (flag_info.equals("0"))
538.                    {
539.                      JOptionPane.showMessageDialog(this,"Cannot  Upload In Read
Only Folder . Try other Folders .  ","Peer 2
Peer...",JOptionPane.INFORMATION_MESSAGE);
540.                    }
541.                    else            // Else if flag = 1
542.                    {
543.                        JFileChooser jfc = new JFileChooser();    // Call an
object of JFileChooser
544.
  // File Dialog to choose the file.
545.
546.                      int button_pressed = jfc.showOpenDialog(this);
547.
548.                      File file_final = jfc.getSelectedFile();
549.                      if (button_pressed == JFileChooser.APPROVE_OPTION)
550.                       {
551.                        str1 = file_final.getPath();               // Get the path of
the file
552.                       }
553.
554.                    String temp = str1.substring(str1.lastIndexOf("\\")+1);
555.                    temp = status_text+temp;
556.
557.                    XmlWriter writer = new XmlWriter();       // Call a class
XMLWRITER to generate
558.
  //  request by using a function
559.                    writer.requestFString("UPLOAD",temp);              //
requestFString...
560.                    String file_data = writer.returnRequest();
561.
562.                    byte file_bytes[] = file_data.getBytes();    // get the  bytes
from the
```

```
563.
     // request...
564.
565.                 BufferedInputStream file_read = new BufferedInputStream(new
 FileInputStream(str1));           // Create an inputstream to that path...
566.
567.                 int upload_file_size = file_read.available();
568.                 int file_size = file_bytes.length;
569.
570.                 byte b[] = new byte[1024];
571.                        // Adjust the request length to 1024
572.                        // (for c#) listeners...
573.
574.                 // another method of the class add_on is used now
(apporpriatelength) this
575.                 // is  used so as to make the request sent by the client to
the listener
576.                 // 1024 in length..(for c#) listeners...
577.
578.                 // The method takes a byte array and its length as parameters
and returns
579.                 // a byte array of length 1024 bytes....
580.
581.                 add_on upload = new add_on();
582.                 b = upload.appropriatelength(file_bytes, file_size);
583.
584.                 out.write(b,0,1024);     // The byte array is written on the
output stream
585.
586.                 int y = 0;
587.                 byte f[] = new byte[1024];
588.                 // Generate a progress monitor to monitor the request...
589.
590.                 ProgressMonitor pm = new ProgressMonitor(this,"Uploading
File..","Uploading Please Wait...",0,upload_file_size);
591.                 int current = 0;
592.                 //pm.setMillisToPopup(5);
593.
594.
595.                 while ((y = file_read.read(f,0,1024))>0)// Read the file and
write on socket
596.                  {
597.                    out.write(f,0,y);
598.                    current = current + y ;
599.                    pm.setProgress(current);             // Monitor the current
activity...
600.                  }
601.
602.                 out.close();
603.                 br_socket.close();                      // Close the streams...
604.         }
605.
606.     }
607.     catch(Exception es)
608.     {}
609.     try
```

```
610.       {
611.         file_socket.close();                    // Close the socket...
612.       }
613.     catch (Exception e)
614.       {
615.         System.out.println( "Some Error while Closing : "+e );
616.       }
617.
618.       }           // End Constructor....
619.     }             // END UPLOAD FILE...
620.
621.   }         // End File_Gui...
```

Code description

◆ Lines 1-8: This includes the basic packages used by the various classes to build this application. The packages include java.net (sockets), java.io (file streams), javax.swing (frames), javax.swing.event (event handling), and so on.

◆ Lines 20-31: This declares a public class (file_gui) that represents the base class for this file. All the variables defined here represent their respective controls that on the frame. These variables include file_open; file_download; file_upload; file_search; and file_close that are of the type JButton, file_listing, which is of the type JTable, and status, which is of the type JLabel, and so on.

◆ Lines 32-45: This declares the user-defined variables used for various purposes during the course of the program. This includes variables for URLConnection; InputStream; sockets; string variables (ip_address, information[][], status_text, flag_info); and variables of the type boolean for various checks during the program.

◆ Lines 59-114: The code between these lines pertains to initializing the variables with parameters and initializing the GUI components (that is, the buttons, the table, and the scrollbar positioning). Mnemonics are supplied for faster access through the keyboard.

◆ Lines 121-127: A condition is applied to disable all buttons except the Close button when the View Files button is pressed; while viewing the files, the client cannot make downloads or uploads.

◆ Lines 129-134: This code pertains to adding all the GUI components to the frame.

◆ Lines 142: An important formatting function is called with the parameter of a Vector value. This helps in extracting information stored in the Vector and placing information in a string two-dimensional array in proper format for later reference; this also places the information on the JTable.

◆ Lines 146-150: Positions and initializes the GUI component (JTable).

◆ Lines 155-161: This adds a scroll facility to the JTable by adding the JScrollpane component and the scrollbar to the frame.

◆ Lines 166-177: This Adds the window listener to the GUI window and adds the ActionListener to various buttons.

◆ Lines 184-290: This includes the code for actions performed on various buttons.

  • 186-219: This includes the code executed when the client selects a particular listing from the table and presses the Open button (file_open).

  • 196: The row selected by the client is identified and based on the selection the information is obtained whether the selection is a file or a folder.

  • 198-209: If a folder is selected and the Open button is pressed, an object of the class add_on is created (request). The object is responsible for sending the request to the listener by using a function of the class search_request. The parameters passed to the function are the folder name, followed by the search criteria. In this case, the parameteris *.*, followed by the `ip_address` of the listener, followed by the flag information of the folder searched for.

- 211-215: If a file is selected, a message box is displayed, as a file cannot be opened over a network.

- 220-223: This includes the code executed when the client presses the Close button. Then the current frame disappears.

- 224-241: This includes the code executed when the client selects an item from the table and presses the Download button to download that option.

- 229-239: When the Download button is pressed, a class called `SwingWorker` provided by Sun is called. This class helps in running a task in a separate thread and thus helps in multithreading involving a GUI. A method `construct` is declared, which returns a class `download_file` responsible for downloading the file. `SwingWorker` can be downloaded from `http://java.sun.com/docs/books/tutorial/uiswing/components/example-swing/SwingWorker.java`.

- 242-263: This includes the code executed when the client presses the Upload button to upload certain files from its system on to the listener's machine if proper permissions are there.

- 248-258: When the Upload button is pressed, a class called `SwingWorker` provided by Sun is called. This class helps in running a task in a separate thread and thus helps in multithreading involving a GUI. A method construct is declared, which returns a class `upload_file`, which is responsible for uploading the file.

- 264-287: This includes the code executed when the client presses the Search option to search for a particular subset of files available. When the Search button is pressed by the client, root information is checked. If `root_information` is "ROOT", a message box is shown indicating that no search can be done if `root_information` is not "ROOT", a class search screen is called that caters to the search.

- 272-275: If `status_text` is "ROOT", a message box is displayed; no search is possible on root.

- 284-285: If search text is not root, create an object of the class `search_screen`; the parameters passed to the constructor are: 1. `Status_text`. 2. The IP address of the listener. 3. The `flag_info` of the folder on which the search is being performed. A GUI is also shown on top of the existing frame; this GUI enables searching by specifying certain criteria.

- Lines 300-394: An important "formating" function is called with the parameter a Vector value. This helps in extracting information stored in the Vector and placing information in a string two-dimensional array in proper format for later reference. This also places information on the `JTable`.

  - 304-319: This checks whether the Vector has more than one value or not. If not, initialize a two-dimensional array of the type `String` with the size of the Vector.

  - 324-370: Loop through the Vector till the end, and extract the information and place it in the information array as well as in the data array (used by the `Jtable`).

  - 383-393: If the size of the Vector is less than 1, simply put the values in both the arrays as nonshareable.

- Lines 400-502: This includes the source code for the inner class `download_file`. This is used when the user selects a file and presses the Download button. This inner class handles all the functionality; that is, connecting to the listener's machine, placing the file on the desired path (`JfileChooser`), showing the progress on the monitor while downloading is in progress, and so on.

  - 407: The row selected by the client is identified and based on the row on which the attribute of the selection is obtained (whether file/folder).

  - 409-410: This creates a `client_socket` on the listener's machine on port 7070.

- 415-417: This attains the output as well as the input Streams on that socket.
- 421-424: If the selection made by the user turns out to be a folder, pop up a message box indicating that the a folder cannot be downloaded and that the user should try opening it instead.
- 427-430: If the request is that of a file, call a class `XmlWriter` to generate a request by using a function.
- 435-447: This calls an object of `JFileChooser` File dialog to place the file and to get the path where the file is being saved.
- 449: This creates an outputstream to that path. (the path obtained by the `JfileChooser`).
- 462-463: A method of the class `add_on` is used now (`appropriatelength`); this is used to make the request sent by the client to the listener 1024 bytes in length (for C# listeners).
- 465: The byte array is written on the output stream.
- 471-473: This generates a progress monitor to monitor the request.
- 475-482: The socket input stream is read and written to the file output stream, also updating the progress monitor in between.
- 484-500: This closes the file streams as well as the sockets and also handles the exceptions through the try… catch blocks.

♦ Lines 509-619: This includes the source code for the inner class `upload_file`. This is used when the user presses the Upload button. This inner class handles all the functionality (that is, checking for permissions, connecting to the listener's machine, placing the file on the desired path (`JfileChooser`), showing the progress on the monitor while the uploading is in progress, and so on.

- 517-518: This creates a `client_socket` on the listener's machine on port 7070.
- 523-525: This attains the output as well as the input streams on that socket.
- 533-540: If the folder in which the user wants to upload the file turns out to be a read-only folder, pop up a message indicating the status. Also, pop up a message if the root folder turns out to be "ROOT".
- 543-555: This calls an object of `JFileChooser` File dialog to choose the file to upload and gets its path.
- 557-560: This calls a class `XMLWRITER` to generate a request by using a function. Also, this appends the filename with the path on the listener's machine.
- 565: This creates an input stream to that path (path of the file to upload)
- 581-582: A method of the class `add_on` is used now (`appropriatelength`). This is used to make the request sent by the client to the listener 1024 bytes in length (for C# listeners).
- 584: The byte array is written on the output stream.
- 590: This generates a progress monitor to monitor the request.
- 595-600: The file input stream is read and written to the socket output stream, also updating the progress on the monitor in between.
- 602-616: This closes the file streams as well as the sockets and also handles the exceptions through the try… catch blocks.

search_screen.java

This class is used when the client/user uses the search option from the previous GUI (see Listing 4-11). This search is different from the server search, as it searches the listener's machine (a particular user) for files specified in the search criteria (see Figure 4-6).

After a search is completed, the class `file_gui.java` is called again to display the search results.

Figure 4-6: search_screen

Listing 4-11: search_screen.java

```
1.   import javax.swing.*;
2.   import javax.swing.event.*;
3.   import java.awt.event.*;
4.   import java.awt.*;
5.   import java.util.*;
6.
7.   /* This class implements Searching for files on the Listener....*/
8.
9.   public class search_screen extends JFrame implements ActionListener
10.  {
11.    JLabel label;                                          //
12.    JTextField search_text;                       // GUI Components
for various purposes..
13.    JButton search_ok,search_cancel;         //
14.
15.    Container contentpane;                       // For  placing
the GUI Componments..
16.
17.    String root_information;
18.    String ip_address;
19.    String flag_info = "";
20.
21.    /* When this class is called from the "file_gui.class" by pressing the
search
22.       button it is provided with three parameters...
23.
24.       root ... The root/directory on which search is being performed. This
cannot be
25.             the root directory...
26.
27.       ip ... The ip address of the listener's machine...
28.
29.       flag ... The flag information of the root/ directory...
30.
31.     */
32.
33.    public search_screen(String root, String ip, String flag )
34.    {
35.     super("Search");
```

```
36.      setSize(270,110);                              // Size of the Search
Screen Frame...
37.
38.      contentpane = getContentPane();
39.      contentpane.setLayout(null);                // Setting the Layout to Absolute
Layout..
40.
41.      label = new JLabel("Search Criteria "); // Initializing the GUI
Component.
42.      label.setBounds(10,10,100,25);                  // Positioning the GUI
Component.
43.
44.      search_text = new JTextField(30);               // Initializing the GUI
Component.
45.      search_text.setBounds(110,10,150,25);    // Positioning the GUI Component.
46.
47.      search_ok = new JButton("Search");              // Initializing the GUI
Component.
48.      search_ok.setMnemonic('S');                        // Setting the
Mnemonic..
49.      search_ok.setBounds(45,50,80,25);            // Positioning the GUI
Component.
50.
51.      search_cancel = new JButton("Cancel");   // Initializing the GUI
Component.
52.      search_cancel.setMnemonic('C');                  // Setting the Mnemonic..
53.      search_cancel.setBounds(150,50,80,25);   // Positioning the GUI Component.
54.
55.      search_ok.addActionListener(this);              // Add action listener to
all the
56.      search_cancel.addActionListener(this);   // Buttons...
57.
58.    // Adding the window  Listener to the gui window
59.    // ie. Code for the "cross"...
60.
61.    addWindowListener (new java.awt.event.WindowAdapter () {
62.        public void windowClosing (java.awt.event.WindowEvent evt) {
63.              setVisible(false);
64.            }
65.        }
66.        );
67.
68.    contentpane.add(label);                                //
69.    contentpane.add(search_text);                    //
70.    contentpane.add(search_ok);                          //       Adding the
GUI Buttons.....
71.    contentpane.add(search_cancel);                  //
72.
73.
74.    root_information = root;     //
75.    ip_address = ip;                          // Initialzing the variables with
parameters...
76.    flag_info = flag;                    //
77.
78.    }
79.
```

```
80.    public void actionPerformed(ActionEvent ae)
81.    {
82.      if (ae.getSource() == search_ok)          // When Ok Button Is pressed....
83.      {
84.            this.setVisible(false);                          // Hide this GUI
screen
85.
86.            // another method of the class add_on is used now (search request)
this
87.            // to send  the listener the search criteria. For sending the search
88.            // criteria the function search_request takes four parameters....
89.            // 1.  root_information .. On Which the search request is being
made..
90.            // 2.  search text ie. the text entered by the user on the text field
91.            //         provided.
92.            // 3.  ip_address of the listener's machine....
93.            // 4.  Flag information of the directory on which request is made...
94.
95.
96.            add_on search_with_condition = new add_on();
97.
   search_with_condition.search_request(root_information,search_text.getText(),ip_
address,flag_info);
98.      }
99.      else if (ae.getSource() == search_cancel)  // When Cancel Button Is
pressed....
100.        {
101.            this.setVisible(false);                          // Hide
this GUI screen
102.        }
103.    }
104.
105.  }
```

Code description

♦ Lines 1-5: This includes the basic packages used by the various classes used to build this application. The packages include javax.swing (frames), javax.swing.event (event handling), and so on.

♦ Lines 9-13: This declares a public class (search_screen) that represents the base class for this file. All the variables defined here represent their respective controls pasted on the frame. These variables include label of the type Jlabel, search_ok, and search_cancel of the type Jbutton, search_text of the type JtextField, and so on.

♦ Lines 17-19: Declares the user-defined variables used for various purposes during the course of the program. This includes string types (that is, Root_information, flag_info, and ip_address).

♦ Lines 33-56: The code between these lines pertains to initializing the GUI components (that is, the buttons, the table, the scrollbar positioning these GUI components on the frame, and their mnemonics for faster access through the keyboard, and so on).

♦ Lines 61-66: This adds WindowListener for handling window events.

♦ Lines 68-71: The code here pertains to adding the various GUI components to the frame.

♦ Lines 74-76: This initializes the variables with parameters.

♦ Lines 80-103: This includes the code for actions performed on various buttons.

- 82-98: This includes the code executed when the client, after entering certain search criteria in the JtextField, presses the Search button to commence the searching operation.

- 96-97: A method of the class add_on is used now (search request). This is used to send to the listener the search criteria. For sending the search criteria, the function search_request takes four parameters: root_information on which the search request is being made; search text, the text entered by the user on the text field provided; the ip_address of the listener's machine; and flag information of the directory on which the request is made.

- 99-102: If the Cancel button is pressed, the search window hides.

add_on.java

This is a multiutility class, as it has functions used by nearly all classes (see Listing 4-12). These functions are as follows:

- ◆ search_request(): Sends the search request to a particular listener. The search request can open/browse a folder, in which case "*.*" is passed or can be requested based on a specific criteria ("*.java", "ja*.ja*", and so on).

- ◆ appropriate_length(): Used to adjust the length of the request sent to the listener to 1024 bytes. This adjustment is made to balance request handling by the "C#" and java listeners.

- ◆ Sorting(): Used to implement sorting (the bubble sort technique is a commonly used technique of sorting records). In this the smallest or the largest record depending upon the condition bubbles comes out after each iteration so that the listeners' names appear in alphabetical order.

- ◆ Start_connection(): Used to send requests to the server; hence, this method is used two times: when the request is sent to the server to provide a list of the users connected at a particular time and when the search_window class is called to implement server-level searches.

Listing 4-12: add_on.java

//© 2001 Dreamtech Software India Inc.
// All rights reserved

```
1.    import java.net.*;
2.    import java.io.*;
3.    import java.util.*;
4.    /* This class file is a mutipurpose class file it contains many functions
which are used
5.       over a series of classes in the project...
6.     */
7.
8.    class add_on
9.    {
10.      Socket file_socket;
11.      String viewfiles[][];
12.      static Vector filenames ; // A vector to maintain the user list (static)
13.
14.
15.      add_on()              // Constructor...
16.      {
17.
18.      }
19.      /*  This function is used to adjust the length of the byte array and to
make it
20.          equal to 1024 bytes. This is done in order to make the size of the
request
```

```
21.             equal to the request accepted by the C# listener...
22.
23.             In the function appropriatelength two parameters are passed
24.             1. Byte array...
25.             2. Length of byte array...
26.
27.             The rest of the bytes (1024 - length) are first converted into
character and
28.             then made into  char '13' and then converted into bytes again..
29.
30.      */
31.
32.      public byte [] appropriatelength(byte[] file_bytes, int file_size)
33.      {
34.              int count = 0;
35.              byte b[] = new byte[1024];
36.              int remaining = 1024-file_size;
37.
38.              for (int i = 0;i<file_bytes.length ;i++ )
39.              {
40.                      b[i] = file_bytes[i];
41.              }
42.
43.              char a[] = new char[remaining];
44.
45.              for (int i = 0;i<remaining ;i++ )
46.              {
47.              a[i] = 13;
48.              }
49.
50.              String tempw = new String(a);
51.              byte d[] = tempw.getBytes();
52.
53.              for (int i=file_size;i<1024 ;i++ )
54.              {
55.              b[i] = d[(i-file_size)];
56.              }
57.
58.              return (b);
59.      }                 // End Appropriate length.....
60.
61.      /* This function is used to issue the search request...
62.          It takes 4 parameters...
63.                  1. Directory information...
64.                  2. Search Criteria..
65.                  3. Ip_address of the listener...
66.                  4. Flag_information of the directory on which search is
made...
67.
68.      */
69.
70.
71.          public void search_request(String directory, String condition, String
ip_address, String flag_info)
72.              {
73.
```

```
74.          try
75.          {
76.                    InetAddress inet = InetAddress.getByName(ip_address);
77.                    file_socket = new Socket(inet,7070); // Create a
client_socket on the
78.
 // Listener's machine at port 7070.
79.
80.                    // Get The output as well as the input Streams on that
socket...
81.                    BufferedOutputStream out = new
BufferedOutputStream(file_socket.getOutputStream());
82.
83.                    BufferedInputStream br_socket = new
BufferedInputStream(file_socket.getInputStream());
84.
85.                    // Now a request is sent to the Listener to show all the
shareable files
86.                    // of the particular directory that satisfy the search
criteria..selected
87.                    // by the user..
88.
89.                    // To send a request a class of the name xmlwriter is used
which has two
90.                    // functions of interest. They are... requestFString(String,
String) and
91.                    // returnRequest(), this xmlwriter is a versatile class as it
is used to
92.                    // generate xml requests for various purposes...
SEARCH,UPLOAD, DOWNLOAD
93.                    // and SHOWFILES... therefore accordingly the requestFString
takes two
94.                    // parameters in case of SHOWFILES the second parameters is
not used.
95.
96.            XmlWriter writer = new XmlWriter(); // Initializing a object
of xmlwriter..
97.                    writer.requestFString("SEARCH",directory+condition);//
calling the
98.
      // function...
99.                    String file_data = writer.returnRequest(); // getting the
request in a
100.
     // temp variable file_data.
101.
102.                        byte file_bytes[] = file_data.getBytes();  // getting
byte array of string
103.
104.                        // An output stream is also initialized this is used
to store all the
105.                        // response from the listener..
106.
107.
108.                    BufferedOutputStream out_file = new
BufferedOutputStream(new FileOutputStream("response.xml"));
```

```
109.
110.                     int file_size = file_bytes.length;
111.
112.
113.                     byte b[] = new byte[1024];          // Initializing a
new byte array of 1024.
114.
115.                     // another method of the same class add_on is used now
(appropriatelength)
116.                     // this is  used so as to make the request sent by the
client to the
117.                     // listener 1024 in length..(for C#) listeners...
118.
119.                     b = appropriatelength(file_bytes, file_size);
120.
121.                     out.write(b,0,1024);  // The byte array is written on
the output stream
122.
123.                     int y = 0;
124.                     byte f[] = new byte[32];
125.
126.                     while ((y = br_socket.read(f,0,32))>0)     // the
socket input stream is read
127.                     {
128.                     out_file.write(f,0,y);        // written on to the file
output stream...
129.                     }
130.
131.                     out.close();         //
132.                     br_socket.close();   //    The filestream and socket
streams are
133.                     out_file.close();    //
134.
135.                     // A class SParser is also used here this class has a
function/method of
136.                     // the name perform which calls the xml parser to
parse the xml file
137.                     // generated by the response from the client socket...
138.
139.                     // the function perform returns a Vector which has the
files/directories,
140.                     // along with their flag information and size in case
of files....
141.
142.                     SParser sp = new SParser();
143.                     Vector parameters = sp.perform("response.xml");
144.                     file_gui showfiles = new
file_gui(parameters,ip_address,directory,flag_info);
145.                     showfiles.show();
146.             }
147.          catch (Exception e)
148.             {
149.                        System.out.println( "Exception in
search_request "+e );
150.
151.             }
```

```
152.
153.               try
154.               {
155.                 file_socket.close();        // Close the Socket...
156.               }
157.               catch (Exception e)
158.               {
159.                       System.out.println( "Some Error while Closing : "+e
);
160.               }
161.
162.         }              // End Search request....
163.
164.
165.      /*  This is a simple sorting function which implements bubble sort
method to
166.          sort the Listeners' names lexicographically...
167.          It takes as its argument a 2-D array of the listeners' names
and a flag
168.          to call
169.      */
170.
171.      public String [][] sorting(String info[][], boolean cond)
172.      {
173.           int  k = 0;
174.           while (k < (info.length-1))
175.           {
176.                int i = 0;
177.                while (i <  (info.length - k - 1))
178.                {
179.                  if((info[i][0] != null)   &&(info[i+1][0] != null))
180.                  {
181.                  if (info[i][0].compareToIgnoreCase(info[i+1][0]) > 0)
182.                    {
183.                        String temp = info[i][0];
184.                        info[i][0] = info[i+1][0];   // Swapping
operation..
185.                        info[i+1][0] = temp;
186.
187.                        temp = info[i][1];
188.                        info[i][1] = info[i+1][1];   // Swapping
operation..
189.                        info[i+1][1] = temp;
190.
191.                        if (cond)
192.                        {
193.                         temp = info[i][2];
194.                         info[i][2] = info[i+1][2]; // Swapping
operation..
195.                         info[i+1][2] = temp;
196.                        }
197.
198.                    }
199.                  }
200.                        i++;
201.                }
```

```
202.
203.                        k++;
204.                    }
205.
206.                return info;              // Returning the 2-D sorted array...
207.          }
208.
209.    /* This function/method is used everytime an object of class Client is
invoked
210.        it is used to get Listeners' List, Search List from the server...After
retrieving
211.        the information, it arranges the information in proper format in a 2_D
array and
212.        returns the array to the class which invoked the function...
213.
214.        The parameters this method takes are..
215.        1. param -- Criteria for calling the function (Search/Root).
216.        2. us -- if param equals Search then this will hold the Search
Criteria..
217.        3. fs -- if param equals Search then this will hold the Search
Criteria..
218.        4. present_users[][] -- Present users connected to the server...
219.
220.    */
221.    public String[][] start_connection(String param,String us, String fs,
String present_users[][])
222.    {
223.        URLConnection urlconnection;
224.        InputStream url_inputstream; // For Connecting and gaining the
information..
225.        String information[][] = {{ " "," "}};
226.        Vector values = new Vector();
227.        boolean go_on = true;
228.        boolean search_flag = false;
229.
230.
231.    try
232.        {
233.        if (param.equalsIgnoreCase("search"))  // if Search
234.        {
235.                // Call The ASP with proper format and parameters and
initialize a vector to
236.                // store the information generated from this request..
237.                urlconnection = (new URL("http://www.s-
cop.com/search.asp?us="+us+"&fs="+fs)).openConnection();
238.            urlconnection.connect();
239.                search_flag= true;
240.                filenames = new Vector();
241.                filenames.add(0,(Object)"filesearch");
242.
243.        }
244.        else   // if root
245.        {
246.        urlconnection = (new URL("http://www.s-
cop.com/userlist.asp")).openConnection();
247.        urlconnection.connect();
```

```
248.          search_flag= false;
249.          }
250.          StringBuffer sb = new StringBuffer();
251.          try
252.          {
253.          url_inputstream = urlconnection.getInputStream(); // get the
inputstream
254.
255.          // read the response from the request and store it in the
response.xml file...
256.          BufferedReader br = new BufferedReader(new
InputStreamReader(url_inputstream));
257.
258.          BufferedWriter file_output = new BufferedWriter(new
OutputStreamWriter(new FileOutputStream("response.xml")),32);
259.
260.          int i = 0;
261.          char[] b = new char[32];
262.          String string = "";
263.          while ((i = br.read(b,0,32)) > 0 )
264.          {
265.          String temp = new String(b,0,i);
266.          string = string +temp;
267.          }
268.          string = string.trim();
269.          char d[] = string.toCharArray();
270.          file_output.write(d,0,d.length);
271.
272.          br.close();          // Close the inputStream..
273.          file_output.close();  // Close the inputStream..
274.
275.          }
276.
277.          catch(Exception ef)
278.          {
279.          }
280.          // A class SParser is also used here this class has a function/method
of
281.          // the name perform which calls the xml parser to parse the xml file
282.          // generated by the response from the client soket...
283.
284.          // the function perform returns a Vector which has the
files/directories,
285.          // along with their flag information and size in case of files....
286.
287.
288.          SParser sp = new SParser();
289.          values = sp.perform("response.xml");
290.
291.
292.          if (param.equalsIgnoreCase("search")) // if the param is search then
293.          {                                                          //
storing is done in the
294.                                                                     //
following format..
295.
```

```
296.                    information = new String[present_users.length][2];
297.                    viewfiles = new String[values.size()][3];
298.                    int i = 1;
299.                    int g = 0;
300.                    int count = 0;
301.
302.                    while(i<(values.size()))
303.                    {
304.                           viewfiles[g][0] = (String)values.get(i);

305.                           i++;
306.                           viewfiles[g][1] = (String)values.get(i);
307.                           i++;
308.                           viewfiles[g][2] = (String)values.get(i);
309.                           i++;
310.                           String temp= "";
311.                           temp = viewfiles[g][0]+"?"+viewfiles[g][2]+"?";
312.
313.                           if
(viewfiles[g][2].substring(viewfiles[g][2].lastIndexOf("\\")+1).equals(""))
314.                           {
315.                                  temp = temp+"0"+"?";
316.                           }
317.                           else
318.                           {
319.                                  temp = temp + "0"+"?"+"   "+"?";
320.                           }
321.                           filenames.add((Object)temp);
322.                           temp = "";
323.                           g++;
324.                    }
325.
326.                    for (int index = 0;index<present_users.length ;index++ )
327.                    {
328.                           if (present_users[index][0] != null)
329.                           {
330.                             int inf  = present_users[index][0].indexOf("(");
331.                             if (inf != -1)
332.                             {
333.                                    present_users[index][0] =
present_users[index][0].substring(0,inf);
334.                             }
335.
336.                           }
337.                    }
338.
339.
340.                    for (int index = 0;index<present_users.length ;index++ )
341.                    {
342.                           if (present_users[index][0] != null)
343.                           {
344.                            count = 0;
345.                            for (int temp = 0;temp<g ;temp++ )
346.                            {
347.                                   if
(viewfiles[temp][1].length()>=present_users[index][0].length())
```

```
348.                                   {
349.                                 if
(present_users[index][0].equalsIgnoreCase(viewfiles[temp][1].substring(0,present
_users[index][0].length())))
350.                                   {
351.                                       count++;
352.                                   }
353.                               }
354.
355.                           }
356.                     present_users[index][0] = present_users[index][0] + "(
"+count+" )";
357.                       }
358.
359.                   }
360.
361.             information = present_users;
362.
363.
364.         }
365.       else
366.       {
367.         if (values.size()>1)
368.         {
369.             information = new String[values.size()][2];
370.             int i = 1;
371.             int g = 0;
372.             while(i<(values.size()))
373.             {
374.                 information[g][0] = (String)values.get(i);

375.                 i++;
376.                 information[g][1] = (String)values.get(i);
377.                 i++;
378.                 g++;
379.             }
380.
381.         }
382.         else
383.         go_on = false;
384.
385.       }
386.
387.
388.         if (!go_on)
389.         {
390.           information = new String[1][2];
391.           information[0][0] = "Not Connected...";
392.               information[0][1] = " - ";
393.         }
394.         else
395.         {
396.             information = sorting(information,false);   // Sorting is
performed,,,
397.         }
398.       }                 // End Try..
```

```
399.        catch(Exception e)
400.        {
401.            go_on = false;
402.        }
403.
404.                        // End Else....
405.
406.
407.
408.        return (information);        // return the sorted list...
409.
410.  }
411.
412.  public Vector returnfilenames()
413.  {
414.
415.  return filenames;
416.  }
417.  }
```

Code description

♦ Lines 1-3: This includes the basic packages used by the various classes used to build this application. The packages include java.net (sockets), java.io (file streams), and java.util (utility).

♦ Lines 8-12: This declares a public class (client) that represents the base class for this file. This declares the user-defined variables, which are used for various purposes during the course of the program. This includes variables for socket, string, and a static-vector connection.

♦ Lines 32-59: This includes the source code for appropriatelength(). This function is used to adjust the length of the byte array and to make it equal to 1024 bytes. This is done to make the size of the request equal to the request accepted by the C# listener. In the function appropriatelength(), two parameters are passed: byte array and length of byte array. The rest of the bytes (1024-length) are first converted into character and then made into char '13' and then converted into bytes again. This char 13 is used for the compatibility issue, so that the Java client can be used with C# listener. Char 13 is treated as blank white space. Any other character could create a problem while parsing the data.

♦ Lines 71-162: This includes the source code for search_request(). This function is used to issue the search request. This function takes four parameters: Directory information, Search Criteria, Ip_address of the listener, and Flag_information of the directory on which the search is made.

  • 76-77: This creates a client_socket on the listener's machine on the port 7070.

  • 81-83: This gets the output as well as the input streams on that socket.

  • 96-97: Now a request is sent to the listener to show all the shareable files.

  • 108: An output stream is also initialized. This is used to store the response from the listener.

  • 119: A method of the same class add_on is used now (apporpriatelength) to make the request sent by the client to the listener, 1024 bytes in length (for C# listeners).

  • 121: The byte array is written on the output stream.

  • 126-129: The socket input stream is read and written to the file output stream.

  • 131-133: Closing the file streams as well as the sockets and also handling the exceptions through the try… catch blocks.

- 142-143: The class `SParser` is also used here. This class has a function/method of the name perform that calls the XML parser to parse the XML file generated by the response from the client socket. The function returns a Vector, which is stored in the Temp Vector.

- 144-145: The Vector value returned by the XML parser is then passed as one of the parameters to a class named `file_gui`. This class is responsible for displaying a GUI consisting of a table and some buttons, along with the root information and flag.

♦ Lines 171-207: This includes the code for the sorting function. This is a simple sorting function that implements a bubble sort method to sort the listeners names in alphabetical order. The `Sorting` function takes as its argument a two-dimensional array of the listeners' names and a flag and returns an array of the same type as that of the input parameter.

♦ Lines 221-410: This includes the code for the `start_connection` function. This function/method is used every time an object of class `Client` is invoked. It is used to get a listener's list, search list from the server. After retrieving the information, the function arranges the information in a two-dimensional array and returns the array to the class that invoked the function. The parameters this method takes are: `param` (criteria for calling the function Search/Root); us (if `param` equals `search`, then this holds the search criteria for a user search); fs (if `param` equals `search`, this holds the search criteria for a file search); and `present_users[][]` (present users connected to the server).

- 223-228: This declares the user-defined variables used for various purposes during the course of the program; this includes variables for `URLConnection`, `inputstream`, and variables of the type `boolean` for various checks during the program.

- 233-243: If the param value is equal to "SEARCH," an ASP (search.asp) is called. This also initializes a Vector to store the information generated from this request.

- 244-249: Otherwise, an ASP (userlist.asp) is called.

- 253: This gets an inputstream to the URL connection created either in line no. 233-243 or 244-249.

- 258: An output stream is also initialized, which is used to store the response from the listener.

- 263-270: Read from the socket and write to file.

- 272-273: Close the streams.

- 288-289: Class `SParser` is also used here. This class has a function/method of the name perform, which calls the XML parser to parse the XML file generated by the response from the client socket. The function returns a Vector, which is stored in the Temp Vector.

- 292-364: If the parameter passed is `"Search"`, arrange the Vector received in proper format by applying the proper delimiters "?".

- 365-385: If the param is not `"Search"`, arrange the values in the Vector in the array `information[][]`.

- 388-393: If no value is in the Vector, indicate in the array that no files are shareable.

- 394-397: If information has some values, function sorting is called to sort the values.

- 408: Information is returned.

♦ Lines 412-416: A function `returnfilenames` is called here. This just returns the file names to the calling program; this function is called when the client presses the View Files button in the class `client.java`.

Summary

This chapter explained how to create a full-fledged peer-to-peer application using Java 2 Standard Edition and XML.

We have explained the concept of Peer to Peer Application by discussing the role of XML in our application, along with how to parse the XML (`SParser.java`). The class parses the XML response returned from the server and returns a Vector to the calling program. Another class has been discussed (`XMLWriter.java`).This class is used by both the listener program and the browser program as, it generates the XML requests, thus illustrating the fact that the XML forms the basis of client/server communication.

The listener program was explained. This program forms the basis of the peer-to-peer application. It makes use of a class `Login.java`, which registers the listener onto the server and then listens for requests on a specified port (7070, in our case). The listener program shares the files/folders to be viewed by the browser by using a class `shareddilog.java`. For implementing the listener-level search facility, the program uses the `check_directory.java` class. It has various features to implement any kind of search using wildcards.

After the listener program, the browser program was explained. The browser browses the list of all connected users and then connects to a user; the browser browses for files and folders shared on the user machine and uploads and downloads the files on his or her machine. The browser uses various classes. The most important class is `client.java`, which searches for various listeners connected . The `file_gui`, on the other hand, provides the detail of files/folders shared by a listener. The `search_screen.java` and the `search_window.java` implement listener-level and server-level searches, respectively.

In Chapter 5, we discuss the implementation of the peer-to-peer application by using C#.

Chapter 5

The P2P Application (C#)

This chapter introduces you to the task of cracking code and illustrates all aspects of detailed programming. In the C# version of this P2P application, the implementation is explained in detail so that you gain a sound understanding of the concepts. The code in this chapter has been written in Microsoft Visual Studio .NET Beta 2. As soon as the final version of Microsoft Visual Studio .NET is released, you can download the executables for this application from www.dreamtechsoftware.com/download.

The code explanation starts with a discussion on the ServerCommunication class (Listing 5-1), which is in the WorkingWithXML namespace. This class carries functions that are very handy to use, such as functions for communicating with the server, getting the IP address for a particular machine, and so on. Further, WorkingWithXML describes the class used to create XML requests/responses, the XMLCreater class, which also resides in the WorkingWithXML namespace. The functions of this class take some parameters, and depending upon the parameters, they either generate a request or a response. Finally, one more class is in the same namespace: XMLParser. This class is used for the parsing of the XML request/response.

While going through the chapter, you may find some lines of code in the WorkingWithXML class that are required by the add-ons (discussed in Chapters 6 and 7). You may skip these lines of code now, but you may need to come back and refer to them while going through Chapters 6 and 7.

After discussing the building blocks of our application, we discuss the application itself. This comprises a listener software and a browser software (client). These two interact with each other to give final shape to this P2P application. The listener, as the name suggests, listens to the requests sent by the browser and also sends a response to listeners. The browser is responsible for showing the response in a user-friendly manner so that the end user can interpret it.

ServerCommunication Class

namespace: WorkingWithXML

The name of the class is ServerCommunication, which is responsible for communication with the server.

Listing 5-1: ServerCommunication Class

// © 2001 Dreamtech Software India Inc.
// All rights reserved

```
1 namespace WorkingWithXML
2 {
3  using System;          // Provides the basic functionality of .NET
4  using System.Net;          // Provides the net related functionality
5  using System.IO;          // Provides the I/O functionality
6  using System.Text;          // Provides text based manipulations
7  using System.Windows.Forms; // Provides the use of graphic interface
8  using System.Web;
```

```
 9
10      /// <summary>
11      ///      Summary description for ServerCommunication.
12      ///      This class is responsible for all the communication with
13      ///      the server as well as Listener
14      ///      It has got some handy functions which can be very helpful
15      ///      like: GetIPAddress, FileDelete etc
16      /// </summary>
17      public class ServerCommunication
18      {
19          /// <summary>
20          /// Default constructor of the class
21          /// This constructor of the class is generated automatically
22          /// by the IDE
23          /// </summary>
24      public ServerCommunication()
25          {
26          }
27
28      /// <summary>
29      /// Get the response data from server represented by WebAddress
30      /// When the request is made to the server it opens a stream
31      /// to the response and the function reads bytes from that
32      /// response stream and converts them to string and returns the value
33      /// </summary>
34      /// <param name="WebAddress"> </param>
35      public string GetDataFromServer(string WebAddress)
36      {
37          // Declares a local variable webRequest of type HttpWebRequest
38          // which is a part of System.Net package. It is used to form
39          // an HttpRequest and sends it to the server
40          HttpWebRequest webRequest;
41
42          // Declares a local variable webResponse of type HttpWebResponse
43          // which is a part of System.Net package. It is used to get the
44          // response from the server against the HttpWebRequest
45          HttpWebResponse      webResponse;
46
47          // Declares a variable responseStream of Stream type which is
48          // used to get the response from the server's end
49          Stream responseStream;
50
51          // streamBuffer variable is declared here of type Byte array
52          // this is used to read the actual data from the responseStream
53          Byte[] streamBuffer;
54
55          // Declares a variable ReturnData of type string which
56          // at last stores the data which is to be returned
57          string ReturnData;
58
59          // initializes the ReturnData to null
60          ReturnData = null;
61
62          // Creates and initializes a webRequest by calling Create
63          // function of the WebRequestFactory and type cast it to
64          // HttpWebRequest type
```

```
65          webRequest = (HttpWebRequest)WebRequest.Create(WebAddress);
66
67          // After requesting the server for HttpWebRequest
68          // it will open a response for the clients end to read
69          // this response is catched by the following line of code
70          // and assigns it to webResponse
71          webResponse =(HttpWebResponse)webRequest.GetResponse();
72
73          // GetResponseStream method of webResponse actually gets
74          // the response stream and assigns it to the responseStream
75          responseStream = webResponse.GetResponseStream();
76
77          // initialize streamBuffer so that it can read 16 bytes of data
78          // at a time
79          streamBuffer = new Byte[16];
80
81          // Declares  int variable iBytesRead which keeps the
82          // records of how many bytes have been read from the
83          // stream
84          int iBytesRead;
85
86          // Reads 16 bytes from the stream until the stream gets
87          // enpty and the value assigned to iBytesRead is zero
88          while( 0 != (iBytesRead = responseStream.Read(streamBuffer, 0, 16)) )
89
90                  // This will convert the bytes data that is read from the
91                  // stream and stored in streamBuffer to string and
                      concatenates
92                  // it to ReturnData
93                  ReturnData += Encoding.ASCII.GetString(streamBuffer, 0,
                      iBytesRead);
94
95          // Removes the leading and trailing spaces from the Data
96          // that is stored is returnData variable
97
98          if( ReturnData != null )
99          {
100                 ReturnData = ReturnData.Trim();
101 //              ReturnData =
    ReturnData.Substring(0,ReturnData.LastIndexOf("</p2p_lng>") +
    "</p2p_lng>".Length );
102         }
103
104         // Flushes the responseStream
105         responseStream.Flush();
106
107         // Closes the responseStream
108         responseStream.Close();
109
110         // Returns the value of ReturnData variable
111         return ReturnData;
112     }
113
114     /// <summary>
115     /// Get the response data from server represented by WebAddress
116     /// using Proxy server. When the request is made to the server it
```

```
117     /// opens a stream to the response and the function reads bytes
118     /// from that response stream and converts them to string and
119     /// returns the value
120     /// </summary>
121     /// <param name="WebAddress"> </param>
122     public string GetDataFromServerUsingProxy(string WebAddress, string
        ProxyAddress, int Port)
123     {
124         // Declares a local variable webRequest of type HttpWebRequest
125         // which is a part of System.Net package. It is used to form
126         // an HttpRequest and sends it to the server
127         HttpWebRequest webRequest;
128
129         // Declares a local variable webResponse of type HttpWebResponse
130         // which is a part of System.Net package. It is used to get the
131         // response from the server against the HttpWebRequest
132         HttpWebResponse        webResponse;
133
134         // Declares a variable responseStream of Stream type which is
135         // used to get the response from the server's end
136         Stream responseStream;
137
138         // streamBuffer variable is declared here of type Byte array
139         // this is used to read the actual data from the responseStream
140         Byte[] streamBuffer;
141
142         // Declares a variable ReturnData of type string which
143         // at last stores the data which is to be returned
144         string ReturnData;
145
146         // initializes the ReturnData to null
147         ReturnData = null;
148
149         System.Net.IWebProxy ProxyData = new
            System.Net.WebProxy(ProxyAddress,Port);
150
151         // Creates and initializes a webRequest by calling Create
152         // function of the WebRequestFactory and type cast it to
153         // HttpWebRequest type
154         webRequest = (HttpWebRequest)WebRequest.Create(WebAddress);
155         webRequest.Proxy = ProxyData;
156
157         // After requesting the server for HttpWebRequest
158         // it will open a response for the clients end to read
159         // this response is catched by the following line of code
160         // and assigns it to webResponse
161         webResponse =(HttpWebResponse)webRequest.GetResponse();
162
163         // GetResponseStream method of webResponse actually gets
164         // the response stream and assigns it to the responseStream
165         responseStream = webResponse.GetResponseStream();
166
167         // initialize streamBuffer so that it can read 16 bytes of data
168         // at a time
169         streamBuffer = new Byte[16];
170
```

```
171         // Declares  int variable iBytesRead which keeps the
172         // records of how many bytes have been read from the
173         // stream
174         int iBytesRead;
175
176         // Reads 16 bytes from the stream until the stream gets
177         // empty and the value assigned to iBytesRead is zero
178         while( 0 != (iBytesRead = responseStream.Read(streamBuffer, 0, 16)) )
179
180               // This will convert the bytes data that is read from the
181               // stream and stored in streamBuffer to string and
                  concatenates
182               // it to ReturnData
183               ReturnData += Encoding.ASCII.GetString(streamBuffer, 0,
                  iBytesRead);
184
185         // Removes the leading and trailing spaces from the Data
186         // that is stored is returnData variable
187         if( ReturnData != null )
188         {
189               ReturnData = ReturnData.Trim();
190 //                  ReturnData =
ReturnData.Substring(0,ReturnData.LastIndexOf("</p2p_lng>") +
"</p2p_lng>".Length );
191         }
192
193         // Flushes the responseStream
194         responseStream.Flush();
195
196         // Closes the responseStream
197         responseStream.Close();
198
199         // Returns the value of ReturnData variable
200         return ReturnData;
201     }
202
203     /// <summary>
204     /// Writes the DataToWrite to Filename
205     /// This function writes the string data which is stored in
206     /// DataToWrite variable to the file pointed by Filename
207     /// Usually we write XML file
208     /// </summary>
209     /// <param name="Filename"> </param>
210     /// <param name="DataToWrite"> </param>
211     public void WriteDataToFile(string Filename, string DataToWrite)
212     {
213         // Declares and initializes the FileToCreate variable of
214         // type File and passes Filename to its constructor to
215         // associate it with the File
216         //File FileToCreate = new File(Filename);
217
218         // Added for Beta 2
219         FileStream WriteStream = new FileStream(Filename,FileMode.Create);
220
221         // Declares and creates a WriteStream object, used
222         // to write the data to the stream which is present
```

```
223              // in DataToWrite variable
224              //Stream WriteStream = FileToCreate.OpenWrite();
225
226              // Writes the data to the file by converting data
227              // to byte format
228              WriteStream.Write(Encoding.ASCII.GetBytes(DataToWrite), 0,
                 DataToWrite.Length);
229
230              // Closes the written file
231              WriteStream.Close();
232      }
233
234      /// <summary>
235      /// Determine the type of request/response received in XML
236      /// This is done by extracting the attribute value from the
237      /// first node value of first child element of the document
238      /// </summary>
239      /// <param name="XMLFilename"> </param>
240      public string TypeOfXMLRecieved(string XMLFilename)
241      {
242              // Declares and initializes a local variable document
243              // of type IXMLDOMDocument present in MSXML2 class. This
244              // variable is used to point to the XML filename or document
245              MSXML2.IXMLDOMDocument        document = new MSXML2.DOMDocument();
246
247              // Declares a local variable element of type IXMLDOMElement
248              // This is used to point to the elements present in the XML
249              // document
250              MSXML2.IXMLDOMElement element;
251
252              // Declares a local variable node of type IXMLDOMElement
253              // This is used to point to the nodes present in the XML
254              // Document
255              MSXML2.IXMLDOMNode            node;
256
257              // A local variable NodeValue is declared of type string
258              // it is used to store the retrieved value from the XML and
259              // returns it from the function
260              string NodeValue;
261
262              // Read the XML document synchronously
263              document.async = false;
264
265              // Initializes NodeValue to null
266              NodeValue = null;
267
268              // Loads the XML document for reading
269              if( document.load(XMLFilename) )
270              {
271                      // Extract the first element of the XML
272                      element = document.documentElement;
273
274                      // Extract the first child node from the element
275                      // and stores it to the node
276                      node = element.firstChild;
277
```

```
278                     // now extract the first node value from the attributes
279                     // present in the XML and saves it to NodeValue
280                     NodeValue = node.attributes.nextNode().nodeValue.ToString();
281         }
282
283         // Simply returns the NodeValue variable
284         return NodeValue;
285     }
286
287     /// <summary>
288     /// This function is used to delete a file represented by filename
289     /// </summary>
290     /// <param name="Filename"> </param>
291     public void FileDelete(string Filename)
292     {
293         // Declares and initializes an object f of type File which is
294         // present in System.IO package and assigns Filename to it
295         //File f = new File(Filename);
296
297         //Added for Beta 2
298         File.Delete(Filename);
299         // Calls the Delete function of File Class to delete the
300         // file represented by Filename
301         //f.Delete();
302     }
303
304     /// <summary>
305     /// Retrieve the IP Address of the machine represented by
306     /// Hostname. This function makes the use of the DNS class
307     /// for extracting the IP address and returns the first entry
308     /// from the IP list obtained
309     /// </summary>
310     /// <param name="Hostname"> </param>
311     public string GetIPAddress(string Hostname)
312     {
313         // Creates a new local variable named LocalHost of type
314         // IPHostEntry which is present in the System.Net package
315         // It then calls the GetHostByName function of the DNS class
316         // and passes the Hostname to it
317         IPHostEntry        LocalHost = Dns.GetHostByName(Hostname);   // To
retrieve my computer's IP
318
319         // Now the LocalHost has got the list of IPs corresponding
320         // to the hostname and it will return the first entry from the
321         // list
322         return LocalHost.AddressList[0].ToString();
323     }
324     }
325 }
326 }
```

Code description of ServerCommunication class (clsServerCommunication.cs)

♦ Lines 3-8: This includes the basic packages needed for the various classes used to build this application. This also includes packages used for communicating with network, streaming facility, file I/O, text manipulations, and so on.

♦ Line 17: This line declares a public class ServerCommunication.

♦ Lines 24-26: This is the default constructor of the ServerCommunication class and is not used anywhere in our application for any purpose.

♦ Lines 35-112: The GetDataFromServer function retrieves the response from the server's end, that is, the result of calling the ASP pages on the server. The address of the ASP page is passed to this function in the WebAddress parameter of this function. It uses this WebAddress parameter to get the response from the server's end. This response is saved in string format in ReturnData for later use.

  • 40: A webRequest variable of the HttpWebRequest class is declared. This variable is used to create a Web request by calling the ASP page.

  • 45: A webResponse variable of the HttpWebResponse class is used to get the response to the requested ASP page from the server.

  • 49: A responseStream variable of the Stream class type is declared to get the response stream of the server.

  • 53: This streamBuffer variable reads the response from the server that is captured by using the responseStream variable.

  • 57: The ReturnData variable of String type is declared here to store the final data, which is to be returned by this function.

  • 65: Here we call the Create() function of the WebRequest class to call the given ASP page from the server; the created request is then type cast to the HttpWebRequest class and gets stored in the webRequest variable.

  • 71: After creating the Web request, we now need to catch the response from the server. This line of code does this by calling the GetResponse() function of the HttpWebRequest class and assigns the response to the webResponse variable.

  • 75: This line gets the stream where the response data is stored on the server.

  • 79: Variable streamBuffer of Byte type is initialized here to read 16 bytes of data at a time from the response stream that it stores in the responseStream variable.

  • 84: This variable is used to store the number of bytes read from the response stream of the server.

  • 88-111: Read 16 bytes of data from stream until stream gets empty, and convert the bytes data into string; read from stream and store it into ReturnData variable while concatenating it. All leading and trailing spaces are removed, and finally stream is cleaned up and closed. The data stored in ReturnData is returned by the function.

♦ 122-201: The GetDataFromServerUsingProxy() function retrieves the response from the server's end. If you are behind a proxy, you have to give the proxy address and port number to this function, that is, the result of calling the ASP pages on the server. The address of the ASP page is passed to this function in the WebAddress parameter of this function. It uses this WebAddress parameter to get the response from the server's end. This response is saved in string format in the ReturnData variable for later use.

♦ Lines 211-232: This function writes the string data returned by the GetDataFromServerUsingProxy() function in an XML file. The name of the file is passed in the Filename variable, and the data to write is passed in the DataToWrite variable.

  • 219: This creates a stream for writing to the file.

- 228: This writes data to the file by converting it to Byte type.

- 231: The written file is closed here.

♦ Lines 240-285: This function determines the type of the request/response received in XML format. This is done by extracting the type attribute of the XML from the first child node of this XML.

- 245: The document object declared here is of type `IXMLDOMDocument`. This interface is present inside the `MSXML2` class and is created as a reference to this application.

- 250: The `element` object of the `IXMLDOMElement` interface is used to point to the elements present in the XML document.

- 255: The `node` object of the `IXMLDOMNode` interface is used to point to the nodes present in the XML document.

- 260: The `NodeValue` variable is used to store the node value of the type attribute in the XML document.

- 263: This line allows the application to read the XML document synchronously.

- 266: This initializes the `NodeValue` variable to null.

- 269-281: First, the XML document is loaded into memory. Then the first element is extracted from the document, which in turn is used to get the first child node from it, and the actual data is extracted from the first attribute of this child node. This value is then stored in `NodeValue` and returned by the function.

♦ Lines 291-302: This function is used to delete the file represented by the `Filename` variable that is passed to this function.

♦ Lines 311-323: This retrieves the IP address of the machine whose name is passed in the `Hostname` parameter of this function. The function uses this parameter to extract the IP address from the DNS lookup and returns the first-found entry from the list retrieved.

XMLCreater Class

namespace: `WorkingWithXML`

The name of the class is `XMLCreater` and holds the responsibility of creating different kinds of requests. The entire coding has been numbered for better clarity and wider legibility (see Listing 5-2).

Listing 5-2: XML CreaterClass

// © 2001 Dreamtech Software India Inc.
// All rights reserved

```
1 namespace WorkingWithXML
2 {
3    // basic package includes
4        using System;
5        using System.Windows.Forms;
6        using System.IO;
7
8        ///    Creates requests and appropriate responses
9        public class XMLCreater
10       {
11       // member variables for storing Apllication path of
12       // application that's using this class
13       // and path to pick up share.ini from
14       string ResponsPath;
15       string SharedResourceInfoPath;
16
```

```
17        // constructor to initiliaze both the paths
18         public XMLCreater(string responsePath,string sharedResourceInfoPath)
19         {
20      ResponsPath = responsePath;
21      SharedResourceInfoPath = sharedResourceInfoPath;
22      }
23
24        // creates an XML document
25        private MSXML2.IXMLDOMDocument CreateDocument()
26        {
27        // create a document object and return that
28        MSXML2.IXMLDOMDocument document = new MSXML2.DOMDocument();
29        return document;
30 }
31
32 // saves and closes XML document
33 private void SaveAndCloseDocument(MSXML2.IXMLDOMElement
         responseElem,MSXML2.IXMLDOMDocument  document)
34 {
35  document.async = false;
36  // create Processing Instruction for XML document
37  MSXML2.IXMLDOMProcessingInstruction procsInstruct =
         document.createProcessingInstruction("xml",
         "version=\"1.0\"encoding=\"utf-8\"");
38  // create primary element
39  MSXML2.IXMLDOMElement elem = document.createElement("p2p_lng");
40
41  // add response object passed to the primary element as child node
42  elem.appendChild(responseElem);
43  // add Processing Instruction object and primary object to document
44  // object passed as child nodes and save the document
45  document.appendChild(procsInstruct);
46  document.appendChild(elem);
47  document.save(ResponsPath);
48 }
49
50
51 // determines the request type passed in the given XML document
52 public string DetermineRequestType(string path,out int
   UploadDownloadPrint,out string[] chatInfo)
53 {
54      int b = 0;
55      string scopeVal = "";
56      bool flag = false;
57      string[] st = new string[3];
58
59      try
60      {
61      // load the XML document
62      MSXML2.IXMLDOMDocument document = new MSXML2.DOMDocument();
63      if(!document.load(path))
64      throw new Exception("XML request found corrupted.");
65
66        // retrieve the request element
67      MSXML2.IXMLDOMElement element = document.documentElement;
68      MSXML2.IXMLDOMNode node = element.firstChild;
```

```
69      MSXML2.IXMLDOMNamedNodeMap nodemap = node.attributes;
70      // retrieve its attributes
71      MSXML2.IXMLDOMNode childNode = nodemap.nextNode();
72
73      if(0 == node.nodeName.CompareTo("request"))
74      {
75      // see what value does the element request holds
76      // and react appropriately
77      switch(childNode.nodeValue.ToString())
78      {
79      case "CHAT":
80      {
81      b = 4;
82      MSXML2.IXMLDOMNode scope = node.firstChild;
83      MSXML2.IXMLDOMNamedNodeMap nodemap2 = scope.attributes;
84      MSXML2.IXMLDOMNode childNode2 = nodemap2.nextNode();
85      MSXML2.IXMLDOMNode childNode3 = nodemap2.nextNode();
86      MSXML2.IXMLDOMNode childNode4 = nodemap2.nextNode();
87      // set file name to upload to "path" parameter
88      st.Initialize();
89      st.SetValue(childNode2.nodeValue.ToString(),0);
90      st.SetValue(childNode3.nodeValue.ToString(),1);
91      st.SetValue(childNode4.nodeValue.ToString(),2);
92      break;
93      }
94      case "SEARCH":
95      {
96      WriteSearchResponse(node);
97      break;
98      }
99      case "SHOWFILES":
100     {
101     WriteShowfileResponse("SHOWFILES");
102     break;
103     }
104     case "DOWNLOAD":
105     {
106     // set flag that it's download request
107     b = 2;
108     flag = true;
109     break;
110     }
111     case "UPLOAD":
112     {
113     // set flag that its upload request
114     b = 1;
115     flag = true;
116     break;
117     }
118     case "PRINT":
119     {
120     // set flag that its print request
121     b = 3;
122     flag = true;
123     break;
124     }
```

```
125
126        case "STREAMING":
127        {
128        // set flag that its Streaming request
129        b = 5;
130        flag = true;
131        break;
132        }
133
134        default:
135        throw new Exception("Request type could not be resolved.");
136    }
137
138        if(flag)
139        {
140        MSXML2.IXMLDOMNode scope = node.firstChild;
141        MSXML2.IXMLDOMNamedNodeMap nodemap2 = scope.attributes;
142        MSXML2.IXMLDOMNode childNode2 = nodemap2.nextNode();
143        // set file name to upload to "path" parameter
144        scopeVal = childNode2.nodeValue.ToString();
145        }
146        }
147    }
148        catch(Exception e)
149        {
150        WriteErrorResponse(e.Message);
151        }
152
153        chatInfo = st;
154        UploadDownloadPrint = b;
155        return scopeVal;
156    }
157
158    // writes error XML responses
159    public void WriteErrorResponse(string error)
160    {
161        // create a document object
162        MSXML2.IXMLDOMDocument document = CreateDocument();
163        // create response and error info elements
164        MSXML2.IXMLDOMElement responseElem =
           document.createElement("response");
165        MSXML2.IXMLDOMElement errorInfoElem=
           document.createElement("errorinfo");
166
167        // set attribute of response element
168        responseElem.setAttribute( "type", "ERROR");
169        // set attribute of errorinfo element
170        errorInfoElem.setAttribute( "errorcode", "1");
171        errorInfoElem.setAttribute( "severity", "Error" );
172        errorInfoElem.setAttribute( "description", error);
173        // add errorinfo element to response object as a child
174        responseElem.appendChild(errorInfoElem);
175        // save the document
176        SaveAndCloseDocument(responseElem, document);
177    }
178
```

```
179    // writes request XML according to the parameter passed
180    public void WriteRequest(string type,string searchValue,string mask)
181    {
182        // create a document object
183        MSXML2.IXMLDOMDocument document = CreateDocument();
184
185        // create request element
186        MSXML2.IXMLDOMElement requestElem =
           document.createElement("request");
187
188        // set attributes of request element
189        requestElem.setAttribute( "type", type);
190
191        // if one of these kinds of request is to be made
192        // specify the filename and pertaining info too.
193        if(type.CompareTo("SHOWFILES") != 0)
194        {
195        string ReqType = "";
196        if(type.CompareTo("CHAT") == 0)
197        ReqType = "message";
198        else
199        ReqType = "scope";
200
201        MSXML2.IXMLDOMElement file_infoElem =
           document.createElement(ReqType.ToString());
202
203        if(type.CompareTo("CHAT") == 0)
204        {
205        file_infoElem.setAttribute("sendername",
           searchValue.Substring(0,searchValue.IndexOf("(")));
206        file_infoElem.setAttribute("senderIP",
           searchValue.Substring(searchValue.IndexOf("(")+1).Substring
           (0,searchValue.Substring(searchValue.IndexOf("(")+1).Length-1));
207        file_infoElem.setAttribute("chatmsg",mask);
208        }
209        else
210        {
211        file_infoElem.setAttribute("type",searchValue);
212        file_infoElem.setAttribute("mask",mask);
213        }
214        requestElem.appendChild(file_infoElem);
215        }
216
217        // close and save the documdent
218        SaveAndCloseDocument(requestElem,document);
219 }
220
221
222 private void WriteShowfileResponse(string reqType)
223 {
224        // create a document object
225        MSXML2.IXMLDOMDocument document = CreateDocument();
226        // create response and error info elements
227        MSXML2.IXMLDOMElement responseElem =
           document.createElement("response");
228        // set attribute of response element
```

```
229         responseElem.setAttribute( "type", reqType);
230
231         // open share.ini for reading
232         StreamReader readfile = new StreamReader(SharedResourceInfoPath);
233         string readData;
234
235         // read entire file
236         while((readData = readfile.ReadLine()) != null)
237         {
238         try
239         {
240         // for each entry in share .ini create a fileinfo element
241         // and fill it with required information
242         MSXML2.IXMLDOMElement file_infoElem =
            document.createElement("fileinfo");
243         int index = readData.IndexOf("=",0);
244         file_infoElem.setAttribute( "filename",readData.Substring(0,index));
245         file_infoElem.setAttribute( "mask", readData.Substring(index+1,1));
246
247         int secindex = -1;
248         if(-1 != (secindex = readData.IndexOf("=",index+1)))
249         file_infoElem.setAttribute( "filesize",
            readData.Substring(secindex+1));
250
251         // add this element to response element as child
252         responseElem.appendChild(file_infoElem);
253         }
254         catch(Exception e)
            {
            MessageBox.Show("Problem faced while responding : " + e.Message);
            }
255         }
256         // close and save the documdent
257         SaveAndCloseDocument(responseElem,document);
258 }
259
260 // responds for search requests
261 private void WriteSearchResponse(MSXML2.IXMLDOMNode node)
262 {
263         try
264         {
265         MSXML2.IXMLDOMNode scope = node.firstChild;
266         MSXML2.IXMLDOMNamedNodeMap nodemap = scope.attributes;
267         MSXML2.IXMLDOMNode childNode = nodemap.nextNode();
268         MSXML2.IXMLDOMNode    childNode2 = nodemap.nextNode();
269         string scopeVal = childNode.nodeValue.ToString();
270         string maskVal = childNode2.nodeValue.ToString();
271
272         // make sure that search request has criteria specified in it
273         if(0 != scope.nodeName.CompareTo("scope"))
274         return;
275
276         // validated that directory's existing
277         if(!Directory.Exists(scopeVal.Substring(0,
```

```
              scopeVal.LastIndexOf("\\")+1)))
278           throw new Exception("Directory does not exist any more");
279
280           MSXML2.IXMLDOMDocument document = CreateDocument();
281           MSXML2.IXMLDOMElement responseElem =
              document.createElement("response");
282           responseElem.setAttribute( "type", "SHOWFILES");
283
284           int i = 0;
285           // get files in the specified directory satisfying the
286           // given criteria
287           string[] files = Directory.GetFiles(scopeVal.Substring(0,
              scopeVal.LastIndexOf("\\")+1),scopeVal.Substring(
              scopeVal.LastIndexOf("\\")+1));
288           files.Initialize();
289
290           while(i < files.Length)
291           {
292           // make fileinfo elements and fill then up with
293           // required
294           MSXML2.IXMLDOMElement file_infoElem =
              document.createElement("fileinfo");
295           file_infoElem.setAttribute( "filename",files[i]);
296           file_infoElem.setAttribute( "mask",maskVal);
297           file_infoElem.setAttribute(
              filesize",Convert.ToString(files[i].Length));
298           ++i;
299
300           // add them to response element as children;
301           responseElem.appendChild(file_infoElem);
302           }
303
304           // get files in the specified directory satisfying the
305           // given criteria
306           string[] dirs = Directory.GetDirectories(scopeVal.Substring(0,
              scopeVal.LastIndexOf("\\")+1),scopeVal.Substring(
              scopeVal.LastIndexOf("\\")+1));
307           dirs.Initialize();
308
309           i = 0;
310           while(i < dirs.Length)
311           {
312           // make fileinfo elements and fill then up with
313           // required
314           MSXML2.IXMLDOMElement file_infoElem =
              document.createElement("fileinfo");
315           file_infoElem.setAttribute( "filename",dirs[i] + "\\");
316           file_infoElem.setAttribute( "mask",maskVal);
317           ++i;
318
319           // add them to response element as children;
320           responseElem.appendChild(file_infoElem);
321           }
322           // close and save the document
323           SaveAndCloseDocument(responseElem,document);
324           }
```

```
325          catch(Exception e) { WriteErrorResponse(e.Message); }
326          }
327      }
328 }
```

Code description of XMLCreater class (clsXMLCreater.cs)

- Lines 4-6: This includes necessary packages to build the application.

- Lines 9-15: Ths public class `XMLCreater` has been declared with two strings for storing the path of the application using this class and for storing the `share.ini` file path, respectively.

- Lines 18-22: This is the implementation of the constructor `XMLCreater`() of the `XMLCreater` class. It initializes the two previously mentioned specified paths with values passed.

- Lines 25-30: The `CreatingDocument()` function creates an XML document object and returns it to the caller function.

- Lines 33-48: The `SaveAndCloseDocument()` function saves and closes the passed XML document after putting in it other required elements and the passed response element.

  - 37: Process Instructions are created for this XML document.

  - 39: The primary element of the XML document (p2p_lng) is created and stored in the `MSXML2.IXMLDOMElements element` object.

  - 42: This adds a response object passed to the primary element as its child node.

  - 45: Here, process-instructions are added to the document and appended to it as a child node.

  - 46: The primary element is added to the document.

  - 47: The document is saved on the application path.

- Lines 52-156: The `DetermineRequestType()` function loads the XML request document sent by the browser, determines the kind of request sent, and reacts appropriately.

  - 62-64: XML document is loaded by calling `IXMLDOMDocument`'s `load`.

  - 67-69: Primary elements are retrieved through, which its child elements (request) and then its attributes are retrieved and stored in a `IXMLDOMNamedNodeMap` element;

  - 71: Here, the first attribute of the child element is received and stored in an object of the `MSXML2.1XMLDOMNode` class named `childNode`.

  - 79-93: Here we are checking what the request element holds. If the request type is chat, information pertaining the user who has initiated the chat process is retrieved and stored in variables for returning to the listener at the end of this function.

  - 94-103: This determines what kind of request it is and reacts appropriately by calling appropriate functions.

  - 104-132: Here we are extracting the child node of the request (scope element) element and storing it into a scope object. In the next line, the attributes of this element are taken in a `IXMLDOMNamedNodeMap` element, and the value of the first attribute is extracted and stored in a string variable for returning at the end of the function.

  - 134-136: In case the request made is exceptional and not understood by these functions, an error message is thrown to the end user by calling `WriteErrorResponse` in a catch block.

  - 138-145: Here we extract the child node of the request (scope element) element and store it into a `scope` object. In the next line, the attributes of this element are taken in a `IXMLDOMNamedNodeMap` element, and the value of the first attribute is extracted and stored in a string variable for returning at the end of the function to the caller function; upload, print, download, and streaming processes are signaled by setting the flag value according to the type of request.

- 152-156: The values extracted previously are assigned to the outgoing parameters, and the information is returned to the caller.

♦ Lines 159-177: The `WriteErrorResponse()` function holds the responsibility of writing error XML responses. An XML document is created. A response element is created, and its type attribute is set to *error*. In the following lines error XML attributes are set to indicate the error message, sources, and so on.

  - 165: An element called `errorinfo` is created.

  - 167-172: In these lines, we set the request type to ERROR, and `errorinfo`'s attributes, such as `errorcode`, `severity`, and `description`, are set to their appropriate values.

  - 174-176: The `errorinfo` element, bundled with its attributes, is added to the response object as a child; the document is saved and closed.

♦ Lines 180-219: The `WriteRequest()` function is used generally by the browser to create XML requests to send to the listener.

  - 183: An XML `document` object is created.

  - 186: A `request` element is created.

  - 189: An attribute called type is associated to XML `document` object.

  - 193-213: If request type to be created is SEARCH, PRINT, CHAT, STREAMING, DOWNLOAD, or UPLOAD, a scope element is created to specify the search criteria and folder to carry out a search operation on or files to download or upload or print or streaming and their masks if required. If request is found to be CHAT, unlike other types of requests with which the scope element is assigned type and mask attributes, `sendername`, `senderIP` and `chatmsg` are associated to it.

  - 218: The document is saved and closed.

♦ Lines 222-258: This function writes the response on an XML document to show files.

  - 224-230: Here we are making an object of `XMLDOMDocument` and an object of `XMLDOMElement` called `response`. Next, we are associating an attribute to a response object called type with the value SHOWFILES.

  - 231-232: We are making an object of the `StreamReader` class, passing it the path and name of share.ini file.

  - 235-255: This while loop keeps reading the file, and, for each file or folder found, it creates a `fileinfo` element and sets its attributes such as `filename`, `mask` and `filesize`. The filesize attribute is not set if the found resource is a folder.

  - 241-242: In each iteration, the `fileinfo` element created is added to the request element, which is sent to `SaveAndCloseDocument()` for saving and closing the document.

♦ Lines 260-328: `WriteSearchResponse()` makes a response XML Document for the search request.

  - 265: The Scope element, with its list of attributes, is retrieved.

  - 266: The First attribute of the scope element is retrieved here.

  - 268: The Second attribute of scope element is retrieved here.

  - 269-271: Value of the First and Second attribute is received.

  - 275: Search criteria is extracted from first attribute of the scope element and is passed to the `Directory` class's object.

  - 276-278: Here we are checking the physical existence of the directory on the hard disk of the computer.

- 280-283: An `XMLDocument` and an `XMLDOMElement` object are created. The `XMLDOMelement` represents the response element, and we have coupled it with an attribute called type with that has the value `SHOWFILE`.

- 287-288: The list of files in the directory specified in the XML search request is obtained by using the `Directory` object's `GetFiles()` function, passing the `path` and `criteria` as arguments.

- 291-303: We are filling up information of each file as attributes to an XMLDOM element called `fileinfo`, created for each file found. Attributes for this element are `filename`, the value of which is the full name of the file; `mask`, whose value is the mask of the directory specified in the search request; and `filesize`, the file size in bytes of the file found. In iterations, we add this element to response element as child node.

- 305-309: We are calling the `Directory` class object's other function called `GetDirectories()`, passing it the `path` and `criteria`. This function returns an array of Directory objects for directories satisfying the given search criteria.

- 310-321: We are iterating through the retrieved array. In iterations, we are creating an XML element called `fileinfo` and setting its attributes. Attributes are `filename` and `mask` values of which will be the directory name of the directory found and mask value of the directory specified in the search criteria, respectively.

- 324: Here the response element is passed to `SaveAndCloseDocument()` to write this response XML element to a response `XMLDocument`.

- 325: If any exception is caught, it is passed to a `WriteErrorResponse()` function, which makes an XML response document with a response-type error that specifies the error message in the `errorinfo` element's attributes.

XMLParser Class

The entire coding in Listing 5-3 has been numbered and explained.

Listing 5-3: XML Parser Class

// © 2001 Dreamtech Software India Inc.
// All rights reserved

```
1  namespace WorkingWithXML
2  {
3    using System;            // Provides the basic functionality of .NET
4    using System.Net;        // Provides the net related functionality
5    using System.IO;         // Provides the I/O functionality
6    using System.Text;       // Provides text based manipulations
7
8    /// <summary>
9    ///   Generic structure used for parsing the XML data
10   ///   This structure composes of various sub structures
11   ///   Each sub structure represents and XML request in whole
12   ///   Every XML is parsed into its corresponding structure to
13   ///   fill its values TypeOfXMLRecieved() function of
14   ///   ServerCommunication class will determine that which structure
15   ///   has to be filled
16   /// </summary>
17   public struct XMLSTRUCT
18   {
19     /// <summary>
20     /// This structure is used to store the parsed
```

```
21      /// values of the AUTH XML which is returned
22      /// after login process
23      /// </summary>
24      public struct __AUTHENTICATION
25      {
26          /// <summary>
27          /// Stores the Code value in it 0(successful)
28          /// or 1(some error occured)
29          /// </summary>
30          public int iCode;
31
32          /// <summary>
33          /// This will stores the status of the login process
34          /// and any error message if occured while login
35          /// </summary>
36          public string sStatus;
37
38          /// <summary>
39          /// This is used for cross checking the IP address
40          /// which is sent to the server that login is successful
41          /// or not
42          /// </summary>
43          public string sIPAddress;
44      }
45
46      /// <summary>
47      /// This structure is used to store the List of all
48      /// the Listeners from the server that are currently
49      /// The values are returned in the USERLIST response XML
50      /// running
51      /// </summary>
52      public struct __USERLIST
53      {
54          /// <summary>
55          /// Name by which the Listener has logged in
56          /// </summary>
57          public string sUsername;
58
59          /// <summary>
60          /// IP Address of that Listener
61          /// </summary>
62          public string sIPAddress;
63      }
64
65      /// <summary>
66      /// This is used to store the values which are parsed
67      /// from the SHOWFILES response XML from the Listener
68      /// It contains the Files and Folders which are to
69      /// be shown to the user
70      /// </summary>
71      public struct __SHOWFILES
72      {
73          /// <summary>
74          /// Stores the Filename or Folder name
75          /// </summary>
76          public string sFilename;
```

```
77
78          /// <summary>
79          /// Stores the FileSize, 0 in case of folders
80          /// </summary>
81          public int          iFileSize;
82
83          /// <summary>
84          /// Mask stores the mask value of a file or folder
85          /// 0(readonly file/folder) 1(read/write access)
86          /// </summary>
87          public int          iMask;
88      }
89
90      /// <summary>
91      /// In case of any Error an ERROR response XML is
92      /// thrown from the Listener. The values are parsed into
93      /// this structure
94      /// </summary>
95      public struct __ERROR
96      {
97          /// <summary>
98          /// Stores the error code
99          /// </summary>
100         public int          iErrCode;
101
102         /// <summary>
103         /// Stores the severity of the error
104         /// Message or Warning or Error
105         /// </summary>
106         public string sSeverity;
107
108         /// <summary>
109         /// The actual error description is stored in this
110         /// variable
111         /// </summary>
112         public string sDescription;
113     }
114
115     /// <summary>
116     /// no XML parser has been made for this structure,
117     /// since it is not used in this version
118     /// </summary>
119     public struct __UPDNLOAD
120     {
121         public string sFilename;
122         public int          iMask;
123     }
124
125     /// <summary>
126     /// no XML parser has been made for this structure,
127     /// since it is not used in this version
128     /// </summary>
129     public struct __MESSAGE
130     {
131         public string sSenderName;
132         public string sMessage;
```

```
133          public string sIPAddress;
134    }
135
136    /// <summary>
137    /// this structure stores the values from the
138    /// SERVERSEARCH XML that is returned by the Server
139    /// as the result of search
140    /// </summary>
141    public struct __SERVERSEARCH
142    {
143        /// <summary>
144        /// IP address of the machine where the file or folder
145        /// is found
146        /// </summary>
147        public string sIPAddress;
148
149        /// <summary>
150        /// Username i.e login name of the machine
151        /// </summary>
152        public string sUsername;
153
154        /// <summary>
155        /// Name of the file found for search criteria is
156        /// in this variable
157        /// </summary>
158        public string sFilename;
159    }
160
161    /// <summary>
162    /// Global varibales which are used
163    /// in different parts of the code
164    /// for their specific structures
165    /// </summary>
166    public __AUTHENTICATION          AUTH;
167    public __USERLIST[]                    USERLIST;
168    public __SHOWFILES[]             SHOWFILES;
169    public __SHOWFILES[]             SEARCH;
170    public __SERVERSEARCH[]     SERVERSEARCH;
171    public __ERROR                        ERROR;
172    public __MESSAGE                 MESSAGE;
173    }
174
175    /// <summary>
176       ///      Summary description for clsXMLParser.
177       ///      This class is used to parse any XML that is received
178       ///      by the Listener of Browser(Client)
179       ///      and stores the values to their corresponding
180       ///      structures so that the application could use them
181       /// </summary>
182    public class XMLParser
183       {
184    /// <summary>
185    /// Stores the Filename to write when login response
186    /// when has arrived to the Browser
187    /// </summary>
188    public string                                        LOGINXML;
```

```
189
190    /// <summary>
191    /// Stores the Filename to write when USERLIST response
192    ///  has arrived to the Browser
193    /// </summary>
194    public string                                          USERLISTXML;
195
196    /// <summary>
197    /// Stores the Filename to write when SERVERSEARCH response
198    ///  has arrived to the Browser
199    /// </summary>
200    public string
SERVERSEARCHRESULTXML;
201
202    /// <summary>
203    /// stores the number of tags that are found
204    /// in the response XML
205    /// </summary>
206    protected int                                          iTags;
207
208    /// <summary>
209    /// Used to store the counter that is how many time
210    /// a loop is running
211    /// </summary>
212    protected int                                          iCounter;
213
214    /// <summary>
215    /// This document variable points to the XML documet
216    /// </summary>
217    protected MSXML2.IXMLDOMDocument          document;
218
219    /// <summary>
220    /// Points to the element of the XML document
221    /// </summary>
222    protected MSXML2.IXMLDOMElement               element;
223
224    /// <summary>
225    /// Points to the node of the XML
226    /// </summary>
227    protected MSXML2.IXMLDOMNode                      node, ChildNode;
228
229    /// <summary>
230    /// points to the node list of the XML document
231    /// Stores the node list of the XML
232    /// </summary>
233    protected MSXML2.IXMLDOMNodeList          nodeList;
234
235    /// <summary>
236    /// Stores the node map of the XML document
237    /// </summary>
238    protected MSXML2.IXMLDOMNamedNodeMap      nodeMap;
239
240    /// <summary>
241    /// Default constructor
242    /// </summary>
243    public XMLParser()
```

```
244              {
245              }
246
247     /// <summary>
248     /// Initialize some important variables
249     /// </summary>
250     protected void InitVariables()
251     {
252          iTags=0;
253          iCounter = 0;
254          document = new MSXML2.DOMDocument();
255     }
256
257     /// <summary>
258     /// This function is responsible for parsing the XML
259     /// Actually this function will call the exact parse function
260     /// depending upon the type of XML Received
261     /// </summary>
262     /// <param name="XMLFilename"> </param>
263     /// <param name="outStruct"> </param>
264     /// <param name="TagName"> </param>
265     public int ParseXML(string XMLFilename, out XMLSTRUCT outStruct, string
TagName)
266     {
267          // Declare and initializes the iElements to 0
268          int iElements = 0;
269
270          // Initializes the outStruct variable of this function
271          // this structure is used to store the values of parsed XML
272          outStruct = new XMLSTRUCT();
273
274          // The following 12 lines of code checks the Type of XML recieved
275          // and calls are made to the corresponding parser function
276          // which actually are reponsible for parsing the XML
277          // all the parse functions are user defined functions
278          // the Number of Parsed records are stores in the iElements
279          // variable which is returned by the function
280          if( 0 == TagName.CompareTo("AUTH") )
281                 iElements = ParseAUTHXML(XMLFilename, out outStruct);
282          else if( 0 == TagName.CompareTo("USERLIST") )
283                 iElements = ParseUSERLISTXML(XMLFilename, out outStruct);
284          else if( 0 == TagName.CompareTo("SHOWFILES") )
285                 iElements = ParseSHOWFILESXML(XMLFilename, out outStruct);
286          else if( 0 == TagName.CompareTo("SEARCH") )
287                 iElements = ParseSHOWFILESXML(XMLFilename, out outStruct);
288          else if( 0 == TagName.CompareTo("ERROR") )
289                 iElements = ParseERRORXML(XMLFilename, out outStruct);
290          else if( 0 == TagName.CompareTo("SERVERSEARCH") )
291                 iElements = ParseSERVERSEARCHXML(XMLFilename, out outStruct);
292          else if( 0 == TagName.CompareTo("CHAT") )
293                 iElements = ParseCHATXML(XMLFilename, out outStruct);
294
295          // Returns the iElements variable to the calling function
296          return iElements;
297     }
298
```

```
299    protected int ParseCHATXML(string Filename, out XMLSTRUCT outStruct)
300    {
301
302        // initializes all the required variables
303        InitVariables();
304
305        // Initialize outStruct variable of this function
306        outStruct = new XMLSTRUCT();
307
308        // Process the XML document syncronously
309        document.async = false;
310
311        // load the xml document in memory for parsing
312        if(document.load(Filename))
313        {
314            // get the first element of the XML
315            element = document.documentElement;
316
317            // get the first child of the element
318            node = element.firstChild;
319
320            // extracts the node list present under the node
321            nodeList = node.childNodes;
322
323            // iTags will assigns to the number of nodes present
324            // in node list
325            iTags = nodeList.length;
326
327            // Initialize the AUTH sructure of the outStruct
328            // variable
329            outStruct.MESSAGE = new XMLSTRUCT.__MESSAGE();
330
331            // move the node to the next node of the nodelist
332            node = nodeList.nextNode();
333
334            // Extract each value from its specific node
335            for(iCounter = 0; iCounter < iTags; iCounter++ )
336            {
337
338                // gets the attribute map that is how many attributes
339                // are present in the node
340                nodeMap = node.attributes;
341
342                // extract the next node from the node map
343                ChildNode = nodeMap.nextNode();
344
345                // The following 9 lines of code will extract the
346                // various attribute values from the XML node
347                // and fills it to the outStruct's corresponding
348                // structure
349                do
350                {
351                    if( 0 ==
ChildNode.nodeName.CompareTo("sendername")  )
352                        outStruct.MESSAGE.sSenderName =
ChildNode.nodeValue.ToString();
```

```
353                              else if( 0 ==
ChildNode.nodeName.CompareTo("chatmsg") )
354                                  outStruct.MESSAGE.sMessage =
ChildNode.nodeValue.ToString();
355                              else if( 0 ==
ChildNode.nodeName.CompareTo("ip") )
356                                  outStruct.MESSAGE.sIPAddress =
ChildNode.nodeValue.ToString();
357                      } while( null != (ChildNode = nodeMap.nextNode()) );
358
359                  // now move to next node
360                  node = nodeList.nextNode();
361          }
362      }
363
364      // Return the number of nodes parsed for the values
365      return iCounter==iTags?iCounter:0;
366  }
367
368  /// <summary>
369  /// Actual Parsing of AUTHENTICATION XML
370  /// </summary>
371  /// <param name="Filename"> </param>
372  /// <param name="outStruct"> </param>
373  protected int ParseAUTHXML(string Filename, out XMLSTRUCT outStruct)
374  {
375      // initializes all the required variables
376      InitVariables();
377
378      // Initialize outStruct variable of this function
379      outStruct = new XMLSTRUCT();
380
381      // Process the XML document syncronously
382      document.async = false;
383
384      // load the xml document in memory for parsing
385      if(document.load(Filename))
386      {
387          // get the first element of the XML
388          element = document.documentElement;
389
390          // get the first child of the element
391          node = element.firstChild;
392
393          // extracts the node list present under the node
394          nodeList = node.childNodes;
395
396          // iTags will assigns to the number of nodes present
397          // in node list
398          iTags = nodeList.length;
399
400          // Initialize the AUTH sructure of the outStruct
401          // variable
402          outStruct.AUTH = new XMLSTRUCT.__AUTHENTICATION();
403
404          // move the node to the next node of the nodelist
```

```
405                    node = nodeList.nextNode();
406
407                    // Extract each value from its specific node
408                    for(iCounter = 0; iCounter < iTags; iCounter++ )
409                    {
410
411                        // gets the attribute map that is how many attributes
412                        // are present in the node
413                        nodeMap = node.attributes;
414
415                        // extract the next node from the node map
416                        ChildNode = nodeMap.nextNode();
417
418                        // The following 9 lines of code will extract the
419                        // various attribute values from the XML node
420                        // and fills it to the outStruct's corresponding
421                        // structure
422                        do
423                        {
424                            if( 0 == ChildNode.nodeName.CompareTo("code") )
425                                outStruct.AUTH.iCode =
Convert.ToInt32(ChildNode.nodeValue);
426                            else if( 0 ==
ChildNode.nodeName.CompareTo("status") )
427                                outStruct.AUTH.sStatus =
ChildNode.nodeValue.ToString();
428                            else if( 0 ==
ChildNode.nodeName.CompareTo("ip") )
429                                outStruct.AUTH.sIPAddress =
ChildNode.nodeValue.ToString();
430                        } while( null != (ChildNode = nodeMap.nextNode()) );
431
432                        // now move to next node
433                        node = nodeList.nextNode();
434                    }
435            }
436
437        // Return the number of nodes parsed for the values
438        return iCounter==iTags?iCounter:0;
439    }
440
441    /// <summary>
442    /// Actual Parsing of USERLIST XML
443    /// </summary>
444    /// <param name="Filename"> </param>
445    /// <param name="outStruct"> </param>
446    protected int ParseUSERLISTXML(string Filename, out XMLSTRUCT outStruct)
447    {
448        // initializes all the required variables
449        InitVariables();
450
451        // Initialize outStruct variable of this function
452        outStruct = new XMLSTRUCT();
453
454        // Process the XML document syncronously
455        document.async = false;
```

```
456
457          // load the xml document in memory for parsing
458          if(document.load(Filename))
459          {
460                  // get the first element of the XML
461                  element = document.documentElement;
462
463                  // get the first child of the element
464                  node = element.firstChild;
465
466                  // extracts the node list present under the node
467                  nodeList = node.childNodes;
468
469                  // iTags will assigns to the number of nodes present
470                  // in node list
471                  iTags = nodeList.length;
472
473                  // Initialize the USERLIST sructure of the outStruct
474                  // variable
475                  outStruct.USERLIST = new XMLSTRUCT.__USERLIST[iTags];
476
477                  // move the node to the next node of the nodelist
478                  node = nodeList.nextNode();
479
480                  // Extract each value from its specific node
481                  for(iCounter = 0; iCounter < iTags; iCounter++ )
482                  {
483                          // gets the attribute map that is how many attributes
484                          // are present in the node
485                          nodeMap = node.attributes;
486
487                          // extract the next node from the node map
488                          ChildNode = nodeMap.nextNode();
489
490                          // The following 9 lines of code will extract the
491                          // various attribute values from the XML node
492                          // and fills it to the outStruct's corresponding
493                          // structure
494                          do
495                          {
496                                  if( 0 ==
ChildNode.nodeName.CompareTo("username")  )
497                                          outStruct.USERLIST[iCounter].sUsername =
ChildNode.nodeValue.ToString();
498                                  else if( 0 ==
ChildNode.nodeName.CompareTo("ip")  )
499                                          outStruct.USERLIST[iCounter].sIPAddress
= ChildNode.nodeValue.ToString();
500                          } while( null != (ChildNode = nodeMap.nextNode())  );
501
502                          // now move to next node
503                          node = nodeList.nextNode();
504                  }
505          }
506
507          // Return the number of nodes parsed for the values
```

```
508              return iCounter==iTags?iCounter:0;
509      }
510
511      /// <summary>
512      /// Actual Parsing of SERVERSEARCH XML
513      /// </summary>
514      /// <param name="Filename"> </param>
515      /// <param name="outStruct"> </param>
516      protected int ParseSERVERSEARCHXML(string Filename, out XMLSTRUCT
outStruct)
517      {
518              // initializes all the required variables
519              InitVariables();
520
521              // Initialize outStruct variable of this function
522              outStruct = new XMLSTRUCT();
523
524              // Process the XML document syncronously
525              document.async = false;
526
527              // load the xml document in memory for parsing
528              if(document.load(Filename))
529              {
530                      // get the first element of the XML
531                      element = document.documentElement;
532
533                      // get the first child of the element
534                      node = element.firstChild;
535
536                      // extracts the node list present under the node
537                      nodeList = node.childNodes;
538
539                      // iTags will assigns to the number of nodes present
540                      // in node list
541                      iTags = nodeList.length;
542
543                      // Initialize the SERVERSEARCH sructure of the outStruct
544                      // variable
545                      outStruct.SERVERSEARCH = new XMLSTRUCT.__SERVERSEARCH[iTags];
546
547                      // move the node to the next node of the nodelist
548                      node = nodeList.nextNode();
549
550                      // Extract each value from its specific node
551                      for(iCounter = 0; iCounter < iTags; iCounter++ )
552                      {
553                              // gets the attribute map that is how many attributes
554                              // are present in the node
555                              nodeMap = node.attributes;
556
557                              // extract the next node from the node map
558                              ChildNode = nodeMap.nextNode();
559
560                              // The following 9 lines of code will extract the
561                              // various attribute values from the XML node
562                              // and fills it to the outStruct's corresponding
```

```
563                          // structure
564                          do
565                          {
566                                  if( 0 == ChildNode.nodeName.CompareTo("ip") )
567
outStruct.SERVERSEARCH[iCounter].sIPAddress = ChildNode.nodeValue.ToString();
568                                  else if( 0 ==
ChildNode.nodeName.CompareTo("username") )
569
outStruct.SERVERSEARCH[iCounter].sUsername = ChildNode.nodeValue.ToString();
570                                  else if( 0 ==
ChildNode.nodeName.CompareTo("filename") )
571
outStruct.SERVERSEARCH[iCounter].sFilename = ChildNode.nodeValue.ToString();
572                          } while( null != (ChildNode = nodeMap.nextNode()) );
573
574                          // now move to next node
575                          node = nodeList.nextNode();
576                  }
577          }
578
579      // Return the number of nodes parsed for the values
580      return iCounter==iTags?iCounter:0;
581  }
582
583  /// <summary>
584  /// Actual Parsing of SHOWFILES XML
585  /// </summary>
586  /// <param name="Filename"> </param>
587  /// <param name="outStruct"> </param>
588  protected int ParseSHOWFILESXML(string Filename, out XMLSTRUCT outStruct)
589  {
590      // initializes all the required variables
591      InitVariables();
592
593      // Initialize outStruct variable of this function
594      outStruct = new XMLSTRUCT();
595
596      // Process the XML document syncronously
597      document.async = false;
598
599      // load the xml document in memory for parsing
600      if(document.load(Filename))
601      {
602              // get the first element of the XML
603              element = document.documentElement;
604
605              // get the first child of the element
606              node = element.firstChild;
607
608              // extracts the node list present under the node
609              nodeList = node.childNodes;
610
611              // iTags will assigns to the number of nodes present
612              // in node list
613              iTags = nodeList.length;
```

```
614
615                    // Initialize the SHOWFILES sructure of the outStruct
616                    // variable
617                    outStruct.SHOWFILES = new XMLSTRUCT.__SHOWFILES[iTags];
618
619                    // move the node to the next node of the nodelist
620                    node = nodeList.nextNode();
621
622                    // Extract each value from its specific node
623                    for(iCounter = 0; iCounter < iTags; iCounter++ )
624                    {
625                            // gets the attribute map that is how many attributes
626                            // are present in the node
627                            nodeMap = node.attributes;
628
629                            // extract the next node from the node map
630                            ChildNode = nodeMap.nextNode();
631
632                            // The following 9 lines of code will extract the
633                            // various attribute values from the XML node
634                            // and fills it to the outStruct's corresponding
635                            // structure
636                            do
637                            {
638                                    if( 0 ==
ChildNode.nodeName.CompareTo("filename") )
639                                            outStruct.SHOWFILES[iCounter].sFilename
= ChildNode.nodeValue.ToString();
640                                    else if( 0 ==
ChildNode.nodeName.CompareTo("mask") )
641                                            outStruct.SHOWFILES[iCounter].iMask =
Convert.ToInt32(ChildNode.nodeValue);
642                                    else if( 0 ==
ChildNode.nodeName.CompareTo("filesize") )
643                                            outStruct.SHOWFILES[iCounter].iFileSize
= Convert.ToInt32(ChildNode.nodeValue);
644                            } while( null != (ChildNode = nodeMap.nextNode()) );
645
646                            // now move to next node
647                            node = nodeList.nextNode();
648                    }
649            }
650
651        // Return the number of nodes parsed for the values
652        return iCounter==iTags?iCounter:0;
653    }
654
655    /// <summary>
656    /// Actual Parsing of ERROR XML
657    /// </summary>
658    /// <param name="Filename"> </param>
659    /// <param name="outStruct"> </param>
660    protected int ParseERRORXML(string Filename, out XMLSTRUCT outStruct)
661    {
662        // initializes all the required variables
663        InitVariables();
```

```
664
665             // Initialize outStruct variable of this function
666             outStruct = new XMLSTRUCT();
667
668             // Process the XML document syncronously
669             document.async = false;
670
671             // load the xml document in memory for parsing
672             if(document.load(Filename))
673             {
674                     // get the first element of the XML
675                     element = document.documentElement;
676
677                     // get the first child of the element
678                     node = element.firstChild;
679
680                     // extracts the node list present under the node
681                     nodeList = node.childNodes;
682
683                     // iTags will assigns to the number of nodes present
684                     // in node list
685                     iTags = nodeList.length;
686
687                     // Initialize the ERROR sructure of the outStruct
688                     // variable
689                     outStruct.ERROR = new XMLSTRUCT.__ERROR();
690
691                     // move the node to the next node of the nodelist
692                     node = nodeList.nextNode();
693
694                     // Extract each value from its specific node
695                     for(iCounter = 0; iCounter < iTags; iCounter++ )
696                     {
697                             // gets the attribute map that is how many attributes
698                             // are present in the node
699                             nodeMap = node.attributes;
700
701                             // extract the next node from the node map
702                             ChildNode = nodeMap.nextNode();
703
704                             // The following 9 lines of code will extract the
705                             // various attribute values from the XML node
706                             // and fills it to the outStruct's corresponding
707                             // structure
708                             do
709                             {
710                                     if( 0 == ChildNode.nodeName.CompareTo("code") )
711                                             outStruct.ERROR.iErrCode =
Convert.ToInt32(ChildNode.nodeValue);
712                                     else if( 0 ==
ChildNode.nodeName.CompareTo("severity") )
713                                             outStruct.ERROR.sSeverity =
ChildNode.nodeValue.ToString();
714                                     else if( 0 ==
ChildNode.nodeName.CompareTo("description") )
```

```
715                              outStruct.ERROR.sDescription =
ChildNode.nodeValue.ToString();
716                    } while( null != (ChildNode = nodeMap.nextNode()) );
717
718                // now move to next node
719                node = nodeList.nextNode();
720           }
721       }
722
723       // Return the number of nodes parsed for the values
724       return iCounter==iTags?iCounter:0;
725   }
726    }
}
```

Code description of XML Parser class (clsXMLParser.cs)

- ◆ Lines 3-6: This includes the basic packages needed for the various classes used to build this application. This includes packages used for communicating with the network, streaming facility, file I/O, text manipulations, and so on.

- ◆ Lines 17-173: This declares the structure of the public type named XMLSTRUCT. This structure is used while parsing XML data. This structure is composed of various substructures and represents an XML request in whole. Every XML is parsed into its corresponding structure to fill its value. The TypeOfXMLReceived() function of the ServerCommunication class, determines which structures have to be filled by the response XML returned by the server or listener.

  - • 24-44: This __AUTHENTICATION structure is used to store the parsed XML values of the AUTH XML, which is returned after login.

  - • 52-62: This __USERLIST structure is used to store the parsed XML values of the USERLIST XML, which is returned after calling the user-list ASP on the server.

  - • 71-88: This __SHOWFILES structure is used to store the parsed XML values of the XML, which is returned after the SHOWFILES request has been sent to the listener.

  - • 95-113: This __ERROR structure is used to store the parsed XML values of the error XML, which is returned if any error has occurred at the listener end while making a response to the request.

  - • 119-134: These two structures are not used in this application. They are kept here for future expandability. You may use these structures as needed. The __MESSAGE structure here can be used for integrating an instant-messaging client to this application. No XML parser function is associated with any of these functions.

  - • 140-159: This __SERVERSEARCH structure is used to have the parsed values, which result from the server after calling the search.asp on the server. This structure contains server-search results.

  - • 166-173: Variables for these structures are declared here. These variables are globally accessible in this application.

- ◆ Lines 182: This is the declaration of the XMLParser class.

- ◆ Lines 188-238: Some global variables used in this application are declared here.

  - • 188: LOGINXML stores the name of the response file, which is generated after login.

  - • 194: USERLISTXML stores the name of the response file, which is after requesting for the list of the currently running listeners.

  - • 200: SERVERSEARCHXML stores the name of the response file, which generated after the search process is completed on the server and response data has been sent.

  - • 206: iTags stores the number of tags present in any XML response.

- 212: iCounter is used for bookkeeping purposes here.

- 217: The MSXML2.IXMLDOMDocument document is used to point toward the XML document reference.

- 222: The MSXML2.IXMLDOMElement element is used to point toward the single XML element reference.

- 227: The MSXML2.IXMLDOMNode node, ChildNode, is used to point toward the XML document's main node and its child nodes.

- 233: The MSXML2.IXMLDOMNodeList nodeList is used to point toward the number of nodes in an XML document.

- 238: The MSXML2.IXMLDOMNodeMap nodeMap is used to point toward the map of the nodes present inside an XML document.

- ◆ Lines 243-245: This is for the implementation of the default constructor of this XMLParser class.

- ◆ Lines 250-255: This function is used to initialize the three variables every time it is called.

- ◆ Lines 265-297: This function is called many times in this application. It is used to parse the XML document. Actually for the reason that parsing becomes simple for the user to understand only a single parse function is made to handle every parse request. This function determines the type of XML received from the server or listener and then calls the appropriate function for parsing that XML. It only acts as a router. This function takes three parameters: the name of the XML file to parse, the reference to the structure passed to the actual parse function, and the tag name so that the actual parse function associated with that tag is called.

  - 272: The outStruct variable is initialized here.

  - 280-297 In these lines, the type of XML received is checked. The XML is then passed to the corresponding user-defined parse functions for parsing. The number of parsed records is stored in iElements variable, which is returned by the function after filling the outStruct variable.

- ◆ Lines 299-366: This function processes the parsing of CHATXML.

  - 302-311: In these lines, required variables are initialized. In line 309, document.async property is set to false to process the document synchronously.

  - 312-325: Here the XML document is loaded into memory for parsing. Then the first element of XML is retrieved, followed by retrieval of the first child of the element. Once the first element and its child element are extracted, the node list present under the node is fetched, and the number of fetches is assigned to the iTags variable.

  - 329-332: The MESSAGE structure of the outStruct variable is initialized. The next is to the control to the next node of the node list, meanwhile storing it into the node variable, which points toward the current node.

  - 355-343: Each value is extracted from specific node while getting the attribute map, which indicates how many attributes are present in the node. This process goes on by moving to the next node map.

  - 349-358: Various attributes' values from the XML node are extracted, filled into the outStruct structure, and move to next node.

  - 365: The number of nodes parsed for the values are returned by the iCounter variable, which counts how many times the loop has run and has been returned by the function.

The following functions carry out the same things. Every line in these functions is the same as the preceding lines. The only difference is that the functions fill their corresponding structures after parsing the values. The parsing logic of these functions is same as described previously.

Login Form

namespace: Listener

The name of the following class is frmLogin, which performs the entire task of listening for what browsers connecting to it are demanding and responding appropriately. This class also handles the life cycles of the login form (described in following paragraphs) and the listener's existence on the tray icon.

Figure 5-1 shows the first form that opens when you start the listener application to log to the server. After the logging process is successful, this form disappears, and only the tray icon remains to indicate that the listener is running.

Figure 5-1: The dialog box that opens when the user starts the listener application

- ♦ **Login:** After typing in the LoginID in the text box given, clicking this button logs in to the server.
- ♦ **Share Files/Folder:** This button opens a Share Files/Folders dialog (explained later) for you to share files or folders with other peers.
- ♦ **Quit:** Quit closes the application.

The tray icon in Figure 5-2 shows that the listener is running once the login form is closed and provides you with Quit and Share Files/Folders options in the Short-Cut menu when you right-click it (see Figure 5-3).

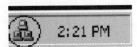

Figure 5-2: The tray icon

Figure 5-3: Quit and Share Files/Folders options.

- ♦ **Quit**: This logs out and quits the application.
- ♦ **Share Files/Folder**: This option opens a Share Files/Folders dialog (explained later) for you to share your files or folders with other peers.

The entire coding in Listing 5-4 has been numbered and explained in this regard.

Listing 5-4: frmLogin

```
1 namespace Listener
2 {
3  // Library includes
4  using System;
5  using System.Drawing;
6  using System.Collections;
7  using System.ComponentModel;
8  using System.Windows.Forms;
9  using System.Net;
   // added for httprequest and responses and hostname resolving
10  using System.IO;                // added for file streaming
11  using System.Text;              // added for text encodings
12  using WorkingWithXML;
13  using System.Net.Sockets;
14  using System.Threading;
15  using System.Runtime.InteropServices;
16  using System.Windows.Forms.Design;
17
18  public class frmLogin : System.Windows.Forms.Form
19  {
20      Socket newSock;
21      [DllImport("Shell32.dll")]
22      public static extern int ShellExecute(int hwnd,
23              string lpVerb,
24              string lpFile,
25              string lpParameters,
26              string lpDirectory,
27              int nShowCmd );
28
29      // State maintainig variables;
30      private bool bLoggedIn;
31      private int IconNo;
32      private bool bShareDialogOpend;
33      private bool bDownLoading;
34
35
36      private Byte[] buffer;
37      private string LoginName;
38      private int ChatWindowCount;
39      //    Variable required in communication with server
40      private ServerCommunication xmlServerComm;
41
42      //    Communcation facilitators on sockets.
43
44      private Socket servSock;
45
46
47      //    Xml requests and responses are created using these objects
48      private XMLCreater xmlCreater;
49      private XMLParser  xmlParser;
50
51      //    Threads of this application's being.
```

```
52          //    Threads for continious update on sys tray
53          //    and for continuous seeking of  connections
54          //    from browsers, respectively.
55      private Thread AcceptThread,ThreadIcon,RespondingThread;
56      private System.ComponentModel.IContainer components;
57      private System.Windows.Forms.Label lbCopyright;
58      private System.Windows.Forms.ToolTip toolTip1;
59      private System.Windows.Forms.MenuItem ctxMenuShare;
60      private System.Windows.Forms.MenuItem ctxMenuQuit;
61      private System.Windows.Forms.TextBox textLoginID;
62      private System.Windows.Forms.Button btnShareFileFolder;
63      private System.Windows.Forms.Label labelLoginID;
64      private System.Windows.Forms.CheckBox chkRemeberID;
65      private System.Windows.Forms.Button btnLogin;
66      private System.Windows.Forms.Button btnQuit;
67      private System.Windows.Forms.MenuItem menuItem1;
68      private System.Windows.Forms.MenuItem ListenCntxtMenu;
69      private System.Windows.Forms.TextBox textBox1;
70      private System.Windows.Forms.NotifyIcon ListenIcon;
71      private System.Windows.Forms.ContextMenu contextMenu;
72      private System.Windows.Forms.Button button1;
73
74      // First functions that gets called in this form's life cycle
75      // Initailizes all the GUI controls and reads username last
76      //used, if any and puts that on the form.
77      public frmLogin()
78      {
79          InitializeComponent();
80          // initialise objects getting used while communication
81          // and parsing
82          xmlServerComm = new WorkingWithXML.ServerCommunication();
83          xmlParser = new WorkingWithXML.XMLParser();
84          xmlParser.LOGINXML = Application.StartupPath + "\\Login.xml";
85          textLoginID.Text = ReadUsername();
86          bLoggedIn                = false;
87          bShareDialogOpend    = false;
88          bDownLoading         = false;
89          IconNo               = 1;
90          ChatWindowCount      = 0;
91          LoginName            = "";
92          AcceptThread         = null;
93          ThreadIcon                = null;
94          RespondingThread     = null;
95      }
96
97      // Reads user name and returns that to the caller
98      public string ReadUsername()
99      {
100         string Username, sTemp;
101         Username = null;
102         if ( File.Exists(Application.StartupPath +
                 "\\UserInfo.ini") )
103         {
104             // open userinof.ini file and read user name
105             Stream fstr = File.OpenRead(Application.StartupPath +
                     "\\UserInfo.ini");
```

```
106             Byte[] buffer = new Byte[Convert.ToInt32(fstr.Length)];
107             fstr.Read(buffer,0,Convert.ToInt32(fstr.Length));
108             sTemp = Encoding.ASCII.GetString(buffer,0,
                    Convert.ToInt32(buffer.Length));
109             Username = sTemp.Substring(sTemp.IndexOf("=")+1);
110             chkRemeberID.Checked = true;
111             fstr.Close();
112         }
113         else
114             chkRemeberID.Checked = false;
115         return Username;
116     }
117
118     // Writes user name to  file for next instantiation
119     public void WriteUsername()
120     {
121         string buffer = "username=";
122         Stream fstr = File.OpenWrite(Application.StartupPath +
"\\UserInfo.ini");
123         buffer += textLoginID.Text;
124         fstr.Write(Encoding.ASCII.GetBytes(buffer),0,buffer.Length);
125         fstr.Close();
126     }
127
128         ///  Clean up resources this application was using.
129         public override void Dispose()
130         {
131             base.Dispose();
132             components.Dispose();
133         }
134
135         /// Required method for Designer support - do not modify
136         /// the contents of this method with the code editor.
137         private void InitializeComponent()
138     {
139         this.components = new System.ComponentModel.Container();
140         System.Resources.ResourceManager resources = new
System.Resources.ResourceManager(typeof(frmLogin));
141         this.contextMenu = new System.Windows.Forms.ContextMenu();
142         this.ctxMenuQuit = new System.Windows.Forms.MenuItem();
143         this.ctxMenuShare = new System.Windows.Forms.MenuItem();
144         this.ListenIcon = new
System.Windows.Forms.NotifyIcon(this.components);
145         this.textBox1 = new System.Windows.Forms.TextBox();
146         this.button1 = new System.Windows.Forms.Button();
147         this.menuItem1 = new System.Windows.Forms.MenuItem();
148         this.btnQuit = new System.Windows.Forms.Button();
149         this.btnLogin = new System.Windows.Forms.Button();
150         this.labelLoginID = new System.Windows.Forms.Label();
151         this.toolTip1 = new System.Windows.Forms.ToolTip(this.components);
152         this.btnShareFileFolder = new System.Windows.Forms.Button();
153         this.textLoginID = new System.Windows.Forms.TextBox();
154         this.chkRemeberID = new System.Windows.Forms.CheckBox();
155         this.ListenCntxtMenu = new System.Windows.Forms.MenuItem();
156         this.lbCopyright = new System.Windows.Forms.Label();
157         this.SuspendLayout();
```

```
158     //
159     // contextMenu
160     //
161     this.contextMenu.MenuItems.AddRange(new
        System.Windows.Forms.MenuItem[] {
162
                          this.ctxMenuQuit,
163
                          this.ctxMenuShare});
164     //
165     // ctxMenuQuit
166     //
167     this.ctxMenuQuit.Index = 0;
168     this.ctxMenuQuit.Text = "Quit";
169     this.ctxMenuQuit.Click += new
        System.EventHandler(this.ctxMenuQuit_Click);
170     //
171     // ctxMenuShare
172     //
173     this.ctxMenuShare.Index = 1;
174     this.ctxMenuShare.Text = "Share File/Folders";
175     this.ctxMenuShare.Click += new
        System.EventHandler(this.ctxMenuShare_Click);
176     //
177     // ListenIcon
178     //
179     this.ListenIcon.ContextMenu = this.contextMenu;
180     this.ListenIcon.Icon =
        ((System.Drawing.Icon)(resources.GetObject("ListenIcon.Icon")));
181     this.ListenIcon.Text = "Peering Peers";
182     this.ListenIcon.Visible = true;
183     //
184     // textBox1
185     //
186     this.textBox1.Location = new System.Drawing.Point(895, 211);
187     this.textBox1.Name = "textBox1";
188     this.textBox1.TabIndex = 6;
189     this.textBox1.Text = "";
190     this.textBox1.Visible = false;
191     this.textBox1.WordWrap = false;
192     //
193     // button1
194     //
195     this.button1.Location = new System.Drawing.Point(450, 72);
196     this.button1.Name = "button1";
197     this.button1.TabIndex = 7;
198     this.button1.Visible = false;
199     //
200     // menuItem1
201     //
202     this.menuItem1.Index = -1;
203     this.menuItem1.Text = "";
204     //
205     // btnQuit
206     //
207     this.btnQuit.BackColor = System.Drawing.SystemColors.Control;
```

```
208        this.btnQuit.DialogResult = System.Windows.Forms.DialogResult.Cancel;
209        this.btnQuit.Location = new System.Drawing.Point(349, 145);
210        this.btnQuit.Name = "btnQuit";
211        this.btnQuit.Size = new System.Drawing.Size(75, 24);
212        this.btnQuit.TabIndex = 5;
213        this.btnQuit.Text = "Quit";
214        this.toolTip1.SetToolTip(this.btnQuit, "Quit and Close");
215        this.btnQuit.Click += new System.EventHandler(this.btnQuit_Click);
216        //
217        // btnLogin
218        //
219        this.btnLogin.BackColor =
           System.Drawing.Color.FromArgb(((System.Byte)(192)),
           ((System.Byte)(192)), ((System.Byte)(0)));
220        this.btnLogin.DialogResult = System.Windows.Forms.DialogResult.OK;
221        this.btnLogin.Font = new System.Drawing.Font(
           "Microsoft Sans Serif", 9F, System.Drawing.FontStyle.Bold,
                   System.Drawing.GraphicsUnit.Point, ((System.Byte)(0)));
222        this.btnLogin.ForeColor = System.Drawing.Color.LemonChiffon;
223        this.btnLogin.Location = new System.Drawing.Point(74, 76);
224        this.btnLogin.Name = "btnLogin";
225        this.btnLogin.Size = new System.Drawing.Size(83, 29);
226        this.btnLogin.TabIndex = 4;
227        this.btnLogin.Text = "Login";
228        this.toolTip1.SetToolTip(this.btnLogin,
                   "Log-in with this LoginID.");
229        this.btnLogin.Click += new System.EventHandler(this.btnLogin_Click);
230        //
231        // labelLoginID
232        //
233        this.labelLoginID.Location = new System.Drawing.Point(18, 30);
234        this.labelLoginID.Name = "labelLoginID";
235        this.labelLoginID.Size = new System.Drawing.Size(54, 14);
236        this.labelLoginID.TabIndex = 2;
237        this.labelLoginID.Text = "Login ID :";
238        //
239        // btnShareFileFolder
240        //
241        this.btnShareFileFolder.BackColor =
                   System.Drawing.SystemColors.Control;
242        this.btnShareFileFolder.Location = new System.Drawing.Point(199,
145);
243        this.btnShareFileFolder.Name = "btnShareFileFolder";
244        this.btnShareFileFolder.Size = new System.Drawing.Size(143, 24);
245        this.btnShareFileFolder.TabIndex = 1;
246        this.btnShareFileFolder.Text = "Share Files/Folders";
247        this.toolTip1.SetToolTip(this.btnShareFileFolder,
                   "Share your folders with other peers");
248        this.btnShareFileFolder.Click += new
                   System.EventHandler(this.btnShareFileFolder_Click);
249        //
250        // textLoginID
251        //
252        this.textLoginID.Location = new System.Drawing.Point(74, 28);
253        this.textLoginID.Name = "textLoginID";
254        this.textLoginID.Size = new System.Drawing.Size(281, 20);
```

```
255        this.textLoginID.TabIndex = 0;
256        this.textLoginID.Text = "";
257        this.toolTip1.SetToolTip(this.textLoginID,
               "Write your Login name here.");
258        //
259        // chkRemeberID
260        //
261        this.chkRemeberID.Location = new System.Drawing.Point(74, 54);
262        this.chkRemeberID.Name = "chkRemeberID";
263        this.chkRemeberID.Size = new System.Drawing.Size(134, 18);
264        this.chkRemeberID.TabIndex = 3;
265        this.chkRemeberID.Text = "Remeber My Login ID";
266        this.toolTip1.SetToolTip(this.chkRemeberID,
               "System will remember LoginID.");
267        //
268        // ListenCntxtMenu
269        //
270        this.ListenCntxtMenu.Index = -1;
271        this.ListenCntxtMenu.Text = "";
272        //
273        // lbCopyright
274        //
275        this.lbCopyright.Location = new System.Drawing.Point(226, 6);
276        this.lbCopyright.Name = "lbCopyright";
277        this.lbCopyright.Size = new System.Drawing.Size(196, 12);
278        this.lbCopyright.TabIndex = 8;
279        this.lbCopyright.Text = "© 2001 www.dreamtechsoftware.com";
280        //
281        // frmLogin
282        //
283        this.AcceptButton = this.btnLogin;
284        this.AutoScaleBaseSize = new System.Drawing.Size(5, 13);
285        this.CancelButton = this.btnQuit;
286        this.ClientSize = new System.Drawing.Size(438, 181);
287        this.ContextMenu = this.contextMenu;
288        this.Controls.AddRange(new System.Windows.Forms.Control[] {
289        this.lbCopyright,
290        this.textLoginID,
291        this.btnShareFileFolder,
292        this.labelLoginID,
293        this.chkRemeberID,
294        this.btnLogin,
295        this.btnQuit,
296        this.textBox1,
297        this.button1});
298        this.Font = new System.Drawing.Font("Microsoft Sans Serif", 8F,
               System.Drawing.FontStyle.Bold);
299        this.ForeColor = System.Drawing.Color.Black;
300        this.FormBorderStyle =
               System.Windows.Forms.FormBorderStyle.FixedDialog;
301        this.Icon =
               ((System.Drawing.Icon)(resources.GetObject("$this.Icon")));
302        this.MaximizeBox = false;
303        this.Name = "frmLogin";
304        this.StartPosition =
               System.Windows.Forms.FormStartPosition.CenterParent;
```

```
305          this.Text = "Peering Peers";
306          this.TransparencyKey = System.Drawing.Color.Olive;
307          this.Closing += new
                     System.ComponentModel.CancelEventHandler(
                         this.frmLogin_Closing);
308          this.ResumeLayout(false);
309
310     }
311
312     // Quit clicked pack up, clean up and leave, and yes
313     // inform server calling "Logout()".
314     protected void ctxMenuQuit_Click (object sender, System.EventArgs e)
315     {
316          Logout();
317          this.Dispose();
318          this.Close();
319          Application.Exit();
320     }
321
322     // Time to be kind to share resoures with others
323     // through "Share Files/Folders" dialog box
324     protected void ctxMenuShare_Click (object sender, System.EventArgs e)
325     {
326          if(!bShareDialogOpend)
327          {
328              // open this dialog box only if it is not opened already
329              bShareDialogOpend = true;
330              // make and object of frmSelection form and show it
331              frmSelection formSelection = new frmSelection();
332              formSelection.ShowDialog();
333              bShareDialogOpend = false;
334          }
335     }
336
337     // another way of popping-up the "Share Files/Folders" dialog box just
338     // in case u didn't like the first one
339     protected void btnShareFileFolder_Click (object sender,
            System.EventArgs e)
340     {
341          frmSelection formSelection = new frmSelection();
342          formSelection.ShowDialog();
343     }
344
345     // Quit clicked pack up, clean up and leave.
346     protected void btnQuit_Click (object sender, System.EventArgs e)
347     {
348          Logout();
349          this.Dispose();
350          this.Close();
351          Application.Exit();
352     }
353
354     // Unless u log-in the log book on server u dont exist for browser
355     protected void btnLogin_Click (object sender, System.EventArgs e)
356     {
357          string ServerAddress;
```

```
358          // URL for ASP to pass on your information to server
359          ServerAddress = "http://webaddress/login.asp?USERID=" +
                  textLoginID.Text + "&IP=" + xmlServerComm.GetIPAddress("");
360          XMLSTRUCT xmlStruct;
361          LoginName = textLoginID.Text;
362
363          try
364          {
365                  if( 0 != textLoginID.Text.Trim().Length )
366                  {
367                          string Share = "";
368
369      // if remember user name check box's checked write username to
"userinfo.ini"
370                          if( chkRemeberID.Checked ) WriteUsername();
371
372                          // else delete that file as it is no longer needed
373                          else xmlServerComm.FileDelete(Application.StartupPath
                                  +"\\Userinfo.ini");
374
375                          // if u had never shared anything set SHARE parameter
to ASP to empty
376                          if( !
File.Exists(Application.StartupPath+"\\Share.ini")  )
377                                  Share = "";
378                          else
379                          {
380                  // else read share.ini and read all the files and folders
381                          // u had shared and set them to SHARE parameter
382                          StreamReader stReader = new
                                  StreamReader(Application.StartupPath
                                  +"\\Share.ini");
383                          string readData;
384                          while((readData = stReader.ReadLine()) != null)
385                          {
386                                  if(!readData.Substring(0,
                                  readData.IndexOf("=")).EndsWith("\\"))
387                                          Share += readData.Substring(0,
                                  readData.IndexOf("=")).Substring(
                                          readData.Substring(0,readData.IndexOf(
                                          "=")).LastIndexOf("\\")+1) + "*";
388                                  else
389                                          Share +=
                                  readData.Substring(0,readData.IndexOf(
                                          "=")) + "*";
390                          }
391                          stReader.Close();
392                          }
393
394                  ServerAddress += "&SHARE=" + Share;
395
396      // make a call to loging.asp and recieve the response in an XML file
397                          xmlServerComm.WriteDataToFile(
                                  xmlParser.LOGINXML,
                                          xmlServerComm.GetDataFromServer(
                                          ServerAddress));
```

```
398
399                    // parse that file and store in XMLSTRUCT
400                    xmlParser.ParseXML(xmlParser.LOGINXML,out xmlStruct,
                            xmlServerComm.TypeOfXMLRecieved(
                            xmlParser.LOGINXML));
401                    // delete XML file
402                    xmlServerComm.FileDelete(xmlParser.LOGINXML);
403
404                    // now check whether login was successful
405                    if( 0 == xmlStruct.AUTH.iCode )
406                    {
407
408                            buffer = new Byte[256];
409
410                            servSock = new Socket(
                                    AddressFamily.InterNetwork,
411                                    SocketType.Stream,
412                                    ProtocolType.Tcp);
413
414                    // if successfull make a socket giving the IP and port
415                            IPAddress localIP = IPAddress.Parse((
                                    xmlServerComm.GetIPAddress("")));
416                            IPEndPoint localEP = new IPEndPoint(
                                    localIP,7070);
417                            servSock.Bind(localEP);
418                            servSock.Listen(40);
419
420
421                            AcceptThread = new Thread( new ThreadStart(
                                    AcceptFunction));
422
423                            AcceptThread.Start();
424
425                    // make a new thread to keep updating the icons on sys tray
426                            ThreadIcon = new Thread( new ThreadStart(IconUpdate));
427                            ThreadIcon.Priority = ThreadPriority.BelowNormal;
428                            ThreadIcon.Start();
429
430                            // hide the login form
431                            this.Hide();
432                    }
433                    else
434                    {
435                            // if unsuccessful show user the error occured
436                            MessageBox.Show(xmlStruct.AUTH.sStatus,
                                    "Peering Peers",MessageBoxButtons.OK,
                                    MessageBoxIcon.Information);
437                            textLoginID.Focus();
438                            textLoginID.SelectAll();
439                    }
440            }
441          else
442          {
443                    // before actually writing your username u cannot
loggin
444                    MessageBox.Show("Blank LoginID detected",
```

```
                                "Peering Peers",MessageBoxButtons.OK,
                                MessageBoxIcon.Error);
445                     textLoginID.Focus();
446                     textLoginID.SelectAll();
447             }
448     }
449     catch( Exception err )
450     {
451             // if logging fails tell user why it did
452             // "Could'nt Login."
453             MessageBox.Show(err.Message,
                        "Peering Peers",MessageBoxButtons.OK,
                        MessageBoxIcon.Error);
454             // and close application
455             this.Dispose();
456             this.Close();
457             Application.Exit();
458     }
459     // declare that logging process's successful
460     bLoggedIn = true;
461 }
462
463 // keep updating ur looks to avoid being overlooked
464 protected void IconUpdate()
465 {
466     try
467     {
468             while(true)
469             {
470                     IconNo += 1;
471
472                     string Filename;
473                     // if something's getting downloaded or uploaded
474                     // pick different icons to put on sys tray.
475                     if(bDownLoading)
476                     {
477                             if((IconNo) == 5)
478                                     IconNo = 1;
479                             Filename = "\\Trans" + IconNo.ToString() +
                                        ".ico";
480                             ListenIcon.Text =
                                        "Downloading or Uploading in Progress";
481                     }
482                     else
483                     {
484             // otherwise keep cycling these four icons on sys tray.
485                             if((IconNo) == 5)
486                                     IconNo = 1;
487                             Filename = "\\Listener" +
                                        IconNo.ToString() + ".ico";
488                             ListenIcon.Text = "Peering Peers";
489                     }
490                     System.Drawing.Icon icon = new System.Drawing.Icon(
                        Application.StartupPath + Filename);
491                     ListenIcon.Icon = icon;
492                     // make the process a bit slow for user to be able to
```

```
493                          // notice it
494                          System.Threading.Thread.Sleep(500);
495                  }
496          }
497          catch(Exception e) { WriteErrorLog(
                     "Updating Sys-tray icon.",e.Message); }
498  }
499
500      // Keep a log of all the exceptions and errors.
501      protected void WriteErrorLog(string Origin, string Message)
502      {
503          StreamWriter stWriter = File.AppendText(Application.StartupPath +
                     "\\Error.log");
504          // write the time of occurence of this error
505          stWriter.WriteLine("Origin = " + Origin +
506                  "            Date & Time (ms-s-m-h  dd/mm/yy/) = "+
507                  DateTime.Now.Millisecond.ToString() +
508                  "-" +
509                  DateTime.Now.Second.ToString() +
510                  "-" +
511                  DateTime.Now.Minute.ToString() +
512                  "-" +
513                  DateTime.Now.Hour.ToString() +
514                  "       " +
515                  DateTime.Now.Day.ToString() +
516                  "/" +
517                  DateTime.Now.Month.ToString() +
518                  "/" +
519                  DateTime.Now.Year.ToString() +
520                  "            Error Message = " + Message);
521
522          stWriter.Close();
523      }
524
525  // Form closing, dispose all the resources used and Exit the Application
526      protected void frmLogin_Closing (object sender,
                         System.ComponentModel.CancelEventArgs e)
527      {
528          Logout();
529
530          this.Dispose();
531          this.Close();
532
533          Application.Exit();
534      }
535
536      // Keeps accepting connections
537      protected void AcceptFunction()
538      {
539          try
540          {
541                  while(true)
542                  {
543                          newSock = servSock.Accept();
544
545                          RespondingThread = new Thread(new
```

```
                                      ThreadStart(RequestResponse));
546                    RespondingThread.Priority = ThreadPriority.Highest;
547                    RespondingThread.Start();
548              }
549       }catch( Exception e ) { WriteErrorLog(
          "Client's attempt of establishing connection failed.",e.Message); }
550  }
551
552  // Respond to the requests made
553  protected void RequestResponse()
554  {
555       Encoding ASCII = Encoding.ASCII;
556       NetworkStream DataStream = new NetworkStream(newSock);
557
558       try
559       {
560              Byte[] readBytes = new Byte[1024],read = new Byte[1024];
561              string[] ChatInfo;
562
563              int bytes = 0,UploadDownloadPrint;
564              bool responseWritten = false;
565              FileStream fs1 = null;
566
567              // read what the browser wrote on its stream and
568              bytes = DataStream.Read(read, 0, read.Length);
569              // make a temporary file
570              FileStream fs = new FileStream(Application.StartupPath +
                        "\\Temp.xml", FileMode.OpenOrCreate);
571
572              // to store that data to
573              BinaryWriter w = new BinaryWriter(fs);
574              w.Write(read, 0, bytes);
575              w.Close();
576              fs.Close();
577
578              // then read file and determine the kind of request
579              xmlCreater = new XMLCreater(Application.StartupPath +
                        "\\Temp1.xml",Application.StartupPath +
                        "\\Share.ini");
580              string DnLoadFile =
                 xmlCreater.DetermineRequestType(Application.StartupPath +
                 "\\Temp.xml",out UploadDownloadPrint,out ChatInfo);
581
582              // if it's download/upload request make file object for
583              // the file browser has requested to upload to
584              // or download from his comp
585              if(DnLoadFile.Length != 0)
586              {
587                     if(UploadDownloadPrint == 1)
588                     fs1 = new FileStream(DnLoadFile,FileMode.CreateNew);
589                     else if(UploadDownloadPrint == 2)
590                     fs1 = new FileStream(DnLoadFile,FileMode.Open);
591                     bDownLoading = true;
592              }
593              else
594              {
```

```
595                     // else make a file object for responding in xml formate
596                             fs1 = new FileStream(Application.StartupPath +
                                    "\\Temp1.xml",FileMode.Open);
597                     responseWritten = true;
598                     }

599                     // write resoponse
600                     if(UploadDownloadPrint == 1)
601                     {
602                     // if it was upload request
603                             BinaryWriter wr = new BinaryWriter(fs1);
604                             int nreadBytes;

605          // read network stream and write data to a loacal file
606                             while( (nreadBytes = DataStream.Read(readBytes,
                                    0, readBytes.Length)) > 0)
607                                     wr.Write(readBytes, 0, nreadBytes);

608                     wr.Close();
609                     fs1.Close();
610                     }
611                     else
612                     {
613                             // write the response or file requested for download
614                             // in browsers stream
615                             BinaryReader r = new BinaryReader(fs1);
616                             int nreadBytes;

617                             // write upon the network stream
618                             while( (nreadBytes = r.Read(
                                    readBytes, 0, readBytes.Length)) > 0)
619                             DataStream.Write(readBytes, 0, nreadBytes);

620                             r.Close();
621                             fs1.Close();
622                     }

623                     // delete all temporary files
624                     if(responseWritten)
625                     File.Delete(Application.StartupPath + "\\Temp1.xml");

626                     File.Delete(Application.StartupPath + "\\Temp.xml");
627                     DataStream.Flush();
628                     newSock.Close();
629                     bDownLoading = false;
630              }
631          catch(SocketException e) {
                    WriteErrorLog("Responding Browser",e.Message);                }
632          }
633          /// The main entry point for the application.
634          public static void Main(string[] args)
635          {
636                     Application.Run(new frmLogin());
637          }

638  // Listener's through, it will inform server that it is making an exit.
```

```
639          public void Logout ()
640          {
641               try
642               {
643               if(bLoggedIn)
644               {
645                    xmlServerComm.GetDataFromServer(
                          "http://webaddress/Logout.asp?ip="
                          +  xmlServerComm.GetIPAddress(""));
646                    MessageBox.Show("Listener Logged-out.",
                               "Process Successfull",
                               MessageBoxButtons.OK,
                               MessageBoxIcon.Information);
647               }

648               //release threads
649               if(ThreadIcon!=null)
650                    if(ThreadIcon.IsAlive)
651                         ThreadIcon.Abort();

652               if(AcceptThread!=null)
653                    if(AcceptThread.IsAlive)
654                         AcceptThread.Abort();

655               if(RespondingThread!=null)
656                    if(RespondingThread.IsAlive)
657                         RespondingThread.Abort();

658               }
659               catch( Exception err ) { MessageBox.Show(err.Message,
                          "Could not Logout properly.",
                          MessageBoxButtons.OK, MessageBoxIcon.Error);}
660          }
661     }
662 }
```

Code description of 'frmLogin' class (frmLogin.cs)

Note: All request/response documents in this application are in XML format.

♦ Lines 3-16: This includes all packages required to build this application.

♦ Lines 18: This declares the class frmLogin, which inherits itself from the
   System.WinForms.Form class.

♦ Lines 19-55: This declares variables and objects, which are used in the class later. Variables and
   objects are declared *private* for use within the class.

♦ Lines 56-73: This declares the GUI component for the application.

♦ Lines 76-96: This implements the constructor frmLogin() of the frmLogin class for intialization
   of GUI components and objects being used while communicating with the server and parsing the
   XML document.

♦ Lines 97-116: The ReadUserName() function opens the userinfo.ini file and reads the login name
   of the last logged-in user (listener), with the help of the stream class's OpenRead() function, and
   returns username to the caller.

- Lines 118-126: The `WriteUserName` function writes the user name to the `userinfo.ini` file with the help of the `stream` class's `OpenWrite()` function for use in next instantiation of this application.

- Lines 128-132: `Dispose()` disposes all resources of the application at its termination.

- Lines 135-310: `InitializeComponent()` initializes all GUI components. This part of coding is IDE generated, and it is recommended that programmers do not modify this code.

  The following functions are related with various buttons placed on forms. These functions provide required functionality and instructions to perform specified tasks. This section incorporates detailed functionality with complete references regarding various options related to the context or shortcut menu. First, we give you the functionality of the context menu or shortcut menu. Some of the functions implemented are detailed later.

- Lines 314-320: The `ctxMenuQuit_Click()` function controls the Quit option of context menu. This function is invoked when you click the Quit option of the shortcut menu. To log out and free the threads, it calls the `Logout()` function, and the application exists.

- Lines 324-335: The `ctxMenuShare_Click` is invoked when you click the Share Resource option of context menu. It opens the Share Files/Folders dialog box.

- Lines 338-344: `btnShareFileFolder_Click()` holds the functionality of the Share button located on the application's form. Once you click this button , it opens the Share File/Folder dialog box.

- Lines 335-352: `btnQuit_Click()` comes into action when you click the Quit button located on the application's form. To log out and free the threads, it calls the `Logout()` function, and the application exists.

- Lines 355-461: This section of code holds for the entire breath of the application. In the lines that follow, you are logging on to the server and communicating with it. (Unless you log in to the log book on the server, you don't exist for the browser.) The role of the Login button holds for the entire working to facilitate logging on to the server. `btnLogin_Click()` is invoked when you click the Login button placed on the application's form.

  - 359: This line is making use of the `ServerCommunication` (defined in the `WorkingWithXML` assembly) class object's `GetIPAddress` function to get the IP address of the computer this application is running on. A list of all the shared files and folders is passed to server, along with the listener's login name during connection to server.

  - 370: This line of code checks whether you have checked the Remember My Login ID checkbox or not. If this checkbox is checked, your user name is written to userinfo.ini for use in the next instantiation of this application by a call to `WriteUserName()`.

  - 373: Just in case you haven't checked the checkbox, the userinfo.ini file is deleted, as it is no longer required.

  - 376-377: This checks the existence of share.ini to make sure you have shared some resources.

  - 378-391: If this file is found, it is opened and all the shared files/folders are read into a string variable, with delimiters after every file/folder name.

  - 393: This information is then concatenated as another parameter, along with `USERID` and IP to the URL of login.asp to make it look like the following:

    ```
    http://webaddress/login.asp?USERID=keith&IP=192.192.192.192&SHARE=sm
    ith.txt*cris.exe*C:\Shared\Temp\*
    ```

  - 397: This calls login.asp by using the `ServerCommunication` class' `GetDataFromServer()`, passing three parameters: `USERID`, `IP`, and `SHARE` (shared resources) and stores the response as an XML document by using the `ServerCommunication` class object's `WriteDataToFile()` function.

- **400:** The XML response document is parsed by `XMLParser`'s `ParseXML()` function. The `XMLParser` class is defined in the `WorkingWithXML` assembly. `ParseXML()` returns the output to the `XMLSTRUCT` variable (defined in the `WorkingWithXML` assembly).

- **405-439:** Now the type of response is determined by checking output and is returned to `XMLSTRUCT`'s variable. Here we are checking the XML response, indicating that authentication is successful, after which the listener begins the process of listening for connections.

- **410-417:** A `socket` is made, giving it the IP address and port number to listen on.

- **421-422:** The `AcceptFunction()` function is then called in a thread to keep on listening for connections. This function is detailed later.

- **423-429:** Another thread is created to keep updating icons on the system tray by passing the `IconUpdate()` function in it, which is coming up next.

- **436-438:** If the login is `unsuccessful`, the message is sent to the user.

- **442-446:** If the login name is detected as blank, the user is taken back to the login name box to write the the login name.

- **447-457:** If the login is `unsuccessful`, the reason given to the user and the application is closed after releasing all resources and threads.

- **459:** A flag is set to indicate that logging is successful.

- ◆ Lines **462-498:** The `IconUpdate()` function is used by this application to show its presence on the machine. It keeps updating the icons on the system tray once the login form is closed, and no other window belonging to this application is open.

  - **474-489:** Check if anything is being downloaded, then change the tray icons accordingly.

  - **490:** The file name generated previously is loaded.

  - **491:** This loaded icon is set to the system tray object's Icon property of this application.

  - **493:** A thread is made to sleep for 500 milliseconds before the next update is made to make the process noticeable to reader.

- ◆ Lines **500-523:** `WriteErrorLog()` is called by other functions as they encounter any internal problem. This function stores errors, their type in error.log, and their time of occurrence as it runs in unattended mode. You can check it any time to see exceptions the application has encountered.

- ◆ Lines **526-534:** `frmLogin_Closing()` is called when the application's Login form is closed by the user either by clicking the Quit button or by clicking the Cross button, in both cases without logging in. It enables the user to dispose all resources the application has been holding and to close the form and finally to terminate the application.

- ◆ Lines **536-550:** The `AcceptFunction()` function keeps accepting connections; that is why use of the `while(true)` looping structure is put into code. The `while(true)` statement runs this process until the thread in which this function is running is aborted. As soon as a connection is detected, the `RequestResponse()` function is called to serve the requests made on this connection.

- ◆ Lines **552-632:** The `RequestResponse()` function appropriately responds to requests made on a connection.

  - **556:** This opens a network stream passing the socket to the calling function.

  - **560-576:** The user (listener) is reading via a network stream whatever the user at other end has written to it and is storing the information to a temporary XML file.

  - **579:** An object of the `XMLCreater` class is created and initialized. The `XMLCreater` class is defined in the `WorkingWithXML` assembly.

- 580: The `DetermineRequestType()` function of the `XMLCreater` class is called to determine the request type and to retrieve the information accordingly.

- 584-591: If the request type is uploading, an empty file is created with the same name as specified in the uploaded request to store the downloaded file. Otherwise, a file is opened for uploading.

- 593-597: If none of these requests is found, an empty XML document is created to store responses for other requests types.

- 600-610: If the request is of uploading type, the file stream for writing is opened, and the network stream is read for the file being written by the browser on it in the form of bytes; read bytes are written in an empty document created earlier.

- 611-622: If it is a download request, search request or merely a show all files request. The listener makes a reader stream either for reading the file to be downloaded or for reading the response file. Either of these read files are written on a network stream for the browser to read on his end.

- 623-630: All temporary files are deleted while closing the connection.

♦ Lines 634-637: `Main()` starts the application and instantiates frmLogin.

♦ Lines 639-660: Once the listener completes its work and its processing, it disposes all resources, releases all threads, and exits the application.

Share Files/Folders Form

namespace: Listener

The `frmSelection` class provides the user at the listener's end with an intuitive interface, facilitating the user with the process of sharing resources (see Listing 5-5).

The dialog box in Figure 5-4 is displayed when you click the Share Files/Folders button on the login form or choose the same option through the tray icon short-cut menu.

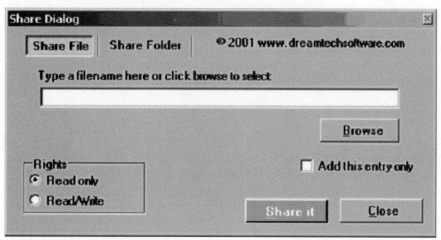

Figure 5-4: The Share Dialog window

♦ **Share File Tab**: This tab is devoted to file sharing.

♦ **Browse**: This opens the File Open dialog box for you to select any file to share.

♦ **Share Folder Tab**: This tab is devoted to file sharing.

♦ **Browse**: This opens the Folder Selection dialog box for you to select any folder to share.

- **Share It**: This shares the file or folder selected under either of the two preceding tabs.

- **Rights**: This group box offers two credential options to choose from to assign to the selected file or folder.

- **Add this entry only**: This checkbox is given for you to indicate whether the dialog box should be closed or not after choosing one file or folder.

- **Close**: This closes the dialog box.

Listing 5-5: frmSelection

// © 2001 Dreamtech Software India Inc.
// All rights reserved

```
 1 namespace Listener
 2 {
 3  // Library includes
 4     using System;
 5     using System.Drawing;
 6     using System.Collections;
 7     using System.ComponentModel;
 8     using System.Windows.Forms;
 9     using System.Windows.Forms.Design;
10     using System.Text;
11     using System.IO;
12
13     ///    Share Files/Folders form class.
14     public class frmSelection : System.Windows.Forms.Form
15     {
16         private System.ComponentModel.IContainer components;
17         private System.Windows.Forms.Label lbCopyright;
18         private System.Windows.Forms.Button btnBrowseFileFolder;
19         private System.Windows.Forms.ToolTip toolTipText;
20         private System.Windows.Forms.CheckBox chkEntry;
21         private System.Windows.Forms.RadioButton rbWrite;
22         private System.Windows.Forms.RadioButton rbRead;
23         private System.Windows.Forms.GroupBox grpRights;
24         private System.Windows.Forms.OpenFileDialog FileOpenDialog;
25         private System.Windows.Forms.Button btnCancel;
26         private System.Windows.Forms.Button btnOK;
27         private System.Windows.Forms.Label label2;
28         private System.Windows.Forms.TextBox txtFoldername;
29         private System.Windows.Forms.Button btnBrowse;
30         private System.Windows.Forms.Label label1;
31         private System.Windows.Forms.TextBox txtFilename;
32         private System.Windows.Forms.TabPage tpFolder;
33         private System.Windows.Forms.TabPage tpShare;
34         private System.Windows.Forms.OpenFileDialog openFileDialog1;
35         private System.Windows.Forms.TabControl tabShare;
36
37         public frmSelection() { InitializeComponent(); }
38
39         // Free resources it was using.
40         public override void Dispose()
41         {
42             base.Dispose();
43             components.Dispose();
44         }
```

```
45
46        /// Required method for Designer support - do not modify
47        /// the contents of this method with the code editor.
48        private void InitializeComponent()
49        {
50        this.components = new System.ComponentModel.Container();
51        this.grpRights = new System.Windows.Forms.GroupBox();
52        this.rbWrite = new System.Windows.Forms.RadioButton();
53        this.rbRead = new System.Windows.Forms.RadioButton();
54        this.chkEntry = new System.Windows.Forms.CheckBox();
55        this.toolTipText = new ystem.Windows.Forms.ToolTip(this.components);
56        this.openFileDialog1 = new System.Windows.Forms.OpenFileDialog();
57        this.label1 = new System.Windows.Forms.Label();
58        this.label2 = new System.Windows.Forms.Label();
59        this.tpShare = new System.Windows.Forms.TabPage();
60        this.btnBrowse = new System.Windows.Forms.Button();
61        this.txtFilename = new System.Windows.Forms.TextBox();
62        this.tabShare = new System.Windows.Forms.TabControl();
63        this.tpFolder = new System.Windows.Forms.TabPage();
64        this.btnBrowseFileFolder = new System.Windows.Forms.Button();
65        this.txtFoldername = new System.Windows.Forms.TextBox();
66        this.btnOK = new System.Windows.Forms.Button();
67        this.FileOpenDialog = new System.Windows.Forms.OpenFileDialog();
68        this.lbCopyright = new System.Windows.Forms.Label();
69        this.btnCancel = new System.Windows.Forms.Button();
70        this.grpRights.SuspendLayout();
71        this.tpShare.SuspendLayout();
72        this.tabShare.SuspendLayout();
73        this.tpFolder.SuspendLayout();
74        this.SuspendLayout();
75        //
76        // grpRights
77        //
78        this.grpRights.Controls.AddRange(new System.Windows.Forms.Control[] {
79        this.rbWrite,
80        this.rbRead});
81        this.grpRights.Location = new System.Drawing.Point(16, 128);
82        this.grpRights.Name = "grpRights";
83        this.grpRights.Size = new System.Drawing.Size(124, 56);
84        this.grpRights.TabIndex = 3;
85        this.grpRights.TabStop = false;
86        this.grpRights.Text = "Rights";
87        //
88        // rbWrite
89        //
90        this.rbWrite.Location = new System.Drawing.Point(6, 36);
91        this.rbWrite.Name = "rbWrite";
92        this.rbWrite.Size = new System.Drawing.Size(96, 14);
93        this.rbWrite.TabIndex = 3;
94        this.rbWrite.Text = "Read/Write";
95        this.toolTipText.SetToolTip(this.rbWrite, "Allows the user to upload
          to this file or folder");
96        //
97        // rbRead
98        //
99        this.rbRead.Checked = true;
```

```
100          this.rbRead.Location = new System.Drawing.Point(6, 16);
101          this.rbRead.Name = "rbRead";
102          this.rbRead.Size = new System.Drawing.Size(95, 14);
103          this.rbRead.TabIndex = 2;
104          this.rbRead.TabStop = true;
105          this.rbRead.Text = "Read only";
106          this.toolTipText.SetToolTip(this.rbRead, "Allows the user to read");
107          //
108          // chkEntry
109          //
110          this.chkEntry.Location = new System.Drawing.Point(296, 128);
111          this.chkEntry.Name = "chkEntry";
112          this.chkEntry.Size = new System.Drawing.Size(120, 16);
113          this.chkEntry.TabIndex = 4;
114          this.chkEntry.Text = "Add this entry only";
115          this.toolTipText.SetToolTip(this.chkEntry, "Quits after adding the
             entry, if checked");
116          //
117          // label1
118          //
119          this.label1.Location = new System.Drawing.Point(8, 8);
120          this.label1.Name = "label1";
121          this.label1.Size = new System.Drawing.Size(248, 14);
122          this.label1.TabIndex = 2;
123          this.label1.Text = "Type a filename here or click browse to select:";
124          //
125          // label2
126          //
127          this.label2.Location = new System.Drawing.Point(8, 8);
128          this.label2.Name = "label2";
129          this.label2.Size = new System.Drawing.Size(232, 14);
130          this.label2.TabIndex = 1;
131          this.label2.Text = "Type a folder name here:";
132          //
133          // tpShare
134          //
135          this.tpShare.Controls.AddRange(new System.Windows.Forms.Control[] {
136          this.btnBrowse,
137          this.label1,
138          this.txtFilename});
139          this.tpShare.Location = new System.Drawing.Point(4, 25);
140          this.tpShare.Name = "tpShare";
141          this.tpShare.Size = new System.Drawing.Size(388, 89);
142          this.tpShare.TabIndex = 0;
143          this.tpShare.Text = "Share File";
144          //
145          // btnBrowse
146          //
147          this.btnBrowse.Location = new System.Drawing.Point(296, 56);
148          this.btnBrowse.Name = "btnBrowse";
149          this.btnBrowse.Size = new System.Drawing.Size(80, 24);
150          this.btnBrowse.TabIndex = 1;
151          this.btnBrowse.Text = "&Browse";
152          this.btnBrowse.Click += new
             System.EventHandler(this.btnBrowseFile_Click);
153          //
```

```
154        // txtFilename
155        //
156        this.txtFilename.Location = new System.Drawing.Point(13, 26);
157        this.txtFilename.Name = "txtFilename";
158        this.txtFilename.Size = new System.Drawing.Size(363, 20);
159        this.txtFilename.TabIndex = 0;
160        this.txtFilename.Text = "";
161        //
162        // tabShare
163        //
164        this.tabShare.Appearance =
           System.Windows.Forms.TabAppearance.FlatButtons;
165        this.tabShare.Controls.AddRange(new System.Windows.Forms.Control[] {
166        this.tpShare,
167        this.tpFolder});
168        this.tabShare.Location = new System.Drawing.Point(16, 8);
169        this.tabShare.Name = "tabShare";
170        this.tabShare.SelectedIndex = 0;
171        this.tabShare.Size = new System.Drawing.Size(396, 118);
172        this.tabShare.TabIndex = 2;
173        //
174        // tpFolder
175        //
176        this.tpFolder.Controls.AddRange(new System.Windows.Forms.Control[] {
177        this.btnBrowseFileFolder,
178        this.label2,
179        this.txtFoldername});
180        this.tpFolder.Location = new System.Drawing.Point(4, 25);
181        this.tpFolder.Name = "tpFolder";
182        this.tpFolder.Size = new System.Drawing.Size(388, 89);
183        this.tpFolder.TabIndex = 1;
184        this.tpFolder.Text = "Share Folder";
185        //
186        // btnBrowseFileFolder
187        //
188        this.btnBrowseFileFolder.Location = new System.Drawing.Point(296,56);
189        this.btnBrowseFileFolder.Name = "btnBrowseFileFolder";
190        this.btnBrowseFileFolder.Size = new System.Drawing.Size(80, 24);
191        this.btnBrowseFileFolder.TabIndex = 2;
192        this.btnBrowseFileFolder.Text = "Browse";
193        this.btnBrowseFileFolder.Click += new
           System.EventHandler(this.btnBrowseFolder_Click);
194        //
195        // txtFoldername
196        //
197        this.txtFoldername.Location = new System.Drawing.Point(13, 26);
198        this.txtFoldername.Name = "txtFoldername";
199        this.txtFoldername.Size = new System.Drawing.Size(363, 20);
200        this.txtFoldername.TabIndex = 0;
201        this.txtFoldername.Text = "";
202        //
203        // btnOK
204        //
205        this.btnOK.BackColor =
           System.Drawing.Color.FromArgb(((System.Byte)(192)),
           ((System.Byte)(192)), ((System.Byte)(0)));
```

```
206        this.btnOK.DialogResult = System.Windows.Forms.DialogResult.OK;
207        this.btnOK.Font = new System.Drawing.Font("Microsoft Sans Serif", 9F,
           System.Drawing.FontStyle.Bold);
208        this.btnOK.ForeColor = System.Drawing.Color.LemonChiffon;
209        this.btnOK.Location = new System.Drawing.Point(240, 168);
210        this.btnOK.Name = "btnOK";
211        this.btnOK.Size = new System.Drawing.Size(85, 25);
212        this.btnOK.TabIndex = 0;
213        this.btnOK.Text = "&Share it";
214        this.btnOK.Click += new System.EventHandler(this.btnOK_Click);
215        //
216        // lbCopyright
217        //
218        this.lbCopyright.Location = new System.Drawing.Point(208, 8);
219        this.lbCopyright.Name = "lbCopyright";
220        this.lbCopyright.Size = new System.Drawing.Size(200, 12);
221        this.lbCopyright.TabIndex = 5;
222        this.lbCopyright.Text = "© 2001 www.dreamtechsoftware.com";
223        //
224        // btnCancel
225        //
226        this.btnCancel.DialogResult =
           System.Windows.Forms.DialogResult.Cancel;
227        this.btnCancel.Location = new System.Drawing.Point(336, 168);
228        this.btnCancel.Name = "btnCancel";
229        this.btnCancel.Size = new System.Drawing.Size(85, 24);
230        this.btnCancel.TabIndex = 1;
231        this.btnCancel.Text = "&Close";
232        //
233        // frmSelection
234        //
235        this.AcceptButton = this.btnOK;
236        this.AutoScaleBaseSize = new System.Drawing.Size(5, 13);
237        this.CancelButton = this.btnCancel;
238        this.ClientSize = new System.Drawing.Size(432, 203);
239        this.Controls.AddRange(new System.Windows.Forms.Control[] {
240        this.lbCopyright,
241        this.chkEntry,
242        this.grpRights,
243        this.btnCancel,
244        this.btnOK,
245        this.tabShare});
246        this.Font = new System.Drawing.Font("Microsoft Sans Serif", 8F,
           System.Drawing.FontStyle.Bold);
247        this.ForeColor = System.Drawing.Color.Black;
248        this.FormBorderStyle =
           System.Windows.Forms.FormBorderStyle.FixedToolWindow;
249        this.HelpButton = true;
250        this.Icon = null;
251        this.Name = "frmSelection";
252        this.ShowInTaskbar = false;
253        this.StartPosition =
           System.Windows.Forms.FormStartPosition.CenterParent;
254        this.Text = "Share Dialog";
255        this.grpRights.ResumeLayout(false);
256        this.tpShare.ResumeLayout(false);
```

```
257          this.tabShare.ResumeLayout(false);
258          this.tpFolder.ResumeLayout(false);
259          this.ResumeLayout(false);
260
261      }
262
263      //Browse folder Button clicked, open folder open dialog
264      protected void btnBrowseFolder_Click (object sender, System.EventArgs e)
265      {
266          BrowseFolder Folder = new BrowseFolder();
267          txtFoldername.Text = Folder.SelectFolder();
268      }
269
270      //   Checkes whether file or folder user's trying to share
271      //   is already shared
272      private bool DoesEntryExists(string Filename, string Data)
273      {
274          bool bFound = false;
275          if( ! File.Exists(Filename) )
276                  return bFound;
277          else
278          {
279          StreamReader stReader = new StreamReader(Filename);
280          string readData;
281          while((readData = stReader.ReadLine()) != null)
282          // what u read's equal or shorter in length than what ur intend to
             share
283          // that means if i've shared "C:\" it'll allow u to share "C:\Shared"
284          // finding substring alone wouldn't have worked here.
285          if(readData.Length <= Data.Length)
286          if( -1 !=
             readData.Substring(0,readData.IndexOf("=")).Trim().IndexOf(Data.Subst
             ring(0,Data.IndexOf("="))) )
287          {
288          bFound = true;
289          break;
290          }
291          stReader.Close();
292          }
293          return bFound;
294      }
295
296      // checks the file of folder passed to it is not shared already,
297      // checks it exists and writes that to the share.ini file.
298      private void WriteDataToFile(string Filename, string Data)
299      {
300          try
301          {
302          // if it's a folder
303          if( 0 == Data.Substring(Data.Length-3,1).CompareTo("\\"))
304          {
305          // check if this entry already exists
306          if( !DoesEntryExists(Filename, Data) )
307          {
308          // if not append this entry to share.ini with its mask
309          StreamWriter stWriter = File.AppendText(Filename);
```

```
310          stWriter.WriteLine(Data);
311          MessageBox.Show("'" + Data.Substring(0,Data.IndexOf("=")) + "' has
             been successfully shared.","Information",MessageBoxButtons.OK,
             MessageBoxIcon.Information);
312          stWriter.Close();
313          }
314          else throw new Exception("Entry already exists");
315          }
316
317          else if( File.Exists(Data.Substring(0,Data.IndexOf("=",0))) )
318          {
319          // else if it's a file and it exists
320          if( !DoesEntryExists(Filename, Data) )
321          {
322          // and if it doesn't exist already append this entry
323          // to share.ini with its size and mask
324          StreamWriter stWriter = File.AppendText(Filename);
325          stWriter.WriteLine(Data);
326          MessageBox.Show("'" + Data.Substring(0,Data.IndexOf("=")) + "' is
             successfully shared.","Information",MessageBoxButtons.OK,
             MessageBoxIcon.Information);
327          stWriter.Close();
328          }
329          else throw new Exception("Entry already exists");
330          }
331          else throw new Exception("File/Folder does not exists");
332          }
333          catch( Exception err )
             {
                     MessageBox.Show(err.Message,"Warning",MessageBoxButtons.OK,
MessageBoxIcon.Warning); }
334          }
335
336   // Share file or folder selected
337   protected void btnOK_Click (object sender, System.EventArgs e)
338   {
339          string ResourceName = null;
340          long fileSize = 0;
341          bool bIsFile = false;
342          try
343          {
344          System.Windows.Forms.TabPage tp = tabShare.SelectedTab;
345          // find the file or folder seleceted
346          if( 0 == tp.Text.Trim().CompareTo("Share File") )
347          {
348          ResourceName = txtFilename.Text;
349          Stream s = File.Open(txtFilename.Text,FileMode.Open);
350          fileSize = s.Length;
351          bIsFile = true;
352          }
353          else if( 0 == tp.Text.Trim().CompareTo("Share Folder") )
354          {
355          ResourceName = txtFoldername.Text;
356          if( !Directory.Exists(ResourceName) )
357          {
358          DialogResult = System.Windows.Forms.DialogResult.None;
```

```
359          throw new Exception("Directory does not exist");
360          }
361
362          if(!ResourceName.Trim().EndsWith("\\"))
363          ResourceName += "\\";
364          }
365
366          // add append mask to it
367          if( 0 < ResourceName.Trim().Length )
368          {
369          if( rbRead.Checked )
370          ResourceName += "=0";
371          else if( rbWrite.Checked )
372          ResourceName += "=1";
373          else
374          {
375          DialogResult = System.Windows.Forms.DialogResult.None;
376          throw new Exception("Rights are missing");
377          }
378
379          if(bIsFile)
380          ResourceName += "=" + fileSize.ToString();
381
382          // and write this entry to share.ini
383          WriteDataToFile(Application.StartupPath +
             "\\Share.ini",ResourceName);
384          if( !chkEntry.Checked )
385          DialogResult = System.Windows.Forms.DialogResult.None;
386          }
387          else
388          {
389          DialogResult = System.Windows.Forms.DialogResult.None;
390          throw new Exception("Cannot add a blank entry");
391          }
392          }
393          catch( Exception err )
    { MessageBox.Show(err.Message,"Warning",MessageBoxButtons.OK,
MessageBoxIcon.Warning); }
394      }
395
396      //   Browse file Button clicked, open file open dialog
397      protected void btnBrowseFile_Click (object sender, System.EventArgs e)
398      {
399          FileOpenDialog.Title = "Select a file to share";
400          if( System.Windows.Forms.DialogResult.OK ==
FileOpenDialog.ShowDialog() )
401                txtFilename.Text = FileOpenDialog.FileName;
402      }
403        }
404 }
```

Code description of 'frmSelection' class (frmSelection.cs)

- Lines 3-12: This includes all packages required in building the application.
- Lines 14: This declares the class frmSelection *inheriting* itself from `System.WinForms.Form`.
- Lines 16-35: This declares the designing variable required in the application.

- Lines 37: `frmSelection()` the constructor is implemented.

- Lines 38-43: `Dispose()` is called at the time of termination of the application to dispose of all the resources used by the application.

- Lines 47-261: `InitializeComponent()` is initializing all the GUI components. Because this part of the code is IDE generated, users are recommended not to alter the code.

- Lines 263-269: `btnBrowseFolder_Click()` is a click-event handler for the Browse button placed on the application's form. Whenever you click it, it makes an object of the BrowseFolder class and calls its `SelectFolder()` function to display the Folder Selection dialog box and puts the name of the folder selected in Folder Name textbox.

- Lines 271-294: `DoesEntryExist()` checks whether entry (file/folder name) passed to it has already been written to `share.ini`, besides checking for the physical existence of that file/folder on hard disk.

  - 275-276: This checks whether the file or folder name selected physically exists on machine or not.

  - 279: A reading stream for share.ini is opened.

  - 297-207: This file is searched for the given resource. If found, the caller function is notified by setting a flag.

  - 281: This flag is returned to the caller at the end of this function.

- Lines 297-334: `WriteDataToFile()` makes sure that the file name or folder name passed to it isn't shared already and exists on the machine. If both these conditions are satisfied, the file/folder name is written to share.ini.

  - 306-314: This function checks whether information passed to it is a file name or a folder name and then makes sure that it exists on the machine. If it is not already in share.ini, it is written to it.

  - 316-333: If it is found to be a file and its entry does not exist in share.ini, it is written in share.ini, along with information pertaining to it (mask and size).

- Lines The 337-395: `btnOK_click()` function is called when you click the Share It button on the File/Folder Selection form. It checks what has been selected, whether it exists on the machine, and makes sure that the resource selected is not shared already and writes that to share.ini. These validations are carried out by using various functions implemented in the same class.

  - 344-365: This checks whether the selected tab is a folder tab or a file tab through its title. Once decided, the name of the selected file/folder is stored in a variable.

  - 367-378: This checks what credentials you have decided to be given to the selected file or folder, and those credentials are appended to a variable used for storing the file or folder name.

  - 379-380: If the selected content is a file, its size is calculated and is appended to the same variable used for storing the file or folder name with its respective credentials.

  - 383: The `WriteDataToFile()` function is called to append this resource to share.ini.

- Lines 396-402: `btnBrowseDialog_Click()` is called when the Browse button placed on the form's File Share tab is clicked to open the File Selection dialog box and puts the selected file in file name textbox.

Client Form

namespace: Client

The name of the class is frmClient, which performs the task of interacting with users (see Listing 5-6).

This window shown in Figure 5-5 is displayed on the startup of the browser application. The main browser window contains the computer name, its IP address, and the search results found in the list. It has five buttons; the function of each button is described in the following list:

- **Open button:** This button is used to open a selected computer. The contents of the selected computer are shown to you in the browser shared window when you click the Open button.

- **Refresh button:** This button updates the list view with the most recent entries from the server. When you click this button, the new user list is requested from the server and displayed to the to you.

- **Search button:** This button allows you to search for a particular file or group of files on the computer. The search window is displayed to enter the search criteria.

- **ViewFiles button:** After the search is complete, the number of searches found are shown in front of their respective computer names. You can select the computer and click the View File button to see the searched files.

- **Quit button:** This button forces the application to terminate. The application closes when you click this button.

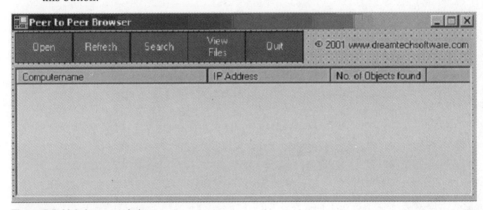

Figure 5-5: Main browser window

Listing 5-6: frmClient

// © 2001 Dreamtech Software India Inc.
// All rights reserved

```
 1 namespace Client        // Copyright 2001 Dreamtech Software India Inc.
 2 {                       // All rights reserved
 3    using System;        // Provides the basic functionality of .NET
 4   using System.Drawing;// Provides the Drawing features, Used for cursors
 5  using System.Collections;// Provides the different type of class
collections
 6  using System.ComponentModel;// Provides the facility of using components
 7  using System.Windows.Forms; // Provides the draring of buttons, listviews
etc
 8  using System.Net;               // Provides the net related
functionality
 9  using System.Text;              // Provides the text manipulation
functions
 10  using System.IO;               // Provides I/O features
 11  using WorkingWithXML;          // Custom Class
 12
 13  /// <summary>
```

```
14    /// This structure is used for book keeping purpose
15    /// The currently running listener list will be requested
16    /// by the server and server sends that list
17    /// Each record in this structure represents the data for the single
18    /// running listener
19    /// </summary>
20    public struct __CONNECTEDCOMPUTERS
21    {
22      /// <summary>
23      /// Declares the string used to store the name of the listener
24      /// This name is in human readable format
25      /// </summary>
26      public string      sComputername;
27
28      /// <summary>
29      /// sIPAddress variable is used to store the IP address of
30      /// the listener
31      /// </summary>
32      public string      sIPAddress;
33
34      /// <summary>
35      /// This will be 0 in starting and consequently filled
36      /// by every search operation
37      /// </summary>
38      public int         iFilesFound;
39    }
40
41    /// <summary>
42      ///      Summary description for frmClient class.
43      /// </summary>
44      public class frmClient : System.Windows.Forms.Form
45      {
46    private System.ComponentModel.IContainer components;
47    private System.Windows.Forms.Button                 btnViewFiles;
48    private System.Windows.Forms.Button                 btnSearch;
49    private System.Windows.Forms.ToolTip        ToolTipText;
50    private System.Windows.Forms.Button                 btnQuit;
51    private System.Windows.Forms.Button                 btnRefresh;
52    private System.Windows.Forms.Button                 btnOpen;
53
54    /// <summary>
55    /// The below declared variables are the user defined variables
56    /// used within this class
57    /// </summary>
58
59    /// <summary>
60    /// Stores the total number of listeners found
61    /// </summary>
62    private int                                 iConnectedComputers;
63
64    /// <summary>
65    /// Stores the number of search results found for
66    /// the matching criteria
67    /// </summary>
68    private int                                 iSearchResult;
69
```

```
70      /// <summary>
71      /// Declares a xmlParser variable of type XMLParser (User defined class)
72      /// </summary>
73      private XMLParser                        xmlParser;
74
75      /// <summary>
76      /// Declares a xmlServerComm variable of type ServerCommunication
77      /// (User defined class)
78      /// </summary>
79      private ServerCommunication             xmlServerComm;
80
81      /// <summary>
82      /// Declares an object xmlStruct of type XMLSTRUCT (User defined class)
83      /// </summary>
84      private XMLSTRUCT                        xmlStruct;
85
86      /// <summary>
87      /// Declares an array of ConnectedComputers of type
88      /// __CONNECTEDCOMPUTERS structures
89      /// </summary>
90      private __CONNECTEDCOMPUTERS[]                        ConnectedComputers;
91      private System.Windows.Forms.ListView           lvComputers;
92      private System.Windows.Forms.ColumnHeader       clhComputername;
93      private System.Windows.Forms.ColumnHeader       clhIPAddress;
94      private System.Windows.Forms.ColumnHeader       clhObjects;
95      private System.Windows.Forms.Label lblCopyright;
96
97      /// <summary>
98      /// declares sSubItems variable as an array of string
99      /// </summary>
100     private System.Windows.Forms.ListViewItem       lvItems;
101
102     /// <summary>
103     /// This is the default constructor of the class
104     /// </summary>
105     public frmClient()
106         {
107             //
108             // Required for Windows Form Designer support
109             //
110             // Auto generated function by the IDE
111         InitializeComponent();
112
113         // Puts the Computer.ico as the form icon
114         this.Icon = new System.Drawing.Icon(Application.StartupPath +
"\\Computer.ico");
115
116         // Creates a new instance of XMLParser class
117         xmlParser = new WorkingWithXML.XMLParser();
118
119         // Creates a new instance of XMLSTRUCT structure
120         xmlStruct = new WorkingWithXML.XMLSTRUCT();
121
122         // Creates a new instance for ServerCommunication class
123         xmlServerComm = new WorkingWithXML.ServerCommunication();
124
```

```
125          // Assigns the global value for USERLISTXML
126          xmlParser.USERLISTXML = Application.StartupPath + "\\userlist.xml";
127
128          // Assigns the global value for SERVERSEARCHXML
129          xmlParser.SERVERSEARCHRESULTXML = Application.StartupPath +
"\\search.xml";
130          try
131          {
132                  // Fills the List view with the values
133                  // these values are the response from the server
134                  if( 0 ==  PopulateList() )
135                          // Displays a message if no computer is connected to
the network
136                          throw new Exception("No computer is connected to the
network. The list will be empty");
137          }
138
139          // Handles every exception that is thrown
140          catch( Exception err ) {
MessageBox.Show(err.Message,"Warning",MessageBoxButtons.OK,
MessageBoxIcon.Warning); }
141          }
142
143          /// <summary>
144          ///     Clean up any resources being used.
145          ///     This is auto generated by the IDE
146          /// </summary>
147          public override void Dispose()
148          {
149              base.Dispose();
150          components.Dispose();
151          }
152
153          /// <summary>
154          ///     Required method for Designer support - do not modify
155          ///     the contents of this method with the code editor.
156          ///      this code is generated automatically by the IDE
157          /// </summary>
158          private void InitializeComponent()
159     {
160          this.components = new System.ComponentModel.Container();
161          this.ToolTipText = new System.Windows.Forms.ToolTip(this.components);
162          this.btnSearch = new System.Windows.Forms.Button();
163          this.btnQuit = new System.Windows.Forms.Button();
164          this.btnViewFiles = new System.Windows.Forms.Button();
165          this.btnRefresh = new System.Windows.Forms.Button();
166          this.btnOpen = new System.Windows.Forms.Button();
167          this.lvComputers = new System.Windows.Forms.ListView();
168          this.clhComputername = new System.Windows.Forms.ColumnHeader();
169          this.clhIPAddress = new System.Windows.Forms.ColumnHeader();
170          this.clhObjects = new System.Windows.Forms.ColumnHeader();
171          this.lblCopyright = new System.Windows.Forms.Label();
172          this.SuspendLayout();
173          //
174          // btnSearch
175          //
```

```
176        this.btnSearch.BackColor = System.Drawing.Color.Chocolate;
177        this.btnSearch.DialogResult =
System.Windows.Forms.DialogResult.Cancel;
178        this.btnSearch.FlatStyle = System.Windows.Forms.FlatStyle.Popup;
179        this.btnSearch.ForeColor = System.Drawing.Color.White;
180        this.btnSearch.Location = new System.Drawing.Point(137, 1);
181        this.btnSearch.Name = "btnSearch";
182        this.btnSearch.Size = new System.Drawing.Size(67, 35);
183        this.btnSearch.TabIndex = 2;
184        this.btnSearch.Text = "&Search";
185        this.ToolTipText.SetToolTip(this.btnSearch, "Search on computers for
filenames");
186        this.btnSearch.Click += new
System.EventHandler(this.btnSearch_Click);
187        //
188        // btnQuit
189        //
190        this.btnQuit.BackColor = System.Drawing.Color.Chocolate;
191        this.btnQuit.DialogResult = System.Windows.Forms.DialogResult.Cancel;
192        this.btnQuit.FlatStyle = System.Windows.Forms.FlatStyle.Popup;
193        this.btnQuit.ForeColor = System.Drawing.Color.White;
194        this.btnQuit.Location = new System.Drawing.Point(270, 1);
195        this.btnQuit.Name = "btnQuit";
196        this.btnQuit.Size = new System.Drawing.Size(67, 35);
197        this.btnQuit.TabIndex = 3;
198        this.btnQuit.Text = "&Quit";
199        this.ToolTipText.SetToolTip(this.btnQuit, "Quit this application");
200        this.btnQuit.Click += new System.EventHandler(this.btnQuit_Click);
201        //
202        // btnViewFiles
203        //
204        this.btnViewFiles.BackColor = System.Drawing.Color.Chocolate;
205        this.btnViewFiles.DialogResult =
System.Windows.Forms.DialogResult.Cancel;
206        this.btnViewFiles.Enabled = false;
207        this.btnViewFiles.FlatStyle = System.Windows.Forms.FlatStyle.Popup;
208        this.btnViewFiles.ForeColor = System.Drawing.Color.White;
209        this.btnViewFiles.Location = new System.Drawing.Point(203, 1);
210        this.btnViewFiles.Name = "btnViewFiles";
211        this.btnViewFiles.Size = new System.Drawing.Size(67, 35);
212        this.btnViewFiles.TabIndex = 5;
213        this.btnViewFiles.Text = "&View Files";
214        this.ToolTipText.SetToolTip(this.btnViewFiles, "View the searched
files");
215        this.btnViewFiles.Click += new
System.EventHandler(this.btnViewFiles_Click);
216        //
217        // btnRefresh
218        //
219        this.btnRefresh.BackColor = System.Drawing.Color.Chocolate;
220        this.btnRefresh.FlatStyle = System.Windows.Forms.FlatStyle.Popup;
221        this.btnRefresh.ForeColor = System.Drawing.Color.White;
222        this.btnRefresh.Location = new System.Drawing.Point(70, 1);
223        this.btnRefresh.Name = "btnRefresh";
224        this.btnRefresh.Size = new System.Drawing.Size(67, 35);
225        this.btnRefresh.TabIndex = 1;
```

```
226         this.btnRefresh.Text = "&Refresh";
227         this.ToolTipText.SetToolTip(this.btnRefresh,  "Refresh the computer
list");
228         this.btnRefresh.Click += new
System.EventHandler(this.btnRefresh_Click);
229      //
230      // btnOpen
231      //
232         this.btnOpen.BackColor = System.Drawing.Color.Chocolate;
233         this.btnOpen.FlatStyle = System.Windows.Forms.FlatStyle.Popup;
234         this.btnOpen.ForeColor = System.Drawing.Color.White;
235         this.btnOpen.Location = new System.Drawing.Point(3, 1);
236         this.btnOpen.Name = "btnOpen";
237         this.btnOpen.Size = new System.Drawing.Size(67, 35);
238         this.btnOpen.TabIndex = 0;
239         this.btnOpen.Text = "&Open";
240         this.ToolTipText.SetToolTip(this.btnOpen,  "Connect to the selected
computer");
241         this.btnOpen.Click += new System.EventHandler(this.btnOpen_Click);
242      //
243      // lvComputers
244      //
245         this.lvComputers.Columns.AddRange(new
System.Windows.Forms.ColumnHeader[] {
246
                              this.clhComputername,
247
                              this.clhIPAddress,
248
                              this.clhObjects});
249      this.lvComputers.Location = new System.Drawing.Point(3, 41);
250      this.lvComputers.Name = "lvComputers";
251      this.lvComputers.Size = new System.Drawing.Size(530, 146);
252      this.lvComputers.TabIndex = 7;
253      this.ToolTipText.SetToolTip(this.lvComputers, "Select a computer to
connect");
254      this.lvComputers.View = System.Windows.Forms.View.Details;
255      this.lvComputers.KeyPress += new
System.Windows.Forms.KeyPressEventHandler(this.lvComputers_KeyPress);
256      this.lvComputers.DoubleClick += new
System.EventHandler(this.lvComputers_DoubleClick);
257      this.lvComputers.SelectedIndexChanged += new
System.EventHandler(this.lvComputers_SelectedIndexChanged);
258      //
259      // clhComputername
260      //
261      this.clhComputername.Text = "Computername";
262      this.clhComputername.Width = 222;
263      //
264      // clhIPAddress
265      //
266      this.clhIPAddress.Text = "IP Address";
267      this.clhIPAddress.Width = 142;
268      //
269      // clhObjects
270      //
```

```
271        this.clhObjects.Text = "No. of Objects found";
272        this.clhObjects.Width = 112;
273        //
274        // lblCopyright
275        //
276        this.lblCopyright.Location = new System.Drawing.Point(348, 10);
277        this.lblCopyright.Name = "lblCopyright";
278        this.lblCopyright.Size = new System.Drawing.Size(192, 14);
279        this.lblCopyright.TabIndex = 6;
280        this.lblCopyright.Text = "© 2001 www.dreamtechsoftware.com";
281        //
282        // frmClient
283        //
284        this.AutoScaleBaseSize = new System.Drawing.Size(5, 13);
285        this.CancelButton = this.btnQuit;
286        this.ClientSize = new System.Drawing.Size(536, 190);
287        this.Controls.AddRange(new System.Windows.Forms.Control[] {

288    this.lvComputers,

289    this.lblCopyright,

290    this.btnViewFiles,

291    this.btnSearch,

292    this.btnQuit,

293    this.btnRefresh,

294    this.btnOpen});
295        this.FormBorderStyle =
System.Windows.Forms.FormBorderStyle.FixedDialog;
296        this.MaximizeBox = false;
297        this.Name = "frmClient";
298        this.StartPosition =
System.Windows.Forms.FormStartPosition.CenterScreen;
299        this.Text = "Peer to Peer Browser";
300        this.ResumeLayout(false);
301
302    }
303
304    /// <summary>
305    /// Fills the List view with initial values
306    /// This function is called from the constructor of this class
307    /// </summary>
308    private int PopulateList()
309    {
310        try
311        {
312                // This line of code gets the response from the server
313                // by calling an asp page and writes it in a file
314                // represented by xmlParser.USERLISTXML
315
xmlServerComm.WriteDataToFile(xmlParser.USERLISTXML,xmlServerComm.GetDataFromSe
rver("http://webaddress/userlist.asp"));
```

```
316
317                // This line will parse the returned XML by the server
318                // and saves it in the xmlStruct variable
319                // iConnectedComputers will have value for total
320                // number of connected listeners
321                iConnectedComputers =
xmlParser.ParseXML(xmlParser.USERLISTXML,out xmlStruct,
xmlServerComm.TypeOfXMLRecieved(xmlParser.USERLISTXML));
322
323                // Clears the every item of the list view
324                lvComputers.Items.Clear();
325
326                // Deletes the File represented by xmlParser.USERLISTXML
327                xmlServerComm.FileDelete(xmlParser.USERLISTXML);
328
329                // initialize the ConnectedComputers array to
330                // the number of listeners found connected
331                ConnectedComputers = new
__CONNECTEDCOMPUTERS[iConnectedComputers];
332
333                // Initializes lvItems object
334                lvItems = new System.Windows.Forms.ListViewItem();
335
336                /// The below 17 lines of code is used for sorting the
337                /// USERLIST alphabetically
338                for( int i = 0; i < iConnectedComputers; i++ )
339                {
340                    for( int j = i+1; j < iConnectedComputers; j++ )
341                    {
342                        if(
xmlStruct.USERLIST[i].sUsername.GetHashCode() <
xmlStruct.USERLIST[j].sUsername.GetHashCode()  )
343                        {
344                            string sTemp;
345                            sTemp = xmlStruct.USERLIST[j].sUsername;
346                            xmlStruct.USERLIST[j].sUsername =
xmlStruct.USERLIST[i].sUsername;
347                            xmlStruct.USERLIST[i].sUsername = sTemp;
348
349                            sTemp =
xmlStruct.USERLIST[j].sIPAddress;
350                            xmlStruct.USERLIST[j].sIPAddress =
xmlStruct.USERLIST[i].sIPAddress;
351                            xmlStruct.USERLIST[i].sIPAddress =
sTemp;
352                        }
353                    }
354                }
355                //////////////////////////////////////////////////////
356                ///
357
358
359                // Fills the ConnectedComputer array with user list values
360                for( int i = 0; i < iConnectedComputers; i++ )
361                {
362                    ImageList imgList = new ImageList();
```

```
363
imgList.Images.Add(System.Drawing.Image.FromFile(Application.StartupPath+"\\Com
puter.ico"));
364                        lvComputers.SmallImageList = imgList;
365                        ConnectedComputers[i].sComputername =
xmlStruct.USERLIST[i].sUsername.Trim();
366                        ConnectedComputers[i].sIPAddress =
xmlStruct.USERLIST[i].sIPAddress.Trim();
367                        ConnectedComputers[i].iFilesFound = 0;
368
369                        // Insert the records one by one in the list view
370                        lvItems =
lvComputers.Items.Insert(i,ConnectedComputers[i].sComputername);
371
372
lvItems.SubItems.Add(ConnectedComputers[i].sIPAddress);
373                        lvItems.SubItems.Add("");
374                        lvItems.ImageIndex = 0;
375                }
376            }
377
378        // Cathces any exception that is thrown by the application
379        // and display message
380        catch( Exception err ) {
MessageBox.Show(err.Message,"Error",MessageBoxButtons.OK,  MessageBoxIcon.Error);
}
381
382        // Return the number of connected computers
383        return iConnectedComputers;
384    }
385
386    /// <summary>
387    /// Fills the Listview with the entries as well as with
388    /// the search criteria if performed any
389    /// </summary>
390    private void PopulateWithSearchResults()
391    {
392        // Decrales and initializes the iCounter value to zero
393        int iCounter = 0;
394        try
395        {
396            // Parse the XML Request returned by the server and store
397            // the number of total searches found in iSearchResult
398            iSearchResult =
xmlParser.ParseXML(xmlParser.SERVERSEARCHRESULTXML  ,out xmlStruct,
xmlServerComm.TypeOfXMLRecieved(xmlParser.SERVERSEARCHRESULTXML));
399
400            // Delete the SEARVERSEARCHXML file after parsing
401            xmlServerComm.FileDelete(xmlParser.SERVERSEARCHRESULTXML);
402
403            // The 8 lines of code will find in the search results
404            // and counts the number of matched files found on each
computer
405            // as the result of the search i.e for example
406            // on computer A 10 files are found , on B 3 files are found
etc
```

```
407                    // This code will do the individual level breakup for the
408                    // search results
409                    for( int i = 0; i < ConnectedComputers.Length; i++)
410                    {
411                        for( int j = 0; j < iSearchResult; j++ )
412                            if( 0 ==
xmlStruct.SERVERSEARCH[j].sIPAddress.Trim().CompareTo(ConnectedComputers[i].sIPA
ddress.Trim()) )
413                                iCounter++;
414                        ConnectedComputers[i].iFilesFound = iCounter;
415                        iCounter = 0;
416                    }
417
///////////////////////////////////////////////////////////////////
418            ///
419
420            // initialize lvItems
421            lvItems = new System.Windows.Forms.ListViewItem();
422
423            // Clears the list view items
424            lvComputers.Items.Clear();
425
426            for( int i = 0; i < ConnectedComputers.Length; i++)
427            {
428                ImageList imgList = new ImageList();
429
imgList.Images.Add(System.Drawing.Image.FromFile(Application.StartupPath+"\\Com
puter.ico"));
430                lvComputers.SmallImageList = imgList;
431
432                // Insert the items in the list view
433                lvItems =
lvComputers.Items.Insert(i,ConnectedComputers[i].sComputername);
434
435                // Assigns the IP Address at first subscript
436
lvItems.SubItems.Add(ConnectedComputers[i].sIPAddress.Trim());
437
438                // Assigns the no of search results found
439                // at second subscript
440
lvItems.SubItems.Add(ConnectedComputers[i].iFilesFound.ToString().Trim());
441
442                lvItems.ImageIndex = 0;
443
444            }
445        }
446
447        // catches any exception that is thrown by the application
448        catch( Exception err ) {
MessageBox.Show(err.Message,"Error",MessageBoxButtons.OK, MessageBoxIcon.Error);
}
449    }
450
451    /// <summary>
452    /// Handles the key press events on the list view
```

```
453    /// </summary>
454    /// <param name="sender"> </param>
455    /// <param name="e"> </param>
456    protected void lvComputers_KeyPress (object sender,
System.Windows.Forms.KeyPressEventArgs e)
457    {
458        if( 13 == e.KeyChar || 32 == e.KeyChar )
459            btnOpen_Click(null,System.EventArgs.Empty);
460    }
461
462    /// <summary>
463    /// Invoked when the user double clicks on the list view
464    /// </summary>
465    /// <param name="sender"> </param>
466    /// <param name="e"> </param>
467    protected void lvComputers_DoubleClick (object sender, System.EventArgs
e) { btnOpen_Click(null,System.EventArgs.Empty); }
468
469    /// <summary>
470    /// Invoked, when the user clicks the refresh button
471    /// This will refresh the contents of the listview
472    /// by getting the USERLIST from the server again and
473    /// shows it in the list view
474    /// </summary>
475    /// <param name="sender"> </param>
476    /// <param name="e"> </param>
477    protected void btnRefresh_Click (object sender, System.EventArgs e)
478    {
479        try
480        {
481            if( 0 == PopulateList() )
482                throw new Exception("No computer is connected to the
network. The list will be empty");
483        }
484        catch( Exception err ) {
MessageBox.Show(err.Message,"Warning",MessageBoxButtons.OK,
MessageBoxIcon.Warning); }
485    }
486
487    /// <summary>
488    /// Invoked when the user clicks on the Open button
489    /// </summary>
490    /// <param name="sender"> </param>
491    /// <param name="e"> </param>
492    protected void btnOpen_Click (object sender, System.EventArgs e)
493    {
494        // Get the currently selected item from the list view
495        System.Windows.Forms.ListView.SelectedListViewItemCollection items =
lvComputers.SelectedItems;
496
497        try
498        {
499            // if item is found or not
500            if( 0 < items.Count )
501            {
```

```
502                         // Makes the string that is required to pass to the
contructor
503                         // of the frmShare class
504
505                         // Appends the "(" and ")" at the begin and end of the
IPAddress
506                         string SelectedIP = " (" + items[0].SubItems[1].Text +
")" ;
507
508                         // gets the name of the computer from Computername
column
509                         // of the list view
510                         string Computername = items[0].Text;
511
512                         // Concatenates the Computername to IP address
513                         Computername = Computername + SelectedIP;
514
515                         // declares a variable ShareForm of type frmShare
class
516                         // and passes the Computername to it
517                         frmShare ShareForm = new frmShare(Computername);
518
519                         // Shows the frmShare dialog window
520                         ShareForm.Show();
521                     }
522
523                 // Throws the exception
524                 else throw new Exception("No selected computer found");
525         }
526
527         // cathces the exception and shows it in a message box
528         catch( Exception err ) {
MessageBox.Show(err.Message,"Warning",MessageBoxButtons.OK,
MessageBoxIcon.Warning); }
529     }
530
531     /// <summary>
532     /// Performs a quit operation when the user clicks the quit button
533     /// </summary>
534     /// <param name="sender"> </param>
535     /// <param name="e"> </param>
536     protected void btnQuit_Click (object sender, System.EventArgs e) {
Application.Exit(); }
537
538     /// <summary>
539     /// This function is called when you click the View files button
540     /// </summary>
541     /// <param name="sender"> </param>
542
543     /// <param name="e"> </param>
544     protected void btnViewFiles_Click (object sender, System.EventArgs e)
545     {
546         // Creates an ShareForm object from frmShare class and
547         // initializes it
548         frmShare ShareForm = new frmShare();
549
```

```
550        // Get the currently selected item from the list view
551        System.Windows.Forms.ListView.SelectedListViewItemCollection    items
= lvComputers.SelectedItems;
552
553        // Get the IPAddress of the Selected item from IP Address
554        // column
555        string SelectedIP = items[0].SubItems[1].Text.Trim();
556
557        // The followinf 12 lines of code Scans through the
558        // SERVERSEARCH list and insert the values in the List view
559        // of the frmShare class Folder and file wise
560        for( int i = 0; i < iSearchResult; i++ )
561        {
562            if( 0 ==
xmlStruct.SERVERSEARCH[i].sIPAddress.Trim().CompareTo(SelectedIP)  )
563            {
564                ImageList imgList = new ImageList();
565
 imgList.Images.Add(System.Drawing.Image.FromFile(Application.StartupPath+"\\Fol
der.ico"));
566
 imgList.Images.Add(System.Drawing.Image.FromFile(Application.StartupPath+"\\Fil
e.ico"));
567                ShareForm.lvFiles.SmallImageList = imgList;
568
569                if( xmlStruct.SERVERSEARCH[i].sFilename.EndsWith("\\")
)
570                {
571                    lvItems =
ShareForm.lvFiles.Items.Insert(i,xmlStruct.SERVERSEARCH[i].sFilename);
572                    lvItems.ImageIndex = 0;
573                }
574                else
575                {
576                    lvItems =
ShareForm.lvFiles.Items.Insert(i,xmlStruct.SERVERSEARCH[i].sFilename);
577                    lvItems.ImageIndex = 1;
578                }
579            }
580        }
581        ////////////////////////////////////////////////////////////////
582        ///
583
584        // Shows the ShareForm window
585        ShareForm.ShowDialog();
586    }
587
588    /// <summary>
589    /// Whenever the user changes the selection in the List view
590    /// This function is called
591    /// </summary>
592    /// <param name="sender"> </param>
593    /// <param name="e"> </param>
594    protected void lvComputers_SelectedIndexChanged (object sender,
System.EventArgs e)
595    {
```

```
596           // Declare a local variable iTemp to store the number of
597           // individual search result return by the GetNumberOfObjectsFound
598           // function
599           int iTemp;
600
601           // calls to the GetNumberOfObjectsFound function and the
602           // value is returned in iTemp, out here is declared because the
603           // GetNumberOfObjectsFound function throws the value out in iTemp
604           // variable
605           GetNumberOfObjectsFound(out iTemp);
606
607           // Checks if the iTemp is zero than disbale view file button
608           // else enable that button
609           if( iTemp > 0 )
610                   btnViewFiles.Enabled = true;
611           else
612                   btnViewFiles.Enabled = false;
613     }
614
615     /// <summary>
616     /// This function returns the total object found in search
617     /// for a particular selected entry so the the state of
618     /// View Files button can be toggled
619     /// </summary>
620     /// <param name="iReturn"> </param>
621     private int GetNumberOfObjectsFound( out int iReturn )
622     {
623           // get the currently selected item from the list view
624           System.Windows.Forms.ListView.SelectedListViewItemCollection    items
= lvComputers.SelectedItems;
625
626           // Declare and initialize the iIndex variable to -1
627           int iIndex = -1;
628
629           // initialize the iReturn valiable to -1
630           iReturn = -1;
631
632           // check that if items variable has some data or not
633           if( 0 < items.Count )
634           {
635                   // get the index of the selected item
636                   iIndex = items[0].Index;
637
638                   // get the corresponding iFilesFound value from the
639                   // List that we have maintained by supplying the
640                   // iIndex value to it
641                   iReturn = ConnectedComputers[iIndex].iFilesFound;
642           }
643
644           // Also returns the iIndex number which is selected,
645           // iIndex contains -1 if nothing is selected
646           return iIndex;
647     }
648
649     /// <summary>
650     /// Invoked when the search button is clicked
```

```
651    /// Shows the search form to enter the search criteria
652    /// </summary>
653    /// <param name="sender"> </param>
654    /// <param name="e"> </param>
655    protected void btnSearch_Click (object sender, System.EventArgs e)
656    {
657        try
658        {
659                // Declare and initialize a new variable SearchForm
660                // of type frmSearch class
661                frmSearch SearchForm = new frmSearch();
662
663                // enables the text box control of the search Form
664                SearchForm.txtSearchOn.Enabled = true;
665
666                // enables the label control of the search Form
667                SearchForm.lblSearchOn.Enabled = true;
668
669                // Sets the bFlag of search form to true
670                SearchForm.bFlag = true;
671
672                // if Search is pressed from within the search form
673                if( System.Windows.Forms.DialogResult.OK ==
SearchForm.ShowDialog() )
674                {
675                        // get the search response from the server by calling
676                        // an asp file and getting the data returned by that
file
677                        // which is in XML format. Later save that data in the
678                        // SERVERSEARCHRESULTXML for parsing
679
xmlServerComm.WriteDataToFile(xmlParser.SERVERSEARCHRESULTXML,xmlServerComm.Get
DataFromServer("http://webaddress/search.asp?US=" + SearchForm.SearchOn + "&FS="
+ SearchForm.SearchFor));
680
681                        // calls the PopulateWithSearchResults function
682                        PopulateWithSearchResults();
683                }
684        }
685
686        // Catches any exception thrown by the application and shows it in
the
687        // message box
688        catch( Exception err ) { MessageBox.Show(err.Message,
"Error",MessageBoxButtons.OK, MessageBoxIcon.Error); }
689    }
690
691    /// <summary>
692        /// The main entry point for the application.
693        /// This is auto generated by the IDE
694        /// </summary>
695      public static void Main(string[] args) { Application.Run(new
frmClient()); }
696      }
}
```

Code description of 'frmClient' class (frmClient.cs)

♦ **Lines 3-11:** This includes the basic packages needed for the various classes used to build this application. This include packages used for communicating with network, streaming facility, file I/O, text manipulations, and so on.

- **10:** This includes a user-defined class called `WorkingWithXML`; this class is used to communicate with the server, parse XML data, and create XML requests.

♦ **Lines 20-39:** A structure is declared here with public access. This structure is used to store the information about each running listener. This information is received from the server by calling an ASP page. Three variables are declared in this structure. The variable `sComputername` is used to store the human-readable name for the connected listener. The second variable, `sIPAddress`, is used to store the IP address of the computer represented by `sComputername`. The last variable, `iFilesFound`, is declared here to store the information about the number of searches found on a particular computer.

♦ **Lines 44 -52:** These lines of code are generated automatically by the C# environment.

- **45:** This declares a public class frmClient, the default class created for this file. This class is inhereted from `System.Windows.Forms`.

- **52:** Some designer variables are declared. These variables represent the various controls created at the design time of this form.

♦ **Lines 62-91:** These lines declare some important user-defined variables. These variables are used at various places in this class.

- **62:** The `iConnectedComputers` variable stores the total number of currently running listeners that are successfully connected with the server.

- **68:** The `iSearchResult` variable is used to store the number of results found for a specific search criteria.

- **73:** This line declares an object `xmlParser` for the `XMLParser` class present inside the `WorkingWithXML` assembly created for this application.

- **79:** The `xmlServerComm` object of the `ServerCommunication` class is declared here to access the functions present in `ServerCommunication` class. This class is user defined and has its source in the `WorkingWithXML` assembly.

- **84:** The `xmlStruct` variable of the `XMLSTRUCT` structure is declared here to have the parsed data to store in their respective places.

- **90:** This Makes an array of the `_CONNECTEDCOMPUTERS` structure represented by the `ConnectedComputers` variable.

♦ **Lines 100:** This declares a ListViewItem variable `lvItems`.

♦ **Lines 105-141:** These lines of code implement the default contructor for this class. Some extra coding has been done in this contructor for the purpose of retrieving the list of the listeners from the server. This is furnished by calling the `PopulateList()` function of this class.

- **117 -123:** New instances of user-defined classes (`XMLParser`, `XMLSTRUCT`, and `ServerCommunication`) are created.

- **126-129:** Here we are assigning the filename to the `USERLISTXML` variable of `XMLParser` class. The userlist XML returned by the server is stored by this filename on the local machine. The next variable `SERVERSEARCHRESULTXML` does the same thing. It stores the name of the file in which the search result XML response is to be stored.

- **134 -141:** With the help of the `PopulateList()` function in this class, the list view is filled with values, which are retrieved as the response from the server. In case no computer is connected to the network, an error message is displayed, and the list is empty.

♦ Lines 147-151: The main purpose of the function is to clear and release all resources held up by the application. This coding is autogenerated by IDE and is called on the closing event of this form.

♦ Lines 158-302: This method is used to initialize and assign the user-interface variables. This is generated automatically by the C# environment. It is advisable not to manipulate these lines of code unless you know where the impact is going to be shown.

♦ Lines 308-384: This `PopulateList()` function is used to populate the list view with the entries retrieved from the userlist XML.

- 315: The response from the server is received by calling an ASP page on the server. This response is then saved in the file represented by the `USERLIST` variable of `XMLParser` class.

- 321: The `xmlStruct` variable stores the parsed data from the XML returned by the server, in response to calling the ASP page. After parsing, the `iConnectedComputer` variable stores the total number of listener entries found on the server.

- 324-354: Each time this function is called, the contents of list view are first cleared and then updated with the recent list. The parsed XML file is then deleted from the system, as we have data saved in the `XMLSTRUCT` structure. The next step is to sort the list by `Computername`.

- 360-376: The array represented by the `iConnectedComputers` variable is being filled here by the values present in the `USERLIST` structure of `XMLSTRUCT`.

- 380: In case the application encounters an error, the message is displayed.

- 383: Lastly, this function returns the number of entries populated in the list view.

♦ Lines 390-449: This function does the same thing described for `PopulateList()` and also populates the *number of objects found column* of the list view with the search results.

♦ Lines 456-461: This function handles the key-press events of the Enter and SpaceBar keys when pressed while some item is selected on the list view.

♦ Lines 467: Whenever you double click the list view, this function comes into action. It calls the click function associated with the Open button, as double click indicates that you want to open or connect to the selected computer from the list view.

♦ Lines 477-485: When you click the Refresh button placed on the application's form, this function is invoked. This function refreshes the contents of the list view by retrieving the fresh `USERLIST` from server again and shows it in the list view. The error message is displayed if no listener is connected to the network. As in constructor, the `PopulateList()` function is called.

♦ Lines 492-529: This function comes into action when you click the Open button. Here the currently selected computer from the computer list view is extracted seperately with its IP address and a string is made out of that (for example, `COMPUTERNAME (IP ADDRESS)`). This string is then passed to the contructor of the frmShare class by making its object ShareForm; after that, the form is displayed on the screen (line 481).

♦ Lines 536: This performs the quit operation when you click the Quit button placed on the application's form.

♦ Lines 544-586: This function is inviked when you click the View button. This function is used to view the searched files.

- 548: An object of the `frmShare` class is initialized as `ShareForm`.

- 560-580: These lines scan through the `SERVERSEARCH` list and insert the values in the list view of the `frmShare` class. Values are inserted in Folder/File as a hierarchy. Finally the results are displayed.

♦ Lines 594-613: Whenever you change the selection in the list view, this function is activated. This function is responsible for enabling or disabling the `ViewFiles` button. If no searches are found on the computer, the `ViewFiles` button becomes disabled when you selects that computer from the list view.

- 599: The local variable `iTemp` of integer type is declared to store the number of individual search results returned by the `GetNumberOfObjectsFound()` function.

- 605: The `GetNumberOfObjectsFound()` function is called, and its values are stored in the local variable `iTemp`.

- 609: If `iTemp` is 0, the ViewFiles button is disabled, if the `iTemp` variable is not zero than keep the ViewFiles button enabled.

♦ Lines 621-647: This function returns the total objects found in the search for a selected entry so that the state of view file can be toggled.

- 624: This retrieves the currently selected item from the list view.

- 627-630: Variables `iIndex` and `iReturn` are initialized to -1.

- 633-646: After verifying that `items` variables have something to read, the index of selected item is extracted and placed into `iIndex` variable. Then the corresponding value for the `iFilesFound` variable is extracted from the `ConnectedComputer` array. Finally, the index and the value of the `iFilesFound` variable are returned.

- Lines 655-689: This function is invoked when the Search button is clicked. A form is displayed at this point to enter the search criteria. Search criteria are then returned to the caller of the form and passed to an ASP page on the server. The server handles the request and fetches the matching records, making an XML and returning the response to the request. This XML is then parsed in the `PopulateWithSearchResults()` function and used to display the values in the list view.

♦ Lines 695: This is the main entry point of this application. This function has the same task as the `main()` function in C or C++. Execution starts here.

frmShare Class

The window shown in Figure 5-6 allows youto see the shared contents of a selected computer. It shows the files/folders, their size, and the type of files/folders on the remote computer.

♦ **Upload button:** This button allows you to select any file from your local machine and to transfer that file on the connected machine. For example, if you want to send a file to the listener, you can use this button.

♦ **Download Button:** To download any file from the remote machine, select a file, and click the Download button to save that file on the local machine over the network.

♦ **Search Button:** This button allows you to search for a specific file in the current folder being viewed.

♦ **Close Button:** This button does not close the application; instead, it closes this window and brings you back to the main application window.

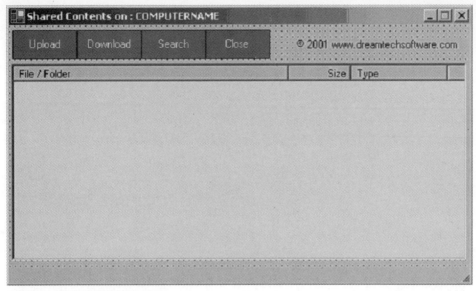

Figure 5-6: Shared Content window

Listing 5-7 describes the code for frmShare.

Listing 5-7: frmShare

//© 2001 Dreamtech Software India Inc.
// All rights reserved

```
 1 namespace Client          // Copyright 2001 Dreamtech Software India Inc.
 2 {                         // All rights reserved
 3
 4  using System;            // Provides the basic functionality of .NET
 5  using System.Drawing;    // Provides the Drawing features, Used for
    cursors
 6    using System.Windows.Forms;// Provides the drawing of buttons, listviews
etc
 7  using System.Net;        // Provides the net related functionality
 8  using System.Net.Sockets; // Provides the functionality of sockets
 9  using System.Text;       // Provides the text manipulation functions
10  using System.IO;         // Provides I/O features
11  using WorkingWithXML;    // Custom class
12  using System.Collections; // Provides the different type of class
collections
13    using System.ComponentModel;// Provides the facility of using components
14
15  /// <summary>
16    /// Summary description for frmShare.
17    /// </summary>
18    public class frmShare : System.Windows.Forms.Form
19    {
20        private System.ComponentModel.IContainer components;
21        private System.Windows.Forms.OpenFileDialog FileOpenDialog;
22        public System.Windows.Forms.Button btnClose;
23        public System.Windows.Forms.StatusBar sBar;
24        private System.Windows.Forms.SaveFileDialog FileSaveDialog;
25        private System.Windows.Forms.ToolTip toolTipText;
```

```
26          public System.Windows.Forms.ListView lvFiles;
27          public System.Windows.Forms.Button btnSearch;
28          public System.Windows.Forms.Button btnDownload;
29          public System.Windows.Forms.Button btnUpload;
30          private System.Windows.Forms.ColumnHeader clhFilename;
31          private System.Windows.Forms.ColumnHeader clhFileSize;
32          private System.Windows.Forms.ColumnHeader clhType;
33
34   /// <summary>
35   /// User defined variables.
36   /// </summary>
37
38   /// <summary>
39   /// stores the number of bytes written or read from any stream
40   /// </summary>
41   private int iBytes;
42
43   /// <summary>
44   ///  These variables are used to store the name of the computer
45   ///  to which you have connected and the parent folder name.
46   ///  Parent folder name is the name of the folder of the contents
47   ///  which you are viewing in the window
48   /// </summary>
49   private string                                    COMPUTERNAME, PARENTFOLDER;
50
51   /// <summary>
52   /// Stores a new created socket of type TCPClient(System defined class)
53   /// used to communicate with the listener
54   /// </summary>
55   private TcpClient ClientSocket;
56
57   /// <summary>
58   /// creates a variable for XMLCreater(User defined class) to
59   /// create XML requests for the listener
60   /// </summary>
61   private XMLCreater xmlCreate;
62
63   /// <summary>
64   /// StreamTCP points to the NetworkStream(System defined class)
65   /// which is used for transfer data over the Socket connection
66   /// </summary>
67   private NetworkStream StreamTCP;
68
69   /// <summary>
70   /// fileStream is an object of type FileStream(System defined class)
71   /// used to have I/O capabilities for files which are used
72   /// in this program
73   /// </summary>
74   private FileStream fileStream;
75
76   /// <summary>
77   /// ReadBuffer and WriteBuffer Byte arrays used for
78   /// Reading and Writing any file.
79   /// </summary>
80   private Byte[] ReadBuffer,WriteBuffer;
81
```

```
82     /// <summary>
83     /// xmlParser is of type XMLParser(User defined class)
84     /// It is used to have the access for Parsing the XML file
85     /// This class is present in WorkingWithXML
86     /// </summary>
87     private XMLParser  xmlParser;
88
89     /// <summary>
90     /// xmlStruct is of type XMLSTRUCT(User defined structure)
91     /// It is used to store the different records obtained
92     /// from parsing the XML. This structure is present in WorkingWithXML
93     /// </summary>
94     private XMLSTRUCT  xmlStruct;
95
96     /// <summary>
97     /// strArray if of Type SHOWFILES of XMLSTRUCT Structure and
98     /// used to save the corresponding Files/Folder which are seen in the
99     /// the List view at run time
100    /// </summary>
101    private XMLSTRUCT.__SHOWFILES[] strArray;
102
103
104    /// <summary>
105    /// The below variables are readonly variables that u cannot
106    /// assign a new value to these variables again. They are
107    /// constant type variables
108    /// </summary>
109
110    /// <summary>
111    /// REQUESTFILE has the name of the file which has to be created
112    /// for a particular request
113    /// </summary>
114    public readonly string REQUESTFILE = Application.StartupPath +
"\\Request.xml";
115
116    /// <summary>
117    /// RESPONSEFILE has the name of the file which has to be created
118    /// for a particular request
119    /// </summary>
120    public readonly string RESPONSEFILE = Application.StartupPath +
"\\Response.xml";
121    private System.Windows.Forms.Label lblCopyright;
122
123    /// <summary>
124    /// MAX_SIZE defines the maximum size of the read or write buffer
125    /// which is used for reading or writing a file
126    /// </summary>
127    public readonly int MAX_SIZE = 512;
128
129    /// <summary>
130    /// This is the default contructor of the this class
131    /// This is called from the View files button
132    /// </summary>
133    public frmShare()
134        {
135            //
```

```
136                  // Required for Windows Form Designer support
137                  //
138                  // Auto generated code line by the IDE
139         InitializeComponent();
140
141         // Puts the Computer.ico as the form icon
142         this.Icon = new System.Drawing.Icon(Application.StartupPath +
"\\Computer.ico");
143
144         // Changes the Caption of this dialog box
145         this.Text = "Search Result";
146         sBar.Text = "Root";
147         COMPUTERNAME = null;
148         PARENTFOLDER = null;
149          }
150
151   /// <summary>
152   /// This is a user defined constructor called from the
153   /// Open button in the frmClient
154   /// Computername is passed to this function, which you
155   /// have selected from the Main window
156   /// </summary>
157   /// <param name="Computername"> </param>
158   public frmShare(string Computername)
159   {
160              //
161              // Required for Windows Form Designer support
162      // This line is not auto generated, instead it has been copied from
163      // default constructor
164          InitializeComponent();
165
166         // Puts the Computer.ico as the form icon
167         this.Icon = new System.Drawing.Icon(Application.StartupPath +
"\\Computer.ico");
168
169         // COMPUTERNAME is a global variable used to store the name
170         // and IP Address of the computer to which you are currently
171         // connected
172         COMPUTERNAME = Computername;
173
174         // Open connection is a user defined function responsible for
175         // opening a socket connection for listener. This function
176         // returns a bool value
177         if( OpenConnection(COMPUTERNAME)  )
178         {
179              // This will creates a SHOWFILE request XML for seding it
180              // to the listener
181              CreateRequest("SHOWFILES","","");
182
183              // This will actually send the REQUESTFILE to the listener
184              SendDataToListener(REQUESTFILE);
185
186              // This will get the response of the above request from
187              // listener and stores that response in a RESPONSEFILE
188              GetDataFromListener(RESPONSEFILE);
189
```

```
190                    // This will Parse that response XML File and results are
191                    // shown to the user
192                    Parsing(RESPONSEFILE);
193
194                    // Closes any Opened socket or stream connection
195                    CloseConnection();
196
197                    // Since this constructor is called at the root level
198                    // therefore no parent folder is associated with it
199                    PARENTFOLDER = null;
200
201                    // Changes the caption of this dialog box
202                    this.Text = "Shared contents on: " + Computername.ToUpper();
203
204                    // Sets the text for the Status bar
205                    sBar.Text = "Root";
206            }
207    }
208
209    /// <summary>
210    /// This is also a user defined constructor called from the
211    /// Search button to view the search results
212    /// This constructor is called from within this code only
213    /// it is used to pass any type of request if needed at the time of
214    /// its construction
215    /// </summary>
216    /// <param name="Computername stores the name of the computer to
connect"> </param>
217    /// <param name="Request stores what type of request you want to send to
the listener"> </param>
218    /// <param name="Scope scope value needed, if any"> </param>
219    /// <param name="Mask mask value needed if any"> </param>
220    public frmShare(string Computername, string Request, string Scope, string
Mask)
221    {
222                // Required for Windows Form Designer support
223        // This line is not auto generated, instead it has been copied from
224        // default constructor
225            InitializeComponent();
226
227        // Puts the Computer.ico as the form icon
228        this.Icon = new System.Drawing.Icon(Application.StartupPath +
"\\Computer.ico");
229
230        // COMPUTERNAME is a global variable used to store the name
231        // and IP Address of the computer to which you are currently
232        // connected
233        COMPUTERNAME = Computername;
234
235        // Open connection is a user defined function responsible for
236        // opening a socket connection for listener. This function
237        // returns a bool value
238        if( OpenConnection(COMPUTERNAME) )
239        {
240                // Creates an XML request with scope and mask
241                CreateRequest(Request,Scope,Mask);
```

```
242
243                // Sends this request to listener
244                SendDataToListener(REQUESTFILE);
245
246                // get the response from listener
247                GetDataFromListener(RESPONSEFILE);
248
249                // Parse that response for records and show those records
250                Parsing(RESPONSEFILE);
251
252                // Closes the active connection
253                CloseConnection();
254
255                // Assign scope to sText local variable
256                string sText = Scope;
257
258                // Extract the name of the PARENTFOLDER
259                sText = sText.Substring(0, sText.LastIndexOf("\\")+1);
260
261                // changes the caption of this dialog box
262                this.Text = sText + " on '" + Computername + "'";
263
264                // Assign the value for PARENTFOLDER
265                PARENTFOLDER = sText;
266
267                // Changes the text of the status bar
268                sBar.Text = sText;
269            }
270    }
271
272    /// <summary>
273        ///     Clean up any resources being used.
274        ///     auto generated function by IDE
275        /// </summary>
276        public override void Dispose()
277        {
278            base.Dispose();
279            components.Dispose();
280        }
281
282        /// <summary>
283        ///     Required method for Designer support - do not modify
284        ///     the contents of this method with the code editor.
285        ///     These are also auto generated lines of code
286        /// </summary>
287        private void InitializeComponent()
288    {
289        this.components = new System.ComponentModel.Container();
290        this.clhType = new System.Windows.Forms.ColumnHeader();
291        this.toolTipText = new System.Windows.Forms.ToolTip(this.components);
292        this.btnClose = new System.Windows.Forms.Button();
293        this.btnSearch = new System.Windows.Forms.Button();
294        this.btnUpload = new System.Windows.Forms.Button();
295        this.btnDownload = new System.Windows.Forms.Button();
296        this.lvFiles = new System.Windows.Forms.ListView();
297        this.clhFilename = new System.Windows.Forms.ColumnHeader();
```

```
298        this.clhFileSize = new System.Windows.Forms.ColumnHeader();
299        this.sBar = new System.Windows.Forms.StatusBar();
300        this.FileOpenDialog = new System.Windows.Forms.OpenFileDialog();
301        this.FileSaveDialog = new System.Windows.Forms.SaveFileDialog();
302        this.lblCopyright = new System.Windows.Forms.Label();
303        this.SuspendLayout();
304        //
305        // clhType
306        //
307        this.clhType.Text = "Type";
308        this.clhType.Width = 108;
309        //
310        // btnClose
311        //
312        this.btnClose.BackColor = System.Drawing.Color.Chocolate;
313        this.btnClose.DialogResult =
System.Windows.Forms.DialogResult.Cancel;
314        this.btnClose.FlatStyle = System.Windows.Forms.FlatStyle.Popup;
315        this.btnClose.ForeColor = System.Drawing.Color.White;
316        this.btnClose.Location = new System.Drawing.Point(217, 5);
317        this.btnClose.Name = "btnClose";
318        this.btnClose.Size = new System.Drawing.Size(71, 31);
319        this.btnClose.TabIndex = 3;
320        this.btnClose.Text = "&Close";
321        this.toolTipText.SetToolTip(this.btnClose, "Exist from this window");
322        this.btnClose.Click += new System.EventHandler(this.btnClose_Click);
323        //
324        // btnSearch
325        //
326        this.btnSearch.BackColor = System.Drawing.Color.Chocolate;
327        this.btnSearch.Enabled = false;
328        this.btnSearch.FlatStyle = System.Windows.Forms.FlatStyle.Popup;
329        this.btnSearch.ForeColor = System.Drawing.Color.White;
330        this.btnSearch.Location = new System.Drawing.Point(146, 5);
331        this.btnSearch.Name = "btnSearch";
332        this.btnSearch.Size = new System.Drawing.Size(71, 31);
333        this.btnSearch.TabIndex = 2;
334        this.btnSearch.Text = "&Search";
335        this.toolTipText.SetToolTip(this.btnSearch, "Search for file(s) or
folder(s)");
336        this.btnSearch.Click += new
System.EventHandler(this.btnSearch_Click);
337        //
338        // btnUpload
339        //
340        this.btnUpload.BackColor = System.Drawing.Color.Chocolate;
341        this.btnUpload.Enabled = false;
342        this.btnUpload.FlatStyle = System.Windows.Forms.FlatStyle.Popup;
343        this.btnUpload.ForeColor = System.Drawing.Color.White;
344        this.btnUpload.Location = new System.Drawing.Point(4, 5);
345        this.btnUpload.Name = "btnUpload";
346        this.btnUpload.Size = new System.Drawing.Size(71, 31);
347        this.btnUpload.TabIndex = 0;
348        this.btnUpload.Text = "&Upload";
349        this.toolTipText.SetToolTip(this.btnUpload, "Writes the file to
current location");
```

```
350        this.btnUpload.Click += new
System.EventHandler(this.btnUpload_Click);
351        //
352        // btnDownload
353        //
354        this.btnDownload.BackColor = System.Drawing.Color.Chocolate;
355        this.btnDownload.Enabled = false;
356        this.btnDownload.FlatStyle = System.Windows.Forms.FlatStyle.Popup;
357        this.btnDownload.ForeColor = System.Drawing.Color.White;
358        this.btnDownload.Location = new System.Drawing.Point(75, 5);
359        this.btnDownload.Name = "btnDownload";
360        this.btnDownload.Size = new System.Drawing.Size(71, 31);
361        this.btnDownload.TabIndex = 1;
362        this.btnDownload.Text = "&Download";
363        this.toolTipText.SetToolTip(this.btnDownload, "Download file to this
computer");
364        this.btnDownload.Click += new
System.EventHandler(this.btnDownload_Click);
365        //
366        // lvFiles
367        //
368        this.lvFiles.Columns.AddRange(new System.Windows.Forms.ColumnHeader[]
{
369
                      this.clhFilename,
370
                      this.clhFileSize,
371
                      this.clhType});
372        this.lvFiles.ForeColor = System.Drawing.SystemColors.WindowText;
373        this.lvFiles.FullRowSelect = true;
374        this.lvFiles.HideSelection = false;
375        this.lvFiles.Location = new System.Drawing.Point(3, 41);
376        this.lvFiles.MultiSelect = false;
377        this.lvFiles.Name = "lvFiles";
378        this.lvFiles.Size = new System.Drawing.Size(502, 211);
379        this.lvFiles.TabIndex = 4;
380        this.toolTipText.SetToolTip(this.lvFiles, "Double click an entry to
open");
381        this.lvFiles.View = System.Windows.Forms.View.Details;
382        this.lvFiles.KeyPress += new
System.Windows.Forms.KeyPressEventHandler(this.lvFiles_KeyPress);
383        this.lvFiles.DoubleClick += new
System.EventHandler(this.lvFiles_DoubleClick);
384        //
385        // clhFilename
386        //
387        this.clhFilename.Text = "File / Folder";
388        this.clhFilename.Width = 303;
389        //
390        // clhFileSize
391        //
392        this.clhFileSize.Text = "Size";
393        this.clhFileSize.TextAlign =
System.Windows.Forms.HorizontalAlignment.Right;
394        this.clhFileSize.Width = 69;
```

```
395          //
396          // sBar
397          //
398          this.sBar.Location = new System.Drawing.Point(0, 259);
399          this.sBar.Name = "sBar";
400          this.sBar.Size = new System.Drawing.Size(508, 16);
401          this.sBar.TabIndex = 5;
402          //
403          // FileOpenDialog
404          //
405          this.FileOpenDialog.Filter = "*.* (All files)|";
406          this.FileOpenDialog.Title = "Select a file to upload";
407          //
408          // lblCopyright
409          //
410          this.lblCopyright.Location = new System.Drawing.Point(314, 14);
411          this.lblCopyright.Name = "lblCopyright";
412          this.lblCopyright.Size = new System.Drawing.Size(192, 14);
413          this.lblCopyright.TabIndex = 6;
414          this.lblCopyright.Text = "© 2001 www.dreamtechsoftware.com";
415          //
416          // frmShare
417          //
418          this.AutoScaleBaseSize = new System.Drawing.Size(5, 13);
419          this.CancelButton = this.btnClose;
420          this.ClientSize = new System.Drawing.Size(508, 275);
421          this.Controls.AddRange(new System.Windows.Forms.Control[] {
422
        this.lblCopyright,
423
        this.btnClose,
424     this.sBar,
425          this.lvFiles,
426          this.btnSearch,
427          this.btnDownload,
428          this.btnUpload});
429          this.FormBorderStyle =
             System.Windows.Forms.FormBorderStyle.FixedDialog;
430          this.MaximizeBox = false;
431          this.Name = "frmShare";
432          this.Text = "Shared Contents on : COMPUTERNAME";
433          this.ResumeLayout(false);
434
435     }
436
437     /// <summary>
438     /// This function is used to extract the mask value for
439     /// a given filename
440     /// </summary>
441     /// <param name="Filename"> </param>
442     private int GetMask(string Filename)
443     {
444          // assigns -1 to a local variable. If no matching file is found then
return -1
445          int iReturn = -1;
446
```

```
447              // take one by one entry and check it for the matching value
448          for(int i = 0; i < strArray.Length; i++)
449               // if match is found
450               if( 0 ==
strArray[i].sFilename.Substring(0,Filename.Length).CompareTo(Filename)  )
451                        // assign the actual mask value of the match to
iReturn
452                        iReturn = strArray[i].iMask;
453
454        //returns the value for iReturn
455        return iReturn;
456    }
457
458    /// <summary>
459    /// Invoked when Upload button is clicked
460    /// </summary>
461    /// <param name="sender"> </param>
462    /// <param name="e"> </param>
463    protected void btnUpload_Click (object sender, System.EventArgs e)
464    {
465        try
466        {
467            //Since you cannot upload at root level
468            // This line check that if you are at root level or not
469            if( null != PARENTFOLDER )
470            {
471            // if Mask is 0 or less than 0 then you cannot upload a file
472                if( 0 < GetMask(PARENTFOLDER) )
473                {
474                    // Since we have used OpenFileDialog to select
the
475                    // filename to save. This initialises
InitialDirectory
476                    // property of the FileOpenDialog to The path
from where
477                    // the application is running
478                    FileOpenDialog.InitialDirectory =
Application.StartupPath;
479
480                    // If use press OK in the FileOpenDialog box
481                    if( System.Windows.Forms.DialogResult.OK ==
FileOpenDialog.ShowDialog() )
482                    {
483                        // Assigns a local variable to the name
of the
484                        // to upload
485                        string LocalFilename =
FileOpenDialog.FileName;
486
487                        // Assigns a local variable to the name
of the
488                        // to upload which is to be sent to the
listener
489                        string RemoteFilename = LocalFilename;
490
```

```
491                                          // Extract the filename from the Full
Qualified name
492                                          RemoteFilename =
RemoteFilename.Substring(RemoteFilename.LastIndexOf("\\") + 1);
493
494                                          // Open a connection
495                                          if( OpenConnection(COMPUTERNAME) )
496                                          {
497                                              // Temporary varable used to
store the current value of the
498                                              // status bar text and to replace
it further
499                                              string sTemp = sBar.Text;
500
501                                              // Creates an UPLOAD request with
the filename and mask
502
CreateRequest("UPLOAD",PARENTFOLDER +
RemoteFilename,GetMask(PARENTFOLDER).ToString());
503
504                                              // sends this request to the
listener
505                                              SendDataToListener(REQUESTFILE);
506
507                                              // Show wait cursor while
uploading the file
508                                              Cursor = Cursors.WaitCursor;
509
510                                              // changes the status bar text
511                                              sBar.Text = "Uploading file.
Please wait...";
512
513                                              // first process all the pending
events from the message queue
514                                              // so that application doesnt
seems blocking
515                                              Application.DoEvents();
516
517                                              // Assign fileStream object to
the local file which is
518                                              // to be uploaded
519                                              fileStream = new
FileStream(LocalFilename,FileMode.Open,FileAccess.Read);
520
521                                              // bReader is used to read data
from the file in
522                                              // binary mode. BinaryReader is a
System defined class
523                                              // Create a new object for Binary
reader link it
524                                              // to the filestream which is
created above
525                                              BinaryReader bReader = new
BinaryReader(fileStream);
526
```

```
527                                              // Initialized the ReadBuffer
variable here
528                                              // to read only 512 bytes at a
time
529                                              ReadBuffer = new Byte[MAX_SIZE];
530
531                                              // Read only 512 bytes at a time
from the file
532                                              // and writes to the socket
stream.
533                                              // This read continues until the
control reaches the
534                                              // end of file
535                                              while( 0 != (iBytes =
bReader.Read(ReadBuffer,0,ReadBuffer.Length)) )
536
StreamTCP.Write(ReadBuffer,0,iBytes);
537
538                                              // now close the binary reader
since it is no longer needed
539                                              bReader.Close();
540
541                                              // closes the fileStream object
542                                              fileStream.Close();
543
544                                              // close the socket connection
545                                              CloseConnection();
546
547                                              // Restore the staus bar text
548                                              sBar.Text = sTemp;
549
550                                              // restore the cursor
551                                              Cursor = Cursors.Default;
552                                    }
553                          }
554                }
555
556                // If mask is 0 or less than 0 then throw the
exception
557                else throw new Exception("Read Only folder detected.
Access Denied");
558            }
559            // Throw the exception os root level it detected
560            // since you cannot upload at root level
561            else throw new Exception("Cannot upload at Root level");
562        }
563
564    // Catches any thrown exception
565    catch( Exception err ) {
MessageBox.Show(err.Message,"Error",MessageBoxButtons.OK,  MessageBoxIcon.Error);
}
566    }
567
568    /// <summary>
569    /// Handles any key press events in the list view
570    /// </summary>
```

```
571     /// <param name="sender"> </param>
572     /// <param name="e"> </param>
573     protected void lvFiles_KeyPress (object sender,
System.Windows.Forms.KeyPressEventArgs e)
574     {
575           // if Enter key(13) or Space bar Key(32) is pressed
576           // than call the Listview double click function
577           if( 13 == e.KeyChar || 32 == e.KeyChar )
578                   lvFiles_DoubleClick(null,System.EventArgs.Empty);
579     }
580
581     /// <summary>
582     /// Called when close button is clicked
583     /// </summary>
584     /// <param name="sender"> </param>
585     /// <param name="e"> </param>
586     protected void btnClose_Click (object sender, System.EventArgs e) {
this.Close(); /* closes this dialog box*/ }
587
588     /// <summary>
589     /// This Function creates all XML requests
590     /// by given Request Scope and Mask
591     /// </summary>
592     /// <param name="Request"> </param>
593     /// <param name="Scope"> </param>
594     /// <param name="Mask"> </param>
595     public void CreateRequest(string Request, string Scope, string Mask)
596     {
597           // creates a new object for xmlCreate variable
598           xmlCreate = new XMLCreater(REQUESTFILE,"");
599
600           // Actually writes the XML request. This is a user defined function
601           xmlCreate.WriteRequest(Request,Scope,Mask);
602     }
603
604     /// <summary>
605     /// Opens a Socket connection for every transaction
606     /// </summary>
607     /// <param name="Computername"> </param>
608     public bool OpenConnection(string Computername)
609     {
610           bool IsConnected = false;
611           try
612           {
613                   // Initializes the local bool variable to false
614                   // value of this variable will be returned by the function
615
616                   // extract the IP address from the Computername
617                   string AddressIP =
Computername.Substring(Computername.IndexOf("(")+1);
618                   AddressIP = AddressIP.Substring(0, AddressIP.Length - 1);
619
620                   // defines the remote end point. That is where to connect
621                   // and at which port to connect to the listener
622                   // IPEndPoint is a system define class
```

```
623                 IPEndPoint RemoteEP = new IPEndPoint(
IPAddress.Parse(AddressIP),7070 );
624
625                 // initializes the cLientSocket variable
626                 ClientSocket = new TcpClient();
627
628                 // Performs a remote connection operation
629                 ClientSocket.Connect(RemoteEP);
630
631                 // Enable the various buttons
632                 btnDownload.Enabled = true;
633                 btnSearch.Enabled = true;
634                 btnUpload.Enabled = true;
635
636                 // gets the stream for the currently connected socket
637                 // This stream is used to send and recieve data
638                 // from and to the listener
639                 StreamTCP = ClientSocket.GetStream();
640
641                 // assigns the true value to IsConnected variable
642                 IsConnected = true;
643
644                 //return the value for IsConnected variable
645             }
646         catch( Exception err ) {
MessageBox.Show(err.Message,"Error",MessageBoxButtons.OK, MessageBoxIcon.Error);
}
647
648         return IsConnected;
649     }
650
651     /// <summary>
652     /// This function sends any type of request to the listener
653     /// which is present in a file represented by filename
654     /// </summary>
655     /// <param name="Filename"> </param>
656     public void SendDataToListener(string Filename)
657     {
658             // Creates a new object for fileStream with File open mode
659         fileStream = new FileStream(Filename,FileMode.Open);
660
661     // initializes and assigns the ReadBuffer with the
662     // length of the file
663     ReadBuffer = new Byte[Convert.ToInt32(fileStream.Length)];
664
665     // read whole file in one shot in ReadBuffer variable
666     fileStream.Read(ReadBuffer,0,ReadBuffer.Length);
667
668     // close the fileStream
669     fileStream.Close();
670
671     // Delete the RequestFile
672     new ServerCommunication().FileDelete(REQUESTFILE);
673
674         // Write the read data to the Socket stream...This data is read by
the
```

```
675              // listener
676              StreamTCP.Write(ReadBuffer,0,ReadBuffer.Length);
677     }
678
679     /// <summary>
680     /// After sending the request, the response will be handled
681     /// by this function. The response will be written in a file
682     /// represented by the filename. This is used to read the response
683     /// that is sent by the listener
684     /// </summary>
685     /// <param name="Filename"> </param>
686     public void GetDataFromListener(string Filename)
687     {
688              // Initializes the WriteBuffer variable to hold
689              // 512 character at a time
690              WriteBuffer = new Byte[MAX_SIZE];
691
692              // Creates a File stream to store the response data.
693              fileStream = new FileStream(Filename,FileMode.Create);
694
695              // Creates a binary write by which we can write to the file
696              BinaryWriter bWriter = new BinaryWriter(fileStream);
697
698              // Read only 512 bytes at a time from the socket
699              // stream and writes to the File.
700              // This read continues until the control reaches the
701              // finds no more bytes to read
702              while( 0 != (iBytes =
StreamTCP.Read(WriteBuffer,0,WriteBuffer.Length)) )
703                      bWriter.Write(WriteBuffer,0,iBytes);
704
705              // Closed the binary writer
706              bWriter.Close();
707
708              // Closed the fileStream Object
709              fileStream.Close();
710     }
711
712     /// <summary>
713     /// Invoked when user double clicks on the list view
714     /// </summary>
715     /// <param name="sender"> </param>
716     /// <param name="e"> </param>
717     protected void lvFiles_DoubleClick (object sender, System.EventArgs e)
718     {
719              // local variable to store index value
720              int             index;
721
722              // local variable to store the name of the entry at which user
723              // double clicks
724              string Filename;
725
726              try
727              {
728                      // Get the selected entry from the list view,
729                      // its name and its index at which it is present
```

```
730                    index = GetSelectedItemFromListView(out Filename);
731
732                    // Index must be greater than -1
733                    if( -1 != index )
734                    {
735                        // if Filename is null then directory is selected
736                        if( null == Filename )
737                        {
738                            // This will send the request to listener with
the name of the folder
739                            // whose contents are to be shown
740                            frmShare ShareForm = new
frmShare(COMPUTERNAME,"SEARCH",strArray[index].sFilename +
"*.*",strArray[index].iMask.ToString());
741
742                            //Now show the contents here
743                            ShareForm.Show();
744                        }
745
746                        // if the user double clicks on the file then
747                        // download that file
748                        else DownloadFile(index,Filename,false);
749                    }
750
751                    // if index is -1 then displays an appropriate error message
752                    else throw new Exception("Nothing Selected");
753                }
754
755            // Catch and show any system error message here
756            catch( Exception err ) {
MessageBox.Show(err.Message,"Warning",MessageBoxButtons.OK,
MessageBoxIcon.Warning); }
757    }
758
759    /// <summary>
760    /// This function gets the value coressponding to the array
761    /// which is currently selected in a list view
762    /// It returns the value in sReturn and function returns the
763    /// index of this value in the array
764    /// </summary>
765    /// <param name="sReturn"> </param>
766    private int GetSelectedItemFromListView( out string sReturn )
767    {
768        // This will get the selected items from the list
769        // in our case only one item is selected
770        System.Windows.Forms.ListView.SelectedListViewItemCollection    items
= lvFiles.SelectedItems;
771
772        // initialize ant assign iIndex to -1
773        int iIndex = -1;
774
775        // This value will be returned by the function in out string sReturn
776        sReturn = null;
777
778        // if nothing is selected dont go inside this iteration
779        if( 0 < items.Count )
```

```
780        {
781                // Get the index of the selected item
782                iIndex = items[0].Index;
783
784                // finds the actual filename by the given index from the list
785                // which we have maintained
786                string Filename = strArray[iIndex].sFilename;
787
788                // Checks whether the selected entry is a Folder or File
789                // if Folder is selected then return the name of the folder
790                // else return null
791                if( !Filename.EndsWith("\\") )
792                     sReturn =
Filename.Substring(Filename.LastIndexOf("\\") + 1);
793                else sReturn = null;
794        }
795        return iIndex;
796    }
797
798    /// <summary>
799    /// This function parses any XML response and displays it in the window
800    /// The Response is in a file denoted by  Filename
801    /// </summary>
802    /// <param name="Filename"> </param>
803    public bool Parsing(string Filename)
804    {
805        // This variable is returned by the function, if the value
806        // of this variable is true then Parsing is successfull else
807        // Parsing Failed
808        bool bReturn = false;
809
810        // This line of code will create a new instance of
811        // XMLParser class and assigns it to the xmlParser variable
812        xmlParser = new WorkingWithXML.XMLParser();
813
814        // This will create a new instance of the XMLSTRUCT structure
815        // and assigns it to the xmlStruct variable
816        xmlStruct = new WorkingWithXML.XMLSTRUCT();
817
818        // This will check whether the correct XML is received by the browser
819        // or not if correct XML is received then only parse that XML
820        // The XML response must me of type "SHOWFILES"
821        if( 0 == new
ServerCommunication().TypeOfXMLRecieved(RESPONSEFILE).CompareTo("SHOWFILES")  )
822        {
823                // The ParseXML function is present in the XMLParser class
824                // which is represented by xmlParser variable, and it will
825                // return the number of records parsed by the parser
826                int iEntries = xmlParser.ParseXML(RESPONSEFILE, out
xmlStruct,new ServerCommunication().TypeOfXMLRecieved(RESPONSEFILE));
827
828                // If number of records greater than zero then continue
829                // further, else dont go inside
830                if( 0 < iEntries )
831                {
832                     /// This block of code is used to sort the records
```

```
833                          /// first the Folders should come and than the files
834                          /// are to be sorted by their sizes
835                          for( int i = 0; i < iEntries; i++ )
836                          {
837                              for( int k = i + 1 ; k < iEntries; k++ )
838                              {
839                                  if(
!xmlStruct.SHOWFILES[i].sFilename.EndsWith("\\") &&
xmlStruct.SHOWFILES[k].sFilename.EndsWith("\\") ||
xmlStruct.SHOWFILES[i].iFileSize > xmlStruct.SHOWFILES[k].iFileSize )
840                                  {
841                                      string Temp;
842                                      Temp =
xmlStruct.SHOWFILES[i].sFilename;
843                                      xmlStruct.SHOWFILES[i].sFilename
= xmlStruct.SHOWFILES[k].sFilename;
844                                      xmlStruct.SHOWFILES[k].sFilename
= Temp;
845
846                                      Temp =
xmlStruct.SHOWFILES[i].iFileSize.ToString();
847                                      xmlStruct.SHOWFILES[i].iFileSize
= xmlStruct.SHOWFILES[k].iFileSize;
848                                      xmlStruct.SHOWFILES[k].iFileSize
= Convert.ToInt32(Temp);
849
850                                      Temp =
xmlStruct.SHOWFILES[i].iMask.ToString();
851                                      xmlStruct.SHOWFILES[i].iMask =
xmlStruct.SHOWFILES[k].iMask;
852                                      xmlStruct.SHOWFILES[k].iMask =
Convert.ToInt32(Temp);
853                                  }
854                              }
855                          }
856                          /////////////////////////////////////////////////////////
857                          /////////////////////////////////////////////////////////
858
859                          // A temporary array is maintained for the inner
860                          // purpose of programming the entries in this strArray
861                          // variables are not shown anywhere to the user
862
863                          // This line declares a instance of the __SHOWFILES
864                          // struct equals to the number of Records found in the
865                          // XML and assigns to the global variable strArray
866                          strArray = new XMLSTRUCT.__SHOWFILES[iEntries];
867
868                          // declares an array of two string
869                          //string[] sSubItem = new string[2];
870
871                          // Added for beta 2
872                          System.Windows.Forms.ListViewItem lvItems = new
System.Windows.Forms.ListViewItem();
873
874                          // declaration of a local variable fName
875                          // used to store temporary data
```

```
876                     string fName;
877
878                     // This will take one by one record from the SHOWFILES
879                     // structure of the XMLSTRUCT
880                     for( int i = 0; i < iEntries; i++ )
881                     {
882                         ImageList imgList = new ImageList();
883
    imgList.Images.Add(System.Drawing.Image.FromFile(Application.StartupPath+"\\Fol
der.ico"));
884
    imgList.Images.Add(System.Drawing.Image.FromFile(Application.StartupPath+"\\Fil
e.ico"));
885                         lvFiles.SmallImageList = imgList;
886
887                         // assigns the filename present in the
SHOWFILES struct
888                         // to fName variable
889                         fName = xmlStruct.SHOWFILES[i].sFilename;
890
891                         // Fills the strArray structure with its values
////////
892                         strArray[i].sFilename = fName;
893                         strArray[i].iMask =
xmlStruct.SHOWFILES[i].iMask;
894
895                         // not used in this version, but kept for
future
896                         strArray[i].iFileSize =
xmlStruct.SHOWFILES[i].iFileSize;
897
    ////////////////////////////////////////////////////
898
899                         // Checks whether the value present in fName is
Folder
900                         // or file, because folder name ends with
backslash
901                         if( fName.EndsWith("\\") )
902                         {
903                             // This will remove the trailing
backslashes from the
904                             // fName
905                             fName = fName.Substring(0,fName.Length -
1);
906
907                             // This will insert a single record in
the listview
908                             // represented by fName and sSubItems
which includes
909                             // size and type. 0 Here displays the
0th image from
910                             // the image list which is the image of
the folder
911                             lvItems = lvFiles.Items.Insert(i,fName);
912
```

```
913                                    // Item 0 represents  the size, Since
there
914                                    // is no size for the directory so this
is null
915                                         lvItems.SubItems.Add("");
916
917                                    // Assigns the folder value to the 1
item, since
918                                    // it is a folder
919                                         lvItems.SubItems.Add("Folder");
920
921                                         lvItems.ImageIndex = 0;
922                               }
923
924                          // The control will come into this code only if
the record is a
925                          // File not folder
926                          else
927                          {
928                                    // Extracts only filename from Full
qualified path
929                                    fName =
fName.Substring(fName.LastIndexOf("\\")+1);
930
931                                    // This will insert a single record in
the listview
932                                    // represented by fName and sSubItems
which includes
933                                    // size and type. 1 Here displays the
1st image from
934                                    // the image list which is the image of
the file
935                                    lvItems = lvFiles.Items.Insert(i,fName);
936
937                                    // Assigns the file size
938                                    lvItems.SubItems.Add(
xmlStruct.SHOWFILES[i].iFileSize.ToString());
939
940                                    // extract the extension of the fileand
assigns it to the
941                                    // last element of sSubItem
942
  lvItems.SubItems.Add(fName.Substring(fName.LastIndexOf(".")  + 1) + " File");

943
944                                         lvItems.ImageIndex = 1;
945                               }
946                          }
947                     // assigns a true value to bReturn variable to
indicate that
948                     // parsing and displaying of the records are
successful
949                     bReturn = true;
950               }
951
952               else
```

```
953                      {
954                              // Calls the DisableUI function
955                              DisableUI();
956
957                              // Displays the Message Box
958                              MessageBox.Show("No result found for this
request","Warning",MessageBoxButtons.OK, MessageBoxIcon.Warning);
959                      }
960              }
961
962      // The case if any error has occured at the listener's side
963      // is informed by the Error XML. If SHOWFILES XML is not
964      // returned then parse the ERROR XML and Show the error to the user
965      else
966      {
967              // Parses the error XML returned by the listener
968              xmlParser.ParseXML(RESPONSEFILE, out xmlStruct,new
ServerCommunication().TypeOfXMLRecieved(RESPONSEFILE));
969
970              // calls DisableUI to disable various the Userinterface
controls
971              DisableUI();
972
973              // Popup the message box and displays the error message
974              MessageBox.Show(xmlStruct.ERROR.sDescription,
xmlStruct.ERROR.sSeverity,MessageBoxButtons.OK, MessageBoxIcon.Error);
975      }
976
977      // Delete the File containing the XML Response from the listener
978      new ServerCommunication().FileDelete(RESPONSEFILE);
979
980      // returns the value for bReturn Variable
981      return bReturn;
982  }
983
984  /// <summary>
985  /// Disable the buttons when not needed
986  /// </summary>
987  private void DisableUI()
988  {
989      btnUpload.Enabled = false;
990      btnDownload.Enabled = false;
991      btnSearch.Enabled = false;
992      lvFiles.Enabled = false;
993  }
994
995  /// <summary>
996  /// Closes the current TCP and Stream Connections
997  /// </summary>
998  public void CloseConnection() { StreamTCP.Close(); ClientSocket.Close();
}
999
1000 /// <summary>
1001 /// This function performs a download operation of a file
1002 /// from the listener's end. This function returns the actual
1003 /// download path from the remote machine. It takes the index
```

```
1004    /// of the selected item in list view, name of the file to download
1005    /// and bDelete, whether to delete a file after downloading bDelete
1006    /// is always false in this case. You can use it for any further
1007    /// purpose. If bDelete if true the file will be deleted after
1008    /// downloading.
1009    /// </summary>
1010    /// <param name="index"> </param>
1011    /// <param name="Filename"> </param>
1012    /// <param name="bDelete"> </param>
1013    private string DownloadFile(int index, string Filename, bool bDelete)
1014    {
1015        // Change the title of the File savedialog box
1016        FileSaveDialog.Title = "Download As";
1017
1018        // Pops up the File save dialog box with the default filename
1019        FileSaveDialog.FileName = Filename;
1020
1021        // Assigns the Initial directory of the File save dialog box
1022        // to the application's startup path
1023        FileSaveDialog.InitialDirectory = Application.StartupPath;
1024
1025        // Declares an initialize the variable sReturn which is used
1026        // to return the value by function. This stores the name of the
1027        // file which is to be downloaded from the remote end
1028        string sReturn = null;
1029
1030        // If user chooses OK from the File Save dialog box then only
1031        // download can begin
1032        if( System.Windows.Forms.DialogResult.OK ==
FileSaveDialog.ShowDialog() )
1033        {
1034            // Stores the current text of the status bar is temporary
1035            // variable sTemp
1036            string sTemp = sBar.Text;
1037
1038            // Writes new text on the status bar
1039            sBar.Text = "Downloading File. Please wait...";
1040
1041            // Show the hour glass cursor while downloading the file
1042            Cursor = Cursors.WaitCursor;
1043
1044            // process all the pending events first from the message loop
1045            Application.DoEvents();
1046
1047            // Opens socket connection to the listener and checks
1048            // whether connected or not
1049            if( OpenConnection(COMPUTERNAME) )
1050            {
1051                // Creates a DOWNLOAD request for a particular
1052                // file to download.
1053
 CreateRequest("DOWNLOAD",strArray[index].sFilename,"");
1054
1055                // Sends this request to the listener
1056                SendDataToListener(REQUESTFILE);
1057
```

```
1058                    // Assigns the sReturn variable to the filename
choosen for
1059                    // download
1060                    sReturn = FileSaveDialog.FileName;
1061
1062                    // Get the download data from the listener and save it
1063                    // in the filename represented by the Filename
property
1064                    // of File save dialog box
1065                    GetDataFromListener(FileSaveDialog.FileName);
1066
1067                    // Close the currently opened socket connection
1068                    CloseConnection();
1069
1070                    //Delete the file if bDelete is true
1071                    if( bDelete ) new
ServerCommunication().FileDelete(Filename);
1072
1073                    // Restore the previos text of the status bar
1074                    sBar.Text = sTemp;
1075            }
1076        }
1077
1078        // restore the default cursor state
1079        Cursor = Cursors.Default;
1080
1081        // returns the filename with Full qualified path
1082        return sReturn;
1083    }
1084
1085    /// <summary>
1086    /// Invoked when the download button is clicked
1087    /// </summary>
1088    /// <param name="sender"> </param>
1089    /// <param name="e"> </param>
1090    protected void btnDownload_Click (object sender, System.EventArgs e)
1091    {
1092        // Declares a local Filename variable
1093        string Filename;
1094
1095        // Get the currently selected item from the List view
1096        int index = GetSelectedItemFromListView(out Filename);
1097        try
1098        {
1099                // Checks whether any entry is selected or not
1100                if( -1 != index)
1101
1102                    // Checks whether a filename is selected for
downloading
1103                    // or not
1104                    if( null != Filename )
1105
1106                        // If filename is selected then download it
1107                        DownloadFile(index,Filename,false);
1108
```

```
1109                          // else throw an exception, Folders cannot be
downloaded
1110                          else throw new Exception("Cannot download folder");
1111
1112                  // If nothing is selected than displays an error message
1113                  else throw new Exception("Nothing Selected");
1114          }
1115
1116      // catches any system generated error message and displays it
1117      // to the user
1118      catch( Exception err ) {
MessageBox.Show(err.Message,"Warning",MessageBoxButtons.OK,
MessageBoxIcon.Warning); }
1119      }
1120
1121   /// <summary>
1122   /// Invoked when the search button is clicked
1123   /// </summary>
1124   /// <param name="sender"> </param>
1125   /// <param name="e"> </param>
1126   protected void btnSearch_Click(object sender, System.EventArgs e)
1127   {
1128          try
1129          {
1130                  // Check that if search is performed at root level or not,
1131                  // since root level search is not possible from here
1132                  if( null != PARENTFOLDER )
1133                  {
1134                          // Creates a new object for frmSearch and initializes
it
1135                          frmSearch SearchForm = new frmSearch();
1136
1137                          // This statememt restricts the search form from
1138                          // Showing Search on: criteria Textbox
1139                          SearchForm.bFlag = false;
1140
1141                          // If user presses OK in the search form then go
inside
1142                          if( System.Windows.Forms.DialogResult.OK ==
SearchForm.ShowDialog() )
1143                          {
1144                                  // Get the search criteria from the SearchFor
variable
1145                                  // of the frmSearch class and passes it to the
constructor
1146                                  // of this class with some more details
1147                                  frmShare ShareForm = new
frmShare(COMPUTERNAME,"SEARCH",PARENTFOLDER +
SearchForm.SearchFor,GetMask(PARENTFOLDER).ToString());
1148
1149                                  // Again show this dialog with the search
results
1150                                  ShareForm.ShowDialog();
1151                          }
1152                  }
1153
```

```
1154                    // Displays an error message
1155                    else throw new Exception("Cannot search at root level here");
1156        }
1157
1158        // Catches any system generated error and displays it
1159        catch( Exception err ) {
MessageBox.Show(err.Message,"Error",MessageBoxButtons.OK,  MessageBoxIcon.Error);
}
1160    }
1161      }
1162 }
```

Code description of 'frmShare' class (frmShare.cs)

♦ Lines 4-13: This includes the basic packages needed for the various classes used to build this application. This includes packages used for communicating with network, streaming facility, file I/O, text manipulations, and so on. Line 11 includes a user-defined class called `WorkingWithXML`. This class is used to communicate with the server, to parse XML data, and to create XML requests.

♦ Line 18: This declares a public class `frmShare` that represents the base class for this file. This class is derived from `System.Windows.Forms`. All the variables defined here represent their respective controls that are pasted on the form. C# automatically generates these lines of code.

♦ Lines 20-32: In these lines of code, the designer variables for the form are declared. These variables are declared automatically by the C# editor and represent the various controls that are drawn at the design time window on the form.

♦ Lines 41-127: These are the user-defined global variables. They are used in various situations in this application; each of these either represents a class or a data type.

- 41: This variable, `iBytes`, is used to store the number of bytes that are either read or written to the stream on the socket or in file using the file stream.

- 49: The variables `COMPUTERNAME` and `PARENTFOLDER` declared here are used to store the name of the computer to which you are currently connected, along with its IP address, and `PARENTFOLDER` stores the name of the parent folder, the contents of which you are viewing.

- 55: The `ClientSocket` object of `TcpClient` class declared here is used to establish a socket connection between the listener and the browser (client). This object is also used to get the stream of the listener and to send the request over that socket stream.

- 61: `XMLCreater` class's object `xmlCreater` is declared here to have the functionality of creating the XML requests to be sent over the socket to the listener. This is a user-defined class and is defined in the `WorkingWithXML` assembly.

- 67: This object, `StreamTCP`, of the `NetworkStream` class is used to get the stream object for the current TCP socket connection. By using this stream object, we have the ability to transfer the data between the listener and browser (client) or vice-versa.

- 74: This global object, `fileStream`, of the `FileStream` class is generally used to have the I/O capabilities over the files. Any I/O performed in a file in this application uses this object.

- 80: `ReadBuffer` and `WriteBuffer` are byte arrays used to read or write data to the file in byte format. These variables are initialized later in this application where they are needed and are initialized to store 512 bytes at a time.

- 87: The `xmlParser` object of the user-defined class `XMLParser` present in the 'WorkingWithXML' assembly is used to acquire the capabilities for parsing an XML file being generated in this application.

- 94: The `xmlStruct` variable of the `XMLSTRUCT` structure is used to store the parsed values from the XML. These parsed values are the output from the preceding `XMLParser` class.

- 101: The variable `strArray` declared here is used to store the corresponding files/folders, which are currently being shown in the window. This array is used only for internal purposes by this application, not for user-interaction purposes.

- 114-120: These two string-type variables are used to store the names of the request and response files, respectively. These names are used to store the contents of the XML.

♦ Lines 133-149: This is the default constructor for the frmShare class. This is used to show the results generated when you search for a file on a particular computer by using the Search button present in the main window, where the computer-name list is shown.

♦ Lines 158-207: This is not a default constructor and is not generated automatically; rather, it is a user-defined constructor created to show all the shared files when you select a particular remote computer you want to connect. This is called from the Open button situated on the main window where the computer name list is shown. The name of the computer along with its IP address is passed to this constructor in the `Computername` parameter. This constructor makes use of this parameter and extracts the IP address from it, which is later used to make a connection to the computer represented by that IP address. This constructor by default creates a `SHOWFILES` request, which is sent to the listener.

♦ Lines 220-270: Once again, implementation of the user-defined constructor is associated in this application. But this time the constructor is invoked when you click the Search button when viewing files/folders, for searching a particular file on the connected computer. In this constructor implementation, four strings are passed for storing specific target information about computer name. The strings are: Type of Request user wants to send to listener, scope and mask values if there are any, along with the computername. This information is passed to this constructor.

♦ Lines 276-280: The `Dispose()` function declared here is automatically generated by the C# environment. It is used to free all the resources acquired by this class.

♦ Lines 287-435: This initializes various designer variables required for the smooth running of the application. This part of the code is autogenerated by IDE, and users are advised not to modify the contents.

♦ Lines 442-456: This function is used to retrieve the mask for a particular file/folder from the `strArray` array. This mask is used to distinguish between read-only files and read-write access files. A selected name of the file/folder is passed as a parameter to this function in the `Filename` variable. The function then looks up the name in the list and returns the associated mask value for that file/folder. If no file/folder is presented by the `Filename` variable, the function returns -1.

♦ Lines 463-566: This function is invoked when the you clicks the Upload button in the view files window. This function is responsible for sending a particular selected file to the listener's end.

- 469: Uploading cannot be done at the root level as well as in situations in which the mask is '0'(read-only access). These lines are for checking these conditions.

♦ 478: This initializes the `InitialDirectory` property of the `FileOpenDialog`, which is set to the default path from where the application is running.

♦ 481: If you click the Save button in the `FileOpenDialog` box, the filename from the fully qualified name is extracted and is stored in the `RemoteFilename` variable.

- 495: Here the connection to the remote listener is opened via the `OpenConnection()` function of this class. The computer name with its IP address is passed to this function.

- 502-511: An upload request is created with the `filename` and `mask`. The request is sent to the listener via the `SendDataToListener()` function, and, in the mean time, the cursor is changed into 'wait cursor' along with the change in the text of the status bar.

- 515: All pending events are processed from the message queue so that the application might not block.

- 519-535: A file stream object is assigned to the local file, which is to be uploaded. The `BinaryReader` class's object `bReader` is used to read 512 bytes at a time from the file and transmits over the socket stream. This reading continues until control reaches the end of the file.

- 536: Data is then written on the network stream by using the `Write()` function of the `StreamTCP` object.

- 539-551: After completion of their tasks, `BinaryReader` and `FileStream` objects are closed, as they are no longer needed. Connection to the socket is closed, too, and text on the status bar and cursor is restored.

- 557-566: Error messages are trapped and shown to you if uploading has failed anywhere.

- Lines 573-579: This function handles any key-press events in the list view of the `frmShare` class.

◆ Line 586: The function is invoked when you press the Close button to exit from this form. It is incorporated by using the `Close()` function of this class.

◆ Lines 595-602: This function is responsible for creating the XML request queries for the listener. These requests are created on the basis of the request type, the scope of that request, and the access mask. The requests are created in the `filename` represented by the `REQUESTFILE` variable used in the second line of the function.

◆ Lines 608-649: This function opens a socket connection to the remote computer and returns true in case of a successful connection and false if not connected successfully. Apart from this, it enables all the buttons on a successful connection. Line 597 of this function gets the network stream of this socket, which is used to transfer data between two applications. This function is called every time you need to send a request or get a response from the listener.

- 618-619: The IP address is extracted from the `Computername` variable.

- 623: A remote endpoint is mentioned in this line, which states where and at which port to connect to the listener.

- 629: The remote connection operation is performed here.

◆ Lines 656-677: The `SendDataToListener()` function sends any type of request in a file represented by `Filename` to the listener. This has been incorporated for reading the file byte by byte and sending it over the network stream of the listener.

◆ 672: The `requestfile` is deleted, as data has been read from it and stored in the `ReadBuffer` variable.

- 686-710: The main purpose of this function, after the request is sent, is to read the response sent by the listener. The response is written to a file, which is later parsed for its data.

◆ 690: The `WriteBuffer` variable is initialized to hold 512 Bytes at a time.

◆ 693: A `FileStream` is created to store data, which is being read from the network stream over the socket.

- 702-703: Only 512 bytes of data are read at a time and written to the file. This reading and writing of data continues to operate until the stream becomes empty and no data is left to read.

◆ 706-709: Finally, the `BinaryWriter` and `FileStream` are closed.

◆ Lines 717-757: This function is invoked when you double click any item in the list view box. First, the selected item is retrieved from the list. It is checked whether it is a file or a folder. If a file is selected, the application opens a dialog box and asks you where to download this selected file. If a folder name is selected, the application opens a new window in which the contents of the selected folder are shown.

- 720-724: This is a locally declared variable index store zero-based index position of the selected item from the list view. The `Filename` variable stores the name of the file/folder that is selected when you double click it.

- 733-736: If the `Filename` variable stores a null value and the index is greater than -1, a folder is selected or else a filename.

- Lines 766-796: This function retrieves the original name of the selected item from the list view, corresponding to the array `strArray`.

♦ Lines 803-982: This function is responsible for parsing the XML response sent by the listener. When the parsing of the XML document is successful, this function shows the parsed data in tabular form in a list view.

- 808: The value of this bool-type variable is returned by the function. If the parsing is successful and no error response is returned, the value of this variable `bReturn` is true; otherwise, it is false.

- 812: A new instance of `XMLParser` class is created and assigned to the `xmlParser` object.

- 816: A new instance of `XMLSTRUCT` is created here. It is used to store the parsed values from the XML document.

- 821: This line checks the type of XML response received by the browser.

- 826: This is responsible for parsing the response XML received by the browser. To this function, we pass the name of the file to parse and the reference to the structure where the parsed results are stored and the type of XML received, so that the parsed results are stored in their respective structures. This function returns the number of records parsed from the XML. This number is then used to extract the exact records and fills them in the list view.

- 835-855: The code given in these lines is used to sort the records present in `xmlSruct`, first folder-wise and then file size-wise.

- 866-946: In these lines of code, the `strArray` is initialized to hold the number of records that are parsed previously. These records are then manipulated accordingly. A check has been made for the files and folder, as a folder name always ends with a backslash(\). While inserting the items in the list view, if a folder is found, a folder icon is being used and a file icon in the case of files.

- 952-959: These lines are executed only if no record is parsed from the XML.

- 965-975: If the `SHOWFILES` response XML is not returned here check for the `ERROR` XML. If this error XML is returned, it is being parsed for the Error and error descriptions. After parsing, the error description is popped up to the user, the popup shows the exact error information that has occurred on the istener's end.

♦ Line 998: This `CloseConnection()` function does very little work. It closes the socket connection and the network stream associated with this socket connection. After opening every connection, you find an associated `CloseConnection()` function being called.

♦ Lines 1013-1083: This function holds the responsibility of handling download operations of a file from the listener. This function performs a download operation and, after downloading successfully it, returns the path along with the name of the downloaded file. When downloading, double click a file, or click the Download button after selecting a file. The Download As window appears; choose the location on your local computer indicating where to download that file, and press the Enter button. While downloading, the text of the status bar is changed, and the wait cursor is displayed. If download is successful, these two are restored.

- 1019: This assigns the default filename to the Download dialog box, which you have selected.

- 1023: This assigns the initial directory of the File Save dialog box to the application's startup path.

- 1032: This checks whether you have selected to download the file or not.

- 1049-1082: A new socket connection is opened toward the listener and checks the connectivity. Then the download request is made for the same file and sent to the listener. A file selected for downloading is then being saved into the sReturn variable. Once the file is downloaded via GetDataFromListener() function, it is saved on the local machine wherever you choose. Lastly, the connection is closed. The text and the cursor are restored. In the case that a connection with the listener cannot be established, an error message is displayed.

♦ Lines 1090-1119: This function is invoked when the Download button is clicked, which is placed on the application's form. The purpose of this function is to gather the required information about the file selected for downloading and to pass that information to the DownloadFile() function discussed previously.

- 1096: This retrieves the currently selected item from the list view, which contains many files or a folder. It is then checked that only files are valid for downloading.

- 1107: Here the actual download function is called to download the selected file from the listener. The index, Filename, and a flag (false) is passed to the DownloadFile() function. This flag determined whether to delete the file after downloading or not. The appropriate error messages are displayed wherever necessary.

♦ Lines 1126-1160: This function is invoked when you click the Search button while viewing the files/folders. A search form is displayed. Enter the search criteria in this form. These criteria are passed to this function and are used to make an XML request. This request is then sent to the listener by calling the constructor of the frmShare class, and all the matched files to that criteria are shown in a new window.

- 1132: Here we are checking whether the search is happening on the root-level, as such a search cannot be done from this point. You cannot search if there is no parent folder for the items that you are currently viewing.

- 1135: This creates a new object for the frmSearch class and initializes it.

- 1139: Setting the variable to false restricts the Search Form from showing Search on: criteria box.

- 1142-1151: When you click the OK button on the Search dialog box, search criteria are retrieved from the SearchFor variable of the frmSearch class and it are passed to the constructor of this class (frmShare) with some details.

- 1155-1159 If you perform a search at root level, an appropriate error message is displayed along with any system-generated error.

Search Window

The window in Figure 5-7 allows you to search for a specific file or folder on a single computer or multiple computers. In the Search on box, enter the computer name (ABC), or use wild cards (A*). In the Search for box, enter the file/folder name, and wildcards are also supported here.

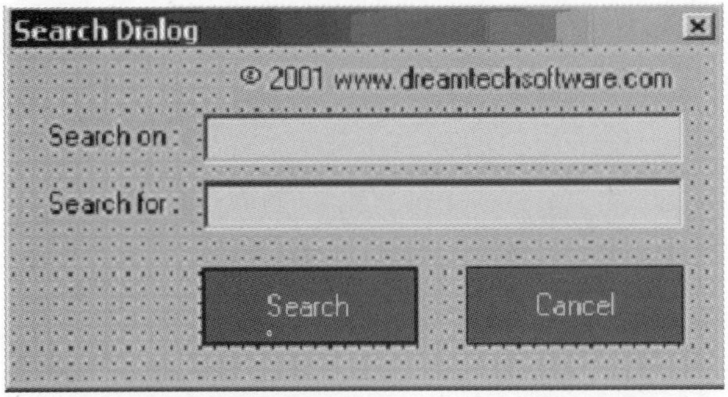

Figure 5-7: The Search dialog box

Search Form

namespace: Client

frmSearch provides you with an intuitive interface to perform searches at various levels and of different types. The entire coding in Listing 5-8 has been numbered for better legibility.

Listing 5-8: frmSearch

//© 2001 Dreamtech Software India Inc.
// All rights reserved

```
1  namespace Client      // Copyright 2001 Dreamtech Software India Inc.
2  {                     // All rights reserved

3      using System;     // Provides the basic functionality of .NET
4      using System.Drawing;// Provides the Drawing features, Used for cursors
5      using System.Windows.Forms;// Provides the darwing of buttons,
       //listviews etc
6      using System.Collections;// Provides the different type of class
       //collections
7      using System.ComponentModel;// Provides the facility of using
       //components
8
9      /// <summary>
10     /// Summary description for frmSearch.
11     /// </summary>
12     public class frmSearch : System.Windows.Forms.Form
13     {
14         private System.ComponentModel.IContainer components;
15         private System.Windows.Forms.Label label1;
16         public System.Windows.Forms.TextBox txtSearchFor;
17         public System.Windows.Forms.Label lblSearchFor;
18         private System.Windows.Forms.ToolTip toolTipText;
19         private System.Windows.Forms.Button btnCancel;
20         private System.Windows.Forms.Button btnSearch;
21         public System.Windows.Forms.TextBox txtSearchOn;
22         public System.Windows.Forms.Label lblSearchOn;
23
24         /// <summary>
25         /// The below variables are user defined variables
26         /// used to store various transient values.
27         /// </summary>
28         public string SearchOn;// Stores the value for first search scope
29         public string SearchFor;// Stores the value for second search scope
30         public bool   bFlag; // Determines whether to perform SearchOn
           //validation
31
32         /// <summary>
33         /// Default constructor of the class
34         /// </summary>
35         public frmSearch()
36         {
37             //
38             // Required for Windows Form Designer support
39             //
40             InitializeComponent();  // auto generated line by the IDE
```

```
41          }
42
43          /// <summary>
44          ///     Clean up any resources being used.
45          ///     This function is auto generated by the IDE
46          /// </summary>
47          public override void Dispose()
48          {
49                  base.Dispose();
50                  components.Dispose();
51          }
52
53           /// <summary>
54           ///     Required method for Designer support - do not modify
55           ///     the contents of this method with the code editor.
56           ///     This function is auto generated by the IDE
57           /// </summary>
58           private void InitializeComponent()
59           {
60                  this.components = new System.ComponentModel.Container();
61                  System.Resources.ResourceManager resources =
                                new System.Resources.ResourceManager
                                (typeof(frmSearch));
62                  this.lblSearchFor = new System.Windows.Forms.Label();
63                  this.toolTipText = new
                    System.Windows.Forms.ToolTip(this.components);
64                  this.txtSearchOn = new System.Windows.Forms.TextBox();
65                  this.txtSearchFor = new System.Windows.Forms.TextBox();
66                  this.btnSearch = new System.Windows.Forms.Button();
67                  this.btnCancel = new System.Windows.Forms.Button();
68                  this.lblSearchOn = new System.Windows.Forms.Label();
69                  this.label1 = new System.Windows.Forms.Label();
70                  this.SuspendLayout();
71                  //
72                  // lblSearchFor
73                  //
74                  this.lblSearchFor.Location = new System.Drawing.Point(13,
            55);
75                  this.lblSearchFor.Name = "lblSearchFor";
76                  this.lblSearchFor.Size = new System.Drawing.Size(63, 13);
77                  this.lblSearchFor.TabIndex = 4;
78                  this.lblSearchFor.Text = "Search for :";
79                  //
80                  // txtSearchOn
81                  //
82                  this.txtSearchOn.Enabled = false;
83                  this.txtSearchOn.Location = new System.Drawing.Point(80, 26);
84                  this.txtSearchOn.Name = "txtSearchOn";
85                  this.txtSearchOn.Size = new System.Drawing.Size(199, 20);
86                  this.txtSearchOn.TabIndex = 0;
87                  this.txtSearchOn.Text = "";
88                  this.toolTipText.SetToolTip(this.txtSearchOn,
                    "Write the search criteria here
                    (For ex:  *, A* or HAR* etc. for
                    matching computer" +
89                  "names)");
```

```
90                //
91                // txtSearchFor
92                //
93                this.txtSearchFor.Location = new System.Drawing.Point(80,
         53);
94                this.txtSearchFor.Name = "txtSearchFor";
95                this.txtSearchFor.Size = new System.Drawing.Size(199, 20);
96                this.txtSearchFor.TabIndex = 1;
97                this.txtSearchFor.Text = "";
98                this.toolTipText.SetToolTip(this.txtSearchFor,
                  "Write the search criteria here
                  (For ex:  *, A* or HAR* etc.
                  for matching Filename" +
99                "s)");
100               //
101               // btnSearch
102               //
103               this.btnSearch.BackColor = System.Drawing.Color.Chocolate;
104               this.btnSearch.DialogResult =
                  System.Windows.Forms.DialogResult.OK;
105               this.btnSearch.FlatStyle =
                  System.Windows.Forms.FlatStyle.Popup;
106               this.btnSearch.ForeColor = System.Drawing.Color.White;
107               this.btnSearch.Location = new System.Drawing.Point(79, 88);
108               this.btnSearch.Name = "btnSearch";
109               this.btnSearch.Size = new System.Drawing.Size(90, 32);
110               this.btnSearch.TabIndex = 2;
111               this.btnSearch.Text = "&Search";
112               this.toolTipText.SetToolTip(this.btnSearch, "Performs search
                  operation");
113               this.btnSearch.Click += new
                  System.EventHandler(this.btnSearch_Click);
114               //
115               // btnCancel
116               //
117               this.btnCancel.BackColor = System.Drawing.Color.Chocolate;
118       this.btnCancel.DialogResult =
          System.Windows.Forms.DialogResult.Cancel;
119       this.btnCancel.FlatStyle = System.Windows.Forms.FlatStyle.Popup;
120       this.btnCancel.ForeColor = System.Drawing.Color.White;
121       this.btnCancel.Location = new System.Drawing.Point(189, 88);
122       this.btnCancel.Name = "btnCancel";
123       this.btnCancel.Size = new System.Drawing.Size(90, 32);
124       this.btnCancel.TabIndex = 3;
125       this.btnCancel.Text = "&Cancel";
126       this.toolTipText.SetToolTip(this.btnCancel, "Cancel the search and
          close this window");
127       //
128       // lblSearchOn
129       //
130       this.lblSearchOn.Enabled = false;
131       this.lblSearchOn.Location = new System.Drawing.Point(13, 28);
132       this.lblSearchOn.Name = "lblSearchOn";
133       this.lblSearchOn.Size = new System.Drawing.Size(63, 13);
134       this.lblSearchOn.TabIndex = 0;
135       this.lblSearchOn.Text = "Search on :";
```

```
136            //
137            // label1
138            //
139            this.label1.Location = new System.Drawing.Point(93, 5);
140            this.label1.Name = "label1";
141            this.label1.Size = new System.Drawing.Size(192, 14);
142            this.label1.TabIndex = 5;
143            this.label1.Text = "© 2001 www.dreamtechsoftware.com";
144            //
145            // frmSearch
146            //
147            this.AcceptButton = this.btnSearch;
148            this.AutoScaleBaseSize = new System.Drawing.Size(5, 13);
149            this.CancelButton = this.btnCancel;
150            this.ClientSize = new System.Drawing.Size(288, 132);
151            this.Controls.AddRange(new System.Windows.Forms.Control[] {
152            this.label1,
153            this.txtSearchFor,
154            this.lblSearchFor,
155            this.btnCancel,
156            this.btnSearch,
157            this.txtSearchOn,
158            this.lblSearchOn});
159            this.FormBorderStyle =
               System.Windows.Forms.FormBorderStyle.FixedToolWindow;
160            this.Name = "frmSearch";
161            this.StartPosition =
               System.Windows.Forms.FormStartPosition.CenterParent;
162            this.Text = "Search Dialog";
163
164            // Puts the Computer.ico as the form icon
165            this.Icon = new System.Drawing.Icon(Application.StartupPath +
               "\\Computer.ico");
166
167            this.ResumeLayout(false);
168        }
169
170        /// <summary>
171        /// Invoked when click on the search button
172        /// </summary>
173        /// <param name="sender"> </param>
174        /// <param name="e"> </param>
175        protected void btnSearch_Click (object sender, System.EventArgs e)
176        {
177            // Start of the try block
178            try
179            {
180                    // Validates for the correctness of the SearchFor Variables
181                    // and check that the user has entered correct search scope
                      //or not.
182                    if( 0 < txtSearchFor.Text.Trim().Length )
183                            SearchFor = txtSearchFor.Text.Trim();       // Assigns
                      //the value of Textbox text to "SearchFor" variable
184                    else
185                    {
```

```
186                                    DialogResult = System.Windows.Forms.DialogResult.None;
                                       // This line stops the dialog from returning
187                                    throw new Exception("Cannot search for blank values");
                                       // Displays an Error message in Messagebox
188                        }
189
190                   if( bFlag )// Checks whether to validate SearchOn or not
191                   {
192                           // Validates for the correctness of the SearchOn
                              //Variables
193                           // and check that the user has entered correct search
                              //scope or not.
194                           if( 0 < txtSearchOn.Text.Trim().Length )
195                           SearchOn = txtSearchOn.Text.Trim(); // Assigns the
                              value of Textbox text to "SearchOn" variable
196             else
197             {
198                           DialogResult = System.Windows.Forms.DialogResult.None;
                              // This line stops the dialog from returning
199                           throw new Exception("Cannot search for blank values");
                              // Displays an Error message in Messagebox
200                        }
201                }
202         }
203    // This block catches any system generated error message and
204    // stops the program from crashing
205    catch( Exception err ) { MessageBox.Show(err.Message,"Warning",
                                        MessageBoxButtons.OK,
                                        MessageBoxIcon.Warning);}
206        }
207    }
208 }
```

Code description of 'frmSearch' class (frmSearch.cs)

♦ Lines 3-7: This Includes necessary packages used for the basic functionality of our application.

♦ Line 12: This is an automatically generated code line, which represents your base class for this file. It is *inherited* from System.Windows.Forms.Form.

♦ Lines 14-22: C# generates these lines of code automatically. The variables declared in these lines represent the user interface controls drawn on the form.

♦ Lines 28-30: This declares three user-defined variables. These are used to store the values of the two text boxes used for entering the search criteria. The third variable determines whether to show the search for computer text box or not.

♦ Lines 35-41: This is the default constructor for this class. It is implemented by C# automatically.

♦ Lines 47-51: This function is used to clean up all the memory and to free resources acquired by this class. This is automatically called on the closing of the form created in this class.

♦ Lines 58-168: This Initializes various designer variables required for the smooth running of the application. This code is autogenerated by IDE, and users are advised not to modify the contents.

♦ Lines 175-206: This function is invoked when you click the Search button on this form.

• 182-188: This checks the correctness of the search criteria entered for searching for files/folders. This validates the search (that is, it cannot be empty and must not have special characters of unwanted signs). The search pattern entered here is stored in the SearchFor variable.

- 194-201: This checks the correctness of the search pattern entered for searching for files/folders on a specific computer or group of computers. This validates the search (that is, it cannot be empty and must not have special characters of unwanted signs). The search criteria entered is stored in the `SearchOn` variable.

Summary

In this chapter, we take up the advanced-level programming of the C# version of our P2P application. We have used the Microsoft XML parser 3.0 (you can download this parser from `http://msdn.microsoft.com/msxml`) for parsing the XML responses being generated as a result of each request. Several classes have been integrated to give our application the proper constitution. The `ServerCommunication` class is responsible for all the communication with the server. The `XMLParser` class is responsible for parsing the XML responses. Similarly, the `xmlCreater` class is responsible for creating the XML requests. The other classes are the individual parts of their forms (for example, the `frmShare` class, `frmLogin`, and so on). These classes have been crafted so that they can be perfectly integrated to build our P2P application.

Chapter 6

Streaming in the P2P Application

For quite some time, streaming has been the major tool for sharing digital audio/video data over computer networks. It has indeed revolutionized the very concept of availing audio/video data. Before the advent of streaming, users had to endure long hours of waiting for downloading a single file before they could actually play it. Worse, in case of an error occurring while downloading the file, the user could not play even that amount of data already downloaded after waiting patiently for hours. Thus, the conventional method was far from being time effective.

With the emergence of streaming, handling audio/video data became very easy — audio/video data is streamed for the user, which means that chunks of data are directed to the destination computer so that the user need not download the required audio/video file completely before beginning to use it. Thus, streaming is a process of downloading an audio/video file occurs in consignments. The amount of data that has been streamed can be played or displayed to the user even as the rest of the data is being streamed in the background. Thus, playing and downloading audio/video data occur simultaneously, which proves to be highly time effective for the user.

Because audio/video data is received in a compressed form, a media player is needed to uncompress it for display. Several media players are available on the market such as Windows Media Player and Real Player. The streaming add-on described in this chapter uses Windows Media Player. You can download the latest version of the Windows Media Player from http://www.msdn.Microsoft.com.

Streaming in the Application

The design of our application permits new concepts to be implemented. We may avail the opportunity for streaming the audio/video data between two remotely located peers over the Internet. In our application, Windows Media Player 6.0 or higher can be used as the default.

The Streaming Process

At the start up of the streaming process, a number of valid audio/video sources are specified that serve as the reservoir for unformatted media data. If any of the selected sources is not eligible for the streaming process, an error message is displayed to the user, and the streaming process stops immediately. On the other hand, if valid media sources are selected, an environment is set-up by adding the various sources of audio/video data to form a Source Group, which is subsequently added to a Source Collection Group.

Before the encoding session starts, attributes such as display information, title, author name, and so on, are assigned. Although the encoding session can proceed without assigning these attributes, it is advisable to assign these attributes, as they offer a complete reference to the session at the receiving end. Once you are through with selecting the media sources and assigning the attributes, set the protocol and the port number over which data is to be broadcasted.

After setting all the associated properties, the encoding engine is prepared to begin encoding. The task of encoding is done through the Windows Media Encoder, which converts data into Windows Media-based format. This filtered data is written on a network stream, which is received by the user at the receiving end. The process of converting data into Windows Media Format continues until no more media data remains to be encoded (see Figure 6-1).

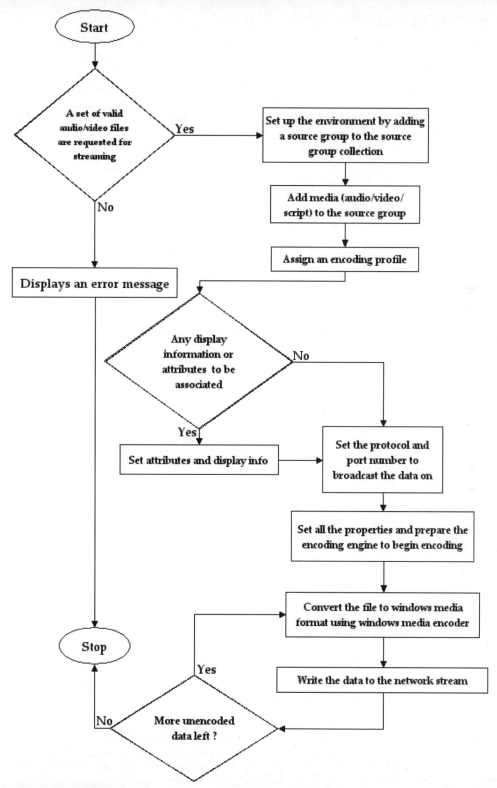

Figure 6-1: The flow of streaming

Windows Media Encoder SDK

Encoding and broadcasting can be done using either Window Media SDK or DirectShow. Of these, Windows Media SDK gives developers better control of media through the Windows Media Encoder SDK, which provides:

- APIs to encode a range of media types in Windows Media Format
- Deeper access to the processes of encoding and streaming over the network to give applications a higher degree of control over media streams in Window Media Format
- COM-based components to support unicast or multicast delivery of encoded media data
- The following codecs for capturing and delivering Windows Media files and streams:
  - The Windows Media Audio version 2 codec, for high-fidelity music and mixed audio
  - The Sipro ACELP.net codec, for voice applications
  - The Microsoft MPEG-4 version 3 codec, for music and video
- Support for receiving media inputs from microphones, video cameras, or stored media files to encode them into Window Media Format to either store as a local file or to broadcast

We have chosen Windows Media Encoder for Encoding and Broadcasting the media data. The tools required apart from Visual C++ 6.0 are listed in the following section.

Windows Media Encoder SDK for Visual C++ 6.0

DirectX 8.0 SDK for supporting nonWindows Media Formats, as Windows Media SDK uses some DirectShow component to render and play back nonWindows Media Formats (like rendering services for the Windows Media Player are provided by DirectShow through the audio renderer, video renderer, and Overlay Mixer filters).

Because the client interface has already been designed using C#, it is more rational to develop this extension in C# only, but the two SDKs listed previously work specifically with VC++6.0 and VB 6.0. We have decided on VC++6.0 as the development tool for this extension, as it lets developers understand the technology better and provides for deeper access and improved control over the various tasks involved in encoding and broadcasting media data over Internet.

This extension is developed as a COM component used by our C# application to broadcast media data over the Internet. The following sections present the code that accomplishes the task of encoding the data into Windows Media Format and then broadcasting it. Every code file is followed by an explanation that clarifies the details.

Uses of Streaming in P2P

Although the basic form of this application provides users, the facility to share any kind of file including media files, this is not the only facility users seek. At times users may want to play a part of media files before actually downloading the entire file. Besides, there is always the probability that users might want to play the song or video online without letting anything be written on the hard drives. This is the case when a user is using wireless mobile devices to listen to a media file or is watching online news that includes audio or video data. There are also cases in which users have to economize on storage capacity and cannot afford to download huge media files on their storage devices. Streaming presents the solution to all such storage restrictions.

The incorporation of streaming in this application enables developers to extend this application for many more commercially useful purposes such as live chat, which can be done by combining this extension with the chat extension described later. Also, users can maintain a radio station, which is possible because this extension gives developers access to media devices installed on computers. By virtue of this extension, developers can use video cameras and attached audio-media devices to broadcast news or presentations over the Internet.

Design Considerations

The incorporation of this extension in our application demands a few changes both on the listener and on the browser side. Because the communication media has always been XML files, this part of the structure does not change. Only a new request type called STREAMING has to be introduced.

Listeners have been made aware of this new request type, whereas the browser has to be modified a bit to be able to make such requests. To serve both these purposes, the shared assembly WorkingWithXML has been changed to make it capable of creating such requests upon the browser's demand and of parsing these requests for the listener.

Because this extension has been built on Windows Encoder SDK for VC++ 6.0, which is not available for C# yet, a component named BroadcastIt has been written in VC++ 6.0, which has been embedded in the listener. The listener makes an instance of this component to cater to streaming requests made by browsers.

The entire code of this component has been given in this chapter module-wise, and every module has been explained immediately after its code. The changes made on the browser and listener and the request XML design used for this purpose also have been explained.

Before beginning to explore the code for the streaming component (Listing 6-1), let's learn a few facts about that:

Component Name	BroadcastIt
Executable file	BroadcastDll.dll
Interface	IBroadcastIt
Declaration file (for the Interface)	BroadcastDll.idl
Implementing class	CBroadcastIt (Interface implemented apart from IBroadcastIt, ISupportsErrorInfo)

Listing 6-1: Declaration of CBroadcastIt class

Declaration file	BroadcastIt.h

```
 1 // BroadcastIt.h : Declaration of the CBroadcastIt
 2
 3 #ifndef __BROADCASTIT_H_
 4 #define __BROADCASTIT_H_
 5
 6 #include "resource.h"       // main symbols
 7 #include <atlctl.h>
 8 #include "BroadcastDllCP.h"
 9
10
11
//////////////////////////////////////////////////////////////////////////////
12 // CBroadcastIt
13 class ATL_NO_VTABLE CBroadcastIt :
14  public CComObjectRootEx<CComSingleThreadModel>,
```

```
15  public CStockPropImpl<CBroadcastIt, IBroadcastIt, &IID_IBroadcastIt,
               &LIBID_BROADCASTDLLLib>,
16  public CComControl<CBroadcastIt>,
17  public IPersistStreamInitImpl<CBroadcastIt>,
18  public IOleControlImpl<CBroadcastIt>,
19  public IOleObjectImpl<CBroadcastIt>,
20  public IOleInPlaceActiveObjectImpl<CBroadcastIt>,
21  public IViewObjectExImpl<CBroadcastIt>,
22  public IOleInPlaceObjectWindowlessImpl<CBroadcastIt>,
23  public ISupportErrorInfo,
24  public IConnectionPointContainerImpl<CBroadcastIt>,
25  public IPersistStorageImpl<CBroadcastIt>,
26  public ISpecifyPropertyPagesImpl<CBroadcastIt>,
27  public IQuickActivateImpl<CBroadcastIt>,
28  public IDataObjectImpl<CBroadcastIt>,
29  public IProvideClassInfo2Impl<&CLSID_BroadcastIt,
&DIID__IBroadcastItEvents,
 &LIBID_BROADCASTDLLLib>,
30  public IPropertyNotifySinkCP<CBroadcastIt>,
31  public CComCoClass<CBroadcastIt, &CLSID_BroadcastIt>,
32  public CProxy_IBroadcastItEvents< CBroadcastIt >,
33  public CProxy_IConfigureEvents< CBroadcastIt >
34 {
35 public:
36  CBroadcastIt()
37  {
38   m_bWindowOnly = TRUE;
39   bSession = FALSE;
40   video       =      FALSE;
41   audio       =      FALSE;
42   shUseDevice = 0;
43   shUseScript = 0;
44   bEncoder = FALSE;
45  }
46
47 DECLARE_REGISTRY_RESOURCEID(IDR_BROADCASTIT)
48
49 DECLARE_PROTECT_FINAL_CONSTRUCT()
50
51 BEGIN_COM_MAP(CBroadcastIt)
52  COM_INTERFACE_ENTRY(IBroadcastIt)
53  COM_INTERFACE_ENTRY(IDispatch)
54  COM_INTERFACE_ENTRY(IViewObjectEx)
55  COM_INTERFACE_ENTRY(IViewObject2)
56  COM_INTERFACE_ENTRY(IViewObject)
57  COM_INTERFACE_ENTRY(IOleInPlaceObjectWindowless)
58  COM_INTERFACE_ENTRY(IOleInPlaceObject)
59  COM_INTERFACE_ENTRY2(IOleWindow, IOleInPlaceObjectWindowless)
60  COM_INTERFACE_ENTRY(IOleInPlaceActiveObject)
61  COM_INTERFACE_ENTRY(IOleControl)
62  COM_INTERFACE_ENTRY(IOleObject)
63  COM_INTERFACE_ENTRY(IPersistStreamInit)
64  COM_INTERFACE_ENTRY2(IPersist, IPersistStreamInit)
65  COM_INTERFACE_ENTRY(ISupportErrorInfo)
66  COM_INTERFACE_ENTRY(IConnectionPointContainer)
67  COM_INTERFACE_ENTRY(ISpecifyPropertyPages)
```

```
 68   COM_INTERFACE_ENTRY(IQuickActivate)
 69   COM_INTERFACE_ENTRY(IPersistStorage)
 70   COM_INTERFACE_ENTRY(IDataObject)
 71   COM_INTERFACE_ENTRY(IProvideClassInfo)
 72   COM_INTERFACE_ENTRY(IProvideClassInfo2)
 73   COM_INTERFACE_ENTRY_IMPL(IConnectionPointContainer)
 74 END_COM_MAP()
 75
 76 BEGIN_PROP_MAP(CBroadcastIt)
 77   PROP_DATA_ENTRY("_cx", m_sizeExtent.cx, VT_UI4)
 78   PROP_DATA_ENTRY("_cy", m_sizeExtent.cy, VT_UI4)
 79   PROP_PAGE(CLSID_Configure)
 80 END_PROP_MAP()
 81
 82 BEGIN_CONNECTION_POINT_MAP(CBroadcastIt)
 83   CONNECTION_POINT_ENTRY(IID_IPropertyNotifySink)
 84   CONNECTION_POINT_ENTRY(DIID__IBroadcastItEvents)
 85   CONNECTION_POINT_ENTRY(DIID__IConfigureEvents)
 86 END_CONNECTION_POINT_MAP()
 87
 88 BEGIN_MSG_MAP(CBroadcastIt)
 89   CHAIN_MSG_MAP(CComControl<CBroadcastIt>)
 90   DEFAULT_REFLECTION_HANDLER()
 91 END_MSG_MAP()
 92
 93 // ISupportsErrorInfo
 94   STDMETHOD(InterfaceSupportsErrorInfo)(REFIID riid)
 95   {
 96     static const IID* arr[] =
 97     {
 98         &IID_IBroadcastIt,
 99     };
100     for (int i=0; i<sizeof(arr)/sizeof(arr[0]); i++)
101     {
102         if (InlineIsEqualGUID(*arr[i], riid))
103             return S_OK;
104     }
105     return S_FALSE;
106   }
107
108 // IViewObjectEx
109   DECLARE_VIEW_STATUS(VIEWSTATUS_SOLIDBKGND | VIEWSTATUS_OPAQUE)
110
111 // IBroadcastIt
112 public:
113   STDMETHOD(InitializeBroadcaster)();
114   STDMETHOD(get_UseScript)(/*[out, retval]*/ short *pVal);
115   STDMETHOD(put_UseScript)(/*[in]*/ short newVal);
116   STDMETHOD(PrepareToEncode)();
117   STDMETHOD(SendURL)(/*[in]*/ BSTR bstrURL);
118   STDMETHOD(SendScript)(/*[in]*/ BSTR bstrScript); .
119   STDMETHOD(get_AudioDevices)(/*[out, retval]*/ VARIANT *pVal);
120   STDMETHOD(get_VideoMedia)(/*[out, retval]*/ BSTR *pVal);
121   STDMETHOD(put_VideoMedia)(/*[in]*/ BSTR newVal);
122   STDMETHOD(get_AudioMedia)(/*[out, retval]*/ BSTR *pVal);
123   STDMETHOD(put_AudioMedia)(/*[in]*/ BSTR newVal);
```

```
124   STDMETHOD(Status)();
125   STDMETHOD(CloseSession)();
126   STDMETHOD(MakeSession)();
127   STDMETHOD(get_ProfilesList)(/*[out, retval]*/ VARIANT *pVal);
128   STDMETHOD(HeraldThisMessage)(/*[in]*/ BSTR bstr);
129   STDMETHOD(get_Port)(/*[out, retval]*/ short *pVal);
130   STDMETHOD(put_Port)(/*[in]*/ short newVal);
131   STDMETHOD(get_Profile)(/*[out, retval]*/ short *pVal);
132   STDMETHOD(put_Profile)(/*[in]*/ short newVal);
133   STDMETHOD(Broadcast)();
134
135   HRESULT OnDraw(ATL_DRAWINFO& di)
136   {
137    RECT& rc = *(RECT*)di.prcBounds;
138    Rectangle(di.hdcDraw, rc.left, rc.top, rc.right, rc.bottom);
139
140    SetTextAlign(di.hdcDraw, TA_CENTER|TA_BASELINE);
141    LPCTSTR pszText = _T("BroadcastIt Dll © Dreamtech Softwares Inc., India
Developed By                                      Ankur Verma");
142    TextOut(di.hdcDraw,
143         (rc.left + rc.right) / 2,
144         (rc.top + rc.bottom) / 2,
145         pszText,
146         lstrlen(pszText));
147
148    return S_OK;
149   }
150
151   short shUseDevice;
152   short shPortNo;
153   short shProfile;
154   short shUseScript;
155
156   bool video,audio,bEncoder;
157   CComBSTR bstrAudioMedia;
158   CComBSTR bstrVideoMedia;
159
160   IWMEncoder* pEncoder;
161   IWMEncSourceGroupCollection* pSrcGrpColl;
162   IWMEncSourceGroup* pSrcGrp;
163
164   BOOL bSession;
165
166   short m_nAppearance;
167   OLE_COLOR m_clrBackColor;
168   LONG m_nBackStyle;
169   OLE_COLOR m_clrBorderColor;
170   LONG m_nBorderStyle;
171   BOOL m_bBorderVisible;
172   LONG m_nBorderWidth;
173   CComBSTR m_bstrCaption;
174   LONG m_nDrawMode;
175   LONG m_nDrawStyle;
176   LONG m_nDrawWidth;
177   BOOL m_bEnabled;
178   OLE_COLOR m_clrFillColor;
```

```
179    LONG m_nFillStyle;
180    CComPtr<IFontDisp> m_pFont;
181    OLE_COLOR m_clrForeColor;
182    CComPtr<IPictureDisp> m_pMouseIcon;
183    LONG m_nMousePointer;
184    CComPtr<IPictureDisp> m_pPicture;
185    BOOL m_bTabStop;
186    CComBSTR m_bstrText;
187    BOOL m_bValid;
188    };
189
190    #endif //__BROADCASTIT_H_
191    #endif //__BROADCASTIT_H_
```

Code description (CBroadcastIt class declaration)

♦ Lines 1-34: CBroadcastIt class declaration. This class inherits itself from IDispatch interface, apart from others like ISupportErrorInfo that makes it more powerful.

♦ Lines 35-46: Constructor of the class initializing some variables.

♦ Lines 47-74: Com map specifying the interfaces supported by this component.

♦ Lines 75-80: Property map defining the properties and property pages supported by this component.

♦ Lines 81-86: Connection point map specifying the sink interface IDs through CONNECTION_POINT_ENTRY macro.

♦ Lines 88-106: Implementation of InterfaceSupportsErrorInfo function that the clients call to determine whether this component supports ISupportInfo or not.

♦ Lines 108-134: Method declaration for this component class.

♦ Lines 135-149: Painting tasks are handled through this function.

♦ Lines 150-158: Variable declarations to carry the property values.

♦ Lines 159-162: Interfaces used for accessing the capabilities of the encoder component.

♦ Line 164: Local variable to keep track of when the session is active.

♦ Lines 165-187: Ambient property-value carriers.

A brief description of the functions exposed by this component follows:

♦ **MakeSession:** This function is called to make a session for encoding and broadcasting the specified media sources, in addition to associating proper attributes and displaying information to this session.

♦ **Broadcast:** This function is called to start the encoding session after the required attributes and media sources have been specified.

♦ **CloseSession:** This function is called to cease the session after realizing all the occupied resources and releasing the media sources being used.

♦ **Status:** This is an optional function and is not required to be called to get the encoder to initialize and begin encoding. But it can be used to get the statistics of running the encoding session.

♦ **SendScript:** This function can be called only if script-media source is supported in a given session to send actual messages along with audio/video media data.

♦ **SendURL:** Like SendScript, this function works only if a script-media source has been supported by the given encoding session; this function is used to send companion URLs that are opened in default browsers as soon as they are received on the other end.

- **PrepareToEncode:** Having specified the attributes of audio and video-script media sources along with the port and the protocol to broadcast the media data on, this function is called for assigning all these properties to the encoding session.

- **InitializeBroadcaster:** This function is called to initialize the encoder component to carry out any kind of media encoding and broadcasting.

- **put_Profile:** This function is called to specify the index of the profile in the given list of available profiles for this session.

- **put_Port:** This function is called to specify where to broadcast the data.

- **put_AudioMedia:** This function is called to specify an audio-media source for this encoding session.

- **put_VideoMedia:** This function is called to specify a video-media source for this encoding session.

- **put_UseScript:** This function is called to instruct the encoding session to support script media. Script media enables the users to sent site links to the reciver end (that is, the reciver of the broadcast). These site links are opened at the reciver end as soon as they are received. This feature facilitates organization of presentation sessions which may include Web sites as well as voice and video media.

- **get_Profile, get_Port, get_AudioMedia, get_VideoMedia, get_UseScript:** These are used to retrieve the values of the properties set previously.

- **get_AudioDevices:** Before you decide whether to use an archive audio file or an audio device installed on your computer for audio input for this encoding session, you need to have the list of all the audio devices installed on your computer. This list can be obtained by calling this function.

- **get_ProfilesList:** Based on the audio and video-script media you have chosen for this encoding session, the profiles available can be obtained by calling this function.

Now that we are through with the declarations of the class that implements the `IBroadcastIt` interface, let's proceed to the code for implementation.

Listing 6-2 shows the implementation file for this class.

Listing 6-2: Implementation for CBroadcastIt class

Implementation file   BroadcastIt.cpp

```
1 // BroadcastIt.cpp : Implementation of CBroadcastIt
2
3 #include "stdafx.h"
4 #include "BroadcastDll.h"
5 #include "BroadcastIt.h"
6 #include "Events.h"
7 #include <comdef.h>
8
9 // CBroadcastIt
10
11 STDMETHODIMP CBroadcastIt::HeraldThisMessage(BSTR bstr)
12 {
13   Fire_BroadcastStatus(bstr);
14   return S_OK;
15 }
16
```

```
17
18 STDMETHODIMP CBroadcastIt::MakeSession()
19 {
20  HRESULT hr;
21  if(!bEncoder)
22   return S_FALSE;
23
24  if(bSession)
25   return S_FALSE;
26
27  bSession = TRUE;
28
29
30
31  CComPtr<IWMEncAttributes> pAttr;
32  CComBSTR m_bstrName;
33  long cnt;
34  CComVariant m_varValue;
35  CComVariant m_varIndex;
36  VARIANT_BOOL* vbAutoStop = 0;
37  IWMEncDisplayInfo* pDispInfo;
38  CComBSTR m_bstrAuthor("Ankur Verma.");
39  CComBSTR m_bstrCopyright("© 2000 Dreamtech Softwares Inc., India.");
40  CComBSTR m_bstrDescription("Media Data.");
41  CComBSTR m_bstrRating("");
42  CComBSTR m_bstrTitle("The Dreamtech P2P Streaming Demo");
43
44  hr = pEncoder->get_Attributes(&pAttr);
45
46  _bstr_t bName[] =
47  {
48   _bstr_t("Title: "),
49   _bstr_t("Author: "),
50   _bstr_t("Copyright: "),
51   _bstr_t("Date Created: "),
52   _bstr_t("Time Created: "),
53   _bstr_t("File Content: ")
54  };
55
56  SYSTEMTIME sysTime;
57  GetLocalTime(&sysTime);
58  TCHAR SysDate[20];
59  TCHAR SysTime[20];
60
61  wsprintf(SysTime,"%d : %d :
%d",sysTime.wHour,sysTime.wMinute,sysTime.wSecond);
62  wsprintf(SysDate,"%d : %d :
%d",sysTime.wDay,sysTime.wMonth,sysTime.wYear);
63
64  USES_CONVERSION;
65  Fire_BroadcastStatus(T2OLE(SysTime));
66  Fire_BroadcastStatus(T2OLE(SysDate));
67
68  _variant_t vVal[] =
69  {
70   _variant_t("The P2P Media Streaming Demo"),
```

```
71     _variant_t("Ankur Verma"),
72     _variant_t("© Dreamtech Softwares Inc., India"),
73     _variant_t(SysTime),
74     _variant_t(SysDate),
75     _variant_t("multimedia data"),
76     };
77
78     for(int i=0;i<6;i++)
79     {
80      pAttr->Add(bName[i],vVal[i]);
81     }
82
83     pAttr->get_Count(&cnt);
84     TCHAR dh[100];
85     for (i=0; i<cnt; i++)
86     {
87      pAttr->Item(i, &m_bstrName, &m_varValue);
88      wsprintf(dh,"%s : %s" , OLE2T(m_bstrName),OLE2T(m_varValue.bstrVal));
89      Fire_BroadcastStatus(T2OLE(dh));
90     }
91
92         pEncoder->put_AutoStop(VARIANT_TRUE);
93
94         pEncoder->get_AutoIndex(vbAutoStop);
95
96
97     hr = pEncoder->get_DisplayInfo(&pDispInfo);
98
99     hr = pDispInfo->put_Author(m_bstrAuthor);
100    hr = pDispInfo->put_Copyright(m_bstrCopyright);
101    hr = pDispInfo->put_Description(m_bstrDescription);
102    hr = pDispInfo->put_Rating(m_bstrRating);
103    hr = pDispInfo->put_Title(m_bstrTitle);
104
105
106    if(shUseScript == 1)
107    {
108     CComPtr<IWMEncSource> pScriptSrc;
109     hr = pSrcGrp->AddSource(WMENC_SCRIPT, &pScriptSrc);
110     CComBSTR bstrScript(L"UserScript://");
111     hr = pScriptSrc->SetInput(bstrScript);
112    }
113
114    IWMEncSource* pAudSrc;
115    IWMEncSource* pVidSrc;
116
117    if(audio)
118    {
119
120     hr = pSrcGrp->AddSource(WMENC_AUDIO, &pAudSrc);
121
122
123     if(FAILED(hr))
124     {
125         Fire_BroadcastStatus(L"Specifing Audio Source Failed");
126         return S_FALSE;
```

```
127    }
128    hr = pAudSrc->SetInput(bstrAudioMedia.Copy());
129    if(FAILED(hr))
130    {
131        Fire_BroadcastStatus(L"Setting Audio Media Source Failed");
132        return S_FALSE;
133    }
134    Fire_BroadcastStatus(bstrAudioMedia.Copy());
135 }
136
137
138 if(video)
139 {
140    hr = pSrcGrp->AddSource(WMENC_VIDEO, &pVidSrc);
141    if(FAILED(hr))
142    {
143        Fire_BroadcastStatus(L"Specifing Video Source Failed");
144        return S_FALSE;
145    }
146    hr = pVidSrc->SetInput(bstrVideoMedia.Copy());
147    if(FAILED(hr))
148    {
149        Fire_BroadcastStatus(L"Setting Video Media Source Failed");
150        return S_FALSE;
151    }
152    Fire_BroadcastStatus(bstrVideoMedia.Copy());
153 }
154
155    return S_OK;
156 }
157
158
159 STDMETHODIMP CBroadcastIt::Broadcast()
160 {
161    if(!bEncoder)
162      return S_FALSE;
163
164    HRESULT hr;
165
166    try
167    {
168      hr = pEncoder->Start();
169      if(FAILED(hr))
170      {
171          Fire_BroadcastStatus(L"Could not Start Encoder");
172          return S_FALSE;
173      }
174    }
175    catch(_com_error e)
176    {
177      Fire_BroadcastStatus(L"Error ............ ");
178      char no2[10];
179      itoa(e.Error(),no2,10);
180      Fire_BroadcastStatus(T2OLE(_T(no2)));
181      Fire_BroadcastStatus(T2OLE(e.ErrorMessage()));
182      Fire_BroadcastStatus(L"Error ............ ");
```

```
183  }
184
185
186  return S_OK;
187  }
188
189
190  STDMETHODIMP CBroadcastIt::CloseSession()
191  {
192  if(!bEncoder)
193    return S_FALSE;
194
195  if(bSession)
196  {
197    HRESULT hr;
198
199    short shACount, shVCount,shSCount;
200    CComVariant varIndex;
201    varIndex.vt = VT_I2;
202    varIndex.iVal = 0;
203
204    hr = pSrcGrp->PrepareToEncode(VARIANT_FALSE);
205    if(FAILED(hr))
206        Fire_BroadcastStatus(L"Prepare encode Failed from Source Group");
207
208
209    hr = pSrcGrp->get_SourceCount(WMENC_AUDIO, &shACount);
210    if(FAILED(hr))
211        Fire_BroadcastStatus(L"Getting Audio Source count Failed");
212    else
213        if (shACount != 0)
214            hr = pSrcGrp->RemoveSource(WMENC_AUDIO, varIndex);
215
216    hr = pSrcGrp->get_SourceCount(WMENC_VIDEO, &shVCount);
217    if(FAILED(hr))
218        Fire_BroadcastStatus(L"Getting Video Source count Failed");
219    else
220        if (shVCount != 0)
221            hr = pSrcGrp->RemoveSource(WMENC_VIDEO, varIndex);
222
223    hr = pSrcGrp->get_SourceCount(WMENC_VIDEO, &shSCount);
224    if(FAILED(hr))
225        Fire_BroadcastStatus(L"Getting Script Source count Failed");
226    else
227        if (shSCount != 0)
228            hr = pSrcGrp->RemoveSource(WMENC_SCRIPT, varIndex);
229
230
231      hr = pSrcGrpColl->Remove(varIndex);
232    if(FAILED(hr))
233        Fire_BroadcastStatus(L"Remove Source Group Failed");
234
235    hr = pEncoder->PrepareToEncode(VARIANT_FALSE);
236    if(FAILED(hr))
237        Fire_BroadcastStatus(L"Prepare encode Failed");
238
```

```
239   hr = pEncoder->Stop();
240   if(FAILED(hr))
241       Fire_BroadcastStatus(L"Could not Stop");
242
243   pEncoder->Release();
244   audio = FALSE;
245   video = FALSE;
246   bEncoder = FALSE;
247   }
248   Fire_BroadcastStatus(L"Session Closed");
249   bSession = false;
250   return S_OK;
251 }
252
253 STDMETHODIMP CBroadcastIt::Status()
254 {
255   if(!bSession)
256     return S_FALSE;
257
258   HRESULT hr;
259     IWMEncStatistics* pStatistics;
260     IWMEncOutputStats* pOutputStats;
261     IDispatch* pDispOutputStats;
262
263     short iStreamCount;
264     long lAvgBitrate, lAvgSampleRate;  long lCurrentBitRate,
lCurrentSampleRate;   long lExpectedBitRate,
 lExpectedSampleRate;     CURRENCY qwByteCount, qwSampleCount;    CURRENCY
   qwDroppedByteCount, qwDroppedSampleCount;
265
266   // Initialize the COM library and retrieve a pointer
267   // to an IWMEncoder interface.
268
269     hr = CoInitialize(NULL);
270     CoCreateInstance(CLSID_WMEncoder,
271                     NULL,
272                     CLSCTX_INPROC_SERVER,
273                     IID_IWMEncoder,
274                     (void**) &pEncoder);
275
276   // Retrieve an IWMEncStatistics interface pointer.
277
278     hr = pEncoder->get_Statistics(&pStatistics);
279
280   // Retrieve the number of multiple bit rate output streams.
281
282     hr = pStatistics->get_StreamOutputCount(WMENC_VIDEO,
283                                            0,
284                                            &iStreamCount);
285
286 // Retrieve an IDispatch pointer for the IWMEncOutputStats
287 // interface.
288
289     hr = pStatistics->get_StreamOutputStats(WMENC_VIDEO,
290                                            0,
291                                            0,
```

```
292                                           &pDispOutputStats);
293
294 // Call QueryInterface for the IWMEncNetConnectionStats
295 // interface pointer.
296
297    hr = pDispOutputStats->QueryInterface(IID_IWMEncOutputStats,
298                                         (void**)&pOutputStats);
299
300 // Manually configure the encoder engine or load
301 // a configuration from a file. For an example, see the
302 // IWMEncFile object.
303
304 // You can create a timer to retrieve the statistics
305 // after you start the encoder engine.
306
307    hr = pOutputStats->get_AverageBitrate(&lAvgBitrate);
308    hr = pOutputStats->get_AverageSampleRate(&lAvgSampleRate);
309    hr = pOutputStats->get_ByteCount(&qwByteCount);
310    hr = pOutputStats->get_CurrentBitrate(&lCurrentBitRate);
311    hr = pOutputStats->get_CurrentSampleRate(&lCurrentSampleRate);
312    hr = pOutputStats->get_DroppedByteCount(&qwDroppedByteCount);
313    hr = pOutputStats->get_DroppedSampleCount(&qwDroppedSampleCount);
314    hr = pOutputStats->get_ExpectedBitrate(&lExpectedBitRate);
315    hr = pOutputStats->get_ExpectedSampleRate(&lExpectedSampleRate);
316    hr = pOutputStats->get_SampleCount(&qwSampleCount);
317
318
319  CURRENCY  TimeElpsed;
320  pStatistics->get_EncodingTime(&TimeElpsed);
321  Fire_EncoderStatus(lAvgBitrate,lAvgSampleRate,lCurrentBitRate,
322                                  lCurrentSampleRate, lExpectedBitRate,
323
lExpectedSampleRate,qwByteCount,qwDroppedByteCount,
324                                  qwDroppedSampleCount,qwSampleCount
325                                  ,TimeElpsed);
326
327  return S_OK;
328 }
329
330
331
332 STDMETHODIMP CBroadcastIt::SendScript(BSTR bstrScript)
333 {
334  if(!bSession)
335    return S_FALSE;
336  CComBSTR bstrType(L"TEXT");
337    CComBSTR bstrData(bstrScript);
338    pEncoder->SendScript(0, bstrType, bstrData);
339  return S_OK;
340 }
341
342 STDMETHODIMP CBroadcastIt::SendURL(BSTR bstrURL)
343 {
344  if(!bSession)
345    return S_FALSE;
346  CComBSTR bstrType(L"URL");
```

```
347     CComBSTR bstrData(bstrURL);
348     pEncoder->SendScript(0, bstrType, bstrData);
349   return S_OK;
350 }
351
352
353 STDMETHODIMP CBroadcastIt::PrepareToEncode()
354 {
355   if(!bEncoder)
356     return S_FALSE;
357
358   if(!bSession)
359     return S_FALSE;
360
361   USES_CONVERSION;
362   HRESULT hr;
363
364
365   IWMEncProfileCollection* pProColl;
366   IWMEncProfile* pPro;
367
368   long lCount;
369
370
371   hr = pEncoder->get_ProfileCollection(&pProColl);
372   if(FAILED(hr))
373   {
374     Fire_BroadcastStatus(L"Get Profile Collection Failed");
375     return S_FALSE;
376   }
377
378
379   CComVariant m_varProfile;
380   m_varProfile.vt = VT_DISPATCH;
381
382   hr = pProColl->get_Count(&lCount);
383   if(FAILED(hr))
384   {
385     Fire_BroadcastStatus(L"Get Profile Count Failed");
386     return S_FALSE;
387   }
388
389   CComBSTR m_bstrProfName;
390   if(shProfile<0)
391   {
392     Fire_BroadcastStatus(L"Profile Name ");
393   }
394
395   hr = pProColl->Item(shProfile, &pPro);
396   if(FAILED(hr))
397   {
398     Fire_BroadcastStatus(L"Get Profile Failed");
399     return S_FALSE;
400   }
401
402   hr = pPro->get_Name(&m_bstrProfName);
```

```
403  if(FAILED(hr))
404  {
405   Fire_BroadcastStatus(L"Get Profile Name Failed");
406   return S_FALSE;
407  }
408  Fire_BroadcastStatus(m_bstrProfName);
409
410  m_varProfile.pdispVal = pPro;
411  hr = pSrcGrp->put_Profile(m_varProfile);
412  if(FAILED(hr))
413  {
414   Fire_BroadcastStatus(L"Set Profile Failed");
415   return S_FALSE;
416  }
417
418  IWMEncBroadcast* pBrdcst;
419  long PortNum;
420
421  hr = pEncoder->get_Broadcast(&pBrdcst);
422  if(FAILED(hr))
423  {
424   Fire_BroadcastStatus(L"Problem calling get_Broadcast");
425   return S_FALSE;
426  }
427
428  hr = pBrdcst->get_PortNumber(WMENC_PROTOCOL_HTTP, &PortNum);
429  if(FAILED(hr))
430  {
431   Fire_BroadcastStatus(L"Problem calling get_PortNumber");
432   return S_FALSE;
433  }
434
435  PortNum = shPortNo;
436
437  hr = pBrdcst->put_PortNumber(WMENC_PROTOCOL_HTTP, PortNum);
438  if(FAILED(hr))
439  {
440   Fire_BroadcastStatus(L"Problem calling put_PortNumber");
441   return S_FALSE;
442  }
443
444  char number[10];
445  itoa(shProfile,number,10);
446  Fire_BroadcastStatus(T2OLE(_T(number)));
447
448  char number1[10];
449  itoa(shPortnumber,number1,10);
450  Fire_BroadcastStatus(T2OLE(_T(number1)));
451
452  hr = pEncoder->PrepareToEncode(VARIANT_TRUE);
453  if(FAILED(hr))
454  {
455   Fire_BroadcastStatus(L"Problem calling PrepareToEncode");
456   return S_FALSE;
457  }
458  return S_OK;
```

```
459 }
460
461
462
463 STDMETHODIMP CBroadcastIt::InitializeBroadcaster()
464 {
465  HRESULT hr = CoCreateInstance(CLSID_WMEncoder,
466                     NULL,
467                     CLSCTX_INPROC_SERVER,
468                     IID_IWMEncoder,
469                   (void**) &pEncoder);
470
471  if(FAILED(hr))
472  {
473   Fire_BroadcastStatus(L"Encoder Could not be Initialized");
474   return S_FALSE;
475  }
476
477  hr = pEncoder->get_SourceGroupCollection(&pSrcGrpColl);
478  if(FAILED(hr))
479  {
480   Fire_BroadcastStatus(L"Source Group collection retrieval Failed");
481   return S_FALSE;
482  }
483
484  hr = pSrcGrpColl->Add(L"SG_2", &pSrcGrp);
485  if(FAILED(hr))
486  {
487   Fire_BroadcastStatus(L"Source Group could not be added");
488   return S_FALSE;
489  }
490
491  bEncoder = TRUE;
492  Fire_BroadcastStatus(L"Encoder Initialized");
493  return S_OK;
494 }
495
496
497
498
499 /******************** Properties ********************/
500
501 /***************** Put Properties ******************/
502
503 STDMETHODIMP CBroadcastIt::put_Profile(short newVal)
504 {
505  USES_CONVERSION;
506  shProfile = newVal;
507  char number[10];
508  itoa(shProfile,number,10);
509  HeraldThisMessage(T2OLE(_T(number)));
510  return S_OK;
511 }
512
513 STDMETHODIMP CBroadcastIt::put_Port(short newVal)
514 {
```

```
515  USES_CONVERSION;
516  shPortNo = newVal;
517  char number[10];
518  itoa(shPortNo,number,10);
519  HeraldThisMessage(T2OLE(_T(number)));
520  return S_OK;
521 }
522
523 STDMETHODIMP CBroadcastIt::put_AudioMedia(BSTR newVal)
524 {
525  bstrAudioMedia = newVal;
526  HeraldThisMessage(bstrAudioMedia);
527  audio = TRUE;
528  return S_OK; 529     }
530
531 STDMETHODIMP CBroadcastIt::put_VideoMedia(BSTR newVal)
532 {
533  bstrVideoMedia = newVal;
534  HeraldThisMessage(bstrVideoMedia);
535  video = TRUE;
536  return S_OK;
537 }
538
539 STDMETHODIMP CBroadcastIt::put_UseScript(short newVal)
540 {
541  if((newVal == 0) || newVal == 1)
542    shUseScript = newVal;
543  else
544    Fire_BroadcastStatus(L"Use Script = 1 or Don't use Script = 0");
545  return S_OK;
546 }
547
548
549 /****************** Get Properties ******************/
550

551 STDMETHODIMP CBroadcastIt::get_Profile(short *pVal)            {         *pVal
= shProfile;        return S_OK;}

552 STDMETHODIMP CBroadcastIt::get_Port(short *pVal)           {       *pVal =
shPortNo;    return S_OK;}

553 STDMETHODIMP CBroadcastIt::get_AudioMedia(BSTR *pVal)       {       *pVal =
bstrAudioMedia.Copy();      return
   S_OK;}

554 STDMETHODIMP CBroadcastIt::get_VideoMedia(BSTR *pVal)       {       *pVal =
bstrVideoMedia.Copy();      return S_OK;}

555 STDMETHODIMP CBroadcastIt::get_UseScript(short *pVal)       {       *pVal =
shUseScript;         return S_OK;}

556
557
558 STDMETHODIMP CBroadcastIt::get_AudioDevices(VARIANT *pVal)
559 {
```

```
560   HRESULT hr;
561      IWMEncSourcePluginInfoManager* pSrcPlugMgr;
562      IWMEncPluginInfo* pPlugInfo;
563
564      int j,i;
565      long lPlugCount, lResCount;
566      VARIANT_BOOL bResources;
567
568
569      hr = pEncoder->get_SourcePluginInfoManager(&pSrcPlugMgr);
570      hr = pSrcPlugMgr->get_Count(&lPlugCount);
571
572      for (i=0; i<lPlugCount; i++)
573      {
574          hr = pSrcPlugMgr->Item(i, &pPlugInfo);
575          CComBSTR bstrScheme;
576          hr = pPlugInfo->get_SchemeType(&bstrScheme);
577
578          if (_wcsicmp(bstrScheme, L"DEVICE")==0 || _wcsicmp(bstrScheme,
     L"UserScript")==0)
579          {
580              hr = pPlugInfo->get_Resources(&bResources);
581              if (bResources==VARIANT_TRUE)
582              {
583                  hr = pPlugInfo->get_Count(&lResCount);
584
585
586              VariantInit(pVal);
587              pVal->vt = VT_ARRAY | VT_BSTR;
588              SAFEARRAY *pTheArray;
589              SAFEARRAYBOUND pBounds = {lResCount,0};
590              pTheArray = SafeArrayCreate(VT_BSTR,1,&pBounds);
591              BSTR *bstrArray;
592
     SafeArrayAccessData(pTheArray,reinterpret_cast<void**>(&bstrArray));
593
594
595                  for (j=0; j<lResCount; j++)
596                  {
597                      CComBSTR bstrResource;
598                      hr = pPlugInfo->Item(j, &bstrResource);
599                      bstrArray[j] = bstrResource.Copy();
600                      //MessageBox(OLE2T(bstrResource),"adf",MB_OK);
601                  }
602
603              SafeArrayUnaccessData(pTheArray);
604              pVal->parray = pTheArray;
605              break;
606              }
607          }
608      }
609  return S_OK;
610  }
611
612
613  /****  Get Available Profiles For This Media Types ****/
```

```
614
615 STDMETHODIMP CBroadcastIt::get_ProfilesList(VARIANT *pVal)
616 {
617  if(!bEncoder)
618   return S_FALSE;
619
620  HRESULT hr;
621  IWMEncProfileCollection* pProColl;
622  IWMEncProfile* pPro;
623
624  hr = pEncoder->get_ProfileCollection(&pProColl);
625  if(FAILED(hr))
626  {
627   Fire_BroadcastStatus(L"Retrieving Collection of Profiles Failed");
628   return S_FALSE;
629  }
630
631
632  long lCount;
633  hr = pProColl->get_Count(&lCount);
634  if(FAILED(hr))
635  {
636   Fire_BroadcastStatus(L"Retrieving Count of Profiles Failed");
637   return S_FALSE;
638  }
639
640  VariantInit(pVal);
641  pVal->vt = VT_ARRAY | VT_BSTR;
642  SAFEARRAY *pTheArray;
643  SAFEARRAYBOUND pBounds = {lCount,0};
644  pTheArray = SafeArrayCreate(VT_BSTR,1,&pBounds);
645  BSTR *bstrArray;
646  SafeArrayAccessData(pTheArray,reinterpret_cast<void**>(&bstrArray));
647
648  char ch[100];
649  USES_CONVERSION;
650  for (int i=0; i<lCount; i++)
651  {
652   CComBSTR m_bstrName;
653   hr = pProColl->Item(i, &pPro);
654   hr = pPro->get_Name(&m_bstrName);
655   bstrArray[i] = m_bstrName.Copy();
656
657
658  }
659
660  SafeArrayUnaccessData(pTheArray);
661  pVal->parray = pTheArray;
662  return S_OK;
663 }
```

Code description (CBroadcastIt implementation)

♦ Lines 1-7: This provides the necessary packages required for building this component.

♦ Lines 9-17: Fire_BroadcastStatus is being used here to invoke a user-defined event to send messages back to the user during different stages of encoding.

♦ Lines 18-26: This checks that the encoder has been initialized successfully and that the session has already been created.

♦ Line 27: A variable is initialized positively to signify that the session is being created currently.

♦ Lines 29-45: Some local variables are declared to be fed as the attribute values of the encoder session. A pointer of type `IWMEncAttributes` is retrieved, calling the `get_Attributes` method on `IWMEncoder`'s pointer.

♦ Lines 46-55: A structure of `bstr` type is initialized with the titles of attributes to be associated with the encoding session.

♦ Lines 56-63: Current system date and time are obtained calling `GetLocalTime()` API, passing in a reference of `SYSTEMTIME` object. The obtained date and time are formatted in a legible manner.

♦ Lines 64-77: A structure of type variant is initialized to store the values for attributes assigned to the current encoding session.

♦ Lines 78-82: This session is then assigned all these attributes as name-value pairs, running a loop and making as many iterations as the number of attributes to be assigned.

♦ Lines 83-91: All the attributes assigned previously are signaled back to the user as a confirmation that all the attributes have been assigned successfully.

♦ Lines 92-95: Encoder session is instructed to stop automatically as soon as the media source is completely encoded.

♦ Lines 96-105: A pointer to the `IWMEncDisplayInfo` interface is obtained by invoking the `get_DisplayInfo()` method on `IWMEncoder` pointer initialized previously in the `InitializeBroadcaster()` function. This pointer is used to fill up the information for a session to be displayed on the receiver's end. Values for different information types, such as author name, copyright information, and so on, are fed.

♦ Lines 106-113: If the component is instructed to support scripts, a script-media stream is added to the encoder by calling the `AddSource()` method on `IWMEncSourceGroup` interface's pointer retrieved previously in the `InitializeBroadcaster()` method.

♦ Lines 114-136: If an audio source has been specified, it is added to the media-source group calling `AddSource()` method on the `IWMEncSourceGroup` interface's pointer retrieved previously in the `InitializeBroadcaster()` function.

♦ Lines 137-154: If a video source has been specified, it is added to the media-source group calling `AddSource()` method on `IWMEncSourceGroup` interfaces' pointer retrieved previously in `InitializeBroadcaster()`.

♦ Lines 161-162: This confirms that the encoder has been initialized successfully.

♦ Lines 169-174: `Start method` is called on `IWMEncoder` interface's pointer to start the encoding and broadcasting session.

♦ Lines 175-184: Any error encountered is conveyed back to the user.

♦ Lines 190-194: This makes sure that the encoder has been initialized successfully.

♦ Line 195: This ensures that the session is to be closed down.

♦ Line 204: Media Source Group is instructed to pack up by passing `FALSE` as the parameter while calling `PrepareToEncode` on it.

♦ Lines 207-214: Media Source Group is queried for the number of audio-media sources associated with it, and those sources are released.

♦ Lines 215-221: Media Source Group is queried for the number of video-media sources associated with it, and those sources arereleased.

- Lines 215-228: `Media Source` Group is queried for the number of script-media sources associated with it, and those sources are released.

- Lines 230-234: The media source `SG -2` that was added to the media source group collection in the function `InitializeBroadcaster` is then removed.

- Lines 235-238: Media Encoder is instructed to cease any active encoding session and to close any active source stream, calling `PrepareToEncode()` with the only parameter it takes set as `FALSE`.

- Lines 239-241: Media Encoder is instructed to stop the current encoding session.

- Lines 242-246: Media Encoder component is released, and the variables are assigned negative values to signify that no encoding session is active.

- Lines 247-249: The user receives the message that the session has been closed.

- Lines 250-333: This part of the code gives users an idea of the usage of the interfaces `IWMEncStatistics` and `IWMEncOutputStats` which may be availed for getting the status of the ongoing encoding session.

- Lines 334-335: This makes sure a session is active.

- Line 338: SendScript is called on `IWMEncoder` pointer to broadcast the textual message along with running media specifying the type of script `TEXT`.

- Lines 343-345: This makes sure a session is active.

- Line 348: SendScript is called on `IWMEncoder` pointer to broadcast the textual message along with running media specifying the type of script `URL`, which opens the site associated with this URL on the receiver's end.

- Lines 355-360: This ensures that the encoder is initialized and that a session is active at the moment.

- Lines 371-377: `IWMEncoder`'s `get_ProfileCollection()` method is invoked to retrieve the pointer to `IWMEncProfileCollection` interface. This interface contains the enumerated profiles available to this encoder session. Any error encountered while doing this is conveyed back to the user.

- Lines 378-387: `IWMEncProfileCollection` interface's method `get_Count` is invoked to retrieve the number of profiles available for this encoding session. Any error encountered is conveyed back to the user.

- Lines 395-400: `IWMEncProfileCollection`'s `Item` method is invoked to retrieve the pointer to a `IWMEncProfile` type pointer that represents the profile at the indices specified as the first argument.

- Lines 401-407: `IWMEncProfile`'s `get_Name` method is invoked to get the name of the profile retrieved.

- Lines 408-416: This profile is associated to the Media Source Group.

- Lines 421-427: `IWMEncoder`'s `get_Broadcast` is invoked to retrieve a pointer of type `IWMEncBroadcast`, which manages the port number and the protocol used for broadcasting the encoded media data.

- Lines 428-433: The port already being used for broadcasting is retrieved calling the `get_PortNumber()` method on this interface pointer.

- Lines 437-442: An appropriate port number is set to broadcast the media data.

- Lines 452-457: `PrepareToEncode` is called on `IWMEncoder` to set all the properties set previously and to prepare the encoder engine for starting.

- Lines 463-476: Calling `CoCreateInstance` with the following parameters: the `Class ID` of the Windows Media Encoder; aggregating interface (which is null in this case); constant that specifies whether the present component will run as in-process and the `interface ID` of the Windows

Media Encoder. In case Windows Media Encoder could not be initialized, an error message is passed to the user. If initialization is successful, the pointer of type `IWMEncoder` which is passed as the fifth parameter is allocated memory.

♦ Lines 477-483: Invoke the `get_SourceGroupCollection` method through the pointer of `IWMEncoder` type to get the collection of source groups in a pointer of type `IWMEncSourceGroupCollection`. Any error encountered while retrieving Source-Group collection is passed to the user.

♦ Lines 484-494: To the collection retrieved, a new source group is added, and the reference to it is atained in a pointer of type `IWMEncSourceGroup`. An error is passed back to the user if the Source Group cannot be loaded successfully.

♦ Lines 503-512: For receiving the index number of the profile that the user selects from the list of profiles, the index number is stored in the local variable `shProfile`. The user is then notified that the value has been stored successfully, by sending him a message along with the number that he had passed. Here it is imperative to mention that profile in this discussion means encoding profile that is comprised of the information regarding the use of available bendwidth for voice and video streaming.

♦ Lines 513-522: Thuis specifies the port number for broadcasting the data.The new value passed is stored in the local variable `shPortNo`.

♦ Lines 523-530: This is called to specify the audio source for this encoding session. The new value passed is stored in the local variable `bstrAudioMedia`, and the variable is initialized to a positive value to signify that the encoding session has audio data in it.

♦ Lines 531-538: This is called to specify the video source for this encoding session. The new value passed is stored in the local variable `bstrVideoMedia`, and the variable will be initialized to a positive value to signify that encoding session has video data.

♦ Lines 539-547: This is called to mention whether this encoding session supports `Script Media`. Only 1 and 0 are acceptable; 1 specifying support for Script Media and 0 e specifying no support.

♦ Line 551: The profile number set by the user calling `put_Profile` can be retrieved by calling this function.

♦ Line 552: The port specified by the user can be retrieved by calling this function.

♦ Line 553: The audio source specified by the user calling `put_AudioMedia` function can be retrieved by calling this function.

♦ Line 554: Calling this function can retrieve the video source specified by the user calling the `put_VideoMedia()` function.

♦ Line 555: Whether this encoding session supports script media or not can be known by calling this function.

♦ Lines 556-571: Method `get_SourcePluginInfoManager` is invoked on the interface pointer of type `IWMEncoder` to get a pointer to the `IWMEncSourcePluginInfoManager` interface. The `get_Count` method is called to get the count of installed source plug-ins.

♦ Lines 572-577: For each source plug-in installed, the plug-in information is obtained by calling the Item method on this interface's pointer, which gives a pointer to the `IWMEncPluginInfo` interface to retrieve registry information of plug-ins.

♦ 578-594: Each registry plug-in information retrieved is checked for whether the scheme type is `DEVICE`. When a plug-in information of this type is found, it is checked if it supports any resource by calling `get_Resources` method on the `IWMEncPluginInfo` pointer. If such resources are supported, the number of resources supported by the plug-in is retrieved by calling the `get_Count()` method. A `SAFEARRAY` pointer is made with `SAFEARRAYBOUND`, specifying the number of elements equal to the number of resources supported.

♦ Lines 595-611: The `IWMEncPluginInfo` interface's item method is invoked to iterate through the list of supported resources and is stored in a `BSTR` type array returned by calling `SafeArrayAccessData()` API. Then `SafeArrayUnaccessData` is called to unlock the array. The array is then stored in the outgoing parameter.

♦ Lines 617-619: This makes sure the encoder has been initialized successfully.

♦ Lines 620-631: `IWMEncoder`'s `get_ProfileCollection` method is invoked to retrieve the pointer to the `IWMEncProfileCollection` interface. This interface contains the enumerated profiles that are available to this encoder session. Any error encountered while doing so is conveyed back to the user.

♦ Lines 632-639: `IWMEncProfileCollection` interface's method `get_Count` is invoked to retrieve the number of profiles available for this encoding session. Any error encountered is conveyed back to the user.

♦ Lines 640-647: A `SAFEARRAY` pointer is declared and created specifying the bounds as the number of elements being equal to the number of profiles found for the current session. This array is locked for access calling `SafeArrayAccessData()`.

♦ Lines 648-659: The enumerator is iterated throughout, and the list names of profiles are stored in the array.

♦ Line 660: The array is unlocked calling `SafeArrayUnaccessData`.

♦ Line 661: The array is assigned to the outgoing parameter.

The Windows Media Encoder we are using here to encode media data supports connection points you can use to your advantage to get the status of the active-encoding session at various stages. For this, implement the `_IWMEncoderEvent` interface. This interface is implemented by the `CEvents` class that follows and as shown in Listing 6-3:

Implementing class: CEvents (Interface implemented: _IWMEncoderEvent)

Listing 6-3: Declaration of CEvents class

Declaration and implementation file: Events.h

```
 1 #ifndef __EVENT_H__
 2 #define __EVENT_H__
 3
 4 #include <atlbase.h>
 5 #include <atlcom.h>
 6
 7 #include "wmencode.h"
 8 #include "wmsencid.h"
 9 #include "BroadcastIt.h"
10
11 #define EVENT_ID        100
12 #define LIB_VERMAJOR    1
13 #define LIB_VERMINOR    0
14
15 class CEvents : public IDispEventImpl< EVENT_ID,
16                                        CEvents,
17                                        &DIID__IWMEncoderEvents,
18                                        &LIBID_WMEncoderLib,
19                                        LIB_VERMAJOR,
20                                        LIB_VERMINOR >
```

```
21 {
22
23 public:
24   int a;
25
26     static _ATL_FUNC_INFO StateChangeInfo;
27     static _ATL_FUNC_INFO ErrorInfo;
28     static _ATL_FUNC_INFO ArchiveStateChangeInfo;
29     static _ATL_FUNC_INFO ConfigChangeInfo;
30     static _ATL_FUNC_INFO ClientConnectInfo;
31     static _ATL_FUNC_INFO ClientDisconnectInfo;
32     static _ATL_FUNC_INFO SourceStateChangeInfo;
33     static _ATL_FUNC_INFO IndexerStateChangeInfo;
34
35 BEGIN_SINK_MAP(CEvents)
36     SINK_ENTRY_INFO( EVENT_ID,
37                      DIID__IWMEncoderEvents,
38                      DISPID_ENCODEREVENT_STATECHANGE,
39                      OnStateChange,
40                      &StateChangeInfo )
41     SINK_ENTRY_INFO( EVENT_ID,
42                      DIID__IWMEncoderEvents,
43                      DISPID_ENCODEREVENT_ERROR,
44                      OnError,
45                      &ErrorInfo )
46     SINK_ENTRY_INFO( EVENT_ID,
47                      DIID__IWMEncoderEvents,
48                      DISPID_ENCODEREVENT_ARCHIVESTATECHANGE,
49                      OnArchiveStateChange,
50                      &ArchiveStateChangeInfo )
51     SINK_ENTRY_INFO( EVENT_ID,
52                      DIID__IWMEncoderEvents,
53                      DISPID_ENCODEREVENT_CONFIGCHANGE,
54                      OnConfigChange,
55                      &ConfigChangeInfo)
56     SINK_ENTRY_INFO( EVENT_ID,
57                      DIID__IWMEncoderEvents,
58                      DISPID_ENCODEREVENT_CLIENTCONNECT,
59                      OnClientConnect,
60                      &ClientConnectInfo)
61     SINK_ENTRY_INFO( EVENT_ID,
62                      DIID__IWMEncoderEvents,
63                      DISPID_ENCODEREVENT_CLIENTDISCONNECT,
64                      OnClientDisconnect,
65                      &ClientDisconnectInfo)
66     SINK_ENTRY_INFO( EVENT_ID,
67                      DIID__IWMEncoderEvents,
68                      DISPID_ENCODEREVENT_SRCSTATECHANGE,
69                      OnSourceStateChange,
70                      &SourceStateChangeInfo )
71     SINK_ENTRY_INFO( EVENT_ID,
72                      DIID__IWMEncoderEvents,
73                      DISPID_ENCODEREVENT_INDEXERSTATECHANGE,
74                      OnIndexerStateChange,
75                      &IndexerStateChangeInfo )
76 END_SINK_MAP()
```

```
77
78 public:
79     STDMETHOD(OnStateChange)(/*[in]*/ WMENC_ENCODER_STATE enumState);
80     STDMETHOD(OnSourceStateChange)(
81                 /*[in*/WMENC_SOURCE_STATE enumState,
82                 /*[in*/WMENC_SOURCE_TYPE enumType,
83                 /*[in*/short iIndex,
84                 /*[in]*/BSTR bstrSourceGroup);
85     STDMETHOD(OnError)(/*[in]*/ long hResult);
86     STDMETHOD(OnArchiveStateChange)(
87                 /*[in]*/ WMENC_ARCHIVE_TYPE enumArchive,
88                 /*[in]*/ WMENC_ARCHIVE_STATE enumState );
89     STDMETHOD(OnConfigChange)(/*[in]*/ long hResult, /*[in]*/ BSTR bstr);
90     STDMETHOD(OnClientConnect)(
91                 /*[in]*/ WMENC_BROADCAST_PROTOCOL protocol,
92                 /*[in]*/ BSTR bstr);
93     STDMETHOD(OnClientDisconnect)(
94                 /*[in]*/ WMENC_BROADCAST_PROTOCOL protocol,
95                 /*[in]*/ BSTR bstr);
96     STDMETHOD(OnIndexerStateChange)(
97                 /*[in]*/ WMENC_INDEXER_STATE enumIndexerState,
98                 /*[in]*/ BSTR bstrFile );
99
100    HRESULT CEvents::Init( IWMEncoder* pEncoder )
101    {
102        HRESULT hr = DispEventAdvise( pEncoder );
103        if( FAILED( hr ) )
104        {
105        }
106    return hr;
107    }
108
109    HRESULT CEvents::ShutDown( IWMEncoder* pEncoder )
110    {
111        HRESULT hr = DispEventUnadvise( pEncoder );
112        if( FAILED( hr ) )
113        {
114        }
115        return hr;
116    }
117
118    CEvents(CBroadcastIt* br);
119
120 };
121
122 ////////////////////////////////////////////////////////////
123
124 CEvents::CEvents(CBroadcastIt* br)
125 {
126  broadcast = br;
127  a = 0;
128 }
129
130
131 _ATL_FUNC_INFO CEvents::ArchiveStateChangeInfo= {CC_STDCALL,
132         VT_ERROR, 2, { VT_I4, VT_I4 } };
```

```
133
134 ///////////////////////////////////////////////////////////
135
136 STDMETHODIMP CEvents::OnArchiveStateChange(
137                 WMENC_ARCHIVE_TYPE enumArchive,
138                 WMENC_ARCHIVE_STATE enumState )
139 {
140 switch ( enumArchive )
141     {
142     case WMENC_ARCHIVE_LOCAL:
143         broadcast->HeraldThisMessage(L"WMENC_ARCHIVE_LOCAL");
144          break;
145     default:
146          break;
147     }
148
149 switch ( enumState )
150     {
151     case WMENC_ARCHIVE_RUNNING:
152          // Process the case.
153         broadcast->HeraldThisMessage(L"WMENC_ARCHIVE_RUNNING");
154          break;
155
156     case WMENC_ARCHIVE_PAUSED:
157          // Process the case.
158         broadcast->HeraldThisMessage(L"WMENC_ARCHIVE_PAUSED");
159          break;
160
161     case WMENC_ARCHIVE_STOPPED:
162          // Process the case.
163         broadcast->HeraldThisMessage(L"WMENC_ARCHIVE_STOPPED");
164          break;
165
166     default:
167         broadcast->HeraldThisMessage(L"Archive");
168          break;
169     }
170 return E_NOTIMPL;
171 }
172
173
174 _ATL_FUNC_INFO CEvents::IndexerStateChangeInfo = {CC_STDCALL,
175          VT_ERROR, 2, { VT_I4, VT_BSTR } };
176
177 ///////////////////////////////////////////////
178
179 STDMETHODIMP CEvents::OnIndexerStateChange(
180                 WMENC_INDEXER_STATE enumIndexerState,
181                 BSTR bstrFile )
182 {
183         broadcast->HeraldThisMessage(L"IndexerStateChange");
184     return E_NOTIMPL;
185 }
186
187
188 _ATL_FUNC_INFO CEvents::ClientDisconnectInfo = {CC_STDCALL,
```

```
189                 VT_ERROR, 2, { VT_I4, VT_BSTR } };
190
191 STDMETHODIMP CEvents::OnClientDisconnect(
192                 WMENC_BROADCAST_PROTOCOL protocol,
193                 BSTR bstr)
194 {
195         broadcast->HeraldThisMessage(L"Client Disconnected");
196 return E_NOTIMPL;
197 }
198
199 _ATL_FUNC_INFO CEvents::ClientConnectInfo = {CC_STDCALL,
200           VT_ERROR, 2, { VT_I4, VT_BSTR } };
201
202 //////////////////////////////////////////////////
203
204 STDMETHODIMP CEvents::OnClientConnect(
205                 WMENC_BROADCAST_PROTOCOL protocol,
206                 BSTR bstr)
207 {
208         broadcast->HeraldThisMessage(L"Client Connected");
209 return E_NOTIMPL;
210 }
211
212
213 _ATL_FUNC_INFO CEvents::ConfigChangeInfo
214 = {CC_STDCALL, VT_ERROR, 2, { VT_I4, VT_BSTR } };
215
216 //////////////////////////////////////////////////
217
218 STDMETHODIMP CEvents::OnConfigChange(long hResult, BSTR bstr)
219 {
220
221         broadcast->HeraldThisMessage(L"Configuration Changed");
222         broadcast->HeraldThisMessage(bstr);
223 return E_NOTIMPL;
224 }
225
226
227 _ATL_FUNC_INFO CEvents::ErrorInfo = {CC_STDCALL,
228           VT_ERROR, 1, { VT_I4 } };
229
230 //////////////////////////////////////////////////
231
232 STDMETHODIMP CEvents::OnError(long hResult)
233 {
234
235   broadcast->HeraldThisMessage(L"Started");
236
237 return E_NOTIMPL;
238 }
239
240
241 _ATL_FUNC_INFO CEvents::SourceStateChangeInfo = {CC_STDCALL,
242           VT_ERROR, 3, { VT_I4, VT_I4, VT_I2 } };
243
244 //////////////////////////////////////////////////
```

```
245
246 STDMETHODIMP CEvents::OnSourceStateChange(
247                 WMENC_SOURCE_STATE enumState,
248                 WMENC_SOURCE_TYPE enumType,
249                 short iIndex,BSTR i)
250 {
251 switch ( enumState )
252     {
253     case WMENC_SOURCE_START:
254
255         broadcast->HeraldThisMessage(L"Started");
256
257          break;
258     case WMENC_SOURCE_STOP:
259
260         broadcast->HeraldThisMessage(L"Stop");
261
262          break;
263     default:
264
265         broadcast->HeraldThisMessage(L"Encoding");
266
267          break;
268     }
269
270 switch ( enumType )
271     {
272     case WMENC_AUDIO:
273
274   broadcast->HeraldThisMessage(L"WMENC_AUDIO");
275
276          break;
277     case WMENC_VIDEO:
278
279   broadcast->HeraldThisMessage(L"WMENC_VIDEO");
280
281          break;
282     case WMENC_SCRIPT:
283
284   broadcast->HeraldThisMessage(L"WMENC_SCRIPT");
285
286          break;
287     default:
288
289          break;
290     }
291
292 return E_NOTIMPL;
293 }
294
295 _ATL_FUNC_INFO CEvents::StateChangeInfo = {CC_STDCALL,
296         VT_ERROR, 1, { VT_I4 } };
297
298 /////////////////////////////////////////////////
299
300 STDMETHODIMP CEvents::OnStateChange(WMENC_ENCODER_STATE enumState)
```

```
301 {
302 switch ( enumState )
303     {
304     case WMENC_ENCODER_STARTING:
305
306   broadcast->HeraldThisMessage(L"WMENC_ENCODER_STARTING");
307
308         break;
309   case WMENC_ENCODER_RUNNING:
310
311   broadcast->HeraldThisMessage(L"WMENC_ENCODER_RUNNING");
312
313         break;
314     case WMENC_ENCODER_PAUSED:
315
316   broadcast->HeraldThisMessage(L"WMENC_ENCODER_PAUSED");
317
318         break;
319     case WMENC_ENCODER_STOPPING:
320
321   broadcast->HeraldThisMessage(L"WMENC_ENCODER_STOPPING");
322
323         break;
324     case WMENC_ENCODER_STOPPED:
325
326   broadcast->HeraldThisMessage(L"WMENC_ENCODER_STOPPED");
327
328         break;
329     default:
330
331         break;
332     }
333 return E_NOTIMPL;
334 }/////////////////////////////////////////////////
335
336 #endif // __EVENT_H__
337 #endif // __EVENT_H__
```

Code description (CEvents declaration and implementation)

◆ Lines 1-6: The ATL Support header file is included.

◆ Lines 7-8: The Encoder header file is included.

◆ Lines 15-22: Class CEvents inherited from IDispEventImpl implements events raised by the encoder.

◆ Lines 26-34: _ATL_FUNC_INFO structure objects declarations for each event are described in the type library. These structures are filled later to define the calling conventions, the number of arguments, and the argument types with the return types.

◆ Lines 35-77: Sink Map defines and links all the functions declared in _IWMEncoderEvents interface to the function declared in this class. All the events fired by Encoder are routed through this map to invoke the implementations of event-handler functions.

◆ Lines 78-99: This part of code is a set of function declarations.

◆ Lines 100-107: This function helps Encoder, which is a source of events in this case, to establish a connection with the event sink (that is, the catcher of these events which implements all the events raised by the encoder which essentially means the implementation of the IWMEncoderEvents interface). Internally, this function calls `DispEventAdvise`, implemented in `IDispEventImpl` from which this class is derived, passing the `IUnknown` pointer to the source of events.

♦ Lines 108-116: This function helps Encoder close the connection with the event sink (that is, the implementation of `_IWMEncoderEvents` interface). Once the connection is broken, events are no longer routed to the handler functions listed in the event Sink Map. Internally,this function calls `DispEventUnadvise`, implemented in `IDispEventImpl` from which this class is derived, passing the `IUnknown` pointer to the source of events.

♦ Lines 124-128: The Constructor receives here a pointer of `CBroadcastIt` type for later use when it will be needed to be set as the source of events.

♦ Lines 130-132: `ArchiveStateChangeInfo` object of `_ATL_FUNC_INFO` type is filled to specify the calling convention, number of arguments, argument types, and return type of the handler for the `ArchiveStateChange` event.

♦ Lines 136-171: The `OnArchiveStateChange` receives the event number of notifications for changes while encoding the local (in most cases) media and for different stages such as stopped, running, and paused.

♦ Lines 173-176: The `IndexerStateChangeInfo` structure is filled with information such as calling conventions, argument types, the number of arguments, and the return type for the handler of `IndexerStateChange` event.

♦ Lines 177-185: This function gets indications when the indexing process begins or stops for a Windows Media file.

♦ Lines 186-189: The `ClientDisconnectInfo` structure is filled with information such as calling conventions, argument types, the number of arguments, and the return type for the handler of the `ClientDisconnect` event.

♦ Lines 190-197: As any client closes the connection, this handler is invoked to signal the event.

♦ Lines 198-200: `ClientConnectInfo` structure is filled with information Suc as calling conventions, argument types, the number of arguments, and the return type for the handler of the `ClientConnect` event.

♦ Lines 201-210: While broadcasting the media on a particular port, the connection made by any client is signaled by the Encoder by firing this event, thus calling this handler.

♦ Lines 212-214: The `ConfigChangeInfo` structure is filled with information such as calling conventions, argument types, the number of arguments, and the return type for the handler of the `ConfigChange` event.

♦ Lines 217-224: Any configuration change is notified invoking this event by the Encoder.

♦ Lines 227-228: The `ErrorInfo` structure is filled with information such as calling conventions, argument types, the number of arguments, and the return type for the handler of the `Error` event.

♦ Lines 232-238: Any Error encountered at any stage of the encoding session is signaled, invoking this event.

♦ Lines 241-242: The `SourceStateChangeInfo` structure is filled with information such as calling conventions, argument types, the number of arguments, and the return type for the handler of the `SourceStateChange` event.

♦ Lines 245-294: This handler is invoked to signal different states of the encoding engine, such as Stopped, Stopping, Start, Starting, and Running.

♦ Lines 295-296: The `SourceStateChangeInfo` structure is filled with information such as calling conventions, argument types, the number of arguments, and return type for the handler of the `SourceStateChange` event.

♦ Lines 300-333: This functionis invoked by the encoder to signal when it starts or stops.

Changes on the Browser Side

Now that you are familiar with the changes made on the listener side of the application, we take up changing the browser module. Because every request is generated by the browser and sent to the listener, we have to request the browser for streaming. For this, some changes are needed on the browser side, such as adding a Stream button to facilitate streaming.

In Figure 6-2, you see the Stream button placed at the top, along with the other buttons. Now that you have placed the Stream button, you need the code that is invoked when you click this button.

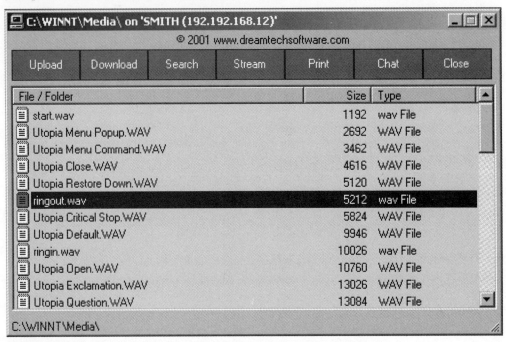

Figure 6-2: The Stream button added on Browser's interface initiates the streaming process.

```
 1     private void btnStream_Click(object sender, System.EventArgs e)
 2   {
 3       // Declares a local Filename variable
 4       string Filename;
 5
 6       // Extract the IP address from the COMPUTERNAME variable
 7       string IPAddress = COMPUTERNAME.Substring(COMPUTERNAME.IndexOf("(")+1);
 8       IPAddress = IPAddress.Substring(0, IPAddress.Length - 1);
 9
10       // Get the currently selected item from the List view
11       int index = GetSelectedItemFromListView(out Filename);
12       try
13       {
14           // Checks whether any entry is selected or not
15   if( -1 != index)
16   {
17       // Checks whether a filename is selected for Streaming
18       // or not
19       if( null != Filename )
20         {
```

```
21    OpenConnection(COMPUTERNAME);
22
23    // Creates a stream request for a particular
24    // file to stream.
25    CreateRequest("STREAMING",strArray[index].sFilename,"");
26
27    // Sends this request to the listener
28    SendDataToListener(REQUESTFILE);
29
30    // Get the response from the listener in lieu of the
31    // above request
32    GetDataFromListener(RESPONSEFILE);
33
34    xmlParser = new WorkingWithXML.XMLParser();
35    xmlStruct = new XMLSTRUCT();
36    xmlParser.ParseXML(RESPONSEFILE,out xmlStruct,new
ServerCommunication().TypeOfXMLRecieved(RESPONSEFILE));
37
38    if( 0 == xmlStruct.ERROR.sDescription.CompareTo("No Error") )
39    {
40        frmStreamer StreamerForm = new frmStreamer(IPAddress);
41        StreamerForm.ShowDialog();
42    }
43    else throw new Exception(xmlStruct.ERROR.sDescription);
44        }
45      else throw new Exception("Cannot stream a folder");
46  }
47  // If nothing is selected then displays an error message
48  else throw new Exception("Nothing Selected");
49      }
50
51      // catches any system generated error message and displays it
52      // to the user
53      catch( Exception err ) {
MessageBox.Show(err.Message,"Warning",MessageBoxButtons.OK,
MessageBoxIcon.Warning); }
54      finally { new ServerCommunication().FileDelete(RESPONSEFILE); }
55 }
```

The preceding function simulates the Stream button click event. When the button is clicked while selecting a file for streaming, the IP address of the connected listener is extracted. The currently selected file is retrieved by calling the `GetSelectedItemFromListView()` function. The control is then passed to the `OpenConnection()` function, which opens the connection to the listener for sending the streaming request. The streaming request is created as follows:

```
<?xml version="1.0" encoding="utf-8"?>
<p2p_lng>
 <request type="STREAMING">
<scope type="C:\WINNT\Media\ringout.WAV" mask=""/>
</request>
</p2p_lng>
```

The preceding request is then sent to the listener by calling the `SendDataToListener()` function and passing the response filename to it. After sending the request, the listener reads it and responds to the browser. This response is then read by calling the `GetDataFromListener()` function. Actually, this response is the `ERROR` response in which `No Error` is written in the description part if the listener successfully listens to the request. Otherwise, the error is returned. This ERROR   XML is then parsed. This check is performed at line 38 in the preceding code. If the streaming request is successful, a new instance of the `frmStreamer` form is created and shown to the user. This window contains the Windows Media Player component to play the selected file via streaming.

For streaming, you have to add a new form and name it `frmStreamer`. Add a Windows Media Player component to it, as in Figure 6-3.

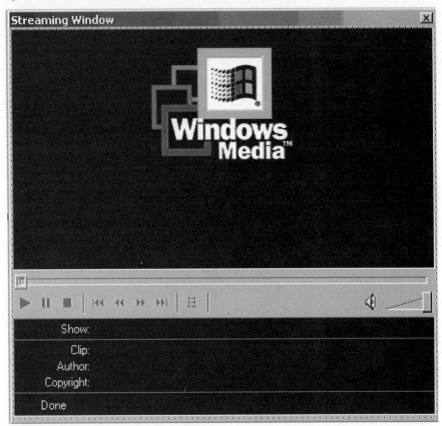

Figure 6-3: The streaming interface for browser

In the default constructor of this form, write the following lines of code below the `InitializeComponent()`:

```
try { axMediaPlayer.FileName = "http://" + IPAddress + ":9090"; }
catch( Exception err ) {
MessageBox.Show(err.Message,"Error",MessageBoxButtons.OK,MessageBoxIcon.Error);

public frmStreamer(string IPAddress)
{
    // Required for Windows Form Designer support
    InitializeComponent();
    try { axMediaPlayer.FileName = "http://" + IPAddress + ":9090"; }
    catch( Exception err ) {
MessageBox.Show(err.Message,"Error",MessageBoxButtons.OK,MessageBoxIcon.Error);
    }
}
```

Because streaming is performed over a network connection, exceptions are likely to happen on either side. To handle these exceptions, we need to catch them. The following lines of code represent the `Error` event of the Windows Media Player, which is automatically invoked in case of an exception. For example, if you are in the middle of a streaming session and the listener closes without notification, or some error occurs on the listener side that stops the listener's streaming session, this event handler warns the user on the browser side and then closes the streaming window.

```
private void axMediaPlayer_Error(object sender, System.EventArgs e)
{
    MessageBox.Show("Some error has been occured while streaming. Cannot
    continue further","Error",MessageBoxButtons.OK,MessageBoxIcon.Error);
    axMediaPlayer.Dispose();
    this.Dispose();
    this.Close();
}
```

After the streaming session is completed successfully and the user is through with the audio/video file, he or she has to close the streaming window to return to the browser window. At this stage, the following event handler is invoked, and it clears all the memory resources that are in use by calling each of the object's `Dispose` functions.

```
private void frmStreamer_Closing(object sender,
                        System.ComponentModel.CancelEventArgs e)
{
    axMediaPlayer.Dispose();
    this.Dispose();
}
```

Changes on the Listener Side

As soon as the request sent by the browser is received at the listener's end, the `RequestResponse()` function that determines the request types and responds to the browser takes control and makes an object of class `StreamIt`, which is written specifically to handle streaming request types.

```
protected void RequestResponse()
{
.
.
    if(UploadDownloadPrint == 5) // this represents a streaming request
    {
    StreamIt streamDlg = new StreamIt(DnLoadFile,new
                    StreamingCallBackDeligates(StreamingCallBack));
    intStreamingThreadIndex = ThreadCount;
    bDownLoading = false;
    return;
    }
.
.
.
}
```

The name of the file requested to be streamed is passed to the object of the `StreamIt` class, as the argument of its constructor. The rest of the job is done by this class.

```
public StreamIt(string MediaFile,StreamingCallBackDeligates callback)
{
.
```

```
callbackFunc            = callback;
.
.
.
this.btnApply_Click(null,null);
}
```

The constructor of the `StreamIt` class stores the filename passed and the `CallBack()` function reference to the respective local-member variables. The `Callback ()` function here is of type `StreamingCallBackDeligates` which has the following signature:

```
public delegate void StreamingCallBackDeligates(string e,StreamIt str);
```

Also, for our purposes, it has the following implementation:

```
public void StreamingCallBack(string e,StreamIt source)
{
 Application.DoEvents();
 if((e.CompareTo("Stopped") == 0))
 {
   if(bStreaming)
    new XMLCreater(Application.StartupPath +
        "\\Temp1.xml","").WriteErrorResponse(
        "A streaming session is already active on this peer");
   else
   {
    new XMLCreater(Application.StartupPath +
        "\\Temp1.xml","").WriteErrorResponse(
        "Problem encountered while initiating the Streaming Session");
    bStreaming = false;
   }
 }
 else if(e.CompareTo("Encoder Stopped") == 0)
   bStreaming = false;
 else if(e.CompareTo("Copy Complete") == 0)
 {
   bStreaming = true;
   new XMLCreater(Application.StartupPath +
        "\\Temp1.xml","").WriteErrorResponse("No Error");
 }
 else
   return;
 .
 .
 .
}
```

The `StreamingCallBack()` function handles various states of the ongoing encoding session and responds accordingly. If the encoder session is found to have experienced a problem, the session is closed, and an error response with the message about the failure is created to be sent to the calling browser later. The information is passed by using the `StreamIt` classes, as explained shortly.

The constructor, after initializing the local variables, calls the `btnApply_Click()` function:

```
private void btnApply_Click(object sender, System.EventArgs e)
{
 axBroadcastIt1.InitializeBroadcaster();
 axBroadcastIt1.Port = 9090;
```

```
    axBroadcastIt1.AudioMedia = strMediaSource;
    axBroadcastIt1.VideoMedia = strMediaSource;
    axBroadcastIt1.MakeSession();
    axBroadcastIt1.PrepareToEncode();
    axBroadcastIt1.Broadcast();
}
```

This function initializes the encoder session calling `InitializeBroadcaster()` function on the object of the `BroadcastIt` COM class (explained in Listing 6-1) and equips it with information such as the port number and the file to stream over the Internet before it calls the `MakeSession()` function to make the encoder session. The `PrepareToEncode()` and `Broadcast()` functions are then called to start the session.

The code that follows defines the `BroadcastStatus()` function that is called by the `BroadcastIt`'s COM object. It is the event handler of `BroadcastStatus` event that the `BroadcastIt` component fires as and when it senses any change in the encoder session's state. The calling of this function ensures that any problem faced during the encoding process leads to the disposal of all the resources being used and that the encoding session terminates gracefully. Any significant change in the encoder session is fired to the login form through the callback function `StreamingCallBack()` to enable it to handle the change accordingly, as described previously.

```
protected int axBroadcastIt1_BroadcastStatus(object  sender,
                AxBROADCASTDLLLib._IBroadcastItEvents_BroadcastStatusEvent  e)
{
   Application.DoEvents();
.
.
   if((e.status.ToString().CompareTo(
           "Second attempt of calling PrepareToEncode failed") == 0)
    || (e.status.ToString().CompareTo("Couldn't Start Encoder") == 0))
   {
    callbackFunc("Stopped",this);
    this.btnCloseSession_Click(null,null);
    this.Dispose();
    this.Close();
   }
   if((e.status.ToString().CompareTo("Encoder Stopped") == 0))
   {
    callbackFunc("Encoder Stopped",this);
    this.btnCloseSession_Click(null,null);
    this.Dispose();
    this.Close();
   }

   if((e.status.ToString().CompareTo("Copy Complete") == 0) ||
           (e.status.ToString().CompareTo("Started") == 0))
    callbackFunc("Copy Complete",this);
   return 1;
}
```

Running the Application

Now that we have seen the coding part needed to incorporate streaming in the current design of our P2P application, we are about to see the code in action. Compile and build the application as described in Microsoft Visual Studio.NET, and double-click the executable file that is generated. Upon executing this file successfully, you are able to see the first window, as shown in Figure 6-4.

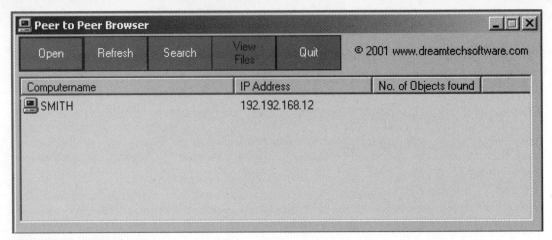

Figure 6-4: The Browser's window

Choose the appropriate media you want to play. In this case, we have shared the Media folder in the window's directory (see Figure 6-5).

File / Folder	Size	Type
start.wav	1192	wav File
Utopia Menu Popup.WAV	2692	WAV File
Utopia Menu Command.WAV	3462	WAV File
Utopia Close.WAV	4616	WAV File
Utopia Restore Down.WAV	5120	WAV File
ringout.wav	5212	wav File
Utopia Critical Stop.WAV	5824	WAV File
Utopia Default.WAV	9946	WAV File
ringin.wav	10026	wav File
Utopia Open.WAV	10760	WAV File
Utopia Exclamation.WAV	13026	WAV File
Utopia Question.WAV	13084	WAV File

C:\WINNT\Media\ on 'SMITH (192.192.168.12)'
© 2001 www.dreamtechsoftware.com
Upload   Download   Search   Stream   Print   Chat   Close
C:\WINNT\Media\

Figure 6-5: Clicking the Stream button starts streaming the selected file.

Select any media file from the window and click the `Stream` button. If the streaming initiates successfully, you see the text `Now Streaming. Please wait`... in the status bar of the browser window (see Figure 6-6).

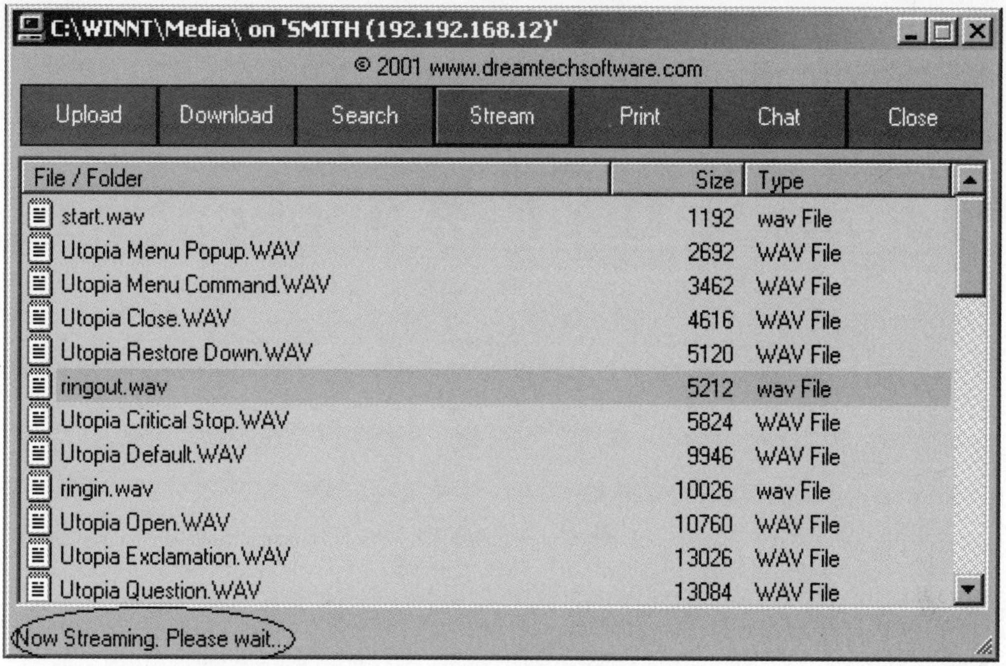

```
C:\WINNT\Media\ on 'SMITH (192.192.168.12)'          _ □ X
              © 2001 www.dreamtechsoftware.com

   Upload    Download    Search    Stream    Print    Chat    Close

 File / Folder                              Size  Type              ▲
 ▤ start.wav                                1192  wav File
 ▤ Utopia Menu Popup.WAV                    2692  WAV File
 ▤ Utopia Menu Command.WAV                  3462  WAV File
 ▤ Utopia Close.WAV                         4616  WAV File
 ▤ Utopia Restore Down.WAV                  5120  WAV File
 ▤ ringout.wav                             5212  wav File
 ▤ Utopia Critical Stop.WAV                 5824  WAV File
 ▤ Utopia Default.WAV                       9946  WAV File
 ▤ ringin.wav                             10026  wav File
 ▤ Utopia Open.WAV                         10760  WAV File
 ▤ Utopia Exclamation.WAV                  13026  WAV File
 ▤ Utopia Question.WAV                     13084  WAV File   ▼
 Now Streaming. Please wait...
```

Figure 6-6: User gets the notification that the streaming process has begun.

You can stream any of the files that are compatible with Windows Media Player; just select that file and click the Stream button. You can create only one streaming session at a time. If some error is encountered while streaming, the application is able to handle that error and to display the error message to the user while stopping the streaming process.

Summary

So far, we have discussed a modest implementation, considering the immense potential of the streaming technology. This technology has virtually unlimited applications in the fast-developing networking environment of today. Now that all software has to work on a network of some kind or other, this technology is of prime significance. Handheld and other wireless mobile devices are so constrained by storage restrictions that carrying media files on them is a far cry from the present. The technology of streaming is endowed with the capacity to bring forth solutions to such problems that have surfaced, along with novel applications. The strength of this technology is that it obviates the need for storing data of any kind before one can actually start availing the data.

This is first time a concerted endeavor has been made to reveal the concept of P2P with the objective of making it of practical value to people. Every effort has been made to discuss all the viable and conceivable extensions to the basic structure of this concept, on which this concept actually stands and works. Streaming and broadcasting (multicast delivery of media data), no new concept to developers, has been tailored in the basic structure of the P2P concept to facilitate carrying this concept beyond conventions and exploiting it to its limits.

The scope for extension this technology harbors is endless. The best of our efforts have been asserted to implement the maximum extensions to this P2P concept and to effect its most pragmatic commercial usage in an open-source learning methodology. Now it is up to you to explore your skills and expertise, which you are bound to have enhanced by perusing this book.

Chapter 7

Add-Ons to the P2P Application

In this chapter, we discuss the enhancements that can be made to the P2P application. These enhancements provide additional features to the users of the application. Enhancements are the following:

- ◆ Chat client
- ◆ Globalized printing
- ◆ P2P Wireless search (for Java version only)

Since the application explained in this book has an open design, it offers opportunities we can try. Readers of this book are free to develop any of their own applications that fit into this model. The add-ons for this application are not part of the application itself and are not included in the accompanying CD-ROM. They are explained only with short snippets of code. The reader can use these code-snippets to build add-ons as needed. The add-ons discussed in this chapter serve as new ideas that can be implemented in the current design.

Chat Client

This P2P application allows its users to share documents. In addition, as described in the previous section, you can send hard copies to other peers by means of printing extensions. Because any communication between two peers begins once they are connected, a chat application can make additional use of this connection.

Chat client is software that allows you to exchange online text messages with other peers. It is commonly used for chatting with other peers over a network. Chatting applications can easily be downloaded for free from the Web sites of software giants such as Yahoo, AOL, and Microsoft. But implementing chatting in a P2P application is open to our readers; it is as efficient and reliable as any other chatting application besides it gives users an opportunity to extend the application's usability to make it work on devices, to add advanced conferencing and presentation features in it and much more, which is possible as it is open source. By following the steps in the code snippets discussed later, you can design your own chat client.

Why is chat client implemented in our application? One simple answer is that we are equipping the application with all possible technologies and thereby extending its approach. But there are several other reasons closely linked with the advantages of chatting, and we can't ignore these:

- ◆ Chatting allows users to communicate with each other in real time over the network.
- ◆ Because messages are directly delivered, chat client saves a lot of time in sending and receiving messages compared with sending e-mails.
- ◆ Because messages can be conveyed to any remotely located peer, chat client is an ideal business tool for handling overseas business operations.

Requirements for implementing chat client in this P2P application are the following:

- ◆ **Source peer (IP address and name):** The user sending the message.

- ♦ **Destination peer (IP address and name):** To whom the message should be delivered.
- ♦ **Message to be delivered:** Contents of the message.
- ♦ **XML for chat message:** Fixed XML format in which the message is converted for delivering to the destination.
- ♦ **XML parser structure:** Values of the chatting message are parsed into this XML Structure; the user receives the values.

Because this application is designed to distribute the workload between two components (the listener and browser), the listener is assigned the responsibility of responding to all kind of requests coming to its way. The listener is responsible for handling multiple chat requests. The listener handles more than one chatting process by opening a window for each chatting request initiated by browsers running on remote peers.

Notice that browsers initiate chatting requests. This expandability takes advantage of the XML format that has been used throughout the development of this application and throughout the addition of extensions.

Establishing a chat session between two peers is depicted in Figure 7-1.

XML Format for Messaging

This XML format has been used for sending and receiving chat messages. This is very much like the other request/response XML formats we have seen in this book. As mentioned earlier, with slight alteration in XML formats, we can add any number of new add-ons to this application in its existing design.

```
<p2p_lng>
  <request type="CHAT">
  <message sendername="SMITH" senderip="192.192.169.11" chatmsg="hello"/>
  </request>
</p2p_lng>
```

Here, the request type is `"CHAT"`; the other information helps the peer receiving this request discover the name and IP of the peer making the request and sending the message. From both sides, message is sent in XML formats only, making it possible for a similar module written in any contemporary language to send and receive messages through this application.

As the browser initiates chatting, it sends a chat request to the concerned listener. Upon receiving such a request, the listener opens a window to indicate that the request has been successfully processed to begin the chatting session.

//© 2001 Dreamtech Software India Inc.
// All rights reserved.

```
if(UploadDownloadPrint == 4)      // this represents a chat request
{
  frmChat oChatFrm = new frmChat(ChatInfo,newSock,LoginName,
    Application.StartupPath + "\\ChatLog.log",++ChatWindowCount);

  oChatFrm.ShowDialog();
```

This window is passed the information such as the name of the peer, who initiated the chat process, and the IP address and the count of chat windows (as there can be more than one chat window running simultaneously on the listener's side).

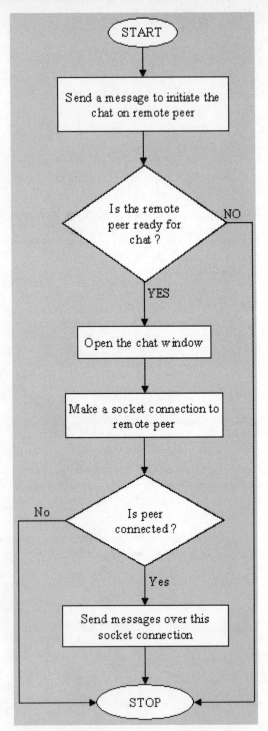

Figure 7-1: Establishing a chat session between two peers

On the browser's end, the user clicks the Chat button (see Figure 7-2) to initiate chatting with an already connected peer.

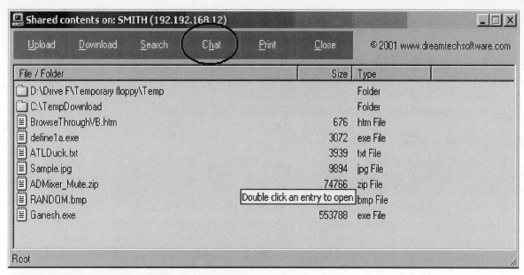

Figure 7-2: Clicking this button initializes the chat session.

A chat window is opened (see Figure 7-3).

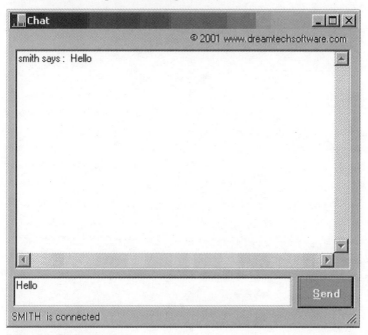

Figure 7-3: The Chat window

These lines are executed when the user clicks the Chat button on the Client's application window.

//© 2001 Dreamtech Software India Inc.
// All rights reserved.

```
protected void btnChat_Click (object sender, System.EventArgs e)
{
  frmChat chat = new frmChat(COMPUTERNAME);
  chat.ShowDialog();
}
```

In the preceding lines, an instance of chat the form class `frmChat` is created, and its `ShowDialog()` function is called to display the chat form.

Implementing the Messaging Mechanism

Implementation of chatting is always linked to messaging techniques. To implement chatting in our P2P application, you must have a thorough understanding of the mechanism for sending and receiving messages.

Sending messages

As soon as this window is displayed, it writes an XML file specifying the request type as chat and information such as the IP address and the name of the peer it is going to connect to. The code snippet that follows shows how this task is accomplished.

//© 2001 Dreamtech Software India Inc.
// All rights reserved.

```
1    if(!Connected)
2    {
3     if( null != Computername )
4     {
5      string AddressIP =
6        Computername.Substring(
7            Computername.IndexOf("(")+1);
8
9      AddressIP = AddressIP.Substring(0,
10                         AddressIP.Length - 1);
11
12      IPEndPoint EPhost = new IPEndPoint(
13      new IPAddress(AddressIP), 7070);
14
15      //Create the Socket for sending data over TCP
16      ClientSocket = new TcpClient();
17
18      // Connect to host using IPEndPoint
19      if(ClientSocket.Connect(EPhost) != 0)
20      {
21         MessageBox.Show("Unable to connect to host");
22         return ;
23      }
24      new frmShare().CreateRequest(
25           "CHAT",Computername,txtMessage.Text);
26
27      FileStream fileStream = new FileStream(
28           new frmShare().REQUESTFILE,FileMode.Open);
29
30      Byte[] ReadBuffer = new Byte[1024];
31      fileStream.Read(ReadBuffer,0,
32           fileStream.Length.ToInt32());
33
34      ClientStream = ClientSocket.GetStream();
35      ClientStream.Write(
36           ReadBuffer,0,fileStream.Length.ToInt32());
37
38      ClientStream.Flush();
39      fileStream.Close();
```

```
40      new ServerCommunication().FileDelete(
41          new frmShare().REQUESTFILE);
42
43      Connected = true;
44      RecivingTimer.Enabled=true;
45    }
46  }
```

The preceding code snippet is executed each time the user clicks the Send button to send messages to the peer with whom he or she is connected.

Code description

♦ Lines 1-23: In this part of the code, the connection is established when the listener specifies the IP address and the port to communicate by using the `TcpClient` class.

♦ Lines 24-25: A new XML file is created specifying the request type as `Chat` and other information such as the IP address and the name of the remote listener by using the `XMLCreator` class's `CreateRequest()` function. The `XMLCreater` class is defined in the `'WorkingWithXML'` namespace.

♦ Lines 27-33: A new file stream is opened for the XML request written and is read in a buffer.

♦ Lines 34-42: A network is opened, and the XML request file read is written on it for other peers to read and is flushed and closed thereafter. The file is deleted, and variables are initialized to indicate a connection has been successfully established.

The chat session opens a new socket after closing the previous one through which it has been connected and sends a request to the listener. The listener keeps this particular socket open unlike other sockets that it closes as soon as it has processed requests received on them. This socket is kept open unless the connection is closed either on the listener side or browser side. A new connection is always opened to keep the normal request/response process running behind the normal chat session.

Once you know how to send messages, we need to address how messages are received. Because the processes of sending and receiving data work in unison, implementing only one of them has no meaning.

Receiving messages

To receive messages sent by other peers, sockets are checked for data availability every 0.2 seconds. This is done by initializing a timer with the time-elapse setting equal to 200 milliseconds (Listing 7-1).

Listing 7-1

```
.
.
.
1  if( Sock.Available>0 )
2  {
3    Byte[] RecvBytes = new Byte[Sock.Available];
4    Sock.Receive(RecvBytes, Sock.Available, 0);
5
6    if(Encoding.ASCII.GetString(RecvBytes,0,RecvBytes.Length).CompareTo(
7      "heistyping") == 0)
8    {
9      ClientTyping = true;
10     lChatSttsBar.Text = ChatUserName + " is typing a message.";
11       return;
```

```
12   }
13
14   rtxtMessages.ForeColor = Color.DarkGray;
15   Font f = new Font("Palatino Linotype",8,FontStyle.Bold);
16   rtxtMessages.Font = f;
17   rtxtMessages.ForeColor = Color.Aquamarine;
18   rtxtMessages.Text += ChatUserName + " says :   ";
19
20   Font f2 = new Font("Palatino Linotype",8,FontStyle.Bold);
21   rtxtMessages.Font = f2;
22   rtxtMessages.ForeColor = Color.Black;
23   rtxtMessages.Text += Encoding.ASCII.GetString(RecvBytes, 0,
24    RecvBytes.Length) + "\r\n";
25   lChatSttsBar.Text = ChatUserName + " is connected";
26 }
```

- ♦ Line 1: This line checks whether data is available on the socket or not.

- ♦ Lines 3-5: A byte buffer is made of a size equal to the amount of data received.

- ♦ Lines 6-13: If this message is just to signify that the other peer is typing a message, information is displayed on the status bar, and the rest of the code is skipped.

- ♦ Lines 14-24: The color and the font settings are set for the box in which incoming messages are displayed and a message is displayed in the box.

- ♦ Line 25: The status bar is rewritten, indicating that the peer is connected.

The Final Touch

To give a professional look to the chat-client extension, a feature has been incorporated through which peers receive notifications when other peers they are connected to are writing messages. The user is notified when the peer he is connected with writes a message (see Figure 7-4). The code for this feature is discussed in the preceding code listing as we discuss the code in lines 6-13.

Figure 7-4: The user is notified that the peer he is chatting with is writing a message.

//© 2001 Dreamtech Software India Inc.
// All rights reserved.

```
if( Typing )
{
 if( Connected && TimeElapse == 1 )
 {
  Byte[] buff = Encoding.ASCII.GetBytes("heistyping");
  ClientStream.Write(buff,0,buff.Length);
  ClientStream.Flush();
 }

 TimeElapse += 1;
 if( TimeElapse >= 10 )
 {
  Typing = false;
  TimeElapse = 0;
 }
}
```

As the first letter is typed, the `Typing` variable is initialized with a positive value to indicate that something has been written, and a message is sent to the listener. This is to indicate that the peer is not away and is writing a message, making this chat extension more interactive.

To accomplish this task, a counter has been maintained to see that the message is sent only after 0.1 seconds of writing. The time counter is kept incrementing to keep track of time intervals.

It is only after not writing anything for 2 seconds that `Typing` variable is initialized to a negative value and the time counter is set back to 0 to indicate that typing has been temporarily halted. From here on, writing anything after a time elapse of 2 seconds causes the message to be sent to the peer.

If the user writes anything, the counter is initialized back to 0; only 2 seconds after the last letter is written is the `Typing` variable initialized to a negative value.

```
protected void txtMessage_KeyPress (object sender,
  System.WinForms.KeyPressEventArgs e)
{
 Typing = true;
 TimeElapse = 0;
}
```

The changes required to achieve the chat mechanism in our P2P application design are shown in the preceding code. The code is only a small snippet and does not to give you the whole picture. We give the user a chance to develop a full-fledged chat application, based on the knowledge that he has acquired so far from the previous code snippets.

Implementing Globalize Printing

Before understanding *Globalize Printing*, you should be familiar with *Network Printing*. Network Printing means sharing a single printer among various users. Such printing is implemented in small networks such as LAN, which allows you to print your own document on a network printer by simply providing a print command from your desktop without requiring you to have your own desktop printer. Apart from escaping the cost of using multiple printers, a single printer easily handles the requirements of all networked users. We take Network Printing one step further in Globalize Printing. Globalize Printing is not restricted to any LAN or Intranet; with Globalize Printing, you can print your desired documents in different locations provided that the person in that location is a registered member with our P2P system. Any remotely located printer can be used for printing.

As mentioned at the outset, one of the features that account for the versatility of the P2P application we have developed is that it provides an ample scope for enhancements to be performed very easily. Globalize Printing is one such feature that many users may seek to incorporate in this application. With Globalize Printing, you can print a remote file that is present on a remote peer to which you are connected. This feature is significant when you are connected to a computer and are browsing its shared contents. To avail this feature, select a file and click the Print button in the browser window. In the same way requests for uploading and downloading files are generated, the request for printing is generated via the XML creater component of this application. The detailed design of the XML request needed for the purpose of printing is the following:

```xml
<?xml version="1.0" encoding="utf-8"?>
<p2p_lng>
 <request type="PRINT">
  <scope type=Filename mask=""/>
 </request>
</p2p_lng>
```

Note that here you have to specify the type of the request as PRINT as indicated in the third line of the preceding XML code. The Filename denotes the file that is to be printed.

You have to make some additions to the existing code:

1. Add a Print button in the browser window.

2. Add code for the Print button when you click the button.

The Print button can be added just as you add a simple button to a form. Just open the frmShare form and add a button to it. Make sure to give the name btnPrint to the button you have inserted. Figure 7-5 shows you where to insert the button.

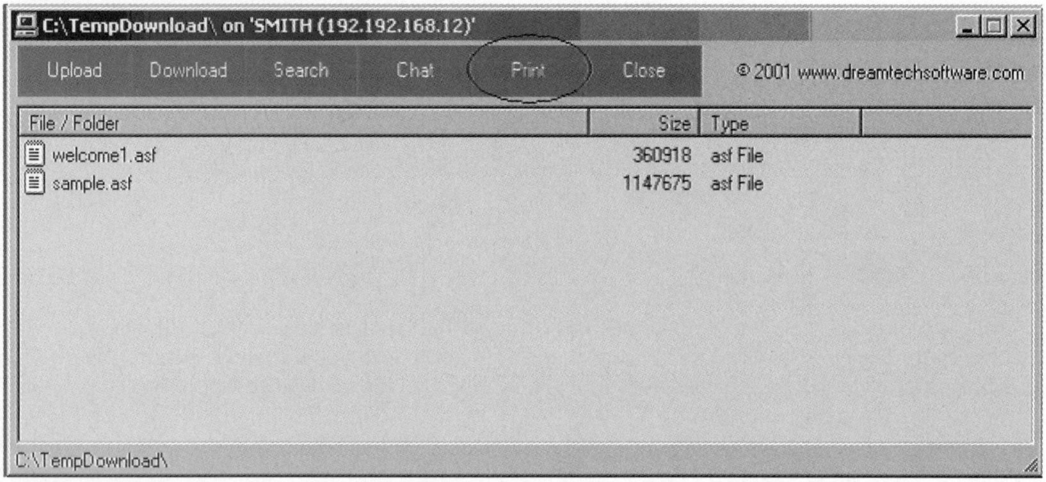

Figure 7-5: Clicking the Print button initiates the Global Printing process on the selected document.

In Figure 7-5, you can see the Print button.

After adding the Print button to the frmShare dialog, you have to add code to it.

Coding for the Print Button (Browser)

The following the lines of code are for the click event of the Print button you have just added.

```
      .
      .
      .
      .
      .
1. protected void btnPrint_Click (object sender, System.EventArgs e)
2. {
3.  string Filename;
4.
5.  // Get the currently selected item from the List view
6.  int index = GetSelectedItemFromListView(out Filename);
7.  try
8.  {
9.   // Checks whether any entry is selected or not
10.   if( -1 != index)
11.
12.     // Checks whether a filename is selected for
 // printing
13.     // or not
14.     if( null != Filename )
15.     {
16.         // If filename is selected then print it
17.         if( OpenConnection(COMPUTERNAME) )
18.         {
19.             // Creates a PRINT request for a
    // particular
20.             // file to PRINT.
21.             CreateRequest("PRINT",strArray
                [index].sFilename,"");
23.
24.             // Sends this request to the
     // listener
25.             SendDataToListener(REQUESTFILE);
26.         }
27.     }
28.     // else throw an exception, Folders cannot be
 // printed
29.     else throw new Exception("Cannot print
     folder");
30.
31.   // If nothing is selected then displays an error
 // message
32.   else throw new Exception("Nothing Selected");
33.  }
34.
35.  catch( Exception err ) { MessageBox.Show(err.Message,
    "Error",MessageBox.IconError); }
36. }
      .
      .
      .
```

.
.

Code description

Starting from line 3, we go into a detailed explanation of the preceding code. We have declared a `string` type object called `Filename`. This object `Filename` is used to store the name of the selected entry from the list view of the browser window. Thereafter, a call is made to the user-defined function `GetSelectedItemFromListView`, and the `Filename` is passed as an `out` parameter to this function. The function returns the index of the selected element in the `index` variable, and the name of the actual entry is returned to the `Filename`. If any folder is selected, the index value returned by the function is greater than -1, and the out parameter `Filename` is NULL. An exception is thrown, and an error message is generated and shown to the user (as shown in Figure 7-6). The function is terminated without executing further.

Figure 7-6: Any exception faced in printing is indicated by an error message.

If, on the other hand, nothing is selected, this function returns -1 as the index value and NULL value in `Filename`. In this case, too, an exception is thrown, and the error message box is displayed (see Figure 7-7) to the user; the function is terminated without executing further.

Figure 7-7: If the printing process is initilated without selecting any document, and error message is displayed.

After checking for the preceding validations, at line 17 we open a socket connection by using the `OpenConnection` function and passing `COMPUTERNAME`. This function returns either true or false, which is checked by the `if` statement. At line 21, the actual print request is being generated by using `CreateRequest`, a user-defined function, and passing arguments to it. The first argument of this function is the request type; in this case, the request type is PRINT. The second argument is the name of the file to be printed. Here the fully qualified filename is extracted from `strArray[index].sFilename` array by giving its index. The third parameter is blank.

At this moment, your request is successfully generated in the folder from which your application is running. Usually, an XML file containing the request data is created for the request. You can run the program to this location by adding a break point on a line below the `CreateRequest` function to check whether the request has been properly generated or not. Once the request is properly generated, a call to the `SendDataToListener(REQUESTFILE)` function is made, and the name of the request file is passed to the function. This function sends your request to the remote peer to whom you are connected; if the peer receives the request successfully, the document is printed on his or her printer.

Coding for the Print Button (Listener)

In the preceding discussion, we have considered the part of coding that is relevant to the browser. The initiation of printing is performed from the browser side, and the work of the listener is less in comparison with that of the browser. The following are the changes you have to make at the listener's end. These changes are to be made in the frmLogin class.

```
namespace Listener
{
    .
    .
    .
    .

 using System.Runtime.InteropServices;

 public class frmLogin : System.WinForms.Form
 {
     .
     .
     .
     .

  [DllImport("Shell32.dll")]
  public static extern int ShellExecute( int hwnd,
          string lpVerb,
                      string lpFile,
          string lpParameters,
          string lpDirectory,
          int nShowCmd );
     .
     .
     .
     .
 }

    .
    .
    .
    .
}
```

Code description

In the beginning of the frmLogin class, where all the necessary namespaces are included, you have to include the System.Runtime.InteropServices namespace in order to achieve the functionality of a Shell32.dll. This is needed for the ShellExecute Win32 SDK function.

Now you need to import the ShellExecute function from the Shell32.dll. For this, the following statements are to be included:

```
  [DllImport("Shell32.dll")]
  public static extern int ShellExecute( int hwnd,
          string lpVerb,
                      string lpFile,
          string lpParameters,
```

```
                      string lpDirectory,
                      int nShowCmd );
```

The first line serves the same purpose as the `LoadLibrary` function in VC++. It loads the `Shell32.dll` file into the application-process space in memory. We have declared the prototype of the `ShellExecute` function that we intend to use in our application. This function is exported to our application from the `Shell32.dll file`. You can use any Win32 SDK function in C# provided that you know the file in which the definition of that function is present.

The code for handling the print request is the following:

//© 2001 Dreamtech Software India Inc.
// All rights reserved.

```
protected void RequestResponse()
{
  .
  .
  .
  .
  if(DnLoadFile.Length != 0)
  {
    if(UploadDownloadPrint == 1)
    {
      fs1 = new FileStream(DnLoadFile,FileMode.CreateNew);
      DnLoadFile.EndsWith("mp3");
    }
    else if(UploadDownloadPrint == 2)
    fs1 = new FileStream(DnLoadFile,FileMode.Open);
    else if(UploadDownloadPrint == 3)
    {
      ShellExecute(0,"print",DnLoadFile,"","",1);
      new File(Application.StartupPath +
    "\\Temp.xml").Delete();
      DataStream.Flush();
      newSock.Close();
      bDownLoading = false;
      return;
    }
    bDownLoading = true;
  }
  .
  .
  .
  .
  .
}
```

You have to add only the part of the code shown in bold. Here the `ShellExecute` function discussed previously is used to print the document. The first parameter to this function is to handle the window, which can be 0; the second parameter represents the action you intend to perform; and the third parameter reveals the name of the file to be printed. The fourth, fifth, and sixth parameters should be exactly as shown in the preceding code. After you send the file to the printer, the next line deletes the temporary file, flushes the stream by using the stream object, closes the socket setting the `bDownload` to false, and returns from the function. These are the necessary changes on the listener side coding of the `frmLogin` form to achieve Globalize Printing.

In the same way, you can print your file on the remote printer or can print a file to multiple printers that are connected to different peers. You will find exploring these possibilities an interesting exercise. Implementations of these are not detailed here, as we have to proceed to some of the other interesting and useful features this project offers.

P2P Searching on Palm Using Java 2 Micro Edition

P2P applications are available for conventional programming environments. This means you can run such applications on your desktop system. But the Internet has gone far beyond PCs and servers to devices such as *Personal Desktop Assistants (PDAs)* and cell phones. We consider these in this chapter. Can P2P work on these devices?

Before we discuss the feasibility of P2P Searching on Palm PDAs or cell phones, we should understand the programming practices and limitations of such devices. PDAs and cell phones have the following limitations:

- **Limited processor power:** Unlike desktop systems, PDAs and cell phones are not exactly bursting with processor power. Because PDAs and cell phones are battery operated, batteries consume more power as processor speed increases.

- **Types of input and output methods:** Unlike desktop systems, PDAs and cell phones do not have a standard "QWERTY" keyboard for input or a monitor for output. Depending on devices, input and output methods vary. Some devices, such as two-way pagers or cell phones, have numeric keypads with alphabet support, yet other devices have a stylus-pads using which one can enter data. Unlike desktop systems, PDAs and cell phones do not boast of a 15-inch or 17-inch screen. Their screen size is limited to a maximum of 160 by 160 pixels.

- **Memory constraints:** Unlike desktop systems, PDAs and cell phones do not boast of gigabytes of memory; they have memory limitations as well as processor limitations. The memory in these devices is divided into heaps, static heaps and dynamic heaps, and is limited.

Taking these limitations into consideration, the programming techniques for these devices are to be modified (that is, because the seemingly unlimited available memory of the desktop is replaced by the limited memory of the PDAs, you must adapt to the memory model of the PDAs). Some techniques for efficient memory utilization are the following:

- Increased use of local variables

- Initializing objects only when they are required

- Smaller applications; that is, only features essential to an application should be created and not those which are only used rarely.

- Deinitializing objects whenever possible, thereby helping the garbage collector

Programming using the J2ME sis not the same as programming using the J2SE because of the memory constraints involved in the Micro Edition. Therefore, the application in this book cannot be simply ported onto the small devices. It requires certain changes; for example, changes in GUI. We cannot use tables now to display information, and only one screen can be shown at a particular time, as opposed to the many screens displayed in the larger version. Also, changes arise in some classes and their methods. The most important change is the way XML parsing is handled. Because of small devices such as cell phones, PDAs, and so on, which have less memory, the XML parser should also be small in light of the memory requirements involved.

The J2ME version does not offer the same functionality as the J2SE version of the application. For instance, it does not allow you to download files. This is understandable, as a device such as a mobile phone cannot be expected or required to store downloaded files. Using this application, you can connect to any user and view shared files, but you cannot download them. For that, you have to use a PC. The idea is that you are at least able to find the required files even while you are on the move.

The explanation of the project follows. First, the user interface is explained, followed by the working of the project and a flow diagram. For the source code of this application, refer to *Wireless Projects Using J2ME* published by Hungry Minds, Inc.

The User Interface

When you start the application, the starting screen shows just two buttons: Start and Exit (see Figure 7-8). When you press the Start button, the next screen shows a scrollable list of users who are currently connected to the same site and using this application. Being connected means that they have logged on to the Internet with this application. Files can be searched in two ways: through a server-level search and a user-level search. A server-level search is useful when you know what files you want, or at least some characters in the names of those files, so that you can use wildcards to conduct the search. For example, if you know that the name of the song you want has the word *rock* in it, you can use this information as the search criteria and can use wildcards (*) for searching it. The other option is to conduct a user-level search. This is useful if you know on whose system the required files are located.

Peer to Peer System..

Start   Exit

Figure 7-8: Screen 1: Starting screen

At its top, the next screen has two buttons, labeled Refresh and Search, respectively. Pressing Refresh updates the list. If you want to search files, you have to press the Search button. Two more buttons, labeled Browse and Exit, respectively, appear at the bottom of the screen. If you decide to see what files are available with a particular user, you can enter your choice in a `TextField` in the form of the user number. Then the user presses the Browse button.

This takes you to a screen showing the listing of shared folders and files on the root directory of that user. If necessary, you may select a folder and again press the Browse button. This can go on until you find the folder of your choice. At any stage of this process, you can press the Search button after entering the directory number in the `TextField`. This gives you a chance to enter your search criterion with any wildcard to locate the required files.

If you do not have an idea where the files are, you may directly press the Search button without pressing the Browse button. With this, you see a screen with two `TextFields`: one field for entering the search criteria for the filename and one field for entering the search criteria for the computer name. After entering these, the Search button is pressed, to show the files found in the search. The search can be cancelled by pressing the Cancel button to go back to the starting screen.

How It Works

This application consists of five class files: `peer_application`, `userlist_screen`, `serversearch`, `searchfiles`, and `showfiles`. In addition, the application uses an external XML parser available in an `org.kxml.parser` package. Executing the first class file (`peer_application`) starts the application. This class performs the following tasks:

♦ Imports the packages required, such as those for handling XML and parsing it (`org.kxml.*`, `org.kxml.io.*`, and `org.kxml.parser`).

♦ Declares variables for the XML parser and parse event, IP address, user list, and the text to be displayed in `ScrollTextBox`.

♦ Uses the `Graphics` class to clear the screen and to display the text welcoming the user through the `clearScreen` and `drawString` methods, respectively.

♦ Paints Start and Exit buttons on the screen by using the `paint` method of the Button class.

♦ Defines event handling for the buttons via the `penDown` method. If the Start button is pressed, the current spotlet is unregistered, and a `startReading` method is called. The callbacks generated by the XML parser in the method `parseData()` are stored in three variables: `ip_address`, `users_connected`, and `text_for_display`.

♦ Calls a method named `startReading`, which is responsible for sending a request to the server for a list of users connected at any time

♦ Instantiates and calls the class `userlist_screen`, which displays the list of users. It takes its parameters as the three variables mentioned previously.

♦ Closes the application in case the user does not want to go on further and presses the Exit button.

♦ Defines the method `startReading`. This method instantiates the preceding three variables and opens an `InputStream` on the ASP file named `userlist.asp`. It also shows an error if an `IOException` occurs.

♦ Defines the method `parseData`. It uses the XML parser mentioned previously and finds the `userinfo` tag with the help of the do...while loop and an `if` block. The attributes of this tag are obtained by using the `getValue` method and are then added to their appropriate position. The vector `ip_address` is then returned to the calling class.

♦ The `parseData` method is available in the parser; it has only to be overridden. But we also need to return two more variables. For this reason, two more methods are defined. One is to return the `text_for_display` variable, and the other is to return the `users_connected` variable.

The class `userlist_screen` (shown in Figure 7-9) is called to display the list of users connected at a particular time. It performs the tasks that follow:

♦ Declares variables for buttons, `ScrollTextBox`; `TextField`; `StreamConnection`; XML parser and parse event; `String` variables; `folder_data`; `file_data`; vectors for the previously mentioned variables; and two more variables (`folder_vector`, `record_of_users`).

♦ Defines constructor of the class to take `text`; `ip_address`; `users_connected`; `viewfile_flag`; and `record_of_users` as the parameters. The parameters are then initialized by the variables earlier defined. The Methods of `Graphics` class are then used such as `drawRectangle()`, and so on, to dislay the user interface elements.

♦ Defines event handling via the `keyDown` and `penDown` methods. The former handles the input if the `TextField` is in focus, and the latter handles the event of buttons being pressed. If necessary, control is transferred to a relevant class.

♦ Defines a method called `appropriatelength`, which is called to make the application compatible with C# listeners. The method is required because the C# listener cannot read less than 1024 bytes at a time. This method takes an array called `file_bytes` and integer `file_size` as parameters and returns a byte array.

Figure 7-9: Screen 2: List of users

The class `showfiles` (shown in Figure 7-10) is called when you have selected a computer to whose files/folders you want to view and have pressed the Browse button. It performs the following tasks:

♦ Creates the user interface for the screen showing shared files and folders.

♦ Provides the user interface for the buttons, `TextField`, and `ScrollTextBox`.

♦ Creates an object of the class `peer_application` and calls the method `startReading` to send a request to the server.

♦ Defines a method `browseDirectory` called when the Browse button is pressed. The screen that follows shows the shared files in that directory.

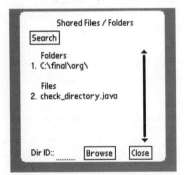

Figure 7-10: Screen 3: Files/folders shared by a particular user

The class `serversearch` is called when you want to search all users (see Figures 7-11 and 7-12). The class serversearch takes care of the following tasks:

♦ Declares variables, buttons, `TextField`, `DataInputStream`, and `vectors` `ip_address` and `users_connected`.

♦ Displays the user interface elements by using the `Graphics` class.

♦ Defines event handling through the `keyDown` method. The code serves the purpose of shifting focus when the Tab key is pressed.

♦ Defines event handling through the `penDown` method. This method handles the events generated by pressing the buttons, such as open, view, exit etc. If the Search button is pressed, the results satisfying the search criterion are displayed.

♦ Defines the method `parseData` that holds the callbacks generated when XML parsing is performed.

Figure 7-11: Screen 4: Implementing server-level search

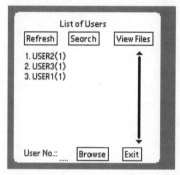

Figure 7-12: Screen 5: Result of the server-level search

The class `searchfiles` is called when the user wants to conduct a search (shown in Figure 7-13). The class `search_files` performs the tasks that follows:

- Declares buttons, `TextField`, Strings (`parent_information`, `text_for_display`, `folder_data`, `file_data`, `host_address`), XML parser and parse event, vector `folder_vector`, `StreamConnection`, `InputStream`, and `OutputStream`.

- Defines the constructor to take address and `parent_information` as parameters. The parameters are initialized with the variables already declared.

- Draws the user-interface elements, including buttons and `TextField`.

- Defines event handling through `penDown` and `keyDown`. The former simply calls the latter if an option has the focus. The penDown method responds to events generated by pressing the buttons such as exit, view, open, and so on.

- The method `appropriatelength` is called to provide compatibility with C# listeners.

Figure 7-13: Screen 6: Implementing the client-level search

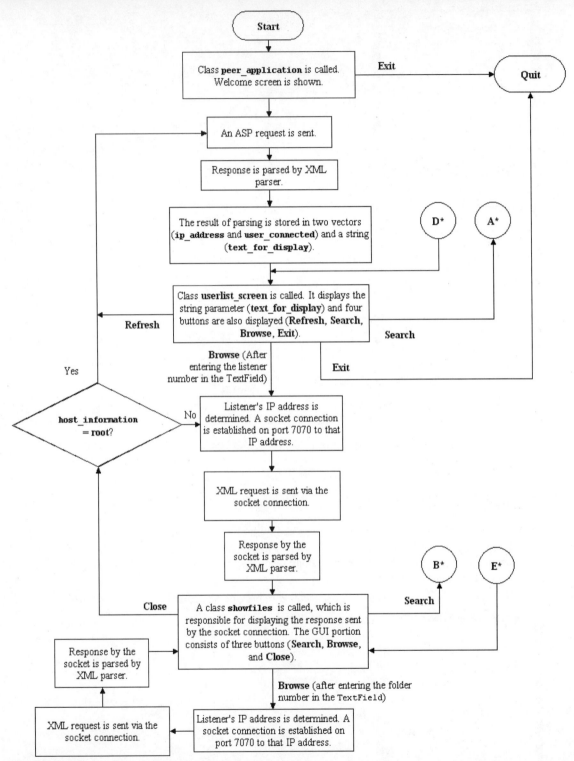

Figure 7-14: The basic flow of the program is shown in the flow chart

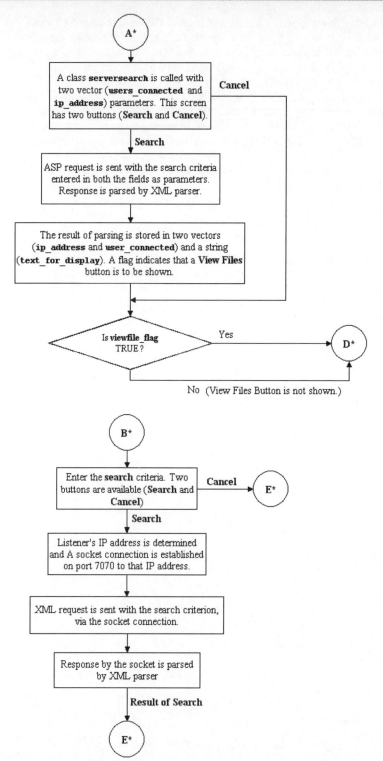

Figure 7-15: Extension of Figure 7-14

When the application starts, a welcome screen appears. After you press the OK button, an asp of the name `userlist.asp` is called, which displays all the users connected at a particular time on the screen. Along with this information, several buttons are presented to you: Refresh (to refresh the list of users currently connected, so as to check whether any new user has joined or not); Search (to implement a server-level search, meaning that the user may search for a file or a group of files on various users connected at a particular time); Exit (to close the application); and Browse. The Browse button is by far the most important. The button is of use when you enter the user number of a particular user and press the button. When you press the button, a socket connection is established between you and the listener, and the listener shows you the list of all shared files and folders. This screen also provides several buttons: Search (when this button is pressed, you can search for files in the list displayed); Browse (this button is used to go deeper into the directory hierarchy); and Close (this button is used to close the socket connection to a particular user) (Figures 7-14 and 7-15).

Summary

In this chapter, you have explored the knowledge you have acquired during your journey through this book. Based on the code presented in this book, you can develop full-fledged commercial applications using P2P communication technology. This chapter shows you how to accomplish the concept of extending the basic P2P functionality by incorporating new coherent add-ons. However, if you are eager to see the full-featured P2P application with add-ons that are discussed previously, you can find them on the accompanying CD-ROM disk.

About the CD-ROM

This appendix provides you with information on the contents of the CD that accompanies this book. For the latest information, please refer to the ReadMe file located at the root of the CD. Here is what you will find:

♦ What's on the CD

♦ Hardware/Software Requirements

♦ Using the CD

♦ Troubleshooting

What's on the CD

The following sections provide a summary of the software and other materials you'll find on the CD.

Author-Created Materials

All author-created material from the book, including code listings and samples, are on the CD in the folder named "P2P Source Code."

The source code is further categorized into three subfolders; namely, JavaVersion, C#Version (the two versions in which this application has been built), and P2PServer. A brief description of the various files in each folder is provided here as an aid to handling the CD-ROM effectively.

JavaVersion Folder

In this folder you will find two more subfolders called Listener and Browser in which you will find their respective source codes.

Listener folder

♦ **org:** This package handles all operations necessary for XML Parsing.

♦ **Login.java:** This class comes into action when the Listener logs on to the server for the first time. This class also invokes login.asp and creates the userinfo.ini file that stores the name of the user.

♦ **Multiserver.java:** This class is responsible for initiating the server on a specific port number to handle the incoming requests and returning the responses generated by the server as per the request made.

♦ **Shared_dialog.java:** This class stores information of all the shared resources in the share.ini file.

♦ **Checkdirectory.java:** This represents the search operation to handle the task of client side searching when the client passes some search criteria.

♦ **XmlWriter.java:** This class is responsible for generating requests and responses in XML format.

♦ **Sparser.java:** This class is responsible for parsing the XML request and responses.

Browser folder

♦ **org:** This package handles all the operations necessary for XML Parsing.

♦ **client.java:** This class is of immense significance since it provides the entry point for the Browser. This class is also responsible for displaying the list of the already logged in users by making the appropriate call `userlist.asp`. It also caters to the GUI components.

♦ **file_gui.java:** This class displays the contents of the selected user. It is also responsible for handling uploading and downloading of files and folders.

♦ **search_screen.java:** This class contains the coding that enables client-side searching.

♦ **add_on.java:** This is a multi-utility class that houses various methods to handle the various tasks. This class is used interchangeably in the lifecycle of this application. The tasks it handles include alphabetically sorting the user names obtained from the server, constructing and sending XML requests to the server, catching responses returned by the server as well as by the Listener. This class is also responsible for making calls to functions which provides compatibility with the Listener that has the C# version.

♦ **search_window.java:** This class is responsible for managing server-side search operations.

♦ **XmlWriter.java:** This class is responsible for generating requests and responses in XML format.

♦ **Sparser.java:** This class is responsible for parsing the XML request and responses.

How to run the application

To run the JAVA version of the application, copy all the folders under the folder JavaVersion on to a folder on the hard disk. To run the Browser, go to the folder Browser and double click the file `client.jar`. Similarly, to run the Listener, go to the folder Listener   and double click the file `login.jar`. The process has been made easier for the users by providing the installation option in the `setup` application for the CD which copies the required files to the location specified by the user.

C#Version Folder

This part describes the contents that are present for the C# version of the P2P application on this CD-ROM:

♦ P2P folder

♦ P2PwithAddons folder

P2P folder

In the P2P folder you will find two folders: Browser and Listener.

This folder contains the full source code for the Browser part of the application. This source code is the basic source code of our application, and includes coding for uploading and downloading files.

♦ **frmClient.cs:** This file has the definition for class `frmClient` which contains the basic coding for the client side.

♦ **frmSearch.cs:** This file contains `frmSearch`. The main task of this class is to handle various search operations performed on the Browser side.

♦ **frmShare.cs:** This file has the definition for the class `frmShare`. This class holds immense responsibility as it caters to all uploading and downloading tasks. Another important function of this class is to display all shared resources of the Listener within the boundary of the Browser.

♦ **frmLogin.cs:** This file contains the definition of the `frmLogin` class which contains the code that governs the overall functionality of the Listener module.

♦ **frmSelection.cs:** This file contains the definition of the `frmSelection` class which helps users to share files and folders.

- **BrowseFolder.cs:** This file contains the definition of the class `BrowseFolder` that is written to provide the folder selection dialog box used by `frmSelection`.

This source code on compiling will generate a class library file named: `WorkingWithXML.dll`. You have to add the reference of this `dll` file in your main project, that is, the P2P project. This `dll` will contain three classes that are described in the ensuing lines.

- **clsServerCommunication.cs:** This class is responsible for handling the communication with server whenever it is required in the lifecycle of the application.

- **clsXMLCreater.cs:** The primary task of this class is to generate request and response XMLs.

- **clsXMLParser.cs:** This class actually parses the request and response XMLs generated by the `clsXMLCreater.cs` class.

P2PwithAddons folder

The application in this folder contains the full source code of the P2P application with the add-ons described in Chapters 6 and 7.

- **frmClient.cs:** This class incorporates all coding necessary for the client side.

- **frmSearch.cs:** This class is responsible for handling all the search operations performed on the Browser side.

- **frmShare.cs:** Apart from handling the regular tasks (uploading, downloading) of this P2P application, this class handles chatting, global printing and streaming.

- **frmStreamer.cs:** This class contains all coding required for streaming.

- **frmChat.cs:** This class is responsible for enabling chatting. All the code required for chatting is inside this class.

- **clsChatSocket.cs:** This class is inherited from the `TcpClient` class. It is used to access the protected functions of the `TcpClient` Class. This class is used only in `frmChat.cs` class.

- **frmLogin.cs:** This file contains the definition of the `frmLogin` class which contains the code that governs the overall functionality of the Listener module.

- **frmSelection.cs:** This file contains the definition of the `frmSelection` class which helps the user to share files and folders.

- **BrowseFolder.cs:** This file contains the definition of the `BrowseFolder` class that is written to provide the folder selection dialog box used by the `frmSelection` class.

- **ThreadIndex.cs:** This file contains the definition of the class that helps the `frmLogin` class to effectively manage threads.

- **FrmChat.cs:** This file holds the code for `frmChat` class, which handles the chat extension to the original P2P application.

- **StreamIt.cs:** This file defines the class `StreamIt`, which holds the code for the streaming extension.

This folder is very similar to the one with the same name in the P2P folder. Since the files names and number of files in the two folders are not different and only the code in the files differ, a description is not needed here.

How to run the application

To build the C# version of this application, copy all the contents of the P2P folder or P2PwithAddons folder to a folder on your hard disk and compile the project files or solution files of the Browser, the Listener and the `WorkingWithXML` projects using Microsoft Visual Studio .NET beta 2. In Browser and in the Listener projects, add a reference to the `WorkingWithXMLdll` which is generated by Microsoft Visual Studio .NET in the Debug folder under the bin folder of this project. Now just double click on the exe files of each, that is, the `Client.exe` and `Listener.exe` that have been generated by the Microsoft Visual Studio .NET environment.

The process has been made easier for the users by providing the installation option in the `setup` application for the CD which copies the required files on the location specified by the user.

P2PServer Folder

Here the contents of the server part on this CD-ROM are discussed.

- ◆ **Login.asp:** The Listener while logging the server calls this page.
- ◆ **Logout.asp:** This page is invoked when the Listener logs out from the server.
- ◆ **Search.asp:** The Browser while performing search operations on the server invokes this page.
- ◆ **Userlist.asp:** The main task of this page is to provide the list of users already logged on the server or which are available when the Browser logs on the server for the first time.

Shareware programs are fully functional, trial versions of copyrighted programs. If you like particular programs, register with their authors for a nominal fee and receive licenses, enhanced versions, and technical support. *Freeware programs* are copyrighted games, applications, and utilities that are free for personal use. Unlike shareware, these programs do not require a fee or provide technical support. *GNU software* is governed by its own license, which is included inside the folder of the GNU product. See the GNU license for more details.

Trial, demo, or evaluation versions are usually limited either by time or functionality (such as being unable to save projects). Some trial versions are very sensitive to system date changes. If you alter your computer's date, the programs will "time out" and will no longer be functional.

eBook version of *Peer-to-Peer Application Development*

The complete text of this book is on the CD in Adobe's Portable Document Format (PDF). You can read and search through the file with the Adobe Acrobat Reader (also included on the CD).

This is the first book to cover the entire code behind a Napster-style, file-sharing model. It contains unique coverage of Windows Media Technology development for making your P2P application multimedia aware. The book is loaded with code, keeping theory to a minimum. The applications, for which the source code is given, are 100 percent tested and working at Dreamtech Software Research Lab. The source code provided in the book is based on commercial applications, which are developed by the software company. Each program of the application is explained in detail so that you get insight into the implementation of the technology in a real-world situation. At the end of the book, some add-ons to this application are given so that you can further explore new developments that are taking place.

This book deals with the design, implementation, and coding of the latest form of the client/server model, the P2P model. The book serves to equip you with enough know-how on the subject so as to enable you to design a P2P model of your own.

The book begins with the history of the P2P model and goes on to explain the various types of P2P models, with detailed diagrams to elucidate the subject. After equipping you with basic concepts, it goes on to develop, step by step, a full-fledged application, which has the scope of being extended with add-ons.

This book is *not* meant for beginners. It teaches you the basics of specific technologies only. The *Cracking the Code* series is meant for software developers/programmers who wish to upgrade their skills and understand the secrets behind professional-quality applications. This book starts where other tutorial books end. It enhances your skills and takes them to the next level as you learn a particular technology. A thorough knowledge of the Java or C# programming languages is the prerequisite for benefiting the most from this book. Experience in network programming is an added advantage. For developing streaming applications, knowledge of Visual C++ is a must. At least a nodding acquaintance with the XML mark-up language is desirable, although the book incorporates a section on XML. Instructions for embedding existing chat-client and audio/video components have been included. You can craft this application in such a way that you are able to send your files to be printed to any part of the globe. Besides Globalize Printing, you can make the application run on wireless models, too. The opportunity is open for you to assess your networking skills and to improve them.

The pivotal feature of the book is that it offers a complete, ready-to-deploy application with source code. The purpose of this book is to acquaint programmers with the subject thoroughly so that they are in a position to write their own codes to build P2P applications. Detailed explanations of the steps involved in writing your own code to build a P2P application in Java as well as in C # have been furnished.

Hardware/Software Requirements

This section lets you know the different S/W and hardware requirements that your system needs to meet to be able to host the applications on the CD.

Hardware Requirements

Make sure that your computer meets the minimum system requirements listed in this section. If your computer doesn't match up to most of these requirements, you may have a problem using the contents of the CD.

For Windows 9x, Windows 2000, Windows NT4 (with SP 4 or later), Windows Me, or Windows XP:

- PC with a Pentium processor running at 120Mhz or faster
- If you are running the Java version of the P2P application, a minimum of 32MB of total RAM installed on your computer; for best performance, we recommend at least 64MB
- To run the C# version of the P2P application, you need to have a minimum of 128MB of total RAM installed on your computer, and for better performance, we recomment 256MB or more. This is because the Microsoft Visual Studio .NET (which has been used to develop the C# version of this application) has not come up with the provision to produce self sustained applications as yet. Thus you need to have Microsoft Visual Studio .NET installed on your computer which requires this much RAM, to be able to run the C# version of the P2P application.
- Ethernet network interface card (NIC) or modem with a speed of at least 28,800 bps
- A CD-ROM drive

For hardware requrements to set up the P2P server, you can refer to Windows 2000 Operating System hardware requirements at `http://www.microsoft.com/windows2000/`.

Software Requirements

This section discusses the software you need to have on your computer to be able to run the two versions of the P2P application on the CD followed by the S/W requirements for setting up the P2P server.

The Java version

Following is the software the user needs to have on his system to run the Java version of this software.

This is the Software Development Kit for developing standard Java applications. The Java version of our application has been developed using this kit. You can download it from: `http://java.sun.com/j2se/1.3/`. It is available on the CD as well.

Forte for Java release

The Forte for Java release software is an integrated development environment used for developing the Java application. You can use this to develop the Java version of our application. It is an IDE provided by

Sun Microsystems. You can download it from: `http://www.sun.com/forte/ffj/`. It is available on the CD as well.

The XML Parser for parsing the XML data. The Java version of the application internally uses this XML Parser. You can get this XML Parser from: `http://xml.apache.org/dist/xerces-j/`. It is available on the CD as well.

The C# version

Following is the software the user needs to have on his system to run the C# version of this software.

The XML Parser class for parsing the XML data. The C# version of the application internally uses this XML Parser. You can get this XML Parser from: `http://msdn.microsoft.com/msxml`.

This SDK is used for developing the streaming extensions of our application. You can download it from: `http://msdn.microsoft.com/windowsmedia/`.

Windows Encoder SDK, which has been used for developing the streaming extensions of our application, internally uses some DirectShow components to render and index some non-streaming media formats. Since the streaming extension could have been developed using this SDK, you may want to explore it. This SDK is available for downloading at: `http://msdn.microsoft.com/directx/`. It is available on the CD as well.

This contains the Window Media Player component that is embedded in the Browser and used to show the audio/video to the user. You can download it from: `http://msdn.microsoft.com/windows/windowsmedia/`.

The P2P server

Following are the software that users need to have on the server to set up the P2P server.

The P2P server can be set up using any of the servers of Windows NT series - 4 or above. P2P server uses the services of Windows NT series server to host its site and to manage database. You can learn more about this O/S at: `http://www.microsoft.com/windows2000/`.

P2P server uses this RDBMS (Relational Data Base Management System) to manage the P2P database. You can learn more about this SQL Server 2000 at: `http://www.microsoft.com/sql/default.asp`.

IIS 5.0

Internet Information Services 5.0 (IIS) is the Windows 2000 Web service that has been used to host the site for P2P. You can learn more about IIS 5.0 at: `http://www.microsoft.com/windows2000/en/server/iis/`.

Apart from the previously discussed software, you will need to have the following.

Software for viewing Adobe PDF files. You will need this software to read the eBook version of *Peer-to-Peer Application Development*. You can download this software from: `http://www.adobe.com/products/acrobat/readermain.html`. It is available on the CD as well.

Using the CD

To install the items from the CD to your hard drive, follow these steps:

1. Insert the CD into your computer's CD-ROM drive.
2. A window will appear with the following options: Install, Explore, eBook, Links and Exit.

- **Install:** Gives you the option to install the supplied software and/or the author-created samples on the CD-ROM.
- **Explore:** Allows you to view the contents of the CD-ROM in its directory structure.
- **eBook:** Allows you to view an electronic version of the book.
- **Links:** Opens a hyperlinked page of web sites.
- **Exit:** Closes the autorun window.

If you do not have autorun enabled or if the autorun window does not appear, follow the steps below to access the CD.

1. Click Start ⇨ Run.

2. In the dialog box that appears, type *d*:\setup.exe, where *d* is the letter of your CD-ROM drive. This will bring up the autorun window described above.

3. Choose the Install, Explore, eBook, Links, or Exit option from the menu. (See Step 2 in the preceding list for a description of these options.)

Troubleshooting

If you have difficulty installing or using any of the materials on the companion CD, try the following solutions:

- ◆ **Turn off any anti-virus software that you may have running.** Installers sometimes mimic virus activity and can make your computer incorrectly believe that it is being infected by a virus. (Be sure to turn the anti-virus software back on later.)

- ◆ **Close all running programs.** The more programs you're running, the less memory is available to other programs. Installers also typically update files and programs; if you keep other programs running, installation may not work properly.

- ◆ **Reference the ReadMe:** Please refer to the ReadMe file located at the root of the CD-ROM for the latest product information at the time of publication.

- ◆ **Make sure that you are online:** The applications (that is, the P2P applications) on this CD are developed assuming the user has an internet/intranet connection. These applications will not work if the user is not connected to internet or intranet.

If you still have trouble with the CD, please call the Hungry Minds Customer Care phone number: (800) 762-2974. Outside the United States, call 1 (317) 572-3994. You can also contact Hungry Minds Customer Service by e-mail at techsupdum@hungryminds.com. Hungry Minds will provide technical support only for installation and other general quality control items; for technical support on the applications themselves, consult the program's vendor or author.

Index

Hungry Minds, Inc.
End-User License Agreement

READ THIS. You should carefully read these terms and conditions before opening the software packet(s) included with this book ("Book"). This is a license agreement ("Agreement") between you and Hungry Minds, Inc. ("HMI"). By opening the accompanying software packet(s), you acknowledge that you have read and accept the following terms and conditions. If you do not agree and do not want to be bound by such terms and conditions, promptly return the Book and the unopened software packet(s) to the place you obtained them for a full refund.

1. **License Grant.** HMI grants to you (either an individual or entity) a nonexclusive license to use one copy of the enclosed software program(s) (collectively, the "Software") solely for your own personal and non-commercial purposes on a single computer (whether a standard computer or a workstation component of a multi-user network). The Software is in use on a computer when it is loaded into temporary memory (RAM) or installed into permanent memory (hard disk, CD-ROM, or other storage device). HMI reserves all rights not expressly granted herein.

2. **Ownership.** HMI is the owner of all right, title, and interest, including copyright, in and to the compilation of the Software recorded on the disk(s) or CD-ROM ("Software Media"). Copyright to the individual programs recorded on the Software Media is owned by the author or other authorized copyright owner of each program. Ownership of the Software and all proprietary rights relating thereto remain with HMI and its licensers.

3. **Restrictions on Use and Transfer.**

    (a) You may only (i) make one copy of the Software for backup or archival purposes, or (ii) transfer the Software to a single hard disk, provided that you keep the original for backup or archival purposes. You may not (i) rent or lease the Software, (ii) copy or reproduce the Software through a LAN or other network system or through any computer subscriber system or bulletin-board system, or (iii) modify, adapt, or create derivative works based on the Software.

    (b) You may not reverse engineer, decompile, or disassemble the Software. You may transfer the Software and user documentation on a permanent basis, provided that the transferee agrees to accept the terms and conditions of this Agreement and you retain no copies. If the Software is an update or has been updated, any transfer must include the most recent update and all prior versions.

4. **Restrictions on Use of Individual Programs.** You must follow the individual requirements and restrictions detailed for each individual program in the What's on the CD-ROM appendix of this Book. These limitations are also contained in the individual license agreements recorded on the Software Media. These limitations may include a requirement that after using the program for a specified period of time, the user must pay a registration fee or discontinue use. By opening the Software packet(s), you will be agreeing to abide by the licenses and restrictions for these individual programs that are detailed in the What's on the CD-ROM appendix and on the Software Media. None of the material on this Software Media or listed in this Book may ever be redistributed, in original or modified form, for commercial purposes.

5. **Limited Warranty.**

    (a) HMI warrants that the Software and Software Media are free from defects in materials and workmanship under normal use for a period of sixty (60) days from the date of purchase of this Book. If HMI receives notification within the warranty period of defects in materials or workmanship, HMI will replace the defective Software Media.

Sun Microsystems, Inc.
Binary Code License Agreement

READ THE TERMS OF THIS AGREEMENT AND ANY PROVIDED SUPPLEMENTAL LICENSE TERMS (COLLECTIVELY "AGREEMENT") CAREFULLY BEFORE OPENING THE SOFTWARE MEDIA PACKAGE. BY OPENING THE SOFTWARE MEDIA PACKAGE, YOU AGREE TO THE TERMS OF THIS AGREEMENT. IF YOU ARE ACCESSING THE SOFTWARE ELECTRONICALLY, INDICATE YOUR ACCEPTANCE OF THESE TERMS BY SELECTING THE "ACCEPT" BUTTON AT THE END OF THIS AGREEMENT. IF YOU DO NOT AGREE TO ALL THESE TERMS, PROMPTLY RETURN THE UNUSED SOFTWARE TO YOUR PLACE OF PURCHASE FOR A REFUND OR, IF THE SOFTWARE IS ACCESSED ELECTRONICALLY, SELECT THE "DECLINE" BUTTON AT THE END OF THIS AGREEMENT.

1. LICENSE TO USE. Sun grants you a non-exclusive and non-transferable license for the internal use only of the accompanying software and documentation and any error corrections provided by Sun (collectively "Software"), by the number of users and the class of computer hardware for which the corresponding fee has been paid.

2. RESTRICTIONS. Software is confidential and copyrighted. Title to Software and all associated intellectual property rights is retained by Sun and/or its licensors. Except as specifically authorized in any Supplemental License Terms, you may not make copies of Software, other than a single copy of Software for archival purposes. Unless enforcement is prohibited by applicable law, you may not modify, decompile, or reverse engineer Software. You acknowledge that Software is not designed, licensed or intended for use in the design, construction, operation or maintenance of any nuclear facility. Sun disclaims any express or implied warranty of fitness for such uses. No right, title or interest in or to any trademark, service mark, logo or trade name of Sun or its licensors is granted under this Agreement.

3. LIMITED WARRANTY. Sun warrants to you that for a period of ninety (90) days from the date of purchase, as evidenced by a copy of the receipt, the media on which Software is furnished (if any) will be free of defects in materials and workmanship under normal use. Except for the foregoing, Software is provided "AS IS". Your exclusive remedy and Sun's entire liability under this limited warranty will be at Sun's option to replace Software media or refund the fee paid for Software.

4. DISCLAIMER OF WARRANTY. UNLESS SPECIFIED IN THIS AGREEMENT, ALL EXPRESS OR IMPLIED CONDITIONS, REPRESENTATIONS AND WARRANTIES, INCLUDING ANY IMPLIED WARRANTY OF MERCHANTABILITY, FITNESS FOR A PARTICULAR PURPOSE OR NON-INFRINGEMENT ARE DISCLAIMED, EXCEPT TO THE EXTENT THAT THESE DISCLAIMERS ARE HELD TO BE LEGALLY INVALID.

5. LIMITATION OF LIABILITY. TO THE EXTENT NOT PROHIBITED BY LAW, IN NO EVENT WILL SUN OR ITS LICENSORS BE LIABLE FOR ANY LOST REVENUE, PROFIT OR DATA, OR FOR SPECIAL, INDIRECT, CONSEQUENTIAL, INCIDENTAL OR PUNITIVE DAMAGES, HOWEVER CAUSED REGARDLESS OF THE THEORY OF LIABILITY, ARISING OUT OF OR RELATED TO THE USE OF OR INABILITY TO USE SOFTWARE, EVEN IF SUN HAS BEEN ADVISED OF THE POSSIBILITY OF SUCH DAMAGES. In no event will Sun's liability to you, whether in contract, tort (including negligence), or otherwise, exceed the amount paid by you for Software under this Agreement. The foregoing limitations will apply even if the above stated warranty fails of its essential purpose.

6. Termination. This Agreement is effective until terminated. You may terminate this Agreement at any time by destroying all copies of Software. This Agreement will terminate immediately without notice from Sun if you fail to comply with any provision of this Agreement. Upon Termination, you must destroy all copies of Software.

7. Export Regulations. All Software and technical data delivered under this Agreement are subject to US export control laws and may be subject to export or import regulations in other countries. You agree to comply strictly with all such laws and regulations and acknowledge that you have the responsibility to obtain such licenses to export, re-export, or import as may be required after delivery to you.

8. **U.S. Government Restricted Rights.** If Software is being acquired by or on behalf of the U.S. Government or by a U.S. Government prime contractor or subcontractor (at any tier), then the Government's rights in Software and accompanying documentation will be only as set forth in this Agreement; this is in accordance with 48 CFR 227.7201 through 227.7202-4 (for Department of Defense (DOD) acquisitions) and with 48 CFR 2.101 and 12.212 (for non-DOD acquisitions).

9. **Governing Law.** Any action related to this Agreement will be governed by California law and controlling U.S. federal law. No choice of law rules of any jurisdiction will apply.

10. **Severability.** If any provision of this Agreement is held to be unenforceable, this Agreement will remain in effect with the provision omitted, unless omission would frustrate the intent of the parties, in which case this Agreement will immediately terminate.

11. **Integration.** This Agreement is the entire agreement between you and Sun relating to its subject matter. It supersedes all prior or contemporaneous oral or written communications, proposals, representations and warranties and prevails over any conflicting or additional terms of any quote, order, acknowledgment, or other communication between the parties relating to its subject matter during the term of this Agreement. No modification of this Agreement will be binding, unless in writing and signed by an authorized representative of each party.

Java(TM) 2 Software Development Kit (J2SDK), Standard Edition, Version 1.3 SUPPLEMENTAL LICENSE TERMS

These supplemental license terms ("Supplemental Terms") add to or modify the terms of the Binary Code License Agreement (collectively, the "Agreement"). Capitalized terms not defined in these Supplemental Terms shall have the same meanings ascribed to them in the Agreement. These Supplemental Terms shall supersede any inconsistent or conflicting terms in the Agreement, or in any license contained within the Software.

1. **Software Internal Use and Development License Grant.** Subject to the terms and conditions of this Agreement, including, but not limited to Section 4 (Java(TM) Technology Restrictions) of these Supplemental Terms, Sun grants you a non-exclusive, non-transferable, limited license to reproduce internally and use internally the binary form of the Software complete and unmodified for the sole purpose of designing, developing and testing your Java applets and applications intended to run on the Java platform ("Programs").

2. **License to Distribute Software.** Subject to the terms and conditions of this Agreement, including, but not limited to Section 4 (Java (TM) Technology Restrictions) of these Supplemental Terms, Sun grants you a non-exclusive, non-transferable, limited license to reproduce and distribute the Software in binary code form only, provided that (i) you distribute the Software complete and unmodified and only bundled as part of, and for the sole purpose of running, your Programs, (ii) the Programs add significant and primary functionality to the Software, (iii) you do not distribute additional software intended to replace any component(s) of the Software, (iv) you do not remove or alter any proprietary legends or notices contained in the Software, (v) you only distribute the Software subject to a license agreement that protects Sun's interests consistent with the terms contained in this Agreement, and (vi) you agree to defend and indemnify Sun and its licensors from and against any damages, costs, liabilities, settlement amounts and/or expenses (including attorneys' fees) incurred in connection with any claim, lawsuit or action by any third party that arises or results from the use or distribution of any and all Programs and/or Software.

3. **License to Distribute Redistributables.** Subject to the terms and conditions of this Agreement, including but not limited to Section 4 (Java Technology Restrictions) of these Supplemental Terms, Sun grants you a non-exclusive, non-transferable, limited license to reproduce and distribute the binary form of those files specifically identified as redistributable in the Software "README" file ("Redistributables") provided that: (i) you distribute the Redistributables complete and unmodified (unless otherwise specified in the applicable README file), and only bundled as part of Programs, (ii) you do not distribute additional software intended to supersede any component(s) of the Redistributables, (iii) you do not remove or alter any proprietary legends or notices contained in or on the Redistributables, (iv) you only distribute the Redistributables pursuant to a license agreement that protects Sun's interests consistent with the terms contained in the Agreement, and (v) you agree to defend and indemnify Sun and its licensors from and against any damages, costs, liabilities, settlement amounts and/or expenses (including attorneys' fees) incurred in connection

with any claim, lawsuit or action by any third party that arises or results from the use or distribution of any and all Programs and/or Software.

4. Java Technology Restrictions. You may not modify the Java Platform Interface ("JPI", identified as classes contained within the "java" package or any subpackages of the "java" package), by creating additional classes within the JPI or otherwise causing the addition to or modification of the classes in the JPI. In the event that you create an additional class and associated API(s) which (i) extends the functionality of the Java platform, and (ii) is exposed to third party software developers for the purpose of developing additional software which invokes such additional API, you must promptly publish broadly an accurate specification for such API for free use by all developers. You may not create, or authorize your licensees to create, additional classes, interfaces, or subpackages that are in any way identified as "java", "javax", "sun" or similar convention as specified by Sun in any naming convention designation.

5. Trademarks and Logos. You acknowledge and agree as between you and Sun that Sun owns the SUN, SOLARIS, JAVA, JINI, FORTE, STAROFFICE, STARPORTAL and iPLANET trademarks and all SUN, SOLARIS, JAVA, JINI, FORTE, STAROFFICE, STARPORTAL and iPLANET-related trademarks, service marks, logos and other brand designations ("Sun Marks"), and you agree to comply with the Sun Trademark and Logo Usage Requirements currently located at http://www.sun.com/policies/trademarks. Any use you make of the Sun Marks inures to Sun's benefit.

6. Source Code. Software may contain source code that is provided solely for reference purposes pursuant to the terms of this Agreement. Source code may not be redistributed unless expressly provided for in this Agreement.

7. Termination for Infringement. Either party may terminate this Agreement immediately should any Software become, or in either party's opinion be likely to become, the subject of a claim of infringement of any intellectual property right.

For inquiries please contact: Sun Microsystems, Inc. 901 San Antonio Road, Palo Alto, California 94303

License Agreement: Forte for Java, release 2.0 Community Edition for All Platforms

To obtain Forte for Java, release 2.0, Community Edition for All Platforms, you must agree to the software license below.

Sun Microsystems Inc., Binary Code License Agreement

READ THE TERMS OF THIS AGREEMENT AND ANY PROVIDED SUPPLEMENTAL LICENSE TERMS (COLLECTIVELY "AGREEMENT") CAREFULLY BEFORE OPENING THE SOFTWARE MEDIA PACKAGE. BY OPENING THE SOFTWARE MEDIA PACKAGE, YOU AGREE TO THE TERMS OF THIS AGREEMENT. IF YOU ARE ACCESSING THE SOFTWARE ELECTRONICALLY, INDICATE YOUR ACCEPTANCE OF THESE TERMS BY SELECTING THE "ACCEPT" BUTTON AT THE END OF THIS AGREEMENT. IF YOU DO NOT AGREE TO ALL THESE TERMS, PROMPTLY RETURN THE UNUSED SOFTWARE TO YOUR PLACE OF PURCHASE FOR A REFUND OR, IF THE SOFTWARE IS ACCESSED ELECTRONICALLY, SELECT THE "DECLINE" BUTTON AT THE END OF THIS AGREEMENT.

1. LICENSE TO USE. Sun grants you a non-exclusive and non-transferable license for the internal use only of the accompanying software and documentation and any error corrections provided by Sun (collectively "Software"), by the number of users and the class of computer hardware for which the corresponding fee has been paid.

2. RESTRICTIONS. Software is confidential and copyrighted. Title to Software and all associated intellectual property rights is retained by Sun and/or its licensors. Except as specifically authorized in any Supplemental License Terms, you may not make copies of Software, other than a single copy of Software for archival purposes. Unless enforcement is prohibited by applicable law, you may not modify, decompile, or reverse engineer Software. You acknowledge that Software is not designed, licensed or intended for use in the design, construction, operation or maintenance of any nuclear facility. Sun disclaims any express or implied warranty of fitness for such uses. No right, title or interest in or to any trademark, service mark, logo or trade name of Sun or its licensors is granted under this Agreement.

3. LIMITED WARRANTY. Sun warrants to you that for a period of ninety (90) days from the date of purchase, as evidenced by a copy of the receipt, the media on which Software is furnished (if any) will be free of defects in materials and workmanship under normal use. Except for the foregoing, Software is provided "AS IS". Your exclusive remedy and Sun's entire liability under this limited warranty will be at Sun's option to replace Software media or refund the fee paid for Software.

4. DISCLAIMER OF WARRANTY. UNLESS SPECIFIED IN THIS AGREEMENT, ALL EXPRESS OR IMPLIED CONDITIONS, REPRESENTATIONS AND WARRANTIES, INCLUDING ANY IMPLIED WARRANTY OF MERCHANTABILITY, FITNESS FOR A PARTICULAR PURPOSE OR NON-INFRINGEMENT ARE DISCLAIMED, EXCEPT TO THE EXTENT THAT THESE DISCLAIMERS ARE HELD TO BE LEGALLY INVALID.

5. LIMITATION OF LIABILITY. TO THE EXTENT NOT PROHIBITED BY LAW, IN NO EVENT WILL SUN OR ITS LICENSORS BE LIABLE FOR ANY LOST REVENUE, PROFIT OR DATA, OR FOR SPECIAL, INDIRECT, CONSEQUENTIAL, INCIDENTAL OR PUNITIVE DAMAGES, HOWEVER CAUSED REGARDLESS OF THE THEORY OF LIABILITY, ARISING OUT OF OR RELATED TO THE USE OF OR INABILITY TO USE SOFTWARE, EVEN IF SUN HAS BEEN ADVISED OF THE POSSIBILITY OF SUCH DAMAGES. In no event will Sun's liability to you, whether in contract, tort (including negligence), or otherwise, exceed the amount paid by you for Software under this Agreement. The foregoing limitations will apply even if the above stated warranty fails of its essential purpose.

6. Termination. This Agreement is effective until terminated. You may terminate this Agreement at any time by destroying all copies of Software. This Agreement will terminate immediately without notice from Sun if you fail to comply with any provision of this Agreement. Upon Termination, you must destroy all copies of Software.

7. Export Regulations. All Software and technical data delivered under this Agreement are subject to US export control laws and may be subject to export or import regulations in other countries. You

agree to comply strictly with all such laws and regulations and acknowledge that you have the responsibility to obtain such licenses to export, re-export, or import as may be required after delivery to you.

8. U.S. Government Restricted Rights. If Software is being acquired by or on behalf of the U.S. Government or by a U.S. Government prime contractor or subcontractor (at any tier), then the Government's rights in Software and accompanying documentation will be only as set forth in this Agreement; this is in accordance with 48 CFR 227.7201 through 227.7202-4 (for Department of Defense (DOD) acquisitions) and with 48 CFR 2.101 and 12.212 (for non-DOD acquisitions).

9. Governing Law. Any action related to this Agreement will be governed by California law and controlling U.S. federal law. No choice of law rules of any jurisdiction will apply.

10. Severability. If any provision of this Agreement is held to be unenforceable, this Agreement will remain in effect with the provision omitted, unless omission would frustrate the intent of the parties, in which case this Agreement will immediately terminate.

11. Integration. This Agreement is the entire agreement between you and Sun relating to its subject matter. It supersedes all prior or contemporaneous oral or written communications, proposals, representations and warranties and prevails over any conflicting or additional terms of any quote, order, acknowledgment, or other communication between the parties relating to its subject matter during the term of this Agreement. No modification of this Agreement will be binding, unless in writing and signed by an authorized representative of each party.

JAVA™ DEVELOPMENT TOOLS FORTE™ FOR JAVA™, RELEASE 2.0, COMMUNITY EDITION SUPPLEMENTAL LICENSE TERMS

These supplemental license terms ("Supplemental Terms") add to or modify the terms of the Binary Code License Agreement (collectively, the "Agreement"). Capitalized terms not defined in these Supplemental Terms shall have the same meanings ascribed to them in the Agreement. These Supplemental Terms shall supersede any inconsistent or conflicting terms in the Agreement, or in any license contained within the Software.

1. Software Internal Use and Development License Grant. Subject to the terms and conditions of this Agreement, including, but not limited to Section 3 (Java(TM) Technology Restrictions) of these Supplemental Terms, Sun grants you a non-exclusive, non-transferable, limited license to reproduce internally and use internally the binary form of the Software complete and unmodified for the sole purpose of designing, developing and testing your [Java applets and] applications intended to run on the Java platform ("Programs").

2. License to Distribute Redistributables. In addition to the license granted in Section 1 (Redistributables Internal Use and Development License Grant) of these Supplemental Terms, subject to the terms and conditions of this Agreement, including, but not limited to Section 3 (Java Technology Restrictions) of these Supplemental Terms, Sun grants you a non-exclusive, non-transferable, limited license to reproduce and distribute those files specifically identified as redistributable in the Software "README" file ("Redistributables") provided that: (i) you distribute the Redistributables complete and unmodified (unless otherwise specified in the applicable README file), and only bundled as part of your Programs, (ii) you do not distribute additional software intended to supercede any component(s) of the Redistributables, (iii) you do not remove or alter any proprietary legends or notices contained in or on the Redistributables, (iv) for a particular version of the Java platform, any executable output generated by a compiler that is contained in the Software must (a) only be compiled from source code that conforms to the corresponding version of the OEM Java Language Specification; (b) be in the class file format defined by the corresponding version of the OEM Java Virtual Machine Specification; and (c) execute properly on a reference runtime, as specified by Sun, associated with such version of the Java platform, (v) you only distribute the Redistributables pursuant to a license agreement that protects Sun's interests consistent with the terms contained in the Agreement, and (vi) you agree to defend and indemnify Sun and its licensors from and against any damages, costs, liabilities, settlement amounts and/or expenses (including attorneys' fees) incurred in connection with any

claim, lawsuit or action by any third party that arises or results from the use or distribution of any and all Programs and/or Software.

3. Java Technology Restrictions. You may not modify the Java Platform Interface ("JPI", identified as classes contained within the "java" package or any subpackages of the "java" package), by creating additional classes within the JPI or otherwise causing the addition to or modification of the classes in the JPI. In the event that you create an additional class and associated API(s) which (i) extends the functionality of the Java platform, and (ii) is exposed to third party software developers for the purpose of developing additional software which invokes such additional API, you must promptly publish broadly an accurate specification for such API for free use by all developers. You may not create, or authorize your licensees to create, additional classes, interfaces, or subpackages that are in any way identified as "java", "javax", "sun" or similar convention as specified by Sun in any naming convention designation.

4. Java Runtime Availability. Refer to the appropriate version of the Java Runtime Environment binary code license (currently located at http://www.java.sun.com/jdk/index.html) for the availability of runtime code which may be distributed with Java applets and applications.

5. Trademarks and Logos. You acknowledge and agree as between you and Sun that Sun owns the SUN, SOLARIS, JAVA, JINI, FORTE, STAROFFICE, STARPORTAL and iPLANET trademarks and all SUN, SOLARIS, JAVA, JINI, FORTE, STAROFFICE, STARPORTAL and iPLANET-related trademarks, service marks, logos and other brand designations ("Sun Marks"), and you agree to comply with the Sun Trademark and Logo Usage Requirements currently located at http://www.sun.com/policies/trademarks. Any use you make of the Sun Marks inures to Sun's benefit.

6. Source Code. Software may contain source code that is provided solely for reference purposes pursuant to the terms of this Agreement. Source code may not be redistributed unless expressly provided for in this Agreement.

7. Termination for Infringement. Either party may terminate this Agreement immediately should any Software become, or in either party's opinion be likely to become, the subject of a claim of infringement of any intellectual property right.

For inquiries please contact: Sun Microsystems, Inc. 901 San Antonio Road, Palo Alto, California 94303